# Guide to UNIX® Using Linux

## COURSE TECHNOLOGY

## Thomson Learning™

ONE MAIN STREET, CAMBRIDGE, MA 02142

Australia • Canada • Denmark • Japan • Mexico • New Zealand • Philippines
Puerto Rico • Singapore • South Africa • Spain • United Kingdom • United States

*Guide to UNIX Using Linux* is published by Course Technology.

| | |
|---|---|
| *Associate Publisher* | Kristen Duerr |
| *Senior Acquisitions Editor* | Stephen Solomon |
| *Product Manager* | Lisa Ayers Egan |
| *Production Editor* | Debbie Masi |
| *Developmental Editors* | Lisa Ruffolo, The Software Resource |
| | Terry Ann Kremer |
| *Quality Assurance* | John Bosco |
| *Associate Product Manager* | Laura Hildebrand |
| *Editorial Assistant* | Tricia Coia |
| *Marketing Manager* | Susan Ogar |
| *Text Designer* | GEX, Inc. |
| *Cover Designer* | Efrat Reis |

**Disclaimer**

Course Technology reserves the right to revise this publication and make changes from time to time in its content without notice.

The Web addresses in this book are subject to change from time to time as necessary without notice.

For more information, contact Course Technology, One Main Street, Cambridge, MA 02142; or find us on the World Wide Web at *www.course.com*.
For permission to use material from this text or product, contact us by

- ■ Web: www.thomsonrights.com
- ■ Phone: 1-800-730-2214
- ■ Fax: 1-800-730-2215

ISBN 0-7600-1096-x

Printed in Canada
 2 3 4 5 WC 02 01 00

# Contents

## chapter 4

# UNIX FILE PROCESSING  101

## chapter 5

# ADVANCED FILE PROCESSING  139

## c h a p t e r    6

## INTRODUCTION TO SHELL PROGRAMMING  *177*

## chapter 11

# THE X WINDOW SYSTEM  417

# Introduction

*Guide to UNIX Using Linux* introduces the fundamentals of the UNIX operating system to the PC user. UNIX is "the operating system of the Internet," powerful and flexible enough for both servers and desktop computers. Taking a hands-on, practical approach, this book guides you through the basics of UNIX system concepts, architecture, and administration. You practice these basic concepts and approaches using Linux, a PC-compatible clone of UNIX that is an ideal teaching tool for mastering UNIX commands. The book achieves its goals with a proven combination of tools that powerfully reinforce both concepts and real-world experience.

This book includes:

- RedHat Linux 6.0 and complete installation instructions
- Comprehensive review and end-of-chapter material, including a command summary, review questions, hands-on exercises, and case projects, which let you practice and master skills as you learn them
- Step-by-step instructions to teach UNIX commands, shell programming, database management, text editing, C programming, debugging, and rapid application development using standard UNIX tools such as awk, sed, and perl
- A proven method to provide a working knowledge of basic system administration requirements and how to achieve them

In addition, the text is carefully structured, clearly written, and accompanied by graphics that provide the visual reinforcement essential to learning. And for instructors using the book in a classroom, a special CD-ROM is available that includes an instructor's manual and an online testing system. Contact customer service or your sales representative to obtain a copy of the CD-ROM.

Coverage is balanced, with one chapter building on the skills and knowledge acquired in the preceding chapters. Operating systems, and UNIX and Linux in particular, are introduced in **Chapter 1**, along with essential information such as using UNIX shells, entering commands, and understanding the role of the system administrator. **Chapter 2** explores the UNIX file system—its partitions and directories—and how to navigate it. **Chapter 3** focuses on the UNIX editors, providing instruction on using the vi and Emacs editors. **Chapter 4** explains the UNIX approach to file processing, while **Chapter 5** covers advanced file processing concepts. **Chapters 6 and 7** introduce you to shell programming, and **Chapter 8** provides practice with UNIX utilities. **Chapters 9 and 10** teach programming tools such as awk, sed, perl, and C/C++. **Chapter 11** covers a recent development in UNIX: the X Window system, which provides a graphical user interface for UNIX.

## Features

In order to ensure a successful learning experience, this book includes the following pedagogical features:

- **Learning Objectives:** Every chapter opens with a list of learning objectives that sets the stage for you to absorb the lessons of the text.
- **Case Approach:** Each chapter opens with a hypothetical case. You solve the problem posed by the case by working through the material in the chapter.
- **Comprehensive Step-by-Step Methodology:** The unique Course Technology methodology keeps students on track. The text introduces new concepts, illustrates them through examples, and guides you through practice steps to achieve mastery of the material.
- **Tips:** Tips, which are marked with the Tip icon, are used to highlight additional helpful information related to the subject being discussed.
- **Summaries:** Following each chapter is a summary that recaps the concepts covered in the chapter, and a table listing the related commands and their options.
- **Review Questions:** Each chapter concludes with meaningful, conceptual review questions that test students' understanding of what they learned in the chapter.
- **Exercises:** The review questions are followed by exercises, which provide students with additional practice using the skills and concepts they learned in the chapter.
- **Discovery Exercises:** Each chapter concludes with Discovery Exercises, which reinforce the chapter concepts and allow for independent study.
- **RedHat Linux 6.0:** Each book is bundled with a copy of RedHat Linux 6.0. Linux is a PC-compatible clone of UNIX that is an ideal teaching tool for many basic and advanced UNIX commands. Course Technology does not offer Technical Support for this software. However, if there is a problem with the media, please contact customer service or your sales representative.

## Supplements

For instructors using this book in a classroom environment, the following teaching materials are available on a single CD-ROM:

**Electronic Instructor's Manual:** The Instructor's Manual that accompanies this textbook includes a list of objectives for each chapter, a detailed chapter lecture notes, suggestions for classroom activities, discussion topics; and solutions.

**Course Test Manager 1.2:** Accompanying this book is a powerful assessment tool known as the Course Test Manager. Designed by Course Technology, this cutting-edge Windows-based testing software helps instructors design and administer tests and pretests. In addition to being able to generate tests that can be printed and administered, this full-featured program also has an online testing component that allows students to take tests at the computer and have their exams automatically graded. The test bank that accompanies this book contains 50–100 questions per chapter.

**PowerPoint Presentations:** This book comes with Microsoft PowerPoint slides for each chapter. This lecture tool covers all of the key points and art for each chapter. The Presentations are included as a teaching aid for classroom presentation, to make available to students on the network for chapter review, or to be printed for classroom distribution.

## System Requirements

To install Red Hat Linux 6, your computer must meet the following minimum requirements:

- Intel 486 processor
- 16 MB of RAM
- 500 MB free hard disk space
- 3.5-inch floppy drive
- CD-ROM drive

To access a UNIX/Linux host on a local-area network to which your computer is connected, you need the following software and information:

- Telnet program
- Either the IP address or the host and domain name of the UNIX system

To access a UNIX/Linux host via the Internet, you need the following software and information:

- Dial-up connection to an Internet Service Provider
- Telnet program
- Either the IP address or the host and domain name of the UNIX system

## Acknowledgments

I would like to thank my wife, Jean, and Lisa Egan at Course Technology for their patience and friendly persuasion when I deserved neither. I would also like to dedicate this book to all my "wide-eyed" students at International Business College, in particular, Adam, a.k.a. Mercedes. Long live free, open, operating systems!

– Jack Dent

Many individuals are responsible for this book's completion. I wish to thank Kristen Duerr and Stephen Solomon for the opportunity to participate in this project. I also wish to thank Lisa Ayers Egan, Lisa Ruffolo, and Terry Ann Kremer for their constant help and encouragement. Working with them was a pleasure. In addition, I wish to thank Debbie Masi, John Bosco, Laura Hildebrand, Tricia Coia, and the countless others at Course Technology who played a role in this book's publication.                     – Tony Gaddis

Thank you to Wendy Abu-Rabi for her contributions to this book.

The following faculty reviewers also deserve special credit. Their comments and suggestions shaped the book into its final form.

Charles Fricks, Kilgore College
Lee Toderick, Pitt Community College
Hans-Peter Appelt, Corning Community College
Darlene De Vida, Lower Columbia College
Phil Reid, Cleveland Community College
Terry Evans, Jackson State Community College
Mark King, Aiken Technological Institute

# The Essence of UNIX

**case** ▶ Dominion Consulting specializes in management systems for large hotels and resorts. Dominion's founders, Eli Addison and Carmen Scott, recognize the need for an in-house computer system that lets their employees work as a team. UNIX is an operating system designed for collaborative development of software, allowing people to work together and share information in controlled ways. Dominion has offered you a position as a UNIX system trainee. Your managers want you to understand the basics of operating systems in general, and UNIX in particular. They ask you to log on to UNIX and learn how to use some basic commands.

After completing this lesson, you should be able to:

- Define operating systems in general and the UNIX operating system in particular
- Describe Linux as it relates to UNIX
- Explain the function of UNIX shells
- Describe options for connecting to a UNIX system
- Define the syntax used for entering UNIX commands
- Use the date, cal, who, man, whatis, and clear commands
- Perform basic command-line editing operations
- Enter multiple commands on a single command line
- Recall a command from the command history
- Log on to and log out of UNIX

# Getting Started with UNIX

This chapter introduces the UNIX operating system and a few of its basic commands. It also explains how you can use Linux to learn UNIX. A variant of UNIX, Linux runs on PCs with Intel processors but uses the same file system and commands as UNIX, which usually runs on a network. Using Linux on your PC is virtually the same as using UNIX on a network.

After you explore essential background information in this chapter, you begin to work with UNIX. If you're familiar with operating systems in general, then some background material may be review for you. This chapter also provides plenty of opportunity for hands-on practice of UNIX commands, primarily in the context of the opening case. The case study reflects a realistic scenario for the tasks you complete in this chapter. You learn to use a variety of basic commands to meet the goals of the scenario.

## Understanding Operating Systems

An **operating system** (OS) is the most important program that runs on a computer. Operating systems enable you to store information, process raw data, use application software, compile your own programs, and access all hardware attached to a computer, such as a printer or keyboard. In short, the operating system is the most fundamental computer program. It controls all the computer's resources and provides the base upon which application programs can be used or written. Figure 1-1 shows a model of an operating system.

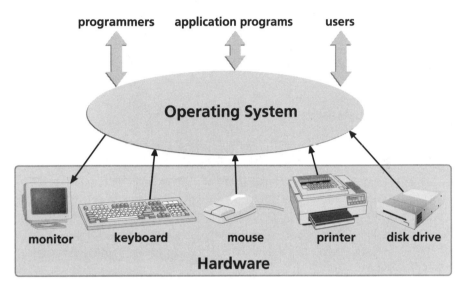

**Figure 1-1:** Operating system model

Different computer systems may have different operating systems. For example, the most common operating systems for personal computers are DOS, OS/2, and Windows. Mainframe computers may use Digital Equipment's VAX operating system or IBM's System 370. Networks also have operating systems, such as Linux and Windows NT. UNIX is the leading operating system for workstations, which are powerful single-user computers linked together on a local-area network.

## PC Operating Systems

A **personal computer** system or **PC** is usually a standalone machine, such as a desktop or laptop computer. A PC operating system conducts all the input, output, processing, and storage operations on a single computer. Figure 1-2 identifies some popular PC operating systems.

**Microsoft Windows**

**Apple Macintosh**

**Linux**

**IBM OS/2**

**Microsoft DOS**

**Figure 1-2:** Common PC operating systems

## Mainframe Operating Systems

A mainframe operating system controls a **mainframe system**, a large computer system with multiple processors that conducts input, output, processing, and storage operations for many users. Historically, mainframe systems have been popular in large corporations and industrial computing. Figure 1-3 shows some recognized mainframe operating systems and their manufacturers.

**Digital Equipment VAX Systems**

**IBM System 370**

**Hewlett Packard HP 9000 Series**

**Figure 1-3:** Common mainframe operating systems

## Network Operating Systems

A computer **network** combines the convenience and familiarity of the personal computer with the processing power of the mainframe. A network lets multiple users share computer resources and files. A **network operating system** controls the operations of a **server** computer, sometimes called a **host** computer, which accepts requests from user programs running on other machines, called **clients**. Figure 1-4 shows the relationship of servers and clients on a network.

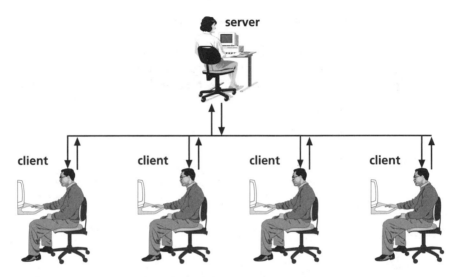

**Figure 1-4:** Relationship of servers and clients on a network

In a centralized approach, all the users' data and applications reside on the server. This type of network is called a **server-based network**. The system administrator secures all the information on the network by securing the server. The system administrator easily maintains the users' applications and performs back-up operations directly on the server. If the server fails, however, the entire network fails.

**Peer-to-peer** networks, which work best for small networks, are more distributed than server-based networks. In a peer-to-peer configuration, each system on the network is both a server and a client. Data and applications are not centrally located but reside on the individual systems in the network. Software upgrades and back-up operations must be performed locally at each computer. Security, which is implemented on each computer, is not uniform. Each user of the network is, to some degree, responsible for administering his or her own system. Despite the disadvantages a peer-to-peer network presents to the system administrator, the individual users do not depend on a central server. If one computer in the network fails, the other systems continue to operate.

# Introducing the UNIX Operating System

UNIX is a multi-user, multitasking operating system with built-in networking functions. It can be used on systems functioning as:

- Dedicated servers in a server-based network
- Client workstations connected to a server-based network
- Client/server workstations connected to a peer-to-peer network
- Standalone workstations not connected to a network

UNIX is a **multi-user system,** which lets many people simultaneously access and share the resources of a server computer. Users must **log on** by typing their user name and a password before they are allowed to use a multi-user system. This validation procedure protects each user's privacy and safeguards the system against unauthorized use. A **multitasking system** lets one user execute more than one program at a time. For example, on a multitasking system, you can update records in the foreground while your document prints in the background.

UNIX is also a portable operating system. Its **portability** means it can be used in a variety of computing environments. In fact, UNIX runs on a wider variety of computers than any other operating system. It also runs on the Internet, regulating popular programs such as **File Transfer Protocol** (FTP), an Internet protocol used for sending files; and **Telnet**, an Internet terminal emulation program. Dominion Consulting chose UNIX as the OS for its computer system because many of its employees must work on a range of computers performing a variety of tasks at the same time.

## A Brief History of UNIX

A group of programmers at Bell Labs originally developed UNIX in the early 1970s. Bell Labs distributed UNIX in its source code form, so anyone who used UNIX could customize it as needed. Attracted by its portability and low cost, universities began to modify the UNIX code to make it work on different machines. Eventually, two standard versions of UNIX evolved: AT&T produced System V and University of California at Berkeley developed BSD. Using features of both versions, Linux may be a more integrated version of UNIX than its predecessors. Currently, the POSIX project, a joint effort of experts from industry, academia, and government, is working to standardize UNIX.

## UNIX Concepts

UNIX pioneered concepts that have been applied to other operating systems. For example, Microsoft DOS and Microsoft Windows adopted original UNIX design concepts, such as the idea of a **shell**—an interface between the user and the operating system—and the hierarchical structure of directories and subdirectories.

The concept of layered components that make up an operating system also originated with UNIX. Layers of software surround the computer system's inner core to protect its vital hardware and software components and to insulate the core system and its users. Figure 1-5 shows how the layers of a UNIX system form a pyramid structure.

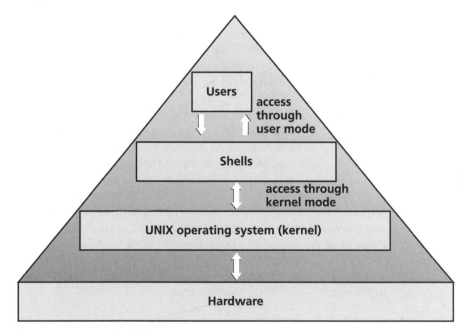

**Figure 1-5:** Layers of a UNIX system

At the bottom of the pyramid is the hardware. At the top are the users. The layers provide insulation, assuring system security and user privacy. The **kernel** is the base operating system, which interacts directly with the hardware and services the user programs. It is only accessible through **kernel mode**, which is reserved for the system administrator. This prevents unauthorized commands from invading the **foundation layer** or the hardware that supports the entire UNIX structure. **User mode** provides access to higher layers where all application software resides.

This layered approach, and all other UNIX features, were designed by programmers, for programmers to use in complex software development. Because the programmers wrote UNIX in the C programming language, it can be installed on any computer that has a C compiler. Its portability, flexibility, and power make UNIX a logical choice for network operating systems. And, with the emergence of a new PC version called Linux, the popularity of UNIX is increasing.

## Linux and UNIX

Linux is a UNIX-like operating system. Linus Torvalds, who released it to the public, free of charge, in 1991, originally created Linux. A number of companies now distribute professional versions of Linux.

Linux offers all the complexity of UNIX at no cost. It is robust enough to handle large tasks with all the networking features of commercial UNIX versions. You can install Linux on your PC, where it can coexist with other operating systems, and test your UNIX skills. All these features make Linux an excellent way to learn UNIX, even when you have access to other computers running on UNIX.

## Introducing UNIX Shells

The **shell** is a UNIX program that interprets the commands you enter from the keyboard. UNIX provides several shells, including the Bourne shell, the Korn shell, and the C shell. Steve Bourne at AT&T Bell Laboratories developed the **Bourne shell** as the first UNIX command processor. Another Bell Labs employee, David Korn, developed the Korn shell. Compatible with the Bourne shell, the **Korn shell** includes many extensions, such as a history feature that lets you use a keyboard shortcut to retrieve commands you previously entered. The **C shell** is designed for C programmers' use. Linux uses the freeware **Bash shell** as its default command interpreter. Its name is an acronym for "Bourne Again Shell," and it includes the best features of the Korn and Bourne shells. No matter which shell you use, your communications with UNIX always take place through a shell interpreter. Figure 1-6 shows the role of the shell in the UNIX operating system.

**Figure 1-6:** Shell's relationship to the user and the hardware

### Choosing Your Shell

Before working with a UNIX system, you need to determine which shell will serve as your command interpreter. Shells do much more than interpret commands: each has extensive built-in commands that, in effect, turn them into first-class programming languages. (You will pursue this subject in depth in Chapters 6 and 7.) You choose a shell when the system administrator sets up your user account. Most users choose the Bash shell, although you can choose any of these:

- Bourne
- Korn
- C shell
- Bash
- tcsh (a freeware shell derived from the C shell)
- zsh (a freeware shell derived from the Korn shell)

### Switching from Shell to Shell

After you choose your shell, the system administrator stores your choice in your account record, and it becomes your assigned shell. UNIX uses this shell any time you log on. However, you can switch from one shell to another by typing the shell's name (such as **tcsh**, **bash**, or **zsh**) on your command line. You work in that shell until you log on again or type another shell name on the command line. Users often use one shell for writing shell scripts (programs) and another for interacting with a program.

## Choosing User Names and Passwords

Before you can work with UNIX and its programs, you must log on by providing a unique user name and password. Decide on a name you want to use to identify yourself to the UNIX system, such as "aquinn." This is the same name others on the UNIX system use to send you electronic mail. UNIX recognizes only the first eight characters of a user name, so choose a user name with eight or fewer characters.

You must also choose a password, which must contain five or more characters. The password should be easy for you to remember but difficult for others to guess, such as your birth date written in a mix of uppercase and lowercase letters, numbers, and hyphens. The password can contain letters, numbers, and punctuation symbols but not control characters.

You can log on to any UNIX or Linux system as long as you have a user account and password on the host (server) computer. A UNIX system administrator creates your account by adding your user name (also called a *login name* or *user id*) and your password. To use this book and the hands-on tutorials, you must connect to and establish an account on a UNIX or Linux system using one of these methods:

- Through a Telnet connection to a remote computer
- As a client on a UNIX client/server network
- As a peer on a peer-to-peer local-area network in which each computer has the Linux operating system installed

- On a standalone PC that has the Linux operating system installed
- Through a log-on terminal, such as a Wyse terminal, connected to a communication port on a UNIX host

The steps you take to connect to a UNIX system vary according to the kind of connection you use. The simplest connection is that of a user terminal that presents the log-on prompt as soon as you turn it on. You can also access the Internet through an Internet Service Provider (ISP) and connect to a remote UNIX host.

## Connecting to UNIX Using Telnet

Telnet is a terminal emulation program for the Internet. It runs on your computer and connects your PC to a server, or host, on the network. You can then log on to a UNIX host and begin working with UNIX.

Each computer on the Internet has an **Internet Protocol** (IP) address. An IP address is a set of four numbers separated by periods, such as *172.16.1.61*. Most systems on the Internet also have a **domain name** such as *Lunar.campus.edu*. Both the IP address and the domain name identify a system on the network. Programs such as Telnet use IP addresses or domain names to access remote systems.

### To access a UNIX host via Telnet:

**1**  Find the remote host's IP address or domain name.

**2**  Connect to the Internet, if necessary. If you use a PPP connection to dial into an ISP, make that connection. If you use a full-time Internet connection at work or school, ignore this step.

**3**  Start your Telnet program and connect to the UNIX system.

Follow the instructions in your Telnet program to connect to a remote host. Usually, you must provide the host name to connect to a UNIX system. For example, you can type the following command after the prompt in a Windows 95/98 MS-DOS window to gain access to the system *Lunar.campus.edu*.

```
telnet Lunar.campus.edu
```

## Logging On to UNIX

After you connect to a UNIX system, you must log on by entering your user name and password. You see a prompt requesting the login or user name and the password. For security reasons, the password does not appear on the screen as you type it. You cannot log on without an authorized user account, if your password fails, or if you wait too long before entering your name and password. Contact your system administrator for help.

After you log on, you are ready to begin using the system.

## Entering Commands

To interact with UNIX, you enter a **command**, text you type after the command prompt. When you finish typing the command, press Enter. UNIX is **case-sensitive**, that is, it distinguishes between uppercase and lowercase letters, so that *John* differs from *john*. You type most UNIX commands in lowercase. Commands are divided into two categories: user-level commands that you type to perform tasks, such as retrieve information or communicate with other users; and system-administration commands, which the system administrator uses to manage the system.

You must know a command's syntax to enter it properly. **Syntax** refers to a command's format and wording, as well as the options and arguments you can use to extend and modify its functions. Most commands are single words, such as *clear*. If you enter a command using correct syntax, UNIX executes the command. Otherwise, you receive a message that UNIX cannot interpret your command.

Appendix A, "Syntax Guide to UNIX Commands," alphabetically lists all the commands in this book and tells you how to enter each command and use its options.

The place on the screen where you type the command is called the **command line**. Commands use the following syntax:

| Syntax | command_name [-options] [arguments] |
| --- | --- |
| Dissection | ■ The **command_name** specifies what operation to perform. In the syntax illustrations in this book, command names appear in boldface. |
| | ■ Command **options** are ways to request that UNIX carry out a command in a specific style, or variation. Options follow command names, separated by a space. They always begin with a hyphen (-). Options are also case-sensitive. For example, **-R** differs from **–r**. You do not need to type an option after every command; however, some commands do not work unless you specify an option. The syntax illustrations in this book list options in square brackets ([ ]) when the command does not require them. |
| | ■ Command **arguments** follow command options, separated by a space. Command arguments are usually file and directory names. In the syntax illustrations in this book, arguments appear in italics. Square brackets surround arguments if the command does not require them. |

### The date Command

Use the UNIX date command to display the system date, which the system administrator maintains. Because the date and time on a multi-user system are critical for smooth processing, only the system administrator can change the date. You start your UNIX training at Dominion Consulting by checking the system date.

**To display your system date:**

**1**  Type **date** in the command line, and press **Enter**.

A date like the one below appears:

```
Mon Apr 20 21:30:08 EST 2000
```

You may see the abbreviation EDT (eastern daylight time) instead of EST (eastern standard time), or another time zone abbreviation, such as PDT (Pacific daylight time) or CST (central standard time). Notice also that UNIX uses a 24-hour clock.

**2**  Type **Date** in the command line, and press **Enter**. You see the following system error message:

```
bash: Date: command not found
```

The system error message appears because you must enter the date command, like most UNIX commands, in lowercase letters.

The date command has an option, -u, which displays the time in Greenwich mean time.

**To display your system date:**

■  Type **date -u** in the command line, and press **Enter**.

A date like the one below appears:

```
Mon Apr 20 23:43:148 UTC 2000
```

## The cal Command

Use the cal command to show the system calendar. Your manager at Dominion, Rolfe Williams, advises you that this is the command commonly used to schedule tasks and events.

**To display your system's default calendar:**

**1**  Type **cal** in the command line, and press **Enter**. Without an option, the cal command shows a calendar of the current month. Assuming the current month is July of the year 2000, you see the default calendar shown in Figure 1-7.

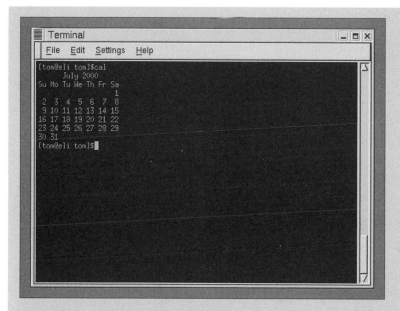

**Figure1-7:** Example of cal command (current month)

**2** Type **cal –j 2000** in the command line, and press **Enter**.

The –j option displays the Julian date format. In other words, it shows the days as numbers starting with 1 and ending with 366, as shown in Figure 1-8.

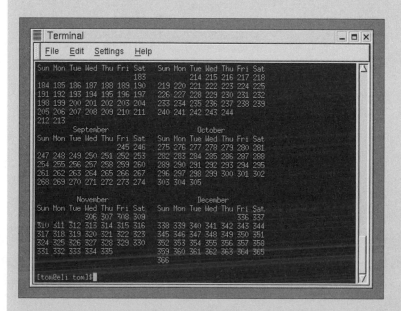

**Figure 1-8:** Example of cal command (full year—Julian dates)

**3**  To determine the day of the week when the Declaration of Independence was signed, type **cal 7 1776** in the command line, and press **Enter**. You should see a calendar similar to the one in Figure 1-9. In this case, the month and year are the command arguments.

**help**

If you type **cal may 1999**, you see an error message because you must use numbers to indicate months, such as *5* for *May*.

```
cal: illegal month value: use 1-12
```

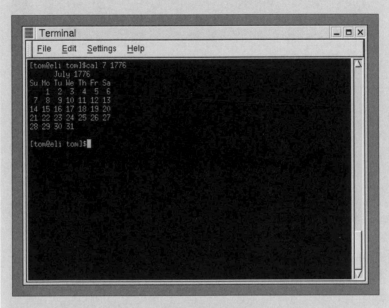

Figure 1-9: Example of cal command (July 1776)

## The who Command

In a multi-user system, knowing who is logged on to the system may be helpful. Use the who command to see who is using the system and their current location. At Dominion, who is a useful command for getting to know your co-workers.

**To use the who command to determine who is logged onto the system:**

**1**  Type **who** in the command line, and press **Enter**.

**2**  You see a list like the one below showing user names, the terminals they are using, and the dates and the times they logged on.

```
root    tty1    Aug 12 07:56
ellen   tty1    Aug 12 08:15
```

```
john    tty2    Aug 12 08:15
jerry   tty3    Aug 12 08:21
```

**3**  To display a line of column headings with the who command's output, type **who –H** and press **Enter**. You see a list like the one below.

```
USER    LINE    LOGIN-TIME      FROM
root    tty1    Aug 12 07:56
ellen   tty1    Aug 12 08:15
john    tty2    Aug 12 08:15
jerry   tty3    Aug 12 08:21
```

If any current users are logged on from a remote host, the FROM column shows the name of the host.

**4**  Idle time is the amount of time that has elapsed with no activity in a user's session. Type **who –i** and press **Enter** to see each user's idle time. You see a list similar to the one below.

```
root    tty1    Aug 12 07:56    00:29
ellen   tty1    Aug 12 08:15    .
john    tty2    Aug 12 08:15    00:01
jerry   tty3    Aug 12 08:21    old
```

The output shows that the person logged on as *root* has performed no activity in the last 29 minutes, and John's session has been idle for one minute. The period on Ellen's line indicates that her session has been active in the last minute. The word *old* on Jerry's line indicates no activity in the past 24 hours.

**5**  If you wish to use multiple options on the same command line, type them all after a single hyphen. For example, type **who –iH** and press **Enter** to see a list of users with idle times and column headings. You see a list similar to the one below.

```
USER    LINE    LOGIN-TIME      IDLE      FROM
root    tty1    Aug 12 07:56    00:29
ellen   tty1    Aug 12 08:15    .
john    tty2    Aug 12 08:15    00:01
jerry   tty3    Aug 12 08:21    old
```

**6**  Type **who –q** and press **Enter** to see a quick list of current users. You see a list similar to the one below, which shows only login names and the total number of users on the system.

```
root ellen john jerry
# users=4
```

**7**  To determine which terminal you are using or what time you logged on, type **who am I** in the command line, and press **Enter**. You see a line similar to the one below. It shows your user name, terminal, and the date and time you logged on.

```
lucky.campus.edu!ellen    tty1    Aug 12 08:15
```

The output above shows that you are logged on to the system lucky.campus.edu as the user ellen.

Note: Any time you provide two arguments to the who command, you'll see the output described in Step 7. For example, you can type who are you, or who x x, to see the same information. Traditionally, UNIX users type who am I to see information describing their session.

## Command-line Editing

Shells support certain keystrokes for performing command-line editing. For example, Bash (which is the default Linux shell) supports the left and right arrow keys, which move the cursor on the command line. Other keys, used in combination with the Ctrl or Alt key, cause other editing operations.

Note: Not all shells support command-line editing in the same manner. The following steps work with the Bash shell.

### To edit a command typed on the command line:

1   To determine which shell you are using, type **echo $SHELL** and press **Enter**. If you are using the Bash shell, you will see the following output.

```
/bin/bash
```

If you are not using the Bash shell, type **bash** and press **Enter**.

2   Type **who am I**, but do *not* press **Enter**.

3   Press the **left arrow** key to move the cursor to the letter **a** in the word *am*.

4   Press **Alt+D** to delete the word "am."

5   Press **Ctrl+K** to delete the command line from the current cursor position.

6   Press **Ctrl+A** to move the cursor to the beginning of the command line.

7   Press **Ctrl+K** again to delete the command line.

8   Retype the command **who am I**, but do *not* press **Enter**.

9   Press **Alt+B** three times. Watch the cursor move to the first character of the previous word each time you press the key combination. The cursor should be positioned at the beginning of the line.

10  Press **Alt+F** three times. Each time you press the key combination, the cursor moves to the position just before the first character of the next word.

11  Press **Ctrl+A**, and then press **Ctrl+K** to clear the command line.

## Multiple Command Entry

You may type more than one command on the command line by separating each command with a semicolon (;). When you press Enter, UNIX executes the commands in the order you entered them.

**To enter multiple commands on the command line:**

■ Type **date ; who –iH** and press **Enter**. You see information similar to the following:

```
Mon Apr 20 21:35:09 EST 2000
USER    LINE    LOGIN-TIME    IDLE      FROM
root    tty1    Apr 20 07:56  00:29
ellen   tty1    Apr 20 08:15    .
john    tty2    Apr 20 08:15  00:01
jerry   tty3    Apr 18 08:21    old
```

The date command produces the first line of the output shown above. The remainder of the output is the result of the who command.

## The clear Command

As you continue to enter commands, your screen may become cluttered. Unless you need to refer to commands you previously entered and their output, you can use the **clear** command to clear your screen. It has no options or arguments.

**To clear the screen:**

■ Type **clear** on the command line, and press **Enter**. The command prompt is now in the upper-left corner of your screen.

## The Command-line History

Often you find yourself entering the same command several times within a short period of time. Most shells keep a list of your recently used commands and allow you to recall a command without retyping it. You can access the command history with the up and down arrow keys. Pressing the up arrow key once recalls the most recently used command. Pressing the up arrow key twice recalls the second most recently used command. Each time you press the up arrow key, you recall an older command. Each time you press the down arrow key, you scroll forward in the command history. When you locate the command you want to execute, press Enter.

**To use the command-line history:**

**1**  Type **date** and press **Enter**.

**2**  Type **who** and press **Enter**.

**3**  Type **who –iH** and press **Enter**.

**4**  Type **clear** and press **Enter**.

**5**  Press the **up arrow** key four times. The date command is recalled to the command line. Do *not* press **Enter**.

**6**  Press the **down arrow** key twice. The who –iH command is recalled to the command line. Press **Enter** to execute the command.

## The man Program

For reference, UNIX includes an online manual that contains all commands, including their options and arguments. The man program in UNIX displays this online manual, called the man pages, for command-line-assistance. Although the man pages for some commands contain more information than others, most man pages list the following items.

- Name: the name of the command and a short statement describing its purpose
- Synopsis: a syntax diagram showing the usage of the command
- Description: a more detailed description of the command than the name item gives
- Options: a list of command options and their purposes
- See Also: other commands or man pages that provide related information
- Bugs: a list of the command's known bugs

The man program usually accepts only one argument—the name of the command about which you want more information. The online manual shows the valid command formats that your system accepts. To close the online manual, type q.

You decide to display information about the who command and the man program for yourself and others at Dominion.

**To display online help for commands:**

**1**  Type **man who** in the command line, and press **Enter**. You see the explanation of the who command illustrated in Figure 1-10.

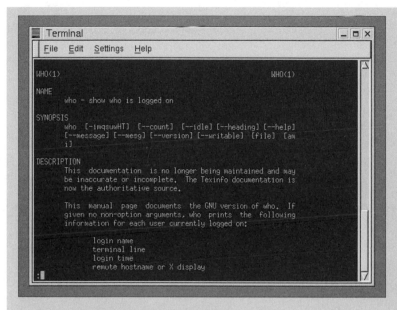

**Figure 1-10:** Manual page

**2** Type **q** to exit the man program.

**3** Type **man man** and press **Enter**. You see the man pages describing the man command.

**4** Type **q** to exit the man program.

## The whatis Command

Sometimes you find that the man pages contain more information than you want to see. To display a brief summary of a command, use the whatis command. The whatis command shows only the name and brief description that appears near the top of a command's man page.

**To display a brief description of a command with the whatis command:**

**1** Type **whatis who** and press **Enter**.

**2** You see a summary of the who command, as shown below.

```
who (1)            - show who is logged on
```

**3** Type **q** to exit the man program.

Note:  The whatis command relies on information stored in a database. The system administrator must execute the makewhatis command, which creates the database, before the whatis command will operate properly. If the whatis command does not display command summaries on your system, the system administrator probably has not executed the makewhatis command.

## Logging Out of UNIX

When you finish your day's work or leave your terminal for any reason, log out of the UNIX system. **Logging out** ends your current process and indicates to UNIX that you are finished. How you log out depends on the shell you are using. For the Bourne, Korn, or Bash shells, type exit on the command line or press Ctrl+D. In the C shell, type logout on the command line.

**To log out of UNIX:**

■  In the command line, type **exit** and press **Enter.**

After completing this lesson, you should be able to:

- Discuss the role of the system administrator
- Identify the system administrator's and the ordinary user's command prompts
- Change your personal password
- View files on your screen using the cat, more, less, head, and tail commands
- Redirect output to a file

# Roles of the System Administrator and Ordinary Users

## Understanding the Role of the UNIX System Administrator

There are two types of users on a UNIX system: the system administrator and ordinary users. As the name suggests, the **system administrator** manages the system by adding new users, deleting old accounts, and ensuring that the system performs services well and efficiently for all users. **Ordinary users** are all other users. The system administrator is also called the **superuser,** because the system administrator has unlimited permission to alter the system. UNIX grants this permission when the operating system is initially installed. The system administrator grants privileges and permissions to regular users.

The system administrator has a unique user name: **root.** The system administrator **owns** the root account, which means no one else can be assigned to that account. The password for the root account is confidential; only the system administrator and a back-up person know it. If the root's password is lost or forgotten, the system administrator uses an emergency rescue procedure to reset the password.

### The System Administrator's Command Line

While ordinary users type their commands after the $ (dollar sign) command prompt, the system administrator's prompt is the # (pound) symbol. The UNIX system generates a default setting for the command prompt for the system administrator in the following format:

```
[root@hostname]#
```

In the prompt, *hostname* is the name of the computer the system administrator logged on to.

For more information on the role of the system administrator, see Chapter 11, "UNIX/Linux System Administration."

### The Ordinary User's Command Line

The $ (dollar sign) is traditionally associated with ordinary users. The UNIX system generates a default setting for the command prompt for ordinary users in the following format:

`[user name@hostname]$`

In the prompt, *user name* is the user's login name, such as *jean*, and *hostname* is the name of the computer the user is logged on to.

## Changing Passwords

Your user name, or login name, identifies you to the system. You may choose your own user name and give it to the system administrator, who then adds you as a new user. As mentioned before, UNIX recognizes up to eight characters in your user name, which is often your first name or nickname. The user name is unique, but not confidential, and may be provided to other users. The password, on the other hand, is confidential and secures your work on the system. You can change your password, if necessary, by using the passwd command. If you do not have a password, use the passwd command to create one.

UNIX lets you change your password only if the new one differs from the old password by at least three characters; the password has more than five characters, including at least two letters and one number; and the password is different from your user name.

The password you chose for the Dominion system—Gscott956—is too similar to another password on the system, so the system administrator asks you to change it.

### To change your password:
**1** Type **passwd** after the command prompt, and press **Enter**.

**2** Type your new password and press **Enter**. Your new password does not appear on the screen as you type.

**3** Retype your new password and press **Enter** so that UNIX can confirm the new password.

 **help**

If the password you retype as confirmation does not match your new UNIX password, UNIX asks you to enter the password again. UNIX may also ask you to choose a different password because you chose one that is too short or too easily guessed, such as *password*.

After changing your password, you should log out and log on again to make sure UNIX recognizes your new password.

**tip**

## Viewing Files Using the cat, more, less, head, and tail Commands

Three UNIX commands let you view the contents of files: cat, more, and less. The more and less commands display a file, one screenful at a time, while the cat command displays the whole file at once. Two other commands, head and tail, let you view the first few or last few lines of a file.

The cat command gets its name from the word **concatenate**, which means to link. You can display multiple files by entering their file names after the cat command and separating each with a space. UNIX then displays the file's contents in the order you entered them.

Your system administrator at Dominion mentions that you can use the cat command to view a file called shells that resides in the /etc directory. This file contains a list of valid shell programs on the system.

**To view the shells file:**

**1** Type **cat /etc/shells** after the command prompt, and press **Enter**.

Use the forward slash (/) to indicate a directory or folder change. You see a list of the available shells, including /bin/bash, /bin/sh, /bin/bsh, /bin/tcsh, /bin/csh, and /bin/zsh.

Sometimes it is helpful to see a file's contents displayed with line numbers. The –n option causes the cat command to display a number at the beginning of each line of output.

**2** Type **cat –n /etc/shells** and press **Enter**. You see the same list of shells as before, but this time a number precedes each line.

You can also view another file in the /etc directory called termcap. This multiple-page file contains many specifications about all terminals supported on the Linux system. The cat command is not a practical way to view this file, which is longer than one screen (23 lines). However, you can use the more and less commands to read a large file screen by screen.

**To view the contents of large files on the screen with the more command:**

**1** Type **more /etc/termcap** after the command prompt, and press **Enter**.

**2** Press the **spacebar** to scroll to the next screen. You cannot use the more command to return to a previously displayed screen.

**3** Terminate the display by typing **q** (for quit).

**To view the contents of large files on the screen with the less command:**

**1**  Type **less /etc/termcap** after the command prompt, and press **Enter**. You see a long file of text on your screen.

**2**  Press the **down arrow** key several times to scroll forward in the file one line at a time.

**3**  Press the **up arrow** key several times to scroll backward in the file one line at a time.

**4**  Press **Pg Dn, Space, z,** or **f** to scroll forward one screen.

**5**  Press **Pg Up** or **b** to return to a previous screen.

**6**  Terminate the display by typing **q** (for quit) when you see a colon (:) at the bottom of a screen.

Sometimes you only need to glimpse part of a file's contents to determine what is stored in the file. The head command shows you the first few lines of a file—by default, the first 10 lines.

**To view the first or last few lines of a file:**

**1**  Type **head /etc/termcap** and press **Enter** to see the first 10 lines of the /etc/termcap file.

**2**  The –n option specifies the number of lines the head command displays. Type **head –n 5 /etc/termcap** and press **Enter**. You see the first five lines of the /etc/termcap file.

**3**  The tail command shows you the last few lines of a file. Like the head command, tail displays 10 lines by default. Type **tail /etc/termcap** and press **Enter** to see the last 10 lines of the /etc/termcap file.

**4**  The –n option specifies the number of lines the tail command displays. Type **tail –n 5 /etc/termcap** and press **Enter**. You see the last five lines of the /etc/termcap file.

## Redirecting Output

In UNIX, the greater than sign (>) is called the redirection symbol. You can use the **redirection symbol** to create a new file or overwrite an existing file by attaching it to a command that produces output. In effect, you "redirect" the output to a disk file instead of the monitor. You already used the who command to find out who was logged on to the system at Dominion. Now you can use the same command with the redirection symbol to save this information in a text file.

**To save to a file that lists persons logged on to the system:**

**1** Type **who > current_users** after the command prompt, and press **Enter**. The who command output does not appear on the screen but is redirected to a new disk file called current_users. UNIX places this text file in the active directory (the folder on the disk where you are currently using the system).

**2** Type **cat current_users** after the command prompt, and press **Enter** to see a list of users currently using the system, similar to the one below.

```
jean      tty1      Feb 7   07:15
joseph    tty2      Feb 7   07:15
becky     tty3      Feb 7   08:05
```

You can also use the redirection symbol with the cal command to save a calendar in a text file. For example, you will be involved in a Dominion development project with a projected deadline in the year 2000. You can save the calendar in a text file.

**To save the year 2000 calendar in a file:**

**1** Type **cal 2000 > year_2000** after the command prompt, and press **Enter**. This creates a text file called year_2000.

**2** Type **less year_2000** and press **Enter** to see the calendar created by the previous command. Use the arrow keys, Pg Dn, Pg Up, and other keys to scroll through the file.

**3** Terminate the display by typing **q** (for quit).

You can also use the cat command to create files from information you type at the keyboard. Type cat>*filename* after the command prompt, where *filename* is the name of the file you are creating. Then press Ctrl+D to end data entry from the keyboard.

Use the redirection symbol (>) to send output to a file that already exists only if you want to overwrite the current file. To append output to an existing file, use two redirection symbols (>>). This adds information to the end of an existing file without overwriting that file.

As you work with UNIX, you remember that Rolfe Williams, your supervisor, asked you to complete a few tasks by the end of the week. You decide to create a notes file of task reminders.

**To create a new file:**

**1** Type **cat > notes** after the command prompt, and press **Enter**.

**2** Type the following: **Remember to order a new CD-ROM and send the report by Thursday**, and press **Enter**.

**3** Press **Ctrl+D**.

**4**  To review the file you just created, type **cat notes** after the command prompt and press **Enter**. The sentence you typed in Step 2 appears on the screen.

After you create the notes file, you remember that Rolfe Williams asked you to complete another task. You can append the reminder to the existing notes file. You also want to include the appropriate monthly calendar in the file for reference.

**To add information to an existing file:**

**1**  Type **cat >> notes** after the command prompt, and press **Enter**.

**2**  Type the following: **Also remember to make reservations for Sept. conference**, and press **Enter**.

**3**  Press **Ctrl+D**.

**4**  To add the calendar to your notes, type **cal 9 2000 >> notes**.

**5**  Type **less notes** to review the file.

# SUMMARY

- The operating system is the most fundamental computer program. It controls all computer resources and provides the base upon which application programs can be used or written.

- A server-based network is centralized. All the users' data and applications reside on the server, which is secured, maintained, and backed up by the system administrator. Each computer in a server-based network relies on the server. All systems in a peer-to-peer network function as both server and client. The security and maintenance of the network is distributed to each system. If one of the systems in a peer-to-peer network fails, the other systems continue to function.

- The UNIX operating system is a multi-user system that lets many people access and share the computer simultaneously. It is also a multitasking operating system: it can perform more than one task at one time.

- UNIX systems may be configured as dedicated servers in a server-based network, client workstations in a server-based network, client/server workstations in a peer-to-peer network, or standalone workstations connected to no network.

- The concept of the layered components that make up an operating system originated with UNIX. Layers of software surrounding the computer system's inner core protect the vital hardware and software components and insulate the core system from users.

- Linux is a UNIX-like operating system that you install on your PC. It coexists with other operating systems such as Windows and MS-DOS.

■ In UNIX, you communicate with the operating system programs through an interpreter called the *shell*, which interprets the commands you enter from the keyboard. UNIX provides several shell programs, including the Bourne, Korn, and C shells. The Bash shell provides enhanced features from the Bourne and the Korn shells. It is the most popular shell on the Linux system.

■ In UNIX, the system administrator sets up accounts for ordinary users. To set up your account and to protect the privacy and security of the system, you select and give the system administrator your user name and password. You can log on to any UNIX or Linux system anywhere as long as you have a user account and password on the host (server) computer. You can also use the Microsoft Windows Telnet program to log on to a remote UNIX system.

■ The commands you type to work with UNIX have a strict syntax that you can learn by referring to the online manual called the *man pages*. Use the man program to display the syntax rules for a command. Use the whatis command to see a brief description of a command. Use the who command to list who is logged in and where they are located. Use the cal command to display the system calendar for all or selected months. To log out when you decide to stop using UNIX, use the exit or logout command.

■ Most shells provide basic command-line editing capabilities and keep a history of your most recently used commands. Use the up and down arrow keys to scroll backward and forward through the list of recently used commands. You may enter multiple commands on a single command line by separating them with a semicolon. UNIX executes the commands in the order you enter them.

■ You can use the view commands to view the contents of files. Use the cat command to create a file by typing information from the keyboard. Use the less and more commands to display multi-page documents. Use the head and tail commands to view the first or last few lines of a file.

 # C O M M A N D     S U M M A R Y

| Chapter 1 commands | | |
| --- | --- | --- |
| Command | Purpose | Options covered in this chapter |
| cal | Show the system calendar | -j displays the Julian date format |
| cat | Display multiple files | -n displays line numbers |

## Chapter 1 commands (continued)

| clear | Clear the screen | |
| date | Display the system date | -u displays the time in Greenwich mean time |
| exit or logout | Exit UNIX | |
| head | Display the first few lines of a file | -n displays the first *n* lines of the specified file |
| less | Display a long file one screen at a time and scroll up and down | |
| man | Display the online manual for the specified command | |
| more | Display a long file one screen at a time and scroll down | |
| passwd | Change your UNIX password | |
| tail | Display the last few lines of a file | -n displays the last *n* lines of the specified file |
| whatis | Display a brief description of a command | |
| who | See who is logged on to UNIX | -H displays column headings<br>-i displays session idle times<br>q displays a quick list of users |

# REVIEW QUESTIONS

1. UNIX commands are case-sensitive. In which case must you type them?
   a. all uppercase
   b. all lowercase
   c. sentence case, so the first letter is capitalized and others are lowercase
   d. any combination of uppercase and lowercase

2. In which order are UNIX commands given?
   a. name, arguments, options
   b. name, options, arguments
   c. options, name, arguments
   d. arguments, options, name

**3.** Which of these statements is false?
   a. Linux is compatible with UNIX.
   b. Ordinary users cannot change the system date.
   c. The UNIX operating system is called the kernel.
   d. You cannot change the shell after you select one.

**4.** In a _____ network, all users' data and applications are centrally located on one system.
   a. peer-to-peer
   b. server-based
   c. standalone
   d. workstation

**5.** UNIX may be configured to run as _____.
   a. a server in a server-based network
   b. a client workstation in a server-based network
   c. a client/server workstation in a peer-to-peer network
   d. all of the above

**6.** What is required to log on?
   a. a user name and password
   b. only a password
   c. a kernel
   d. a shell

**7.** Use the UNIX date command to _____.
   a. display the system calendar
   b. display any date in the future
   c. reset the system date
   d. display the system date

**8.** The man program provides _____.
   a. a programming guide
   b. an online reference for command syntax
   c. a file template
   d. an operating system version

**9.** The whatis command provides _____.
   a. a brief description of a command
   b. a more detailed description of a command than that given by the man program
   c. a description of a hardware device attached to the system
   d. an online tutorial on the UNIX operating system

**10.** By default, the cal command displays _____.
   a. the current system date
   b. a list of shells
   c. the current month and year
   d. the contents of the cal file

11. What type of operating system best describes UNIX?
    a. a multi-user, multitasking operating system
    b. an operating system that conducts all its operations on a standalone PC
    c. an operating system with a graphical user interface
    d. a portable single-user operating system

12. Why is the UNIX operating system designed with layers?
    a. to increase its speed
    b. to permit networking
    c. to allow other operating systems to communicate with it
    d. to insulate the core system from the user environment

13. When viewing a file with the cat command, you can _____.
    a. edit the file
    b. only view the file
    c. spell check the file
    d. delete the file

14. After creating a file with the cat > *filename* command, if you use the command again with the same filename, you _____.
    a. append new information to the file
    b. overwrite the file
    c. create a new file
    d. delete the file

15. The less command fixes the _____ command's scrolling limitation.
    a. cat
    b. more
    c. clear
    d. date

16. UNIX recognizes the first _____ characters in a user, or login, name.
    a. four
    b. six
    c. eight
    d. twelve

17. The –i option used with the who command displays _____.
    a. your login name
    b. column headings
    c. user idle time information
    d. the number of users currently logged in

18. The password should not contain _____.
    a. numbers
    b. uppercase letters
    c. control characters
    d. the underscore character

**19.** The > symbol may be combined with _____ to create output.
   a. only the cat command
   b. any command that produces output
   c. only the who command
   d. only the cal command

**20.** The _____ commands display only the first or last few lines of a file.
   a. first and last
   b. cat –first and cat –last
   c. viewhead and viewtail
   d. head and tail

**21.** Multiple commands entered on the same command line must be separated by a
_____.
   a. space
   b. semicolon (;)
   c. colon (:)
   d. comma (,)

**22.** One major difference between the system administrator and ordinary users is
_____.
   a. the system administrator has unlimited permission to alter the system
   b. the system administrator does not have to log on to the system
   c. the system administrator must enter commands in uppercase letters
   d. ordinary users can change some system settings, but not all

**23.** The symbol that ordinary users see as their command prompt is the _____.
   a. colon (:)
   b. pound sign (#)
   c. slash character (/)
   d. dollar sign ($)

**24.** True or false: If you forget your password, you can use the passwd command to display it on the screen.

**25.** True or false: Your password must be different from your user name.

**26.** Your password must contain at least _____ character(s).
   a. five
   b. eight
   c. twelve
   d. one

**27.** The passwd command requires that you type your password _____ times.
   a. one
   b. two
   c. three
   d. zero

**28.** When using the cat > *filename* command, you must enter _____ to end keyboard input.
   a. *
   b. Ctrl+D
   c. q
   d. exit

**29.** The _____ symbol directs command output to a file.
   a. *
   b. $
   c. >
   d. <

# E X E R C I S E S

**1.** Use the cal command to determine on what day of the week you were born.

**2.** Use the cal command to discover on what day of the week the Declaration of Independence was signed.

**3.** Use the cal command to discover what is unusual about the year 1752.

**4.** Clear the screen and view the online manual for the cal command. What is the explanation for the year 1752?

**5.** Create a file called today containing today's date.

**6.** Create a file called manual_for_date containing the online manual for the date command.

**7.** Use the who command to append a quick list of current users to the date file.

**8.** View the files today and manual_for_date:
   a. individually
   b. in sequence

**9.** View the files today and manual_for_date in sequence by using:
   a. the less command
   b. the more command

**10.** Create a file containing the calendar for next year, and use the more command to view the file and scroll forward through it.

**11.** Use the less command to view the file you created in Exercise 10, and scroll backward through it.

**12.** Use the tail command to view the last 10 lines of the file you created in Exercise 10.

**13.** Create a file listing two tasks on your to-do list.

**14.** Add another task to the list in the file you created in Exercise 13.

# DISCOVERY EXERCISES

1. Use the who command to determine how many users are logged on.

2. Use the option for the who command that displays a heading for the information displayed.

3. Combine the cat and cal commands to create a file containing a memo about a meeting to review a new hotel management program. Attach a calendar for November of 2000 to your memo, and remind the recipients of the meeting dates for Wednesday, Thursday, and Friday of the third week of the month.

4. Use the head command to view the first six lines of the file you created in Step 3.

5. Repeat the command you used in Discovery Exercise 4, but redirect the output to another file. What is stored in the file you created?

6. Your system administrator at Dominion mentions that you can also specify the number of bytes you wish to view with the head and tail commands. Use the man program to discover how this is done. Perform the proper commands to view the first and last 10 characters of the file you created in Discovery Exercise 3.

# Exploring the UNIX File System

**2**

**case ▶** Dominion Consulting is creating a centralized telephone database that will contain each employee's name and phone number information. Currently each department maintains this information and stores it in multiple files located in separate directories. Your job is to consolidate this information in a single master database that everyone in the company can access.

**After studying this lesson, you should be able to:**

■ Discuss and explain the UNIX file system

■ Define a UNIX file system partition

■ Use the mount command to mount a file system

■ Discuss relative and absolute path addressing

■ Diagram the UNIX file system hierarchy

■ Navigate the file system

# Understanding Files and Directories

In this chapter, you explore the UNIX file system, including the basic concepts of files and directories and their organization in a hierarchical tree structure. After you learn to navigate the file system, you practice what you've learned by creating directories and files and copying files from one directory to another. You also have the opportunity to set file permissions, which is important in a multi-user system like UNIX.

## Understanding the UNIX File System

In UNIX, a **file** is the basic component for data storage. UNIX considers everything it interacts with as a file, even attached devices such as the monitor, keyboard, and printer. A **file system** is the UNIX system's way of organizing files on mass storage devices such as hard and floppy disks. A physical file system is a section of the hard disk that has been formatted to hold files. UNIX consists of multiple file systems that form virtual storage space for multiple users. The file system's organization is a hierarchical structure similar to an inverted tree; that is, a branching structure where top-level files contain other files, which in turn contain other files. Figure 2-1 illustrates a typical UNIX directory.

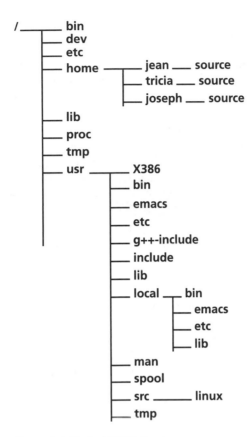

**Figure 2-1:** Typical UNIX directory

## Understanding the Standard Tree Structure

The tree-like structure for UNIX file systems starts at the root level. **Root** is the name of the file at this basic level, and it is denoted by the slash character (/). The slash represents the **root directory**.

A **directory** is a special kind of file that can contain other files and directories. Regular files store information, such as records of employee names and addresses or payroll information, while directory files store the names of regular files and the names of other directories, which are called **subdirectories**. The subdirectory is considered the **child** of the **parent** directory because the child directory is created within the parent directory. In Figure 2-1, the root directory (/) is the parent of all the other directories. The home directory, for example, is the parent of the jean, tricia, and joseph subdirectories.

## Using UNIX Partitions

The section of the disk that holds a file system is called a **partition**. One disk may have many partitions, each separated from the others so that it remains unaffected by external disturbances such as structural file problems associated with another partition. When you install UNIX on your computer, one of your first tasks is deciding how to partition your hard drive.

UNIX partitions are identified with names such as "hda1" and "hda2." The first two letters tell UNIX the device type: "hd," for instance, means hard disk. The third letter, "a," for instance, indicates whether the disk is the primary or secondary disk (a=primary, b=secondary). Partitions on a disk are numbered starting with 1. The name "hda1" tells UNIX that this is the first partition on the disk, and the name "hda2" indicates it is the second partition on the same disk. If you have a second hard disk with two partitions, the partitions are identified as "hdb1" and "hdb2." Computer storage devices such as hard disks are called peripheral devices. Computer **peripherals**, like hard disks, connect to the computer through **electronic interfaces**. The two most popular hard disk interfaces are the **IDE** (integrated drive electronics) and **SCSI** (small computer system interfaces). On PCs, IDE hard disk drives are more common than SCSI (pronounced "scuzzy"). The SCSI is faster and more commonly used on local-area-network servers. If you have a primary SCSI hard disk with two partitions, the two partitions are named "sda1" and "sda2." Figure 2-2 shows two partition tables: one with an IDE drive and the other with a SCSI drive.

```
Disk/dev/hda: 128 heads, 63 sectors, 767 cylinders
Units = cylinders of 8064 * 512 bytes

     Device Boot  Begin    Start    End   Blocks   Id  System
/dev/hda1     *       1        1    242   975712+    6  DOS 32-bit >=32M
/dev/hda2           243      243    767  2116899    5  Extended
/dev/hda3           243      243    275   127024+  83  Linux native
/dev/hda6           276      276    750  1028224+  83  Linux native
/dev/hda7           751      751    767    68512+  82  Linux swap

Command (m for help):  _
```

This partition table is from a Linux system with an IDE drive

```
Disk /dev/sda: 255 heads, 63 sectors, 1106 cylinders
Units = cylinders of 16065 * 512 bytes

     Device Boot  Begin    Start    End   Blocks   Id  System
/dev/sda1            1        1     64   514048+  83  Linux native
/dev/sda2           65       65   1106  8369865    5  Extended
/dev/sda5           65       65   1084  8193118+  83  Linux native
/dev/sda6         1085     1085   1100   128488+  82  Linux swap

Command (m for help):  _
```

This partition table is from a Linux system with a SCSI drive

**Figure 2-2:** Two partition tables

Note that the first table in Figure 2-2 identifies "hda" as the device, which indicates an IDE drive. The second table identifies "sda" as the device, which indicates a SCSI drive.

## Setting Up File System Partitions

Partitioning your file systems protects and insulates each file system. If one file system fails, you can work with another. This section provides general guidelines on how to partition hard disks. These recommendations are suggestions only. How you partition your hard drive may vary depending on your system's configuration, number of users, and planned use. Partition size is measured in megabytes (MB, a million characters). You should have at least three separate partitions to store your file systems: root, swap, and /usr.

Begin by setting up a partition for the root file system. A partition must be mounted before it becomes part of the file system. The kernel mounts the root file system when the system starts. The kernel has no other information about the computer's other file systems, so all the information and programs the kernel needs to start the system must be present on the root partition. To protect this critical information, isolate the root partition from the other partitions.

Large partitions have a greater chance of being corrupted than small partitions do. The root partition should be small to avoid file corruption. A corrupted root file system makes the system unbootable. Red Hat and most Linux distributors recommend a root partition size of no more than 120 MB.

After creating the root partition, you should set up the **swap** partition. The swap partition acts like an extension of memory, so that UNIX has more room to run large programs. Linux distributors suggest that your swap space be twice the size of your computer's internal memory (RAM). For example, if your computer has 16 MB of RAM, you should allocate 32 MB for the swap partition. Linux distributors recommend not allocating more than 128 MB of swap space, because doing so wastes space. See Appendix C, "Installing Red Hat 5.x," for more information.

The **/usr** partition stores all the non-kernel operating system programs that make the computer useful. These programs include software development packages that support computer programming, networking, Internet access, graphical screens (including X-Windows), and the large number of UNIX **utilities** (programs that perform utilitarian operations like copying files, listing directories, and communicating with other users). The usr partition should be the largest of the three partitions, at least 600 MB.

In addition to these three separate partitions, you can create a **/home** partition, the home directory for all users' directories. A separate home partition protects and insulates users' personal files from the UNIX operating system software.

For example, Dominion Consulting partitions a PC with 16 MB of RAM and allocates 2 GB of hard disk space for UNIX, allowing 120 MB for the root partition, 1400 MB for the /usr partition, 32 MB for the swap partition, and 448 MB for the /home partition.

### The /usr Partition

The /usr partition is a large partition that stores most operating system files and programs. Most Linux distributors, including Red Hat, offer you the option to "install everything" from their CD-ROM and store most of these files in the /usr partition. This is true of other UNIX systems as well. Software development tools such as language compilers, shared libraries, and header files needed for program creation are also stored in a hierarchy of subdirectories starting at /usr.

### The /home Partition

The /home partition is the storage space for all users' work. If the /root partition (or any other partition) crashes, having a /home partition ensures that you do not lose all the users' information. Although you are restricted from reading information in other partitions, you own and can access most files in your home directory. You can grant or deny access to your files as you choose. See "Setting File Permissions" later in this chapter for more information on file ownership.

The size of the partition on a system for all users' home directories depends on how many users the system supports. Thirty users probably need a total of 3000 MB, that is, 3 GB (3 billion characters). This scheme gives users 100 MB each to store their work. The space allocated depends on how much data each user needs to store.

### The /swap Partition

Swap partitions support **virtual memory**. Virtual memory means you have an unlimited memory resource—swap partitions try to meet this goal by providing swap space on disk and treating it like an extension of memory (RAM). It is called swap space because the system can use it to swap information between disk and RAM. Setting up swap space makes your computer run faster and more efficiently. If your computer has 16 MB of RAM or less, you must allocate some disk space to a swap partition. Even if your computer has more than 16 MB of RAM, swap space is recommended for all UNIX systems. The minimum amount of swap space should equal your RAM.

............................................................................................

**The largest possible swap space is 127 MB on Linux systems; any additional space is wasted. You can create and use more than one swap partition if you want more than 127 MB, although this is only necessary for large server installations.**

............................................................................................

# Exploring the Root File System

The root (/) file system is mounted by the kernel when the system starts. To **mount** a file system is to connect it to the directory tree structure. The system administrator uses the mount command to mount a file system. The syntax of the mount command is:

| Syntax | **mount** *device-name mount-point* |
|---|---|
| Dissection | ■ *device-name* identifies the partition (file system) to mount. |
| | ■ *mount-point* identifies the directory where you want to mount the file system. |

See "Using the mount Command" later in this chapter for more information about the mount command.

You must mount a file system before the system can access it. After mounting, the root file system is accessible for reading only. The root file system contains all essential programs for file system repair, restoring from a backup, starting the system, and initializing all devices and operating resources. It also contains the information for mounting all other file systems. Nothing beyond these essentials should reside in the root partition.

**You can restore a "crashed" root partition using rescue files stored on floppy disks or tape. The installation media that comes with Red Hat Linux creates rescue disks.**

The root directory itself generally contains subdirectories that contain files. The next sections describe the more frequently referenced subdirectories of the root file system.

### The /bin Directory

The /bin directory contains **binaries**, or **executables**, the programs needed to start the system and perform other essential system tasks. This directory holds many programs that all users need to work with UNIX.

### The /boot Directory

The /boot directory often contains the files that the **bootstrap loader** (the utility that starts the operating system) needs and the kernel (operating system) images.

### The /dev Directory

Files in /dev are device drivers. They access system devices and resources such as hard disks, the mouse, printers, consoles, modems, memory, floppy disks, and the CD-ROM drive. All UNIX versions include many device files in the /dev directory to accommodate separate vendor devices that can be attached to the computer. The device files are divided into two major classifications: block types and character types. The type indicates the method of data transmission on the device, either as a block of characters or as a serial flow of characters. You can see the list of device files by typing ls –l /dev after the command prompt. (See "Listing Directory Contents" later in this chapter for more information on the ls command.) The left-most character on the list tells you whether the file is a character device (c) or a block device (b) as shown in Figure 2-3.

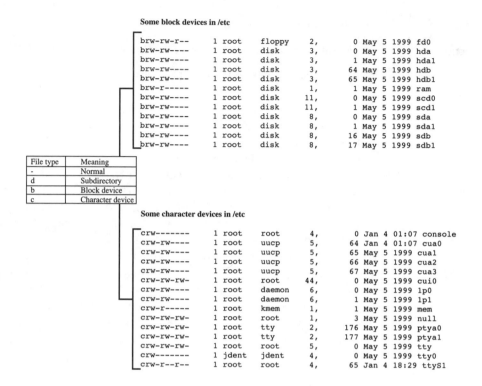

Some block devices in /etc

| | | | | | | | | | |
|---|---|---|---|---|---|---|---|---|---|
| brw-rw-r-- | 1 | root | floppy | 2, | 0 | May | 5 | 1999 | fd0 |
| brw-rw---- | 1 | root | disk | 3, | 0 | May | 5 | 1999 | hda |
| brw-rw---- | 1 | root | disk | 3, | 1 | May | 5 | 1999 | hda1 |
| brw-rw---- | 1 | root | disk | 3, | 64 | May | 5 | 1999 | hdb |
| brw-rw---- | 1 | root | disk | 3, | 65 | May | 5 | 1999 | hdb1 |
| brw-r----- | 1 | root | disk | 1, | 1 | May | 5 | 1999 | ram |
| brw-rw---- | 1 | root | disk | 11, | 0 | May | 5 | 1999 | scd0 |
| brw-rw---- | 1 | root | disk | 11, | 1 | May | 5 | 1999 | scd1 |
| brw-rw---- | 1 | root | disk | 8, | 0 | May | 5 | 1999 | sda |
| brw-rw---- | 1 | root | disk | 8, | 1 | May | 5 | 1999 | sda1 |
| brw-rw---- | 1 | root | disk | 8, | 16 | May | 5 | 1999 | sdb |
| brw-rw---- | 1 | root | disk | 8, | 17 | May | 5 | 1999 | sdb1 |

| File type | Meaning |
|---|---|
| - | Normal |
| d | Subdirectory |
| b | Block device |
| c | Character device |

Some character devices in /etc

| | | | | | | | | | |
|---|---|---|---|---|---|---|---|---|---|
| crw------- | 1 | root | root | 4, | 0 | Jan | 4 | 01:07 | console |
| crw-rw---- | 1 | root | uucp | 5, | 64 | Jan | 4 | 01:07 | cua0 |
| crw-rw---- | 1 | root | uucp | 5, | 65 | May | 5 | 1999 | cua1 |
| crw-rw---- | 1 | root | uucp | 5, | 66 | May | 5 | 1999 | cua2 |
| crw-rw---- | 1 | root | uucp | 5, | 67 | May | 5 | 1999 | cua3 |
| crw-rw-rw- | 1 | root | root | 44, | 0 | May | 5 | 1999 | cui0 |
| crw-rw---- | 1 | root | daemon | 6, | 0 | May | 5 | 1999 | lp0 |
| crw-rw---- | 1 | root | daemon | 6, | 1 | May | 5 | 1999 | lp1 |
| crw-r----- | 1 | root | kmem | 1, | 1 | May | 5 | 1999 | mem |
| crw-rw-rw- | 1 | root | root | 1, | 3 | May | 5 | 1999 | null |
| crw-rw-rw- | 1 | root | tty | 2, | 176 | May | 5 | 1999 | ptya0 |
| crw-rw-rw- | 1 | root | tty | 2, | 177 | May | 5 | 1999 | ptya1 |
| crw-rw-rw- | 1 | root | root | 5, | 0 | May | 5 | 1999 | tty |
| crw------- | 1 | jdent | jdent | 4, | 0 | May | 5 | 1999 | tty0 |
| crw-r--r-- | 1 | root | root | 4, | 65 | Jan | 4 | 18:29 | ttyS1 |

**Figure 2-3:** Device files in /dev

Explanations of the items listed in Figure 2-3 follow:

- **console** refers to the system's console—that is, the monitor connected directly to your system.
- **ttyS1** and **cua1** are devices used to access serial ports. For example, /dev/ttyS1 refers to COM2, the communication port on your PC.
- **cua** devices are "callout" devices used in conjunction with a modem.
- Device names beginning with **hd** access hard drives.
- Device names beginning with **sd** are SCSI drives.
- Device names beginning with **lp** access parallel ports. The lp0 device refers to LPT1, the line printer.
- **null** is a "black hole"—any data sent to this device is gone forever. Use this device when you want to suppress the output of a command appearing on your screen. Chapters 6 and 7 discuss this technique.
- Device names beginning with **tty** refer to "virtual consoles" on your system. (You access them by pressing Alt+F1, Alt+F2, and so on.) Chapter 11 discusses virtual consoles, which let you switch between screens.
- Device names beginning with **pty** are "pseudo-terminals." They are used to provide a terminal to remote login sessions. For example, if your machine is on a network, incoming remote logins would use one of the pty devices in /dev.

## The /etc Directory

The /etc directory contains configuration files the system uses when the computer starts. Most of this directory is reserved for the system administrator, and it contains system-critical information stored in files:

- **passwd,** the user database
- **rc,** scripts or directories of scripts to run when the system starts
- **fstab,** lists of file systems mounted automatically when the system starts
- **group,** the user group database
- **inittab,** the configuration file for the **init** program that performs essential chores when the system starts
- **motd,** the message of the day file
- **printcap,** the printer capability database
- **termcap,** the terminal capability database
- **profile** and **bashrc,** files executed at logon that let the system administrator set global defaults for all users
- **login.defs,** the configuration file for the **login** command

## The /lib Directory

This directory houses the **shared library images,** files that programmers generally use to share code in the libraries rather than creating copies of this code in their programs. This makes the programs smaller and faster. Many files in this directory are symbolic links to files in system libraries. A **symbolic link** is a name that points to and lets you access a file located in a directory other than the current directory. In the directory's long listing, *l* in the leftmost position identifies files that are symbolic links.

## The /mnt Directory

Mount points for temporary mounts by the system administrator reside in the /mnt directory. This directory is often divided into subdirectories such as /mnt/cdrom and /mnt/floppy, to clearly specify device types.

## The /proc Directory

The /proc directory occupies no space on the disk: it is a **virtual file system** allocated in memory only. Files in /proc refer to various processes running on the system, so you can find information about which programs and processes are running.

## The /root Directory

The /root directory is the home directory for the user root, usually the system administrator.

### The /sbin Directory

The /sbin directory is reserved for the system administrator. Programs that start the system, programs needed for file system repair, and essential network programs are stored here.

### The /tmp Directory

Many programs need a temporary place to store data during processing cycles. The traditional location for these files is the /tmp directory.

### The /var Directory

The /var directory holds subdirectories whose sizes often change. These subdirectories contain files such as error logs and other system performance logs that are useful to the system administrator. The /var/spool/mail subdirectory contains mail from the network, which remains there until you read and delete it.

## Using the mount Command

As you learned, UNIX uses the mount command to connect the file system partitions to the directory tree when the system starts. Users can access virtually anything on the system; only the total number of partitions mounted limits access. After the system starts, you can remove this limit by using the mount command to make other file systems accessible. The floppy disk and CD-ROM drives are the two devices that users most commonly need, so you must mount them.

• • • • • • • • • • • • • • • • • • • • • • • • • • • • • • • • • • • • • • • • • • • • • • • • • • • • • • •

**To ensure security on the system, only the root user, usually the system administrator, can use the mount command. However, ordinary users can use several software packages to mount and unmount file systems, particularly on floppy disks and CDs.**

• • • • • • • • • • • • • • • • • • • • • • • • • • • • • • • • • • • • • • • • • • • • • • • • • • • • • • •

Suppose you want to access files on a CD for the Dominion Consulting database. The system administrator mounts a CD-ROM by inserting a disk in the drive and uses the following mount command:

```
mount -t iso9660 -r /dev/cdrom /mnt/cdrom
```

This command mounts the CD on a device called "cdrom" located in the /dev directory. The actual mount point in UNIX is /mnt/cdrom, a directory that references the CD-ROM device. Once the CD is mounted, you can access its files through the /mnt/cdrom directory. UNIX supports several different types of file systems. The type of file system is specified with the –t option. CD-ROMs are classified as iso9660 devices, so the system administrator types –t, followed by the argument iso9660. The –r indicates that the CD-ROM device is read-only.

You also want to store back-up files on a floppy disk. The system administrator mounts a floppy disk in drive A using the command:

```
mount /dev/fd0 /mnt/floppy
```

This command mounts the floppy in drive A, which is the device /dev/fd0, to the mount point, /mnt/floppy, in the UNIX file structure. Any files stored in the directory /mnt/floppy are written to the floppy.

After accessing manually mounted file systems, the system administrator unmounts them using the umount command before removing the storage media, as in these examples:

```
umount /mnt/floppy
umount /mnt/cdrom
```

See Appendix B, "The UNIX Command Syntax Guide to the Linux Shell and Utility Programs," for a complete description of the mount and umount commands.

## Understanding Paths and Pathnames

As you learned, all UNIX files are stored in directories in the file system, starting from the root directory. To specify a file or directory, use its **pathname**, which follows the branches of the file system to the desired file. A forward slash (/) separates each directory name. For example, suppose you want to specify the location of the file phones.502. You know that it resides in the source directory, in Jean's home directory, illustrated in Figure 2-1. You can specify this file's location as /home/jean/source/phones.502.

### Using Your Command-line Prompt

The UNIX command prompt may indicate your location within the file system. For example, the prompt [jean@eli jean]$ is probably the **default prompt** that the system generated when the system administrator first created the login account. The prompt [jean@eli jean]$ means that "jean" is the user working on the host machine called "eli" in her home directory, which bears her user name, "jean." In other words, "jean is at eli in her home directory." When Jean changes her location to /home/jean/source, her prompt looks like:

```
[jean@eli source]
```

**tip**

When the system is initially installed, the default root prompt looks like this: [root@spirit /root]#. To simplify the meaning of the command prompts in this book, the steps use $ to represent the ordinary user's command prompt and # to represent the system administrator's command prompt.

## Customizing Your Prompt

Your login prompt is configured automatically when you login. An environment variable, PS1, contains special formatting characters that determine your prompt's configuration.

**To see the contents of the PS1 environment variable:**

**1**    Type **echo $PS1** and press **Enter**.

**2**    You see the contents of the PS1 variable, which may appear as:

`[\u@\h \W]\$`

Characters that begin with \ are special Bash shell formatting characters. \u prints the user name, \h prints the system host name, and \W prints the name of the working directory. The \$ character prints either a # or a $, depending on the type of user logged on. The brackets, [ and ], and the space that separates \h and \W, are not special characters, so they are printed just as they appear. When Jean is logged on to the system eli and working in her home directory, her prompt appears as [jean@eli jean]$ in the format shown above.

Table 2-1 shows other formatting characters for configuring your Bash shell prompt.

| Formatting character | Purpose |
|---|---|
| \d | Displays the date |
| \h | Displays the host name |
| \n | Displays a new line |
| \nnn | Displays the ASCII character that corresponds to the octal number nnn. |
| \s | Displays the shell name |
| \t | Displays the time |
| \u | Displays the user name |
| \w | Displays the path of the working directory |
| \W | Displays the name of the working directory without any other path information |
| \! | Displays the number of the current command in the command history |

**Table 2-1:** Formatting characters for configuring a Bash shell prompt

| Formatting character | Purpose |
|---|---|
| \# | Displays the number of the command in the current session |
| \$ | Displays a # if root is the user, otherwise displays a $ |
| \[ | Marks the beginning of a sequence of non-printing characters, such as a control sequence |
| \] | Marks the end of a sequence of non-printing characters |
| \\ | Displays a \ character |

**Table 2-1:** Formatting characters for configuring a Bash shell prompt (continued)

**To configure your Bash shell prompt:**

**1** To change your prompt to display the date and time, type **PS1='\d \t>'** and press **Enter**. Type the command with no spaces between the characters. Your prompt now looks similar to:

Tue Jul  5 09:18:33>

**2** To change your prompt to display the current working directory, type **PS1='\w>'** and press **Enter**. Your prompt now looks similar to:

~>

The \w formatting character displays the ~ to represent the user's home directory.

To change your prompt to display the full path of the current working directory, you must use another environment variable, PWD. The PWD variable contains the full pathname of the current working directory.

**3** To display the PWD variable in the prompt, type **PS1='$PWD>'** and press **Enter**. (Notice that you must place the $ sign in front of the environment variable name to extract its contents.) Your prompt now looks similar to:

/home/jean>

**4** Log out of the system, and log back on to reset your prompt to its default configuration.

## The pwd Command

You can use the UNIX pwd command to display your current path (pwd stands for **print working directory**).

**To display your current path:**

■ After the $ command prompt, type **pwd** and press **Enter**. The system displays the path of your current working directory.

## Navigating the File System

To navigate the UNIX directory structure, use the cd (change directory) command. Its syntax is:

| Syntax | cd *directory* |
|---|---|
| Dissection | ■ *directory* is the name of the directory to which you want to change. The directory name is expressed as a path to the destination, with slashes (/) separating subdirectory names. |

When you log on, you begin in your home directory, which is under the /home directory. When you change directories and then want to return to your home directory, type cd and press Enter. (UNIX also uses the tilde character (~) to denote the user's home directory.)

You want to go to the mail subdirectory to see if Dominion employees sent you e-mail.

**To change directories:**

**1** After the $ command prompt, type **cd /etc/mail** and press **Enter**. This moves you to the /etc/mail subdirectory.

**2** Type **cd** and press **Enter**. The change directory command (cd) without arguments returns you to your home directory.

UNIX refers to a path as either an **absolute path** or a **relative path**. An **absolute path** begins at the root level and lists all subdirectories to the destination file. For example, assume that Becky has a directory named lists, located under her home directory. In the lists directory she has a file called todo. The absolute path to the todo file is \home\becky\lists\todo. The path lists each directory that lies in the path to the todo file.

**tip**

••••••••••••••••••••••••••••••••••••••••••••••••••••••••••••••••••••••••••••••••••••

Any time the \ symbol is the first character in a path, it stands for the root directory. All other \ symbols in a path serve to separate the other names.

••••••••••••••••••••••••••••••••••••••••••••••••••••••••••••••••••••••••••••••••••••

A **relative path** takes a shorter journey. You can enter the relative path to begin at your current working directory and proceed from there. In Figure 2-1, jean, tricia, and joseph each have subdirectories located in their /home directories. Each has a subdirectory called "source." Because Jean is working in her home directory, she can change to her source directory by typing the following command and pressing Enter:

```
cd source
```

Jean is changing to her source directory directly from her home directory, /home/jean. This example uses relative path addressing. Her source directory is one level away from her current location, /home/jean. As soon as she enters the change directory command, cd source, the system takes her to /home/jean/source, because it is relative to her current location.

If Tricia, who is in the /home/tricia directory, enters the command cd source, the system takes her to the /home/tricia/source directory. For Tricia to change to Jean's source directory, she can enter:

```
cd /home/jean/source
```

This example uses absolute path addressing, because Tricia starts from the root directory and works through all intervening directories.

---

**To navigate directories:**

**1**   If you are not in your home directory, type **cd** and press **Enter**.

**2**   The parent directory of your home directory is /home. /home is an absolute path name. Type **cd /home** and press **Enter**. The system takes you to the /home directory.

You may now use the relative path with the cd command to return to your home directory. For example, if your user name is phillip, you can type cd phillip.

**3**   Type the **cd** command followed by your user name, and press **Enter**. The system takes you to your home directory.

---

## Using Dot and Dot Dot Addressing Techniques

UNIX interprets a single **dot** character to mean the current directory, and **dot dot** (two consecutive dots) to mean the parent directory. Entering the following command keeps you in the current directory:

```
cd .
```

If you use two dots (known as dot dot), you move back to the parent directory. Do not type a space between the two dots. The next example shows how the user, jean, returns to her home directory, which is /home/jean:

```
cd ..
```

Assume you are Jean in her home directory and want to go to Tricia's source directory. Use the following command:

```
cd ../tricia/source
```

**tip**

Although it is not always required, including a space after all UNIX commands is good practice if the commands include arguments.

In the previous example, the dot dot tells the operating system to go to the parent directory, which is /home. The first / separator followed by the directory name tells the operating system to go forward to the tricia subdirectory. The second "/" separator followed by the directory name tells UNIX to go forward to the source subdirectory, the final destination. If no name follows the slash character, UNIX treats it as the root directory. Otherwise, / separates one directory from another.

**To use dot and dot dot to change your working directory:**

1  If you are not in your home directory, type **cd** and press **Enter**.

2  Type **cd .** and press **Enter**. Since . references your current directory, the system did not change your working location.

3  Type **cd ..** and press **Enter**. The system takes you to the parent directory, which is /home.

4  Type **cd ..** and press **Enter**. The system takes you to the root (/) directory.

5  Type **cd** and press **Enter**. The system takes you to your home directory.

## Listing Directory Contents

Use the ls (list) command to display a directory's contents, including files and other directories. When you use the ls command with no options or argument, it displays the names of all files and directories in your current working directory.

**To see a list of files and directories in your current working directory:**

■  Type **ls** and press **Enter**.

You see a list of file and/or directory names.

You can provide an argument to the ls command to see the listing for a specific file or to see the contents of a specific directory.

**To see a listing for a specific file or directory:**

1  If you are not in your home directory, type **cd** and press **Enter**.

2  In Chapter 1, you used the cat command to create a notes file. You should still have that file in your home directory. Type **ls notes** and press **Enter**. The system displays the listing for the notes file.

**3**   To see the contents of a directory other than your current working directory, give the directory name as an option to the ls command. For example, to see the contents of the /var directory, type **ls /var** and press **Enter**. You see a listing similar to the one below.

```
catman db gdm lib local lock log nis preserve run spool tmp yp
```

You can also use options to display specific information or more information than the command alone provides. The –l option for the ls command generates a long directory listing, which includes complete information about each file. You decide to print a long listing of the /etc and /home directories for the Dominion system.

**To use the ls command with the –l option:**

**1**   Type **ls -l /etc** and press **Enter**.

You see information similar to that in Figure 2-4.

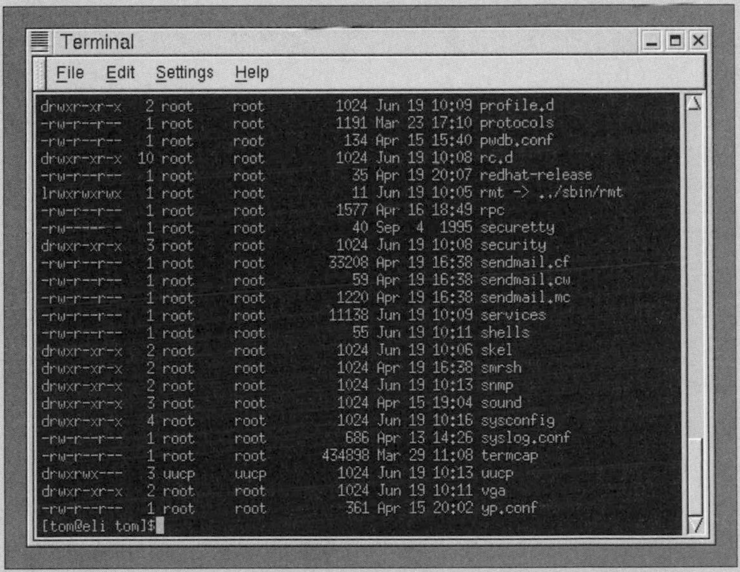

**Figure 2-4:** Contents of /etc directory

**2**   Type **ls –l /** and press **Enter**.

You see information similar to that in Figure 2-5.

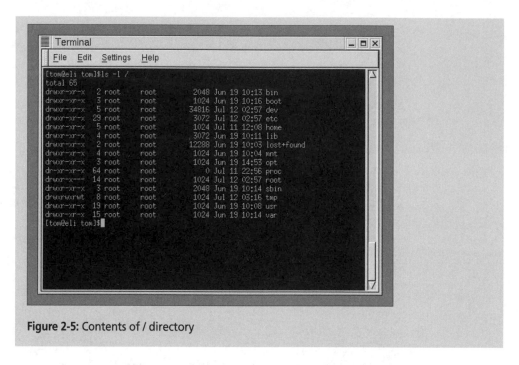

**Figure 2-5:** Contents of / directory

As you can see from the figures, the ls -l command provides more information about each item in the listing than a simple ls command. For example, look at the first item listed in Figure 2-5:

```
drwxr-xr-x    2 root    root        2048 Jun 19   10:13 bin
```

If you look in the rightmost column, you see bin, the name of a file. All the columns to its left contain information about the file bin. Here is a description of the information in each column, from left to right.

- *File Type and Access Permissions*: The first column of information shown is the following set of characters:

  drwxr-xr-x

  The first character in the list, d, indicates the file is actually a directory. If bin were an ordinary file, a hyphen (-) would appear instead. The remainder of the characters indicate the file's access permissions. You will learn more about these later in this chapter, in the section, "Setting File Permissions."

- *Number of Links*: The second column is the number of files that are symbolically linked to this file. (You will learn about symbolic links in Chapter 5.) If the file is a directory, this is the number of subdirectories it contains. The listing for bin shows it contains two subdirectories. (A directory always contains at least two subdirectories: dot and dot dot.)

- *Owner*: The third column is the owner of the file. The root user owns the bin directory.
- *Group*: The fourth column is the group that owns the file. The root group owns the bin directory.
- *Size*: The fifth column shows the size of the file in bytes.
- *Date and Time*: The sixth and seventh columns show the date and time the file was created or last modified.
- *Name*: The eighth column shows the file's name.

You can also use the –a option with the ls command to list **hidden files**, those whose names begin with a dot. The operating system normally uses hidden files to keep configuration information and for other purposes. The system administrator at Dominion tells you that your home directory contains a number of hidden files. You can list them using the –a option with the ls command.

**To list hidden files in your home directory:**

- Type **ls –a** after the command prompt, and press **Enter**.

  You see a list similar to the one in Figure 2-6.

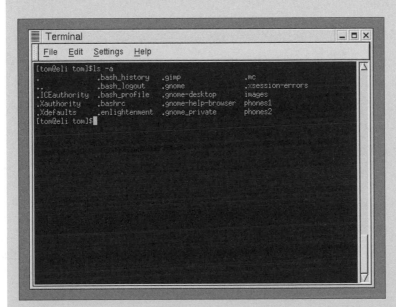

**Figure 2-6:** List of hidden files in the user's home directory

See Appendix B, "The UNIX Command Syntax Guide to the Linux Shell and Utility Programs," for a complete description of the ls command.

## Using Wildcards

A wildcard is a special character that can stand for any other character or, in some cases, a group of characters. Wildcards are useful when you wish to work with several files whose names are similar or with a file whose exact name you cannot remember. UNIX supports several wildcard characters. In this section you will learn about two: * and ?.

The * wildcard represents any group of characters in a filename. For example, assume Becky has these nine files in her home directory:

```
friends
instructions.txt
list1
list2
list2b
memo_to_fred
memo_to_jill
minutes.txt
notes
```

If she enters ls *.txt and presses Enter, she sees the following output:

```
instructions.txt   minutes.txt
```

The argument *.txt causes ls to display the names of all files that end with .txt. If she enters ls memo*, she sees the following output:

```
memo_to_fred   memo_to_jill
```

If she enters the command ls *s and presses Enter, ls displays all filenames that end with s. She sees the output:

```
friends   notes
```

The ? wildcard only takes the place of a single character. For example, if Becky types ls list? and presses Enter, ls displays all files whose names start with *list* followed by a single character. She sees the output:

```
list1   list2
```

She does not see the listing for the file list2b, because two characters follow the word "list" in its name.

**To work with wildcards:**

**1**   To practice using wildcards, you first must create a set of files with similar names. In Chapter 1 you used the cat command to create the notes file. Use the cat command now to create these five files:

first_name: a file containing your first name
middle_name: a file containing your middle name
last_name: a file containing your last name
full_name1.txt: a file containing your full name
full_name22 .txt: another file containing your full name

**2**   Type **ls *name** and press **Enter**. You see first_name, middle_name, and last_name listed.

**3**   Type **ls full_name?.txt** and press **Enter**. You see full_name1.txt listed.

After studying this lesson, you should be able to:

■ Create new directories to store files

■ Copy files from one directory to another

■ Set file permissions to let other users access your directory and files

# Working with Files and Directories

## Creating Directories and Files

As part of your work to create Dominion's centralized telephone database, your manager at Dominion, Rolfe Williams, asks you to create directories for departments 4540 and 4550 and then create files of department phone numbers to store in those directories. You can use the mkdir (make directory) command to create a new directory and the cat command to create the phone files.

**To create new directories and phone files:**

**1** Type **cd** and press **Enter** to make sure you are in your home directory.

**2** Type **mkdir dept_4540** and press **Enter** to make a new directory called dept_4540.

**3** Type **ls** and press **Enter**. You see the dept_4540 directory in the listing.

**4** Type **cd dept_4540** and press **Enter** to change to the new directory. Now you can use the cat command to create a file called phones1. The phones1 file contains fields for area code, phone prefix, phone number, last name, and first name. A colon (:) separates each field.

**5** Type these commands, pressing **Enter** at the end of each line:

```
cat > phones1
219:432:4567:Harrison:Joel
219:432:4587:Mitchell:Barbara
219:432:4589:Olson:Timothy
```

**6** Press **Ctrl+Z**.

**7** Type **cd** and press **Enter** to return to your /home directory.

**8**  Type **mkdir dept_4550** and press **Enter** to make a new directory called dept_4550.

**9**  Type **ls** and press **Enter**. You see the dept_4550 directory in the listing.

**10** Type **cd dept_4550** and press **Enter** to change to the new directory. Now you can use the cat command to create the file phones2, which contains the same fields as the phones1 file.

**11** Type these commands, pressing **Enter** at the end of each line:

**cat > phones2**
**219:432:4591:Moore:Sarah**
**219:432:4567:Polk:John**
**219:432:4501:Robinson:Lisa**

**12** Press **Ctrl+Z.**

You created two new directories using the mkdir command and then created two files of phone number information using the cat command.

Note:  You can delete empty directories by using the remove directory (rmdir) command. First, use the cd command to change to the parent directory of the subdirectory you want to delete. For example, if you want to delete the old directory in /home/old, first change to the home directory. Then type rmdir directory, as in rmdir old, and press Enter.

## Copying Files

You use the UNIX copy command, cp, to copy files from one directory to another. The –i option warns you that the cp command will overwrite the destination file. You can also use the dot location (current directory) as shorthand to specify the destination of a cp command.

After you create the phone file, Rolfe wants you to create a new central directory for Dominion called corp_db and then copy the phones1 file into it. You can use the tilde character (~) to represent the location of your home directory.

**To copy the phones1 file into a new directory, corp_db:**

**1**  Type **cd** and then press **Enter** to return to the /home directory.

**2**  Type **mkdir corp_db** and press **Enter** to make a new directory.

**3**  Type **cd corp_db** and press **Enter** to change to the new directory.

**4**  To copy the phones1 file from the dept_4540 directory to the current directory, type **cp ~/dept_4540/phones1 .** and press **Enter**.

**5**  To copy the phones2 file from the dept_4550 directory to the current directory, type **cp ~/dept_4550/phones2 .** and press **Enter**.

Now the Dominion central database contains two files. You can use the cat command to combine the two files and redirect (>) the output to the corp_phones file, which lists all phone number information for the company.

**To concatenate two files to one:**

**1** Type **cat phones1 phones2 > corp_phones** and press **Enter** to add the contents of the two phone files to one new file called corp_phones.

**2** Type **more corp_phones** and press **Enter** to view the new file's contents.

As you recall from Chapter 1, the more command, which lets you display files one screen at a time, is especially useful for reading long files.

Note: To delete files you do not need, use the remove (rm) command. First, use the cd command to change to the directory containing the file you want to delete. Then type rm *filename*. For example, to delete the file old in the current directory, type rm old. You receive a warning before the file is deleted, so be sure you want to remove a file permanently before using this command. You will learn more about the rm command in Chapter 4.

## Setting File Permissions

Because UNIX is a multi-user system, users can set permissions for files they own so that others can read, write, or execute their files. A file's owner is the person who created it. The permissions the owner sets are listed as part of the file description. Figure 2-7 shows directory listings that describe file types.

| File type | Meaning |
|-----------|---------|
| - | Normal file |
| d | Subdirectory |

```
Excerpt from ls -1 /etc

drwxr-xr-x   12  root    root        1024   Feb  6    1996   X11
-rw-r--r--    1 root    root          10   Oct 15   19:11   adjtime
drwxr-xr-x    1 root    root        1024   Feb 27    2000   cron.daily
```

```
Excerpt from ls -1 /home/jean/source

rw-rw-r--     1 jean    jean         387   Dec 12   23:11   phones.502
```

**Figure 2-7:** File types described in directory listings

Notice the long listing of the two directories. (Remember that the directory is just another file.) The earlier section, "Listing Directory Contents," describes the information presented in a long listing. Now you can look closer at the file permissions. For the first file described, the column on the far left shows the string of letters drwxr-xr-x. You already know the first character indicates the file type. The characters that follow are divided into three sections of file permission specifiers. There are three specifiers in each section, as illustrated in Figure 2-8.

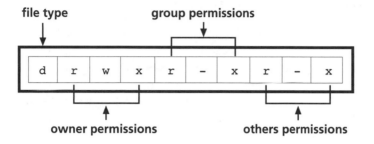

**Figure 2-8:** File permission specifiers

The first section of file permission specifiers indicates the owner's permissions. The owner, like all users, belongs to a group of users. The second section indicates the group's permissions. This specification applies to all users other than the owner who are members of the owner's group. The third section indicates all others' permissions. This specification applies to all users who are not the owner and not in the owner's group. In each section, the first character indicates read permissions. If an "r" appears there, that category of users has permission to read the file. The second character indicates write permission. If a "w" appears there, that category of user has permission to write to the file and delete the file. The third character indicates execute permission. If an "x" appears there, that category of user has permission to execute the file. If a dash (-) appears in any of these character positions, that type of permission is denied.

> Note: If a user is granted read permission for a directory, the user can see a list of its contents. Write permission for a directory means the user can store and delete files in the directory. Execute permission for a directory means the user can make the directory the current working directory.

From left to right, the letters drwxr-xr-x mean:

d   Indicates the file type (d = directory)
r   File's owner has read permission
w   File's owner has write permission
x   File's owner has execute permission (can run the file as a program)
r   Group has read permission
-   Group does not have write permission
x   Group has execute permission

r    Others have read permission

-    Others do not have write permission

x    Others have execute permission

You can change the pattern of permission settings by replacing any of the three letters with a dash (-) to remove, or deny, permission. For example, setting others' permissions to - - - removes all permissions for others. They cannot read, write, or execute the file. In the first line of Figure 2-7, notice that the owner has read, write, and execute (rwx) permissions for the file X11. The r-x indicates that the group of users that shares the same group id as the owner has only read and execute permissions. The system administrator assigns group ids when he or she adds a new user account. **Group ids** give a group of users equal access to files that they all share. Others are all other users who are not associated with the owner's group by a group id, but have read and execute permissions.

Use the UNIX chmod command to set file permissions. In its simplest form, the chmod command takes as arguments a symbolic string followed by one or more file names. The symbolic string specifies permissions that should be granted or denied to categories of users. Here is an example: ugo+rwx. In the string, the characters ugo stand for **u**ser (same as owner), **g**roup, and **o**thers. These categories of users will be affected by the chmod command. The next character, the + sign, indicates that permissions are being granted. The last set of characters, in this case rwx, indicates the permissions being granted. The symbolic string ugo+rwx indicates that read, write, and execute permissions are being granted to the owner, group, and others. Here is an example of how the symbolic string is used in a command, to modify the access permissions of myfile:

```
chmod ugo+rwx myfile
```

Here is a command that grants group read permission to the file customers:

```
chmod g+r customers
```

It is also possible to deny permissions with a symbolic string. The following command denies the group and others write and execute permissions for the file account_info.

```
chmod go-wx account_info
```

See Appendix B, "The UNIX Command Syntax Guide to the Linux Shell and Utility Programs," for a complete description of the chmod command.

Rolfe wants all users to have access to the corp_phones file. To make that possible, he asks you to change the file permissions. First, permit access to your home directory. Next, allow access to the corp_db directory, and then set the permissions for everyone to read the corp_phones file. You can use the execute permission command (x) to grant access to directories.

**To change file and directory permissions:**

**1** Make sure that you are in the parent directory /home.

**2** Type **chmod go+x ~** and press **Enter** to allow access to the home directory.

This command means "make the home directory (~) accessible (+x) to the group (g) and others (o)."

**3** Type **chmod ugo+x ~/corp_db** and press **Enter** to allow access to the corp_db directory.

This command means "make the corp_db directory accessible (+x) for the owner (u), group (g), and others (o)."

**4** Type **chmod ugo+r ~/corp_db/corp_phones** and press **Enter** to set permissions so everyone can read the file.

This command means "make the corp_phones file readable (+r) for the owner (u), group (g), and others (o)."

**Note: From your directory, you can create any subdirectory and set permissions for it. However, you cannot create subdirectories outside your home directory unless the system administrator makes a special provision.**

You used the appropriate UNIX commands to create new directories to store files and set up a central directory for all users, and then you transferred files from other directories to the central directory. Finally, you changed file permissions so other users can access the directories and files you created.

 # S U M M A R Y

- In UNIX, a file is the basic component for data storage. UNIX considers everything to be a file, even attached devices such as the monitor, keyboard, and printer.

- A file system is the UNIX system's way of organizing files on mass storage devices such as hard and floppy disks. Files are stored on a file system, which is a hierarchical structure like a tree where top-level files contain other files, which in turn contain other files.

- Every file can be located by using a correct and unique pathname; that is, a listing of names of directories leading to a particular file.

- The standard tree structure starts with the root (/) directory, which serves as the foundation for a nested group of other directories and subdirectories.

- The section of the disk that holds the file system is called a partition. One disk may have many partitions, each separated from the others so that it remains unaffected by external disturbances such as structural file problems associated with another partition.

- The UNIX file system is a virtual file system, meaning that you can access all partitions once they are mounted in the tree structure.

■ A path, as defined in UNIX, serves as a map to access any file on the system. An absolute path is one that always starts at the root level. A relative path is one that starts at your current location.

■ You may customize your command prompt to display the current working directory name, the date, time, and several other items.

■ The ls command displays the names of files and directories contained in a directory. The ls –l command and its options display all file information on the screen. This display is often called a long listing. The ls –a command shows hidden files.

■ Wildcard characters can be used in a command, such as ls, and take the place of other characters in a file name. The * wildcard can take the place of any string of characters, and the ? wildcard can take the place of any single character.

■ You can use the mkdir command to create a new directory as long as you own the parent directory. A file's owner is the person who creates it and becomes the only one who controls access to it.

■ You can use the chmod command to set permissions for files that you own. The permissions settings are rwx, which mean read, write, and execute, respectively. File permissions are set to control file access by three types of users: the owner, the group, and others. You must remember to change permission settings on any directories you own if you want others to access information in those directories. You use the execute permission (x) command to grant access to directories.

■ You can use the cp command to copy a source file to a destination file. UNIX overwrites the destination file without warning unless you use the –i option. The dot location (current directory) is a shorthand way to specify the destination in a cp command.

##  C O M M A N D   S U M M A R Y

| Chapter 2 commands | | |
| --- | --- | --- |
| Command | Purpose | Options covered in this chapter |
| cd | Change directories | |
| chmod | Set file permissions for specified users | |
| cp | Copy files from one directory to another | -i prevents overwriting of the destination file without warning |
| ls | Display directory's contents, including its files and subdirectories | -a lists the hidden files<br>-l generates a long listing of the directory |

## Chapter 2 commands

| | | |
|---|---|---|
| mkdir | Make a new directory | |
| mount | Connect the file system partitions to the directory tree when the system starts | -r indicates that the mounted device is read-only<br>-t specifies the type of file system |
| pwd | Display your current path | |
| rm | Remove a file | |
| rmdir | Remove an empty directory | |
| umount | Disconnect the file system partitions from the directory tree | |

# R E V I E W    Q U E S T I O N S

1. A UNIX file system _____.
   a. is a directory
   b. is a physical allocation of space on a hard disk or other storage media
   c. has to be formatted to hold files
   d. a and c

2. The standard tree structure starts at _____.
   a. the current directory
   b. the root directory
   c. the first allocated partition
   d. the home directory

3. The absolute path must always start at _____.
   a. the current directory
   b. the root directory
   c. the first allocated partition
   d. the home directory

4. The most important reason to create a disk partition is to _____.
   a. make the system run faster
   b. conserve space on the disk
   c. protect information in that partition
   d. create adequate space to store application software

5. A virtual file system is one that _____.
   a. allows information to be retrieved from anywhere
   b. is created when all partitions are mounted
   c. lets users access virtually anything on the system; the total number of partitions mounted limits access
   d. all of the above

6. A partition named hda2 is _____.
   a. the first partition on the primary hard drive
   b. partition a on hard drive number 2
   c. the second partition on the primary hard drive
   d. the second partition on the secondary hard drive

7. A partition named sda1 is _____.
   a. the first partition on the secondary hard drive
   b. the first partition on the primary SCSI hard drive
   c. the first partition on the secondary SCSI hard drive
   d. none of the above

8. For safety purposes, the most critical file system that should be partitioned is _____.
   a. /
   b. /usr
   c. /home
   d. /bin

9. Most operating system files and programs are stored in the _____ partition.
   a. /
   b. /var
   c. /proc
   d. /usr

10. The _____ partition is the storage space for all users' work.
   a. /home
   b. /
   c. /root
   d. /bin

11. A path is _____.
   a. a tree structure
   b. a long directory listing
   c. a map of partitions
   d. a map to access any file on the system

12. Which of the following serves as virtual memory?
   a. the swap partition
   b. the / root partition
   c. the /etc partition
   d. the /usr partition

**13.** The /dev directory contains _____ .
    a. device driver files
    b. development and programming utilities
    c. the UNIX bootstrap loader
    d. none of the above

**14.** The dot refers to _____ .
    a. the parent directory
    b. the current directory
    c. the home directory
    d. the child directory

**15.** The dot dot refers _____ .
    a. the parent directory
    b. the current directory
    c. the home directory
    d. the child directory

**16.** Which of these statements is false?
    a. You can create a child directory only in a parent directory you own.
    b. You must set the x permission for all directories that you want to access.
    c. You can use the cd .. command to move up one directory in the directory tree.
    d. The dot (.) refers to the parent directory.

**17.** You can use the dot as the location of the _____ .
    a. parent directory
    b. child directory
    c. current directory
    d. root directory

**18.** The \h formatting character, used to customize the prompt, causes _____ to be displayed.
    a. the time in 24-hour format
    b. the host name
    c. the home directory name
    d. none of the above

**19.** The ls –l command is useful for checking _____ .
    a. file permissions
    b. file type
    c. file size
    d. all of the above

**20.** The file type, shown in a long directory listing, for an ordinary file (not a directory) is the character _____ .
    a. f
    b. d
    c. –
    d. space

21. Which of these grants the group read and write access to *filename*?
    a. chmod g+rw *filename*
    b. chmod g+r+w *filename*
    c. chmod o+rw *filename*
    d. chmod g-rw *filename*

22. Which command grants access to directories?
    a. chmod
    b. rwx
    c. execute permission (x)
    d. ls –x

23. The _____ environment variable stores the command-line prompt.
    a. PWD
    b. PROMPT
    c. PATH
    d. PS1

24. When you use the cp command, you should be aware that _____.
    a. the dot destination places the file in the parent directory
    b. the destination file will overlay a file with the same name
    c. it destroys the source file
    d. the source file cannot be relatively addressed

25. The remote directory is in the user's home directory. To copy a file from the remote directory to the current directory, type _____.
    a. cp ~/remote/*filename*
    b. cp +/*filename*
    c. cp > /remote/*filename*
    d. cp/remote/*filename*

26. The –i option, used with the cp command, causes _____.
    a. the cp command to ignore any requests not to overwrite the destination file, if it already exists
    b. the cp command to insert the file being copied into the existing destination file
    c. the cp command to warn you that it will overwrite the destination file
    d. none of the above

27. To list hidden files in a directory, type _____.
    a. hid -a
    b. ls –a
    c. cd\hidden\ls
    d. ls +a

# EXERCISES

1. The file notice.txt is in the directory notices, which is in the directory public. The public directory is in Tom's home directory. (Tom's user name is tom.) What is the absolute path to the notice.txt file?

2. If your current working directory is the notices directory (under Tom's home directory), what is the relative path to the notices.txt file?

3. List an example of the cd command showing how to use absolute path addresses.

4. List an example of the cd command showing how to use relative path addresses. Log on and display the directories in /bin, /sbin, and /etc.

5. List the chmod symbolic string that will grant read and execute permission to a file's owner and group.

6. List the chmod symbolic string that will deny a file's read, write, and execute permission to all users who are not the owner or not in the owner's group.

7. Create a file using the cat command, and copy it to the /home directory. Change permissions so that no one can access that file.

8. Log on as another user, and try to access the files you previously created. Log on again under your account, and modify the files so they are accessible.

# DISCOVERY EXERCISES

1. Use the ls command option to list hidden files in your home directory.

2. Use the absolute path to change to the /etc directory. From the /etc directory, change to the X11 directory using the relative path. Now list the .bashrc file in your home directory using the ls command. (Stay in the current location to do this.)

3. In the command line, type **cd ~/../..** and press **Enter**. Where are you now located in the tree structure? Explain how you got there.

4. In the command line, type **cd ~/../etc/X11** and press **Enter**. Where are you now located in the tree structure? Explain how you got there.

5. Using the relative path from your home directory, enter the cat command to display the contents of the /etc/passwd file.

6. Use the cd command to return to your home directory. Redirect the output of the date command to a file named chap2info. Use the ls command to get a long listing for this file. What permissions do the owner, group, and others have?

7. Change the permissions for the chap2info file to read and write for the owner and deny permissions for anyone else. Look at a long listing to confirm that the changes took effect.

8. Modify your command prompt so it always displays the absolute path of your current working directory.

# CHAPTER 3

# The UNIX Editors

**case ▶** All employees at Dominion Consulting write weekly memos summarizing their activities and accomplishments. They write these memos using a UNIX text editor, which lets you create and modify simple text-based documents. UNIX includes at least two text editors—vi editor and Emacs. As part of your UNIX training, your manager at Dominion Consulting, Rolfe Williams, asks you to use these editors to create two versions of the same memo summarizing basic features of text files.

# LESSON A
## objectives

After studying this lesson, you should be able to:

■ Describe an ASCII text file

■ Explain why operating system editors use ASCII files

■ Create and edit simple documents using the vi editor

# The vi Editor

This chapter introduces two UNIX editors. An **editor** is a program for creating and modifying computer documents such as programs and data files. Files may contain notes, memos, or program source code, for example. A **text editor** is like a simplified word processor; you can use a text editor to create and edit documents, but you cannot format them using boldfaced centered text or other features. All operating systems have a standard editor; many also include alternate editors. In UNIX, the standard editor is the vi editor and the most popular alternate is the Emacs editor.

## Understanding UNIX Files

Almost everything you create in UNIX is stored in a file. All information stored in files is in the form of binary digits. A **binary digit**, called **bit** for short, consists of two numbers, 0 and 1. Because the computer consists of electronic circuits that are either in an "on" or "off" state, binary numbers are perfectly suited to report these states. The exclusive use of 0s (which mean "off") and 1s (which mean "on") as a way to communicate with the computer is known as **machine language**. The earliest programmers had to write their programs using machine language, a tedious and time-consuming process.

### ASCII Text Files

To make information stored in files accessible, computer designers established a standard method for translating binary numbers into plain English. This standard used a string of eight binary numbers, called a **byte,** which is an acronym for "binary term." A byte can be configured into fixed patterns of bits, and these patterns can be interpreted as an alphabetic character, decimal number, punctuation mark, or a special character, such as &, *, or @. Each byte, or **code**, has been standardized into a set of bit patterns known as ASCII codes. **ASCII** stands for the American Standard Code for Information Interchange. Computer files containing nothing but ASCII characters are called **text files**, and files that contain non-ASCII characters, such as machine instructions, are called **binary files**. Figure 3-1 lists the ASCII characters.

| **Printing Characters** (Punctuation Characters) | | | | **Printing Characters** (Alphabet—Upper Case) | | | | **Printing Characters** (Alphabet—Lower Case) | | | |
|---|---|---|---|---|---|---|---|---|---|---|---|
| *Dec* | *Octal* | *Hex* | *ASCII* | *Dec* | *Octal* | *Hex* | *ASCII* | *Dec* | *Octal* | *Hex* | *ASCII* |
| 32 | 040 | 20 | (Space) | 65 | 101 | 41 | A | 97 | 141 | 61 | a |
| 33 | 041 | 21 | ! | 66 | 102 | 42 | B | 98 | 142 | 62 | b |
| 34 | 042 | 22 | " | 67 | 103 | 43 | C | 99 | 143 | 63 | c |
| 35 | 043 | 23 | # | 68 | 104 | 44 | D | 100 | 144 | 64 | d |
| 36 | 044 | 24 | $ | 69 | 105 | 45 | E | 101 | 145 | 65 | e |
| 37 | 045 | 25 | % | 70 | 106 | 46 | F | 102 | 146 | 66 | f |
| 38 | 046 | 26 | & | 71 | 107 | 47 | G | 103 | 147 | 67 | g |
| 39 | 047 | 27 | ' | 72 | 110 | 48 | H | 104 | 150 | 68 | h |
| 40 | 050 | 28 | ( | 73 | 111 | 49 | I | 105 | 151 | 69 | i |
| 41 | 051 | 29 | ) | 74 | 112 | 4A | J | 106 | 152 | 6A | j |
| 42 | 052 | 2A | * | 75 | 113 | 4B | K | 107 | 153 | 6B | k |
| 43 | 053 | 2B | + | 76 | 114 | 4C | L | 108 | 154 | 6C | l |
| 44 | 054 | 2C | , | 77 | 115 | 4D | M | 109 | 155 | 6D | m |
| 45 | 055 | 2D | - | 78 | 116 | 4E | N | 110 | 156 | 6E | n |
| 46 | 056 | 2E | . | 79 | 117 | 4F | O | 111 | 157 | 6F | o |
| 47 | 057 | 2F | / | 80 | 120 | 50 | P | 112 | 160 | 70 | p |

| **(Decimal Numbers—Print)** | | | |
|---|---|---|---|
| *Dec* | *Octal* | *Hex* | *ASCII* |
| 48 | 060 | 30 | 0 |
| 49 | 061 | 31 | 1 |
| 50 | 062 | 32 | 2 |
| 51 | 063 | 33 | 3 |
| 52 | 064 | 34 | 4 |
| 53 | 065 | 35 | 5 |
| 54 | 066 | 36 | 6 |
| 55 | 067 | 37 | 7 |
| 56 | 070 | 38 | 8 |
| 57 | 071 | 39 | 9 |

Continuation of Upper Case and Lower Case:

| *Dec* | *Octal* | *Hex* | *ASCII* | *Dec* | *Octal* | *Hex* | *ASCII* |
|---|---|---|---|---|---|---|---|
| 81 | 121 | 51 | Q | 113 | 161 | 71 | q |
| 82 | 122 | 52 | R | 114 | 162 | 72 | r |
| 83 | 123 | 53 | S | 115 | 163 | 73 | s |
| 84 | 124 | 54 | T | 116 | 164 | 74 | t |
| 85 | 125 | 55 | U | 117 | 165 | 75 | u |
| 86 | 126 | 56 | V | 118 | 166 | 76 | v |
| 87 | 127 | 57 | W | 119 | 167 | 77 | w |
| 88 | 130 | 58 | X | 120 | 170 | 78 | x |
| 89 | 131 | 59 | Y | 121 | 171 | 79 | y |
| 90 | 132 | 5A | Z | 122 | 172 | 7A | z |

| **(Special Characters—Print)** | | | |
|---|---|---|---|
| *Dec* | *Octal* | *Hex* | *ASCII* |
| 58 | 072 | 3A | : |
| 59 | 073 | 3B | ; |
| 60 | 074 | 3C | < |
| 61 | 075 | 3D | = |
| 62 | 076 | 3E | > |
| 63 | 077 | 3F | ? |
| 64 | 080 | 40 | @ |

| **Non-Printing Characters (Abridged)** Control Characters | | | |
|---|---|---|---|
| *Dec* | *Octal* | *Hex* | *ASCII* |
| 0 | 000 | 00 | ^@ (Null) |
| 7 | 007 | 07 | Bell |
| 8 | 010 | 08 | Backspace |
| 9 | 011 | 09 | Tab |
| 10 | 012 | 0A | LineFeed, Newline |
| 11 | 013 | 0B | Vertical Tab |
| 12 | 014 | 0C | Formfeed |
| 13 | 015 | 0D | Carriage return |

**Figure 3-1:** ASCII characters

## GUI Files

Computers are not limited to processing ASCII codes. To work with graphic information, such as icons, illustrations, and other images, binary files can include strings of bits representing white and black dots, where each black dot represents a 1 and each white dot a 0. Graphics files include bit patterns—rows and columns of dots called a **bitmap**—that must be translated by graphics software, commonly called a **GUI** (Graphical User Interface), which transforms a complex array of bits into an infinite variety of images.

### Executable Program Files

Many programmers develop source code for their programs by writing text files; then they compile these files to convert them to executable program files. **Executable program files** contain pure binary or machine language that the computer can immediately use or execute.

## Using Operating System Editors

Operating system editors let you create and edit simple ASCII files. UNIX includes two editors: vi and Emacs. They are **screen editors**: they display the text you are editing one screen at a time and let you move around the screen to change and add text. You can also use a line editor to edit text files. A **line editor** lets you work with only one line or group of lines at a time. Although line editors do not let you see the context of your editing, they are useful for general tasks such as searching, replacing, and copying blocks of text.

## Using the vi Editor

The vi editor is so called because it is visual—it immediately displays on screen the changes you make to text. It is also a **modal editor**; that is, it works in two modes: insert mode and command mode. **Insert mode** lets you enter text; **command mode** lets you enter commands to perform editing tasks, such as moving through the file and deleting text.

Now you're ready to write your first memo using the vi editor. To do so, you complete the following tasks:

- Create a new file in the vi editor
- Insert, edit, and delete text
- Search and replace text
- Add text from other files
- Copy, cut, and paste text
- Print a file
- Save a file and exit vi

### Creating a New File in the vi Editor

Start by creating a file called temp to hold your first memo summarizing the basic features of text files. To start vi and create a file simultaneously, you type vi followed by the new file's name.

**To enter vi and create a new file:**

■ After the $ command prompt, type **vi temp** and press **Enter**. This starts vi and creates a new file called temp. Your screen should look similar to Figure 3-2.

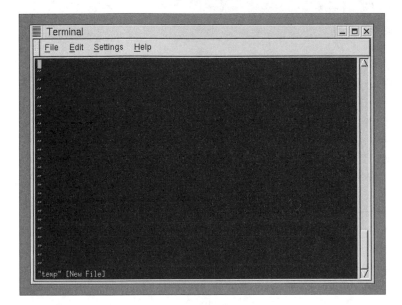

**Figure 3-2:** vi editor's opening screen

In the upper-left corner of your screen, you see the cursor, shown in Figure 3-2 as an underline character. The cursor indicates your current location in the file.

Note:  The line containing the cursor is the **current line**. Lines containing tildes (~) are not part of the file: they indicate lines on the screen only, not lines of text in the file.

## Inserting Text

When you start the vi editor, you're in command mode. This means that the editor interprets anything you type on the keyboard as a command. Before you can insert text in your new file, you must use the i (insert) command.

**To insert text in the Temp file:**

**1**  Type **i**.

Like most vi commands, the i command does not appear (or echo) on your screen. The command switches you from command mode to insert mode; you don't need to press Enter to signal the command's completion.

**2**  Type the text shown in Figure 3-3.

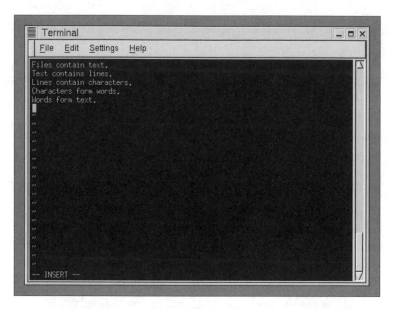

**Figure 3-3:** Inserting text with the vi editor

If you need to delete characters, press Backspace. Press Enter at the end of each line to move to the next line.

Note: In insert mode, every character you type appears on the screen. To switch to command mode, press Esc until "INSERT" is no longer displayed.

## Repeating a Change

Use the repeat ( . ) command to repeat the most recent change you made. Because you just inserted text, the repeat command repeats the insertion, duplicating the inserted text. You can add the next item in your memo by repeating the previous line and then editing it.

**To repeat your last command:**

**1**    Press **ESC** to switch to command mode.

**2**    Type . (period).

The vi editor inserts the last text you typed below the current line. Your screen should look similar to the one in Figure 3-4.

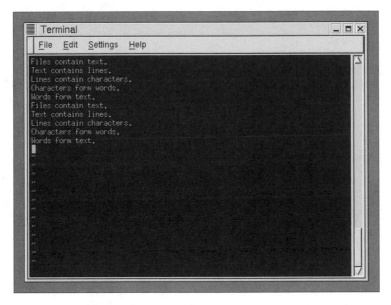

**Figure 3-4:** Repeating a command in the vi editor

Now you're ready to edit the text you just inserted. Start by moving the cursor around the screen and then deleting unnecessary text.

## Moving the Cursor

You can move the cursor when you are in command mode. Start by moving around the screen to get a feel for the commands, and then move to the particular line you want to edit.

**To move the cursor around the screen:**

**1**  Press **ESC** to make sure you are in enter command mode.

**2**  Press the arrow keys to move up, down, left, and right one character at a time.

**3**  Type **H** to move the cursor to the upper-left corner of the screen.

   Note: Make sure you type capital letters as indicated in these steps.

**4**  Type **L** to move the cursor to the last line on the screen.

**5**  Type **G** to go to the beginning of the last line. This is the go to command. You can include a number before the G to indicate which line you want to move to.

**6**  Type **2G** to move to the beginning of the second line.

In addition to these commands, you can use other commands to move the cursor. Table 3-1 summarizes the vi editor's cursor movement keys.

| Key | Movement |
| --- | --- |
| h or left arrow | Left one character position |
| l or right arrow | Right one character position |
| k or up arrow | Up one line |
| j or down arrow | Down one line |
| H | Upper-left corner of the screen |
| L | Last line on the screen |
| $n$G | Go to the line specified by a number, $n$ |
| w | Forward one word |
| b | Back one word |
| 0 (zero) | To the beginning of the current line |
| $ | To the end of the current line |
| Ctrl+U | Up one-half screen |
| Ctrl+D | Down one-half screen |
| Ctrl+F or Pg down | Forward one screen |
| Ctrl+B or Pg up | Back one screen |

**Table 3-1:** vi editor's cursor movement keys

Remember that cursor movement keys only work in command mode.

**Note:** Using the letter keys to move the cursor dates back to the days when UNIX used teletype terminals that had no arrow keys. Designers of vi chose the letter keys because of their relative position on the keyboard.

## Deleting Text

Now that you know how to insert text and move around a file, you are ready to delete text. To do so, move to a character and then type x to delete that character. You can also combine many delete commands with cursor movement commands to delete more than one character. Table 3-2 summarizes the most common delete commands.

| Command | Purpose |
|---------|---------|
| x | Delete the character above the cursor |
| dd | Delete the current line |
| dw | Delete the word above the cursor. If the cursor is in the middle of the word, delete from the cursor to the end of the line. |
| d$ or D | Delete from the cursor to the end of the line |
| d0 | Delete from the cursor to the start of the line |

**Table 3-2:** vi editor's delete commands

Now you can use the delete commands and the cursor movement keys to edit text you inserted in your memo.

**To edit the temp file by deleting text:**

**1** Press **Esc** to make sure you are in command mode.

**2** Type **1G** to move to the first line of the file. You want to delete this line.

**3** To delete the first line, type **dd**.

Your file should now look like Figure 3-5.

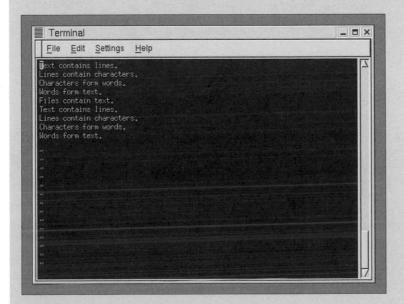

**Figure 3-5:** Memo after deleting first line

**4**  Press **w** to go to the next word, "contains."

**5**  Type **dw** to delete the current word (so the line now reads "Text lines"), and then type **i** to enter insert mode.

**6**  Type **consistss of** between "Text" and "lines." Be sure to include the extra "s."

**7**  Press the arrow keys to move the cursor to the extra "s" in "consistss," and then press **ESC** to switch to command mode.

**8**  To delete the current character (the extra "s"), type **x**.

Your memo should now look like the one in Figure 3-6.

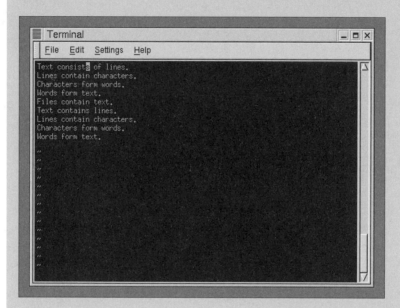

**Figure 3-6:** Memo after editing

Now you want to edit the sentence, "Files contain text" by deleting the last word.

**9**  Press the arrow keys to move to the sentence, "Files contain text," and then move to the first "c" in "contain."

**10**  Type **d$** to delete the text from the cursor to the end of the line, and then type **i** to switch to insert mode.

**11**  Type **consist of words.** to complete the sentence.

Now you can edit the next sentence by replacing the first word.

**12**  Press the arrow keys to move to the next line in the file, move to the space before the word "lines," and then press **ESC** to switch back to command mode.

**13**  Type **d0** to delete the text from the cursor to the beginning of the line, and then type **i** to enter insert mode.

**14**  Type **Words form** to insert that text at the beginning of the sentence.

**15**  Your completed memo should look like the one in Figure 3-7.

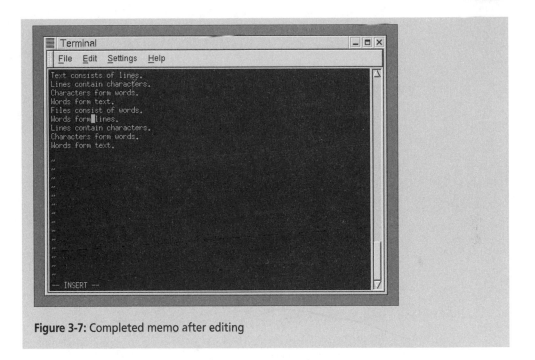

**Figure 3-7:** Completed memo after editing

The vi editor offers you alternatives for copying, cutting, and pasting text.

Note: The delete line command, dd, actually places deleted lines in a buffer. Then you can use the paste command, p, to paste deleted (cut) lines elsewhere in the text. (Position the cursor where you want to paste them.) To copy and paste text, use the yank command, yy, to copy the lines. After yanking the lines you want to paste elsewhere, move the cursor and type p to paste the text in the current location.

## Undoing a Command

If you complete a command and then realize you want to reverse its effects, you can use the undo command. For example, if you delete a few lines from a file by mistake, type u to restore the text. The undo command reverses only your last command.

## Searching for a Pattern

You can search forward for a pattern of characters by typing a forward slash (/), typing the pattern you are seeking, and then pressing Enter. For example, suppose you want to know how many times you used the word "consist" or "consists" in your memo.

## To search for a pattern of text to find either word:

**1**  Press **Esc** to make sure you are in command mode.

**2**  Type **H** to move the cursor to the top of the screen.

**3**  Type **/cons** to search for words that start with "cons."

**4**  Press **Enter**. The cursor moves to the beginning of the word "consists" on line 1.

**5**  To search for the next occurrence of "cons," press **n** (for next). The cursor moves to the beginning of the word "consist" on the fifth line.

   If you had searched for "/con," you would have first found "consist" on line 1 and then "contain" on line 2.

**6**  To see file status information, press **Ctrl+K**. Your screen should look like the one in Figure 3-8.

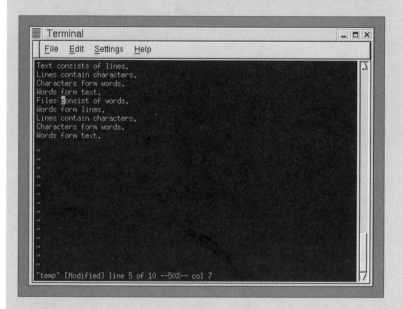

**Figure 3-8:** vi status line

Note: The **status line** at the bottom of the screen displays information, including line-oriented commands (explained later in this lesson) and error messages.

## Searching and Replacing

Let's say you want to change all occurrences of "text" in your memo to "documents." Instead of searching for "text" and then deleting and inserting "documents," you can search and replace with one command. The commands you learned so far are screen-oriented. Commands that can perform more than one action (searching and replacing) are **line-oriented commands.**

> Note: **Screen-oriented commands** execute at the location of the cursor. You do not need to tell the computer where to perform the operation: it takes place relative to the cursor. Line-oriented commands, on the other hand, require you to specify an exact location (an **address**) for the operation. Screen-oriented commands are easy to type, and their changes appear on the screen. Typing line-oriented commands is more complicated, but they can execute independently of the cursor and in more than one place in a file.

A colon (:) precedes all line-oriented commands. It acts as a prompt on the status line. Enter line-oriented commands on the status line, and press Enter when you complete the command.

> Note: In this chapter, all instructions for line-oriented commands include the colon as part of the command.

### To search for a pattern of characters:

**1** Press **Esc** to make sure you are in command mode.

**2** Type **/form** and press **Enter**. This command instructs vi to search for the first occurrence of the word "form" and moves the cursor under that word.

**3** Type **n** to repeat the search. vi locates the next occurrence of the word "form."

### To search for "text" and replace it with "documents":

**1** Press **Esc** to make sure you are in command mode.

**2** Type **:1,$s/text/documents/g.** This command means "From the first line (1) to the end of the file ($), search for 'text' and replace it with 'documents' (s/text/documents/) everywhere it occurs on each line (g)."

**3** Press **Enter.** Your screen should look like the one illustrated in Figure 3-9.

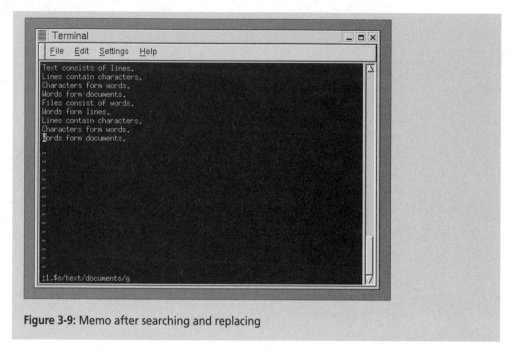

**Figure 3-9:** Memo after searching and replacing

Note that the word "Text" in line 1 remains unchanged because it is capitalized. By default, case matters in searches.

## Saving a File and Exiting vi

As you edit a file, saving your changes is a good idea. You should always save the file before you exit vi; otherwise, you lose your changes.

**To save the temp file:**

■ Type **:x** and then press **Enter** to save your changes, exit the vi editor, and return to the UNIX shell.

The status line provides information about your file, including its name and the number of lines and characters it contains.

Note: While in command mode, you can also use :wq (write and quit) or ZZ to exit the editor after you save the file on disk. To save a file and continue working with the vi editor, type :w.

## Adding Text from Another File

Sometimes the text you want to include in one file is already part of another file. For example, let's say you want a separate copy of the text in the file temp so you can use it to practice editing. Start by creating a new file called practice, and then add text from the temp file by using the line-oriented r (read) command.

### To create a new file and add text from another file:

**1**   Type **vi practice** and press **Enter** to create a new file.

**2**   Press **Esc** to make sure you are in command mode.

**3**   Type **:r temp**.

Your file should look like the one illustrated in Figure 3-10.

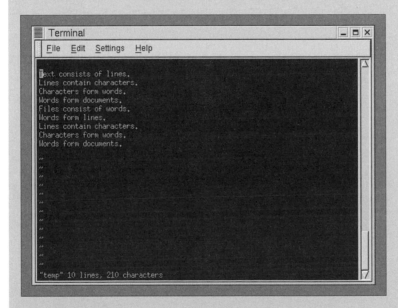

**Figure 3-10:** Adding text from another file

The r command copied the text from temp and put it in the current file, practice. Notice the blank line at the top of the file.

**4**   Move the cursor to the blank line, and type **dd** to delete it.

## Leaving vi Temporarily

If you want to execute other UNIX commands while you work with vi, you can leave vi temporarily. For example, let's say you are working on your memo for Dominion and want to check the current date quickly.

**To leave vi temporarily to find the current date and time:**

**1**  Type :**!date** and press **Enter.**

You see today's date and instructions for returning to command mode.

**2**  Press **Enter** to return to command mode.

## Changing Your Display While Editing

Besides using the vi editing commands, you can also set options in vi to control editing parameters such as line number display and whether case matters in searches. Turn on line numbering when you want to work with a range of lines, for example, when you're deleting or cutting and pasting a block of text. Then you can refer to the line numbers to specify the text. You decide to delete the last three lines from your memo. Turn on line numbering first, and then use a delete command.

**To use automatic line numbering:**

**1**  Type :**set number** and press **Enter.**

Your redrawn screen shows line numbers to the left of the text. Your screen should look like the one in Figure 3-11.

**Figure 3-11:** Changing your display

Line numbers are for reference only. They are not part of the file. Now you can use these reference numbers to delete the last three lines in the file.

**2**  Type **:7,9d** and press **Enter**.

You deleted the last three lines of the file.

## Copying or Cutting and Pasting

You can use the yy command in vi to copy a specified number of lines from a file and place them on the clipboard. To delete the lines from the file and store them on the clipboard, use the dd command. Now you want to reorganize your document so that the first three lines are at the end of the file. You can use cut and paste commands to make this change.

**To cut and paste text:**

**1**  Type **H** to move the cursor to the beginning of line 1.

**2**  Type **3dd** to cut the first 3 lines from the document and store them on the clipboard.

**3**  Type **G** to move the cursor to the end of the file.

**4**  Type **p** to paste the three lines at the end of the file.

## Printing vi files

You can use the lpr (line print) shell command to print a file. Type !lpr and then type the name of the file you want to print.

**To print a file:**

**1**  Press **Esc** to return to command mode.

**2**  Type **!lpr practice** and press **Enter**. This prints the file practice in the current directory on the default printer.

You can also specify which printer you want to use with the –Pprinter option. For example, you may use two printers—lp1 and lp2. To print the practice file on lp2, type !lpr –Plp2 practice and press Enter.

## Canceling an Editing Session

If necessary, you can cancel an editing session, that is, you can undo all the changes you made. If you are working with a new file, vi deletes the file. If you are modifying an existing file, vi restores its original condition. You decide you don't need your practice file, so you can cancel your editing session.

**To cancel your editing session:**

■ Type **:q!** and press Enter.

This cancels all changes you made, and because practice is a new file, vi deletes it.

# SUMMARY

■ Bytes are "computer characters" referred to as "codes." These codes have been standardized and are known as ASCII codes. ASCII stands for the American Standard Code for Information Interchange. Computer files that contain only ASCII characters (bytes) are called text files.

■ The vi editor remains the choice of most UNIX users. All operating systems editors process text files. Text files are also called "flat files" or "ASCII files."

■ The vi editor is a modal editor, because it works in two modes: insert mode and command mode. Insert mode lets you enter text, and command mode lets you navigate the file and modify the text.

■ In the vi editor's insert mode, characters you type are inserted in the file. They are not interpreted as vi commands. To exit insert mode and re-enter command mode, press Esc.

■ With vi, you initially edit a copy of the file placed in the computer's memory. You do not alter the file itself until you save it on disk.

# COMMAND SUMMARY

| Chapter 3, Lesson A commands | |
|---|---|
| Command | Purpose |
| **vi Commands** | |
| . (repeat) | Repeat your most recent change |
| / | Search forward for a pattern of characters |
| :! | Leave vi temporarily |
| :q | Cancel an editing session |
| :r | Read text from one file and add it to another |
| :set | Turns on certain options, such as line numbering |

| Chapter 3, Lesson A commands (continued) | |
|---|---|
| :w | Save a file and continue working |
| :wq | Write changes to disk and exit vi |
| :x | Save changes and exit vi |
| i | Switch to insert mode |
| P | Paste text from the clipboard |
| u | Undo your most recent change |
| vi | Start the vi editor |
| yy | Copy (yank) text to the clipboard |
| ZZ | In command mode, save changes and exit vi |
| *UNIX Commands* | |
| lpr | Print a file |

Note: Table 3-1 lists the vi editor's cursor movement keys. Table 3-2 lists the vi editor's delete commands.

# R E V I E W    Q U E S T I O N S

1. The vi editor is called a modal editor because it _____.
   a. is portable
   b. operates in two modes
   c. makes entering and changing text easy
   d. operates in a single mode

2. Which key do you press to switch from insert mode to command mode?
   a. Esc
   b. :
   c. Ctrl+C
   d. Ins

3. While in command mode, you can exit vi by _____.
   a. typing :quit!
   b. typing :wq!
   c. typing :x
   d. all of the above

4. Why is the vi editor called a "visual editor?"
   a. Because it works with a line editor
   b. Because it is line-oriented
   c. Because it uses a graphical interface
   d. Because text changes appear immediately on the screen

5. In the vi editor, the colon (:) serves as the _____.
   a. status line command prompt
   b. exit command
   c. substitution command
   d. search command

6. In the vi editor's command mode, what single character do you type to start searching for a text pattern?
   a. ?
   b. s
   c. /
   d. :

7. Operating system editors work with _____ files.
   a. executable program
   b. flat
   c. graphical
   d. system

8. Which of these vi commands deletes one line from a file?
   a. d$
   b. d0
   c. dd
   d. x

9. Which of these vi commands is a cursor movement command?
   a. G
   b. l
   c. h
   d. all of the above

10. Which of these vi commands adds text from another file?
    a. r
    b. read
    c. :r
    d. :w

11. Which of these commands displays line numbers in a vi file?
    a. set no
    b. :set
    c. :number
    d. :set number

12. Which vi command causes you to leave vi temporarily?
    a. :t
    b. :wq
    c. :!
    d. :u

**13.** Which vi command repeats your most recent change?

    a. .

    b. :r

    c. :!

    d. :u

**14.** Which vi command copies text to the clipboard?

    a. :y

    b. C

    c. :c

    d. Y

**15.** Which vi command pastes text from the clipboard?

    a. :p

    b. P

    c. :!

    d. :u

**16.** Which vi command undoes your most recent changes?

    a. :wq

    b. u

    c. :o

    d. Z

**17.** What does the H command perform?

    a. causes the cursor to move to the beginning of line 1

    b. causes the cursor to move to the beginning of the current line

    c. holds the contents of the file in memory for future editing

    d. none of the above

**18.** What does the command 7dd perform?

    a. deletes the seventh word on the current line

    b. deletes seven lines

    c. deletes the third line from the current line

    d. none of the above

**19.** What does the command G perform?

    a. grabs text and places it in the clipboard

    b. moves the cursor to the first occurrence of the letter G

    c. moves the cursor to the end of the file

    d. moves the cursor to the end of the current line

**E X E R C I S E S**

1. Using the vi editor:
   a. Create a document with 10 lines.
   b. Enter the word "these" on every line.
   c. Save the file.
   d. Re-open the document and change "these" to "those" throughout the file.

2. Using the vi editor:
   a. Create a document called first.file, and enter a few lines of text in it. Save it.
   b. Create a second document called second.file, and enter a few lines of text in it. Save it.
   c. Create a third document called third.file, by adding the text from the first two files.
   d. Save the third file and exit from the editor.
   e. Type **vi third.file** to be sure third.file contains the text from both files.

3. Delete all text from third.file, and then restore it.

 **D I S C O V E R Y   E X E R C I S E S**

1. Create a file with 10 lines of text. Remove the first four lines, and add them to the end of the file.

2. On a line in the middle of the file, insert your name.

3. Move the cursor to the beginning of the file.

4. Enter the command to search for your first name and replace it with "George." (If your first name happens to be George, replace it with "Abraham.")

5. Save the file but do not exit vi.

6. Without exiting vi, temporarily execute the ls command to confirm that the file was saved.

7. Enter the command that causes line numbers to appear.

8. Enter the command that causes lines 1 through 3 to be deleted.

9. Move to the line of text that contains your last name, cut it, and place the text on the clipboard.

10. Paste your last name at the beginning of the first line in the file.

# The Emacs Editor

## Using the Emacs Editor

Emacs is another UNIX text editor that has gained popularity but, due to its complexity, continues to run second to the vi editor. Unlike vi, Emacs is not modal: it does not switch from command mode to insert mode. This means that you can type a command without verifying that you are in the proper mode. Although Emacs is more complex than vi, it is more consistent. For example, you can enter most commands by pressing Alt or Ctrl key combinations.

Emacs also supports a sophisticated macro language. A **macro** is a set of commands that automates a complex task. Think of a macro as a "super instruction." Emacs also has a powerful command syntax and extensions. Its packaged set of customized macros lets you read electronic mail and news, and edit the contents of directories. Emacs is reputed to have more features than any other UNIX program. You can start learning Emacs by learning its common commands. Table 3-3 lists these commands.

| Alt command | Purpose | Ctrl command | Purpose |
|---|---|---|---|
| Alt+< | Move cursor to start of file | Ctrl+@ | Mark the cursor location. After moving the cursor, you can move or copy text to the mark. |
| Alt+> | Move cursor to end of file | Ctrl+A | Move cursor to start of line |
| Alt+B | Move cursor back one word | Ctrl+B | Move cursor back one character |
| Alt+D | Delete current word | Ctrl+D | Delete the character under cursor |

**Table 3-3:** Common Emacs commands

| Alt command | Purpose | Ctrl command | Purpose |
|---|---|---|---|
| Alt+F | Move cursor forward one character | Ctrl+E | Move cursor to end of line |
| Alt+Q | Reformat current paragraph using word wrap so that lines are full | Ctrl+F | Move cursor forward one character |
| Alt+T | If the cursor is under the first character of the word, transposes word with the preceding word | Ctrl+G | Cancel the current command |
| Alt+U | Capitalize all letters of the current word | Ctrl+H | Use online help |
| Alt+W | Scroll up one screen | Ctrl+K | Delete text to the end of the line |
| Alt+X doctor | Enter doctormode to play a game in which Emacs responds to your statements with questions. Save yourwork first. Not all versions support this mode. | Ctrl+N | Move cursor to next line |
| **Ctrl key combination** | | Ctrl+P | Move cursor to preceding line |
| Ctrl+H+C | Display the command that runs when you press a particular key | Ctrl+T | Transpose the character before the cursor and the character under the cursor |
| Ctrl+H+T | Run a tutorial about Emacs | Ctrl+V | Scroll down one screen |
| Ctrl+X, Ctrl+C | Exit Emacs | Ctrl+W | Delete marked text. Press Ctrl+Y to restore deleted text. |
| Ctrl+X, Ctrl+S | Save the file | Ctrl+Y | Insert text from the file buffer, and place it after the cursor |
| Ctrl+X, U | Undo the last change | | |
| Ctrl+Del | Delete the character under the cursor | | |

**Table 3-3:** Common Emacs commands (*continued*)

Note: In most cases, Ctrl and Alt commands in Emacs are not case-sensitive, so Alt+B and Alt+b are the same command.

You can use Emacs to duplicate your first memo for Dominion Consulting. To do so, you complete the following tasks:

- Create a new file in Emacs
- Edit and delete text
- Copy, cut, and paste text

## Creating a New File in Emacs

You can start Emacs by typing the emacs command. If you type a filename after this command, Emacs creates a new, blank file with that name, or opens an existing file with that name. If you type emacs with no filename, Emacs displays the introductory list of a few important commands, shown in Figure 3-12.

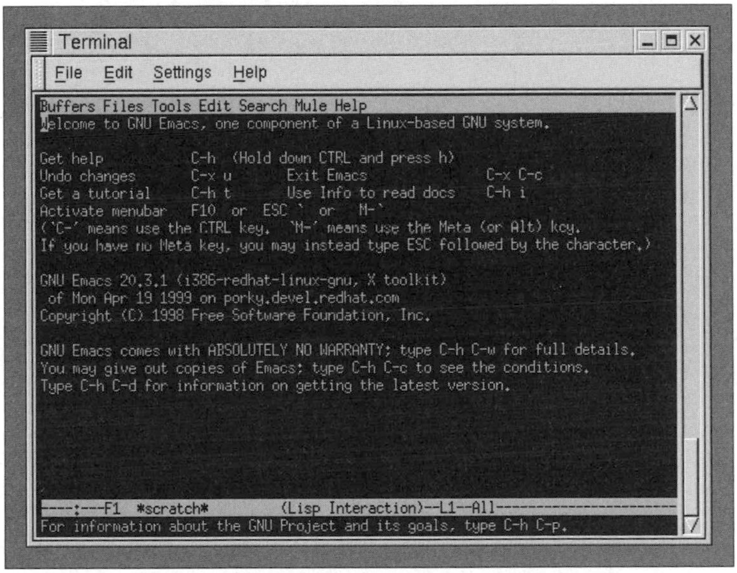

**Figure 3-12:** Emacs opening screen (without a filename)

Start by creating a file called practice that will contain the same text as your original temp memo for Dominion Consulting.

**To start Emacs and create a file called practice:**

**1**    Type **emacs practice.fil** and then press **Enter**.

You see the opening screen; its status bar indicates you are creating a new file.

**2**    To add text to the file, type the text you see in Figure 3-13.

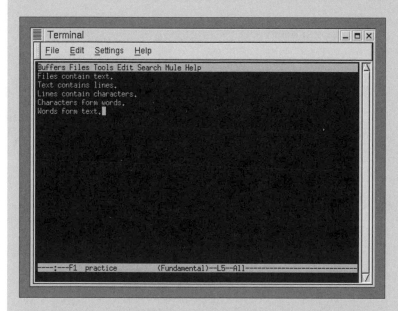

Figure 3-13: Creating a new file in Emacs

**3**    Press **Ctrl+x** and then **Ctrl+s** to save the file.

**4**    Press **Ctrl+x** and then **Ctrl+c** to exit the file.

Note:  In Emacs, you must press the two Ctrl key combinations to save and exit a file.

## Editing an Emacs File

To navigate an Emacs file, you can use either the cursor movement keys—such as the arrow keys, Pg up, Pg down, Home, and End—or Ctrl key combinations. Before editing practice, move around the file.

**To navigate the practice file:**

**1**    To return to Emacs and retrieve your file, type **Emacs practice.fil** and press **Enter**.

**2**    Press **Ctrl+f** to move forward one character, and then press the **right arrow** key.

**3**   Press **Ctrl+b** to move back one character, and then press the **left arrow** key.

**4**   Using the **up arrow** and **down arrow** keys, place the cursor on the line that begins "Lines contain."

### To delete text and undo the deletion:

**1**   Press **Ctrl+k** to delete the current line.

**2**   Press **Ctrl+x** and then type **u** to undo the last change.

**tip**

You can restore the text repeatedly, even after making many changes. Press Ctrl+x, and then u. Use this command to undo your editing commands in sequence. The Emacs undo command offers an advantage over the vi undo command, which only restores your most recent change.

In Emacs, you can insert text simply by typing. You can also insert text by copying and pasting or cutting and pasting. You can copy the first two lines of the practice file and paste them at the end of the file.

### To copy and paste text in Emacs:

**1**   Move the cursor to the beginning of the sentence "Characters form words."

**2**   Press **Ctrl+spacebar**. This marks the starting point for the block of text you want to copy. You see the words "Mark set" in the status bar.

**3**   Press the **down arrow** key twice to move the cursor to the next line.

**4**   Press **Alt+w**. This marks the end of the text block to copy.

       You can also hold down Esc and press w to mark the end of the block.

**5**   Press **Alt+>** to move to the end of the file.

**6**   Press **Ctrl+y** to paste the marked text from the clipboard into the buffer.

**Performance**

**tip**

To cut and paste rather than copy and paste, press Ctrl+w when the cursor is at the end of the block you want cut.

Like the vi editor, Emacs lets you search for specific text. For example, suppose you want to find the text "on" in your practice document.

**To search for specific words:**

**1**  Press **Ctrl+s**. You see the "I-search" prompt in the status line. You can now type the text you are seeking.

**2**  Type **it**.

**3**  Press **Ctrl+s** to search for the next occurrence of "on." Press **Ctrl+s** again.

**4**  Press **Ctrl+r** to search backward for the previous occurrence of "on."

**To reformat the document so lines are full with text:**

**1**  The first and third lines each have the word "contain." On each line, move the cursor to the space after the word "contain" and press **Enter**. This breaks each of the lines into two lines.

**2**  Press **Alt+Q** to reformat the file so the lines are full of text.

After working with the practice document, you're ready to exit Emacs. To do so, follow the instructions in the earlier section, "Creating a New File in Emacs." (Press Ctrl+x and then press Ctrl+c to save and exit the file.)

 # S U M M A R Y

- The Emacs editor has gained popularity, but due to its complexity, it continues to run second to the vi editor.

- Unlike vi, Emacs is not modal. (It does not switch from command mode to insert mode.)

- Emacs has a powerful command syntax and extensions, and supports a sophisticated language of macro commands. A macro is a set of commands designed to simplify a complex task. Emacs' packaged set of customized macros lets you read electronic mail and news, and edit the contents of directories.

- You can start Emacs by typing emacs with or without a filename. If you enter this command and then type a filename, Emacs creates a new, blank file with that name, or opens an existing file with that name. If you type emacs with no filename, Emacs displays an introductory list of a few important commands.

- You can use either the cursor movement keys—such as the arrow keys, Pg up, Pg down, Home, and End—or Ctrl key combinations to navigate an Emacs file.

- You can undo your editing changes in sequence, even after you've made many changes. The Emacs undo command offers an advantage over the vi undo command, which can only restore your most recent change.

■ In Emacs, you can insert text simply by typing. You can also insert text by copying and pasting or cutting and pasting. Like the vi editor, Emacs also lets you search for specific text.

 # COMMAND SUMMARY

| Chapter 3, Lesson B commands | |
|---|---|
| Command | Purpose |
| *Emacs Commands* | See Table 3-3 |
| emacs | Start the Emacs editor |
| *UNIX Commands* | |
| lpr | Print a file |

Note: Table 3-3 lists common Emacs commands.

# REVIEW QUESTIONS

1. The Emacs editor _____.
   a. is modeless
   b. is modal
   c. is capable of both modal and modeless operations
   d. has insert and command modes

2. To issue a command in Emacs, press _____.
   a. down the Ctrl key, and then press a letter
   b. down the Alt key, and then press a letter
   c. the function keys (F1–F12)
   d. a and b

3. Which of these Ctrl key combinations lets you quit the Emacs editor and return to the command line?
   a. Ctrl+c, Ctrl+x
   b. Ctrl+x, Ctrl+c
   c. Ctrl+s, Ctrl+x
   d. Ctrl+x, Ctrl+e

4. Which of these Ctrl key combinations saves your file?
   a. Ctrl+c, Ctrl+x
   b. Ctrl+x, Ctrl+y
   c. Ctrl+x, Ctrl+s
   d. Ctrl+z, Ctrl+s

5. Which of these best compares Emacs to the vi editor?
   a. Emacs is popular, but due to its complexity, continues to run second to the vi editor.
   b. The vi editor has a sophisticated macro language, but Emacs does not.
   c. Both have an insert mode and a command mode.
   d. All of the above are correct.

6. What do you see when you use the Emacs command with no filename to start editing an Emacs file?
   a. A blank screen for an unnamed file
   b. A list of common Emacs commands
   c. The text of the last file you edited
   d. A summary of differences between Emacs and the vi editors

7. Which of these is false?
   a. In Emacs, you can press Del to delete characters.
   b. In Emacs, you can use all the arrow keys to move up, down, left, or right.
   c. In Emacs, you can use Ctrl+h to move the cursor back one space.
   d. In Emacs, you can use Ctrl+a to move text to the beginning of the line.

8. True or false: In most cases, Ctrl and Alt commands in Emacs are not case-sensitive.

9. The _____ command marks the start of the block of text you want to copy.
   a. Ctrl+M
   b. Ctrl+S
   c. Ctrl+spacebar
   d. none of the above

10. The _____ command marks the end of the block of text you want to copy.
    a. Alt+w
    b. Ctrl+w
    c. Alt+spacebar
    d. none of the above

11. The _____ command moves the cursor to the end of the file.
    a. Ctrl+<
    b. Ctrl+>
    c. Alt+<
    d. Alt+>

12. The _____ command inserts text from the clipboard and places it after the cursor.
    a. Ctrl+p
    b. Ctrl+y
    c. Alt+p
    d. Alt+y

13. The _____ command is used to undo the last command.
    a. Ctrl+u
    b. Ctrl+x
    c. Ctrl+u,x
    d. Ctrl+x,u

14. The _____ command causes the current line to be deleted.
    a. Ctrl+k
    b. Ctrl+l
    c. Ctrl+x,k
    d. Alt+k

15. The _____ command invokes the I-search prompt.
    a. Ctrl+s
    b. Alt+s
    c. Ctrl+spacebar
    d. none of the above

16. The _____ command searches backward.
    a. Ctrl+x,b
    b. Ctrl+b
    c. Ctrl+r
    d. none of the above

17. True or false: The Emacs undo command is like the vi undo command. Both can only undo the last command.

# EXERCISES

Use Table 3-3 to find the correct commands for performing the following steps.

1. Using the Emacs editor, create a new file that contains the first 4 lines of Shakespeare's 80th Sonnet:
   O, how I faint when I of you do write,
   Knowing a better spirit doth use your name,
   And in the praise thereof spends all his might,
   To make me tongue-tied, speaking of your fame!

2. Move the cursor to any letter except "b" in the word "better" on the second line.

3. Use the command that causes the current word to be transposed with the one that follows it. After executing the command, the line should read:
   Knowing a spirit better doth use your name,

4. Move the cursor to the word "doth" on the same line.

5. Use the command to delete the current word.

6. Move the cursor to the first character of the word "spirit" on the same line.

7. Use the command that capitalizes the letters of the word.

8. Move the cursor under the letter "y" in the word "your" on the same line.

9. Use the command that deletes the character under the cursor. The line should now read:
Knowing a SPIRIT better use our name,

10. Move the cursor to the word "spends" on the third line.

11. Use the command that deletes text to the end of the line. The line should now read:
And in the praise thereof

12. Move the cursor to the end of the first line.

13. Use the command that puts a mark at the cursor location.

14. Move the cursor to the first character of the first line.

15. Use the command that deletes marked text, that is, deletes the first line.

16. Move the cursor to the end of the file. Use the command that restores deleted text. The text that was the first line of the file is now at the end of the file.

# DISCOVERY EXERCISES

1. Using the practice file, practice copying and pasting the text to rearrange the order of the lines.

2. Add text to the file, and practice using the cursor movement commands.

3. Replace all occurrences of the word "the" with "a."

4. Select five words and convert them to all uppercase.

5. Delete a line and then undo the deletion.

6. Transpose the first two words in each line.

7. Save the file and exit Emacs.

# UNIX File Processing

**case ▶** Your manager at Dominion Consulting, Rolfe Williams, wants you to extract a list of names from the phone number file you created earlier and sort the list. Then he wants you to help a Dominion client, Worldwide Hotels, design a new vendor and product report. The hotel firm wants to produce an alphabetical list of vendors and the products each offers. The vendor and product names reside in separate files: a product file and a vendor file. Both files contain vendor numbers. Rolfe asks you to use the UNIX file processing tools to produce a vendor report using the two files.

After studying this lesson, you should be able to:

- Explain UNIX's approach to file processing
- Use basic file manipulation commands
- Extract characters and fields from a file using the cut command
- Rearrange fields inside a record using the paste command
- Merge files using the sort command
- Create a new file by combining cut, paste, and sort

# Extracting Information from Files

Now that you know how to work with UNIX files and editors, you're ready to learn how to manipulate files and work with their contents. After a brief discussion of UNIX file types and file structures, Lesson A defines file processing and shows you how to use redirection operators when processing files. You also learn how to manipulate files by creating, deleting, copying, and moving them to extract information from files, to combine fields, and to sort a file's contents, all in the context of the opening case. In Lesson B, you learn how to assemble information you extracted from files. You also create a script to automate a series of commands, link files with a common field, and use the awk command to format output. You complete these tasks to meet the goals of the opening case.

## UNIX's Approach to File Processing

UNIX file processing is based on the idea that files should be treated as nothing more than character sequences. This concept of a file as a series of characters offers a lot of flexibility. Because you can directly access each character, you can perform a range of editing tasks, such as correcting spelling errors and organizing information as necessary.

### Understanding UNIX File Types

Operating systems support several types of files. UNIX, like MS-DOS, has regular files, directories, and special files. **Regular files** contain information you create and manipulate, and include either ASCII files, such as the text files you created in Chapter 3, or binary files, such as those you create while compiling source code. You use regular files, also called **ordinary files**, in this chapter. Other file types include directories and special files, such as character files and block files. Chapter 2 explained that directories are system files for maintaining the structure of the file system. **Character special files** are related to serial input/output devices, such as printers. **Block special files** are related to devices, such as disks.

## UNIX File Structures

Files can be structured in several ways. For example, UNIX stores data, such as letters, product records, or vendor reports, in **flat ASCII files**. UNIX structures a file depending on the kind of data it stores, and recognizes three kinds of regular files: unstructured ASCII characters, records, and trees. Figure 4-1 illustrates the three kinds of regular files.

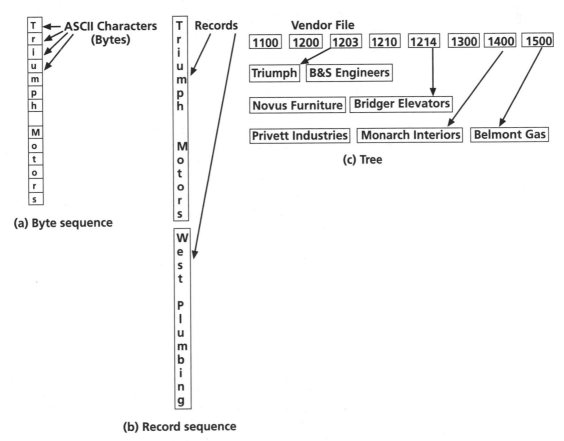

**(a) Byte sequence**

**(b) Record sequence**

**(c) Tree**

**Figure 4-1:** Three kinds of regular files

Figure 4-1(a) shows a file that is an unstructured sequence of bytes and is a typical example of a text file. This file structure gives you the most flexibility in data entry, because you can store any kind of data in any order. However, you can only retrieve the data in the same order, which may limit its overall usefulness. For example, suppose you list Worldwide Hotel's vendors in an unstructured ASCII file. You can only view or print the entire list, not just the vendor names or vendor numbers.

Figure 4-1(b) shows data as a sequence of fixed-length records, each having some internal structure. In this structure, UNIX reads the data as fixed-length records. Although you must enter data as records, you can also manipulate and retrieve the data as records. For example, you can select only certain vendor records to retrieve from the file.

The third kind of file, illustrated in Figure 4-1(c), is structured as a tree of records, not necessarily of the same length. Each record contains a key field, such as a record number, in a fixed position in the record. The key field sorts the tree, so you can quickly search for a record with a particular key. For example, you can quickly find the record for Triumph Motors by searching for record #1203.

## Processing Files

When performing commands, UNIX **processes** data—it receives input from the standard input device (your keyboard) and then sends output to the standard output device (your monitor). System administrators and programmers refer to standard input as **stdin**. They refer to standard output as **stdout**. (The third standard output is called **standard error,** or **stderr**. When UNIX detects errors in processing system tasks and user programs, it directs the errors to stderr, which is the screen by default.)

You can use the redirection operators to save the output of a command or program in a file, or use a file as an input to a process. The redirection operators, therefore, help you process files.

### Using Input and Error Redirection

You can use redirection operators (>, >>, 2>, <, and <<) to retrieve input from something other than the standard input device and to send output to something other than the standard output device.

You already used the output redirection operators in Chapter 1 when you created a new file by redirecting the output of several commands to files. Redirect output when you want to store the output of a command or program in a file. For example, recall that you can use the ls command to list the files in a directory, such as /home. The standard output device for the ls command is the screen, so you see the list on the screen. To redirect the list to a file called homedir.list, use the redirection symbol by typing ls > homedir.list.

You may also redirect the input to a program or command with the < operator. For instance, a program that accepts keyboard input may be redirected to read information from a file instead. In the following steps you create a file for the vi editor to read its commands from, instead of reading them from the keyboard.

**To create a file from which the vi editor reads commands:**

**1** Use the vi editor, or the cat command with output redirection, to create the file testfile, containing the text:

```
This is line 1.
This is line 2.
This is line 3.
This is line 4.
```

**2** In the vi editor,
Create another text file containing some vi commands as follows. Type **cat > commands** and press **Enter**. Type **dd** and press Enter. Type **H** and press **Enter**. Type **p** and press **Enter**. Type **:wq** and press **Enter**. Press **Ctrl+D**.

**3** Type **cat commands** and press **Enter**. You see the contents of the commands file, which are:

```
dd
G
p
:wq
```

**4** Type **vi testfile < commands** and press **Enter**. This loads testfile into the vi editor and redirects vi's input to the text in the command file. The text in the command file is treated as commands typed on the keyboard.

**5** Type **cat testfile** and press **Enter**. You see the contents of testfile after the vi commands execute. The contents are:

```
This is line 2.
This is line 3.
This is line 4.
This is line 1.
```

You may also use the 2> operator to redirect commands or program error messages from the screen to a file.

**To redirect error messages:**

**1** Force the ls command to display an error message by giving it an invalid argument. Assuming you have no file or directory in your /home directory named jojo, type **ls jojo** and press **Enter**. You see the error message:

```
ls: jojo: no such file or directory
```

**2** Redirect the error output of the ls command. Type **ls jojo 2> errfile** and press **Enter**. There is no output on the screen.

**3** Type **cat errfile** and press **Enter**. You see errfile's contents:

```
ls: jojo: no such file or directory
```

# Manipulating Files

When you manipulate files, you work with the files themselves as well as their contents. This section explains how to complete the following tasks:

- Create files
- Delete files
- Copy files
- Move files
- Find files
- Display files
- Combine files
- Cut and paste file contents
- Sort files

## Creating Files

The simplest way to create a file is to use the output redirection operator (>). You learned how to do this to redirect the cat command's output in Chapters 1–3. You can also use the redirection operator without a command to create an empty file.

---

**To create an empty file:**

**1**   After the $ command prompt, type **> newfile1** and press **Enter**.

This creates an empty file called newfile1.

**2**   To list the new file, type **ls –l newfile1** and press **Enter**.

You see only the information listed next, where jean is your user name.

```
-rw-rw-r--  1 jean  jean      0 Nov 1 16:57 newfile1
```

**3**   To create another new file, type **> newfile2** and press **Enter**.

---

You may also use the touch command to create empty files. For example, the following command creates the file newfile3, if the file does not already exist.

```
touch newfile3
```

The primary purpose of the touch command is to change a file's time and date stamp. UNIX maintains the following date and time information for every file:

- Creation date and time: the date and time the file was created
- Access date and time: the date and time the file was last accessed
- Modification date and time: the date and time the file was last modified

Although the touch command cannot change an existing file's creation date and time, it can alter the file's access and modification dates and times. By default, it uses the system date and time for the new values.

**To create a file and alter its date/time stamp with the touch command:**

**1**  Type **touch newfile3** and press **Enter**. This command creates the file newfile3.

**2**  Type **ls –l newfile3** and press **Enter**. You see a long listing for the newfile3 file. Note its modification date and time.

**3**  Wait at least one minute.

**4**  Type **touch newfile3** and press **Enter**. This updates the file's access and modification date and time stamps with the system date and time.

**5**  Type **ls –l newfile3** and press **Enter**. Look at the file's modification time. It should be different now.

Table 4-1 lists and describes the touch command's options.

| Command option | Description |
| --- | --- |
| -a | Updates the access time only |
| -m | Updates the modification time only |
| -c | Prevents touch from creating the file if it does not exist |

**Table 4-1:** Touch command options

## Deleting Files

When you no longer need a file, you can delete it using the rm (remove) command. If you use rm without options, UNIX deletes the specified file without warning. Use the –i (interactive) option to have UNIX warn you before deleting the file. You can use the rm command to delete the new files you just created.

**To delete a file from the current directory:**

**1**  After the $ command prompt, type **rm newfile1** and press **Enter**.

   This permanently deletes newfile1 from the current directory.

**2**  Type **rm –i newfile2** and press **Enter**.

   You see the message, "remove 'newfile2'?".

**3**  Type **y** for yes and press **Enter**.

**To delete a group of files using wildcards:**

1  You can specify multiple filenames as arguments to the touch command. Type **touch file1 file2 file3 filegood filebad** and press **Enter**. This command creates the files file1, file2, file3, filegood, and filebad.

2  Type **ls file*** and press **Enter**. You see the listing for the files you created in Step 1.

3  Type **rm file*** and press **Enter**.

4  Type **ls** and press **Enter**. The files have been erased.

## Removing Directories

When you no longer need a directory, you can use the rmdir command to remove it. The command takes the form:

Syntax          rmdir *directory-name*

Note:  A directory must be empty before you can remove it.

**To remove a directory with the rmdir command:**

1  Type **mkdir newdir** and press **Enter**. This creates a new directory named newdir.

2  Use a relative path with the touch command to create a new file in the newdir directory. Type **touch newdir/newfile** and press **Enter**. This creates the file newfile in the newdir directory.

3  Type **ls newdir** to see a listing of the newfile file.

4  To attempt to remove the directory, type **rmdir newdir** and press **Enter**. You see an error message similar to:

```
rmdir: newdir: Directory not empty
```

5  Use a relative path with the rm command to delete newfile. Type **rm newdir/newfile** and press **Enter**.

6  The directory is now empty. Type **rmdir newdir** and press **Enter**.

7  Type **ls** and press **Enter**. The newdir directory is no longer there.

## Copying Files

Chapter 2 introduced the cp command. Its general form is:

Syntax          cp [-options] *source destination*

The command copies the file or files specified by the source path to the location specified by the destination path. You can copy files into another directory, with the copies keeping the same names as the originals. You can also copy files into another directory with the copies taking new names, or copy files into the same directory as the originals, with the copies taking new names.

For example, assume Tom is in his /home directory (/home/tom). In this directory he has the file reminder. Under his home directory he has another directory, duplicates (/home/tom/duplicates). He copies the reminder file to the duplicates directory with the following command:

```
cp reminder duplicates
```

After he executes the command, a file named reminder is in the duplicates directory. It is a duplicate of the reminder file in the /home/tom directory. Tom also has the file class_of_78 in his home directory. He copies it to a file named classmates in the duplicates directory with the following command:

```
cp class_of_78 duplicates/classmates
```

After he executes the command, the file classmates is stored in the duplicates directory. Although it has a different name, it is a copy of the class_of_78 file. Tom also has a file named memo_to_boss in his home directory. He wants to make a copy of it and keep the copy in his home directory. He types the following command:

```
cp memo_to_boss memo.safe
```

After he executes this command, the file memo.safe is stored in Tom's home directory. It is a copy of his memo_to_boss file.

You may specify multiple source files as arguments to the cp command. For example, Tom wants to copy the files project1, project2, and project3 to his duplicates directory. He types the following command:

```
cp project1 project2 project3 duplicates
```

After he executes the command, copies of the three files are stored in the duplicates directory. You may also use wildcard characters with the cp command. For example, Tom has a directory named designs under his home directory (/home/tom/designs). He wants to copy all files in the designs directory to the duplicates directory. He types the following command:

```
cp designs/* duplicates
```

After he executes this command, the duplicates directory contains a copy of every file in the designs directory.

The cp command is especially useful for preventing data loss: you can use it to make back-up copies of your files. You can create three new files and then copy them to a different directory. Then you can duplicate one file and give it a different name. Start by creating the subdirectory source in your home directory. You can create three new files and then copy them to the source directory.

**To create three files and copy them to a directory:**

**1**   If you do not already have a subdirectory source, make sure you're in your home directory and then create the directory. After the $ command prompt, type **mkdir source** and then press **Enter**.

**2**   To create three files in your home directory, type **> file1** and press **Enter**, type **> file2** and press **Enter**, and then type **> file3** and press **Enter**.

**3**   Now you can copy the three files to the source directory. Type **cp file1 file2 file3 source** and press **Enter**.

Now you can copy of one of the files and give it a different name so you can distinguish it as a back-up file.

**4**   After the $ command prompt, type **cp file1 file1.sav** and press **Enter**.

Now your working directory contains two files with identical contents but different names.

## Recursively Removing Directories

The rm command normally requires that a directory be empty before you can remove it. This can be inconvenient when you need to remove a directory that has several subdirectories under it. The –r option, however, tells the rm command to remove a directory and everything it contains, including subdirectories. It even removes subdirectories of subdirectories. This operation is known as recursive removal.

**To recursively remove a directory with several subdirectories:**

**1**   Create a directory with several subdirectories. Type **mkdir company** and press **Enter**. Type **mkdir company/sales** and press **Enter**. Type **mkdir company/marketing** and press **Enter**. Type **mkdir company/accounting** and press **Enter**.

**2**   Create three empty files in the company directory. Type **touch company/file1 company/file2 company/file3** and press **Enter**.

**3**   Copy the files to the other directories. Type **cp company/file1 company/file2 company/file3 company/sales** and press **Enter**. Type **cp company/file1 company/file2 company/file3 company/marketing** and press **Enter**. Type **cp company/file1 company/file2 company/file3 company/accounting** and press **Enter**. (HINT: The three commands you just typed are very similar. You can reduce your typing by using the Up arrow key to recall the first command.)

**4**   Use the ls command to verify that the files were copied into all three directories.

**5** Remove the company directory and everything it contains. **Type rm –r company** and press **Enter**.

**6** Type **ls** and press **Enter**. The company directory is removed.

Caution: Be very careful with the rm –r command. It can permanently delete massive amounts of information.

## Moving Files

Moving files is similar to copying them, except you remove them from one directory and store them in another. To move a file, use the mv (move) command. The command has the general form:

**Syntax**                 mv [-options] *source destination*

You can also use the mv command to rename a file by moving one file into another file with a different name.

**To move a file from one directory to another:**

**1** To create the new file thisfile in your home directory, type **> thisfile** and then press **Enter**.

**2** Type **mv thisfile source** and press **Enter** to move the new file to the source directory.

**3** Type **ls** and press **Enter**. Thisfile is not listed. Type **ls source** and press **Enter**. You see thisfile listed.

**4** To move more than one file, type the filenames before the directory name. For example, type **mv file1 file1.sav source** and press **Enter**.

**5** To create the new file my_file, type **> my_file** and press **Enter**.

**6** To rename my_file to your_file, type **mv my_file your_file** and press **Enter**.

**7** Type **ls** and press **Enter**. You see your_file listed, but my_file is not listed.

Note: Moving and renaming a file are essentially the same operation.

You can also use the –i option with the mv command. It causes the command to prompt you before it overwrites an existing destination file.

## Finding Files

The find command searches for files that have a specified name. Use the find command to locate files that have the same name or to find a file in any directory. The command has the form:

| Syntax | find *pathname* −name *filename* |
|---|---|
| Dissection | ■ *pathname* is the path name of the directory you want to search. The find command searches recursively; that is, it starts in the named directory and searches down through all files and subdirectories under the directory specified by *pathname*. |
| | ■ **-name** indicates that you are searching for files with a specific filename. You may use wildcard characters in the filename. For example, you may use phone* to search for all filenames that begin with "phone." For other search conditions you can use with find, refer to Appendix B, "Syntax Guide to UNIX Commands." |

The find command prohibits you from searching areas where you do not have system-level permissions. As the search progresses, it passes through protected areas, but you receive a "Permission denied" message each time you enter a directory for which you do not have access permissions.

You can use the find command to find every file named phone1 in the /home directory and all its subdirectories.

**To find a file:**

■ After the $ command prompt, type **find /home −name phone1** and press **Enter**.

Note: Although Linux does not use it, other UNIX versions require the −print option after the filename to display the names of files the find command locates.

## Combining Files

Now you're ready to work on the vendor report for Worldwide Hotels, Dominion's client. Two separate files, illustrated in Figure 4-2, store the data you need—product descriptions and vendor numbers.

```
File Name: products1

Lobby Furniture          1201
Ballroom Specialties     1221
Poolside Carts           1320
Formal Dining Specials   1340
Reservation Logs         1410
```

```
File Name: products2

Plumbing Supplies        1341
Office Equipment         1361
Carpeting Services       1395
Auto Maintenance         1544
Pianos and Violins       1416
```

**Figure 4-2:** Two product description files

You can use the cat command to combine the two files in a new vendor products master file. Do so by redirecting the output of cat to create the product1 file in your home directory. The file contains two colon-separated fields.

**To use the cat command to combine files:**

**1**  After the $ command prompt, type **cat > product1**.

**2**  Type the following text, pressing **Enter** at the end of each line:

> **Lobby Furniture:1201**
> **Ballroom Specialties:1221**
> **Poolside Carts:1320**
> **Formal Dining Specials:1340**
> **Reservation Logs:1410**

**3**  Press **Ctrl+Z**.

Now you can redirect the output of cat to create the product2 file in your home directory. This file also contains two colon-separated fields.

**4**  After the $ command prompt, type **cat > product2**.

**5**  Type the following text, pressing **Enter** at the end of each line:

> **Plumbing Supplies:1423**
> **Office Equipment:1361**
> **Carpeting Services:1395**
> **Auto Maintenance:1544**
> **Pianos and Violins:1416**

**6**  Press **Ctrl+Z**.

**7** Now you can combine the two files in a master products file. After the $ command prompt, type **cat product1 product2 > products** and press **Enter.**

**8** To list the contents of products, type **more products** and press **Enter.** You see the list:

```
Lobby Furniture:1201
Ballroom Specialties:1221
Poolside Carts:1320
Formal Dining Specials:1340
Reservation Logs:1410
Plumbing Supplies:1423
Office Equipment:1361
Carpeting Services:1395
Auto Maintenance:1544
Pianos and Violins:1416
```

## The Paste Command

The paste command combines files line by line, whereas the cat command appends data to the end of the file. When you use paste to combine two files into a third file, the first line of the third file contains the first line of the first file followed by the first line of the second file. For example, Becky has the file vegetables in her home directory. Its contents are:

```
Carrots
Spinach
Lettuce
Beans
```

She also has the file bread in her home directory. Its contents are:

```
Whole wheat
White bread
Sourdough
Pumpernickel
```

After she executes the command paste Vegetables Bread > Food, the vegetables and bread files are combined, line by line, into the file food. The food file's contents are:

```
Carrots      Whole wheat
Spinach      White bread
Lettuce      Sourdough
Beans        Pumpernickel
```

Note: The paste command normally sends its output to the screen. To capture it in a file, use the redirection symbol.

As you can see, the paste command is most useful when you combine files that contain columns of information. When paste combines items into a single line, it separates them with a tab. For example, look at the first line of the food file:

```
Carrots    Whole wheat
```

When paste combined "Carrots" and "Whole wheat," it inserted a tab between them. You can use the –d option to specify another character as a delimiter. For example, to insert a comma between the output fields instead of a tab, Becky types the paste command:

```
paste —d',' vegetables bread > food
```

After Becky's command executes, the food file's contents are:

```
Carrots,Whole wheat
Spinach,White bread
Lettuce,Sourdough
Beans,Pumpernickel
```

Now you can use the paste command to combine the two product files in one. (Use paste instead of cat, because you're combining fields from two or more files.)

---

**To use the paste command to combine files:**

**1**   After the $ command prompt, type **paste product1 product2** and press **Enter**. This means "combine the file called product1 with the file called product2." You see the list of product descriptions:

```
Lobby Furniture:1201      Plumbing Supplies:1341
Ballroom Specialties:1221      Office Equipment:1361
Poolside Carts:1320      Carpeting Services:1395
Formal Dining Specials:1340      Auto Maintenance:1544
Reservation Logs:1410      Pianos and Violins:1416
```

---

## Using the Cut Command to Remove Fields

You have learned that files can consist of records, fields, and characters. You may want to retrieve some, but not all, fields in a file. You can use the cut command to remove specific columns or fields from a file. The syntax of the cut command is:

**Syntax**

**cut** -f *list* [-d *char*] *file1  file2 …*
Or
**cut** -c list *file1  file2 …*

**Dissection**

- **-f** specifies that you are referring to fields.

- *list* is a comma- or hyphen-separated list of integers or range of integers that specifies the field. For example, -f 1 indicates field 1, –f 1,14 indicates fields 1 and 14, and –f 1-14 indicates fields 1 through 14.

- **-d** indicates that a specific character separates the fields.

- *char* is the character used as the field separator (delimiter), for example, a comma. The default field delimiter is the Tab character.

- *file1, file2* are the files from which you want to cut columns or fields.

- **-c** references character positions. For example, -c 1 specifies the first character and –c 1,14 specifies characters 1 and 14.

Recall the vegetables and bread files in Becky's home directory. She also has the file meats. When she uses the command paste Vegetables Bread Meats > Food, the contents of the food file are:

```
Carrots     Whole wheat     Turkey
Spinach     White bread     Chicken
Lettuce     Sourdough       Beef
Beans       Pumpernickel    Ham
```

Becky wants to extract the second column of information (the bread list) from the file and display it on the screen. She types the following command:

```
cut –f2 food
```

The option –f2 tells the cut command to extract the second field from each line. Tab delimiters separate the fields, so cut knows where to find the fields. She sees the following output on the screen:

```
Whole wheat
White bread
Sourdough
Pumpernickel
```

She extracts the first and third columns from the file with the command:

```
cut –f1,3 food
```

The results of the command are:

```
Carrots     Turkey
Spinach     Chicken
Lettuce     Beef
Beans       Ham
```

Now you can complete your work with the Dominion phone number files by extracting a list of names from the files. First, you will create two files: corp_phones1 and corp_phones2. The corp_phones1 file includes five records of variable size, and a colon separates each field in the record. (Figure 4-1(c) illustrates this type of file structure.) The corp_phones2 file also includes five records of fixed length (the type of file structure illustrated in Figure 4-1(b)). Figure 4-3 illustrates the contents of the two files. You can use the cut command with either file to extract a list of names.

```
File Name:  Corp_phones1 (Variable Size Records - Fields separated by colon :)

219:432:4567:Harrison:Joel:M:4540:Accountant:09-12-1985
219:432:4587:Mitchell:Barbara:C:4541:Admin Asst:12-14-1995
219:432:4589:Olson:Timothy:H:4544:Supervisor:06-30-1983
219:432:4591:Moore:Sarah:H:4500:Dept Manager:08-01-1978
219:432:4527:Polk:John:S:4520:Accountant:09-22-1998

Storage space = 279 bytes
```

```
File Name:  Corp_phones2 (Fixed length records)

Character positions
1-3 5-7 9-12 14-25      26-35     36 38-41 43-50         59-68
===========================================================================
219 432 4567 Harrison   Joel      M 4540 Accountant      09-12-1985
219 432 4587 Mitchell   Barbara   C 4541 Admin Asst      1-14-19952
219 432 4589 Olson      Timothy   H 4544 Supervisor      06-30-1983
219 432 4591 Moore      Sarah     H 4500 Dept Manager    08-01-1978
219 432 4527 Polk       John      S 4520 Accountant      09-22-1998

Storage space = 345 bytes
```

**Figure 4-3:** Two versions of the company telephone file

### To create the corp_phones1 and corp_phones 2 files:

**1**  Use the vi or Emacs editor to create the file corp_phones1.

**2**  Type the following lines of text, exactly as they appear. Press **Enter** at the end of each line:

219:432:4567:Harrison:Joel:M:4540:Accountant:09-12-1985

219:432:4587:Mitchell:Barbara:C:4541:Admin Asst:12-14-1995

219:432:4589:Olson:Timothy:H:4544:Supervisor:06-30-1983

219:432:4591:Moore:Sarah:H:4500:Dept Manager:08-01-1978

219:432:4527:Polk:John:S:4520:Accountant:09-22-1998

**3**  Save the file and create a new file named corp_phones2.

**4**  Type the following lines of text, exactly as they appear. Consult Figure 4-3 for the precise position of each character. Press Enter at the end of each line.

219 432 4567 Harrison      Joel        M 4540 Accountant      09-12-1985

```
219 432 4587 Mitchell     Barbara    C 4541 Admin Asst      12-14-1995

219 432 4589 Olson        Timothy    H 4544 Supervisor      06-30-1983

219 432 4591 Moore        Sarah      H 4500 Dept Manager    08-01-1978

219 432 4527 Polk         John       S 4520 Accountant      09-22-1998
```

**5**  Save the file and exit the editor.

You want to extract the first and last names from the corp_phones1 file first. This file includes variable-length records and fields separated by colon characters. You can select the fields you want to cut by specifying their positions and separator character.

## To use the cut command to extract fields from variable-length records:

**1**  After the $ command prompt, type **cut –f4-6 –d: Corp_phones1** and press **Enter**.

This command means "cut the fields (-f) in positions four through six (4–6) that the colon character (-d:) delimits in the corp_phones1 file."

You see the list of names:

```
Harrison:Joel:M
Mitchell:Barbara:C
Olson:Timothy:H
Moore:Sarah:H
Polk:John:S
```

Now you can extract the first and last names from the corp_phones2 file. This file includes fixed-length records, so you can cut by specifying character positions.

## To use the cut command to extract fields from fixed-length records:

**1**  After the $ command prompt, type **cut –c14-25,26-35,36 corp_phones2** and press **Enter**.

This command means "cut the characters (-c) in positions 14 through 25, 26 through 35, and position 36 (14-25,26-35,36) in the corp_phones2 file."

You see the list of names:

```
Harrison      Joel       M
Mitchell      Barbara    C
Olson         Timothy    H
Moore         Sarah      H
Polk          John       S
```

**tip**

••••••••••••••••••••••••••••••••••••••••••••••••••••••••••••••••••••••••••••••

Make sure not to include a space in the code sequence after the dash (-) options in the cut command. For example, the correct syntax is cut (space) –c14-25,26-35,36 (space) /Corp_ /phones2.

••••••••••••••••••••••••••••••••••••••••••••••••••••••••••••••••••••••••••••••

Using the cut command with variable-length or fixed-length records produces similar results. Cutting from fixed-length records creates a more legible display, but requires more storage space. For example, corp_phones2 requires 345 bytes and corp_phones1 requires 279.

## Using the Sort Command

Use the sort command to sort a file's contents alphabetically or numerically. UNIX displays the sorted file on the screen by default, but you can specify that you want to store the sorted data in a particular file.

The sort command offers many options, which Appendix B, "Syntax Guide to UNIX Commands," completely describes. Here is an example of its use:

```
sort file1 > file2
```

In this example, the contents of file1 are sorted and the results stored in file2. (If the output is not redirected, sort displays its results on the screen.) Here is a more complex example:

```
sort +.10 file1 > file2
```

This command specifies a sorting key. A sorting key is a field or character position within each line. The sort command sorts the lines based on the sorting key. The + indicates that sorting does not begin at the first character position, but is offset elsewhere in the file. The period (.) indicates that the offset is measured in characters. (If the period is missing, the offset is measured in fields.) The number of characters to offset follows the period. The sample command tells the sort command that the sort key begins at character position 10.

Sorting the corp_phones1 file is relatively easy, because you can refer to field numbers. As you will see when you perform the next steps, sorting the fixed-length file, corp_phones2, is more difficult. In the first two steps, you sort the corp_phones2 file by last name and first name, respectively. In the third and fourth steps, you do the same thing with corp_phones1. Notice that the output of these four steps goes to stdout (the screen). The last step uses the –o option, instead of output redirection, to write the sorted output to a new disk file, sorted_phones.

**To sort the phones2 file:**

**1**   After the $ command prompt, type **sort +.13 corp_phones2** and press **Enter**.

This sorts the file by last name, starting at character position 13 (+.13). You see the following on your screen:

```
219 432 4567 Harrison    Joel      M 4540 Accountant    09-12-1985
219 432 4587 Mitchell    Barbara   C 4541 Admin Asst    12-14-1995
```

```
219 432 4591 Moore      Sarah     H 4500 Dept Manager   08-01-1978
219 432 4589 Olson      Timothy   H 4544 Supervisor     06-30-1983
219 432 4527 Polk       John      S 4520 Accountant     09-22-1998
```

**2**   Type **sort +.25 corp_phones2** and press **Enter**.

This sorts the file by first name, starting at character position 25 (+.25). You see the following on your screen:

```
219 432 4587 Mitchell   Barbara   C 4541 Admin Asst     12-14-1995
219 432 4567 Harrison   Joel      M 4540 Accountant     09-12-1985
219 432 4527 Polk       John      S 4520 Accountant     09-22-1998
219 432 4591 Moore      Sarah     H 4500 Dept Manager   08-01-1978
219 432 4589 Olson      Timothy   H 4544 Supervisor     06-30-1983
```

**3**   Type **sort –t:+3 corp_ phones1** and press **Enter**.

This sorts the variable-length records (-t:) starting at the Last Name field (+3). You see the following on your screen:

```
219:432:4567:Harrison:Joel:M:4540:Accountant:09-12-1985
219:432:4587:Mitchell:Barbara:C:4541:Admin Asst:12-14-1995
219:432:4591:Moore:Sarah:H:4500:Dept Manager:08-01-1978
219:432:4589:Olson:Timothy:H:4544:Supervisor:06-30-1983
219:432:4567:Polk:John:S:4520:Accountant:09-22-1998
```

**4**   Type **sort –+: +4 corp_phones1** and press **Enter**.

This sorts the variable-length records (-+: indicates the fields are delimited by a colon) starting at the First Name field (+4). You see the following on your screen:

```
219:432:4587:Mitchell:Barbara:C:4541:Admin Asst:12-14-1995
219:432:4567:Harrison:Joel:M:4540:Accountant:09-12-1985
219:432:4567:Polk:John:S:4520:Accountant:09-22-1998
219:432:4591:Moore:Sarah:H:4500:Dept Manager:08-01-1978
219:432:4589:Olson:Timothy:H:4544:Supervisor:06-30-1983
```

**5**   To sort by first name and create the output file Sorted_phones, type **sort –t: +4 –0 sorted_phones corp_phones1** and press **Enter**. This sorts the phones1 file by first name and creates an output file, sorted_phones.

## Putting It All Together

Now you can use the many file processing tools you've learned all at once. First, use the cat command to create the vendors file. The records in the vendor names file consist of two colon-separated fields: the vendor number and vendor name.

**To create the vendors file:**

**1**   After the $ command prompt, type **cat>vendors** and press **Enter**.

**2** Type the following text, pressing **Enter** at the end of each line:

**1201:Cromwell Interiors**
**1221:Design Extras Inc.**
**1320:Piedmont Plastics Inc.**
**1340:Morgan Catering Service Ltd.**
**1350:Pullman Elevators**
**1360:Johnson Office Products**

**3** Press **Ctrl+Z**.

Figure 4-4 shows the two files that Worldwide can use to determine which product each vendor supplies.

```
File Name: vendors

Vendor    Vendor Name
Number
=================================
1201:Cromwell Interiors
1221:Design Extras Inc.
1320:Piedmont Plastics Inc.
1340:Morgan Catering Service Ltd.
1350:Pullman Elevators
1360:Johnson Office Products
```

```
File Name: products

Prod       Product       Vendor
Number     Description   Number
=================================
S0107:Lobby Furniture:1201
S0109:Ballroom Specialties:1221
S0110:Poolside Carts:1320
S0130:Formal Dining Specials:1340
S0201:Reservation Logs:1410
```

**Figure 4-4:** Vendors and products

In the next steps, you use the cut, paste, and sort commands to create a single vendor report for Worldwide Hotels. Start by using the cut command to extract product descriptions and vendor numbers from the products file and storing them in separate files, p1 and p2. Then extract vendor numbers and names from the vendors file, and store them in v1 and v2. Use the paste command to combine the two vendor files (v1 and v2) in a third file, v3. Then combine the two product files (p1 and p2) in a file, p3. Sort and merge the v3 and p3 files, and send their output to the vrep file, the vendor report.

Next use the cat command to create the products file. The records in the products file consist of three colon-separated fields, the product number, the product description, and the vendor number.

**To create the products file:**

**1**   After the $ command prompt, type **cat > products** and press **Enter**.

**2**   Type the following text, pressing **Enter** at the end of each line:

```
S0107:Lobby Furniture:1201
S0109:Ballroom Specialties:1221
S0110:Poolside Carts:1320
S0130:Formal Dining Specials:1340
S0201:Reservation Logs:1410
```

**3**   Type **Ctrl+Z** to end the cat command

**To use the cut, paste, and sort commands to create a report:**

**1**   After the $ command prompt, type **cut –f2 –d: products > p1** and press **Enter**.

This means "extract the data from the second field delimited by a colon in the products file, and store it in the p1 file." It stores these product descriptions in the p1 file:

```
Lobby Furniture
Ballroom Specialties
Poolside Carts
Formal Dining Specials
Reservation Logs
```

**2**   Type **cut –f3 –d: products > p2** and press **Enter**.

This means "extract the data from the third field delimited by a colon in the products file, and store it in the p2 file." It stores these vendor numbers in the p2 file:

```
1201
1221
1320
1340
1410
```

**3**   Type **cut –f1 –d: vendors > v1** and press **Enter**.

This means "extract the data from the first field delimited by a colon in the vendors file, and store it in the v1 file." It stores these vendor numbers in the v1 file:

```
1201
1221
1320
1340
1350
1360
```

**4**   Type **cut –f2 –d: vendors > v2** and press **Enter**.

This means "extract the data from the second field delimited by a colon in the vendors file, and store it in the v2 file." It stores these product descriptions in the v2 file:

```
Cromwell Interiors
Design Extras Inc.
Piedmont Plastics Inc.
Morgan Catering Service Ltd.
Pullman Elevators
Johnson Office Products
```

**5**   Type **paste v1 v2 > v3** and press **Enter**.

This means "combine the data in v1 and v2, and direct it to the file v3. It stores these vendor numbers and product descriptions in the v3 file:

```
1201    Cromwell Interiors
1221    Design Extras Inc.
1320    Piedmont Plastics Inc.
1340    Morgan Catering Service Ltd.
1350    Pullman Elevators
1360    Johnson Office Products
```

**6**   Type **paste p2 p1 > p3** and press **Enter**.

This means "combine the data in p2 and p1, and direct it to a file called p3." It stores these vendor numbers and product descriptions in the p3 file:

```
1201    Lobby Furniture
1221    Ballroom Specialties
1320    Poolside Carts
1340    Formal Dining Specials
1410    Reservation Logs
```

**7**   Type **sort -o vrep -m v3 p3** and press **Enter**.

This means "sort and merge the data in v3 and p3, and direct the output to a file called vrep." It stores these vendor numbers and product descriptions in the vrep file:

```
1201    Cromwell Interiors
1201    Lobby Furniture
1221    Ballroom Specialties
1221    Design Extras Inc.
1320    Piedmont Plastics Inc.
1320    Poolside Carts
1340    Formal Dining Specials
1340    Morgan Catering Service Ltd.
1350    Pullman Elevators
1360    Johnson Office Products
1410    Reservation Logs
```

You used the cut, paste, and sort commands to extract information from files, combine the information, and then sort and merge the information in a new file.

# S U M M A R Y

- Operating systems support regular files, directories, character special files, and block special files. Regular files contain user information. Directories are system files for maintaining the file system's structure. Character special files are related to serial input/output devices, such as printers. Block special files are related to devices, such as disks.

- Files can be structured in several ways. UNIX stores data, such as letters, product records, or vendor reports, in flat ASCII files. UNIX structures files depending on the kind of data they store and recognizes three kinds of regular files: unstructured ASCII characters, records, and trees.

- When performing commands, UNIX processes data—it receives input from the standard input device and then sends output to the standard output device. UNIX refers to the standard devices for input and output as stdin and stdout, respectively. By default, stdin is the keyboard and stdout is the monitor. Another standard device, stderr, refers to the error file that defaults to the monitor.

- Output from a command may be redirected from stdout to a disk file. Input to a command may be redirected from stdin to a disk file. The error output of a command may be redirected from stderr to a disk file.

- The touch command updates a file's time and date stamps and creates empty files.

- When you manipulate files, you work with the files themselves as well as their content. You can use file manipulation commands to create, delete, copy, move, find, and display files.

- The rmdir command removes a directory.

- The cut command removes specific columns or fields from a file. Select the fields you want to cut by specifying their positions and separator character, or you can cut by character positions, depending on the data's organization.

- To combine two or more files, use the paste command. Where cat appends data to the end of the file, the paste command combines files line by line. You can also use paste to combine fields from two or more files.

- Use the sort command to sort a file's contents alphabetically or numerically. UNIX displays the sorted file on the screen by default, but you can also specify that you want to store the sorted data in a particular file.

# R E V I E W   Q U E S T I O N S

1. The UNIX file deletion command is _____.
   a. del
   b. remove
   c. rm
   d. kill
2. A regular file contains _____.
   a. a user program
   b. user information

    c. binary digits

    d. UNIX commands

**3.** Directories are _____.

    a. any files with a tree structure

    b. standard output devices

    c. special files for identifying disks

    d. system files for maintaining the file system's structure

**4.** The stderr device refers to _____.

    a. keyboard errors

    b. the standard error output device

    c. the line printer

    d. an output file

**5.** You can use the redirection operators to _____.

    a. change the file type

    b. redirect stdin, stdout, and stderr to a disk file

    c. combine two or more files

    d. merge sorted data

**6.** The < operator redirects _____.

    a. standard output

    b. standard input

    c. standard error

    d. none of the above

**7.** The 2> operator redirects _____.

    a. standard output

    b. standard input

    c. standard error

    d. none of the above

**8.** The UNIX move command _____.

    a. is identical to the copy command

    b. moves only one file at a time

    c. moves multiple files at once

    d. serves the same purpose as a rename command

**9.** The touch command _____.

    a. updates a file's access date and time

    b. updates a file's modification date and time

    c. updates a file's creation date and time

    d. both a and b

**10.** The command to recursively remove directories and their contents is _____.

    a. rmdir

    b. rmdir –r

    c. rm –r

    d. recurs

**11.** Use the cut command to _____.

    a. extract characters or fields from a file

    b. delete characters or fields from a file

    c. truncate records in a file

    d. reverse the paste command's effects

12. Use the paste command to _____.
    a. place information on the clipboard
    b. combine several files
    c. reverse the cut command's effects
    d. work with the cat command
13. The plus symbol (+) is an option used with the sort command to _____.
    a. offset the sort field
    b. indicate that the starting field should be skipped
    c. add more options to the sort command
    d. a and b
14. UNIX file processing treats files as _____.
    a. a sequence of fixed-length records
    b. a sequence of bytes
    c. a sequence of variable-length records
    d. key fields to index records

# EXERCISES

1. Explain the difference between cat and paste.
2. What does the command rm –r do that rmdir does not?
3. Describe two ways to create an empty file.
4. Write the command line that sorts the records in the corp_phones1 file by date of hire, the last field in the record. Refer to Figure 4-3.
5. Write the command line for the sort you did in Exercise 4, but use the corp_phones2 file instead of the corp_phones1 file.
6. Suppose you have three files: sales1, sales2, and sales3. Write the paste command that combines these files and separates the fields on each line with a ! character. The command should store the results in the file sales4.
7. Write the cut command that extracts the second field from each line of the sales4 file (that you created in Exercise 6). The command should store its results in the file sales5.
8. Write a command that Becky uses to search for the file johnson_account. She knows the file is somewhere in a directory under her home directory.

# DISCOVERY EXERCISES

1. Use the cut command to create the file prod_desc using the products file shown in Figure 4-4. The only field in the file should be the product description.
2. Create a file similar to the products file (Figure 4-4) named prod_desc1. The prod_desc1 file should have the same fields as the products file but contain different data. Use the sort command with the merge option to create an output file, merged_product. Use the input files, prod_desc1 and products.
3. Use any combination of cut and paste to create a new file using the input file, corp_phones2, shown in Figure 4-3. Place the employee's last name, first name, and middle initial in fields 1, 2, and 3.

After studying this lesson, you should be able to:

- Create a script file
- Use the join command to link files using a common field
- Use the awk command to create a professional-looking report

# Assembling Extracted Information

## Using Script Files

As you have seen, command-line entries can become long, depending on the number of options you need to use. You can use the shell's command-line history retrieval feature to recall and re-execute past commands. This feature works well for you, but others who need to execute your commands cannot access them repeatedly. MS-DOS users resolve this problem by creating batch files. UNIX users do the same: they create **shell script files** to contain command-line entries. Like MS-DOS batch files, script files contain commands that can be run sequentially as a set. A good candidate for a script file is the series of cut, paste, and sort commands that you entered in Lesson A. You can use the vi editor to create the script file and then make the script executable with the chmod and x commands.

Rolfe Williams is delighted with your vendor report but wants a way to generate the report whenever the data changes. You can create a script that includes a series of commands for creating the file ven_report.

**To use the vi editor to create a script:**

**1** Change your working directory to the corp_dbdirectory, under your home directory.

**2** After the $ command prompt, type **vi ven_report** and press **Enter**.

The vi editor starts and creates a new file, ven_report.

**3** Enter insert mode and then type the following, pressing **Enter** at the end of every line:

```
a
cut -f2 -d: products > p1
cut -f3 -d: products > p2
cut -f1 -d: vendors  > v1
cut -f2 -d: vendors  > v2
paste v1 v2 > v3
paste p2 p1 > p3
sort -t: -o vrep -m v3 p3
```

These are the same commands you used in Lesson A to create the first vendor report.

**4** Press **Esc**.

**5** Type **:wq** to exit the vi editor.

Now you can make the script executable with the chmod command. The chmod command sets file permissions. In the example that follows, the chmod command and its ugo+x option make the ven_report file executable by **u**sers (owners), **g**roup, and **o**thers. Run a test to make sure it works.

**To make the script executable:**

**1** After the $ command prompt, type **chmod ugo+x ven_report** and press **Enter**.

See "Setting File Permissions" in Chapter 2 for more information on the chmod command.

**2** To make sure the script works, type **./ven_report** and press **Enter**.

You see the same list of vendor numbers and product descriptions that you saw in Lesson A.

## Using the Join Command

The join command differs from the other file processing commands in this chapter, because it is used in relational database processing. **Relational databases** consider files as tables and records as rows. They also refer to fields as columns that can be joined to create new records. The join command is the UNIX method that lets you extract information from two files sharing a common field.

For example, you can use the join command to combine information in the vendor and product files, thereby producing the vendor report for Worldwide's purchasing department. Both the vendor and product reports include the vendor number. The syntax of the join command is:

| | |
|---|---|
| **Syntax** | **join** [options] *file1 file2* |

| | |
|---|---|
| **Dissection** | ■ *file1, file2* are two input files that must be sorted on the join field—the field you want to use join the files. The join field is also called a **key**. You must sort the files before you can join them. When you issue the join command, UNIX compares the two fields. Each output line contains the common field followed by a line from *file1*, followed by a line from *file2*. You can modify output using the options described next. If records with duplicate keys are in the same file, UNIX joins on all of them. You can create output records for unpairable lines, for example, to append data from one file to another without losing records. |

**Options**

■ **-j** specifies the common fields on which the join is to be made.

■ **-o** specifies a list of fields to be output. The list contains blank-separated field specifiers in the form *m.n*, where *m* is the file number and *n* is the position of the field in the file. Thus –o 1.2 means "output the second field in the first file."

■ **-t** specifies the field separator character. By default this is a blank, tab, or new line character. Multiple blanks and tabs count as one field separator.

■ **-a** *n* produces a line for each unpairable line in file *n*, where *n* = 1 or 2.

■ **-e** *str* replaces the empty fields for the unpairable line in the string specified by *str*. The string is usually a code or message to indicate the condition; that is, –e "No Vendor Record."

For an example of join logic, see Figure 4-5.

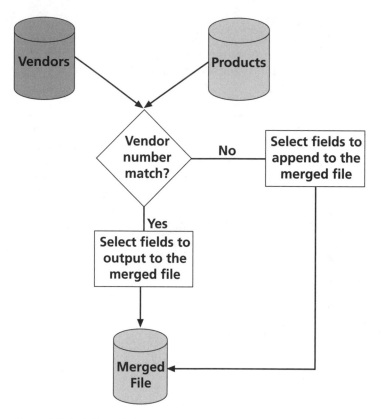

**Figure 4-5:** Relational join

In Figure 4-5, the join command combines fields from the vendor and product files. Then it searches for vendor numbers in the vendor file matching those in the product file. If a field does not match, UNIX selects it and later appends it to the merged file. If the field does match, UNIX sends it to the merged file.

## Using the Join Command to Create the Vendor Report

You can use the join command to create a vendor report showing what products Worldwide's purchasing department has in stock.

**To use the join command to create a report:**

**1**    After the $ command prompt, type **join –a1 –e "No Products" –j1 1 –j2 3 –o 1.2 2.2 –t: vendors products > vreport; cat vreport** and press **Enter.**

In this command, the –j option indicates the first or second specified file, such as vendors or products. Numbers following j1 and j2 specify field numbers used for the join or match. Here, UNIX uses the first field of the vendors record to join the third field of the products file.

The −a option tells the command to print a line for each unpairable line in the file number. In this case, a line prints for each vendor record that does not match a product record.

The −e option lets you display a message for the unmatched (-a 1) record, such as "No Products."

The −o option sets the fields that will be output when a match is made.

The 1.2 indicates that field two of the vendors file is to be output along with 2.2, field two of the products file.

The −t option specifies the field separator, the colon. This join command redirects its output to a new file, vreport. The cat command displays the output on the screen.

The report contains this information:

```
Cromwell Interiors:Lobby Furniture
Design Extras Inc.:Ballroom Specialties
Piedmont Plastics Inc.:Poolside Carts
Morgan Catering Service Ltd.:Formal Dining Specials
Pullman Elevators:No Products
Johnson Office Products:No Products
```

## A Brief Introduction to Awk

Awk, a pattern-scanning and processing language, helps to produce professional-looking reports. Although you can use the cat and more commands to display the output file that you create with your join program, the awk command (which starts the Awk program when you type it on the command line) lets you do the same thing more quickly and easily. The syntax of the awk command is:

| Syntax | awk [-Fsep] ' pattern {action} ..' filenames |
|---|---|
| Dissection | ■ awk checks to see if the input records in the specified files satisfy the *pattern* and, if they do, awk executes the *action* associated with it. If no *pattern* is specified, the *action* affects every input record. |
| | ■ -F: means the field separator is a colon. |

**To generate and format the vendor report:**

**1** After the $ command prompt, type **awk −F: '{printf "%-28s\t %s\n", $1, $2}'** **vreport** and then press **Enter**. This command is explained in detail after Step 2.

**2**   You see the vendor report, including vendor names and product descriptions:

```
Cromwell Interiors              Lobby Furniture
Design Extras Inc.             Ballroom Specialties
Piedmont Plastics Inc.         Poolside Carts
Morgan Catering Service Ltd.   Formal Dining Specials
Pullman Elevators              No Products
Johnson Office Products        No Products
```

The parts of the awk command you typed in Step 1 are:

- **awk –F:** calls the Awk program and identifies the field separator as a colon.
- **'{printf "%-28s\t %s\n", $1, $2}'** represents the *action* to take on each line that is read in. Single quotes enclosed the action.
- **printf** is a print formatting function from the C language. It lets you specify an edit *pattern* for the output. The code inside the double quotes defines this pattern. The code immediately following the % tells how to align the field to be printed. The – sign specifies left alignment. The number that follows, 28, indicates how many characters you want to display. The trailing s means that the field consists of non-numeric characters, also called a "string." The \t inserts a tab character into the edit pattern. The %s specifies that another string field should be printed. You do not need to specify the string length in this case, because it will be the last field printed (the product name). The \n specifies to skip a line after printing each output record. The $1 and $2 separated with a comma indicates that the first and second fields in the input file should be placed in the edit pattern where the two s's appear. The first field is the vendor name, and the second is the product description.
- **vreport** is the name of the input file.

## Using the Awk Command to Refine the Vendor Report

To refine and automate the vendor report, you can create a shell script, as you did at the beginning of this lesson. This new script, however, includes only the awk command, not a series of separate commands. You then call the Awk program using awk with the –f option. This option tells awk that the code is coming from a disk file, not from the keyboard. You can present the *action* statements inside the Awk program file in a different way. The program file includes additional lines needed to print a heading and the current date for the report.

The next steps show what happens when you enter the Awk program in a file like this. You use the FS variable to tell the program what the field separator is, in this example, a colon. FS is one of many variables that awk uses to advise the program about the file being processed. Other codes you see here set up an initial activity that executes once when the program loads. BEGIN followed by the opening curly brace ({) indicates this opening activity. The closing curly brace (}) marks the end of actions performed when the program first loads. These *actions* print the headings, date, and dash lines that separate the heading from the body of the report.

## To create the awk script:

**1** After the $ command prompt, type **vi awrp** and press **Enter** to start the vi editor and create the file awrp.

**2** Type the code:

```
BEGIN {
       { FS = ":"}
       { print "\t\tVendors and Products" }
       { "date" | getline d }
       { printf "\t    %s\n",d }
       { print "Vendor Name\t\t\t Product Names" }
       {print"=============================================\n" }
       }
       { printf "%-28s\t%s\n",$1, $2 }
```

**3** Press **Esc**.

**4** Type **:wq** to exit the vi editor.

**5** After the $ command prompt, type **awk –f awrp vreport > v_report**, and press **Enter**.

This means "using the Awk program, combine the fields from the awrp file with the fields from the vreport file, and send them to a new file called v_report."

**6** Type **cat v_report** and press **Enter**.

You see the following report:

```
          Vendors and Products
      Sun Dec 20 21:03:41 EST 1998
Vendor Name                      Product Names
==========================================================

Cromwell Interiors               Lobby Furniture
Design Extras Inc.               Ballroom Specialties
Piedmont Plastics Inc.           Poolside Carts
Morgan Catering Service Ltd.     Formal Dining Specials
Pullman Elevators                No Products
Johnson Office Products          No Products
```

**7** To print the report on the default printer, type **lpr v_report** and press **Enter**.

You produced a vendor and product name report and then formatted and printed the report.

# S U M M A R Y

- To automate command processing, include commands in a script file that you can later execute like a program. Use the vi editor to create the script file and the chmod command to make it executable.

- Use the join command to extract information from two files sharing a common field. You can use this common field to join the two files. You must sort the two files on the join field—the one you want to use to join the files. The join field is also called a "key." You must sort the files before you can join them.

- Awk is a pattern-scanning and processing language useful for creating a formatted and professional-looking report. You can enter the Awk language instructions in a program file using the vi editor and call it using the awk command.

# C O M M A N D    S U M M A R Y

| Chapter 4 commands | | |
|---|---|---|
| Command | Purpose | Options covered in this chapter |
| awk | Start the Awk program to format output | -F identifies the field separator<br>–f indicates code is coming from a disk file, not the keyboard |
| cp | Copy one or more files | |
| cut | Extract specified columns or fields from a file | -c refers to character positions<br>-d indicates a specified character separates the fields<br>-f refers to fields |
| find | Find files | -name specifies the name of files you want to locate |
| join | Combine files having a common field | -a *n* produces a line for each unpairable line in file *n*<br>-e *str* replaces the empty fields for an unpairable file with the specified string<br>-j uses specified common fields when joining<br>-o outputs a specified list of fields<br>-t indicates a specified character separates the fields |

## Chapter 4 commands (continued)

| | | |
|---|---|---|
| less | Display the file's contents, pausing at the end of each screen | |
| lpr | Print the command output on the default printer | |
| more | Display the contents of a file, pausing at the end of each screen | |
| mv | Move one or more files | |
| paste | Combine fields from two or more files | |
| rm | Remove one or more files | −i specifies that UNIX should request confirmation of file deletion before removing the files<br>−r specifies that directories should be recursively removed |
| rmdir | Remove a directory | |
| sort | Sort the file's contents | +n sorts on the field specified by n<br>.+ designates the position that follows an offset (+) as a character position, not a field position<br>−t indicates that a specified character separates the fields<br>−m means to merge files before sorting<br>−o redirects output to the specified file |
| touch | Update an existing file's date and time stamp command or creates empty new files | −a specifies that only the access date and time is to be updated<br>−m specifies that only the modification date and time is to be updated<br>−c specifies that no files are to be created |

# R E V I E W   Q U E S T I O N S

1. Which of these statements is false?
   a. The join program requires that you sort files by the join field.
   b. A script file is similar to an MS-DOS batch file.
   c. The Awk program eliminates the need to write high-level languages.
   d. You can make your script files executable.

2. The join command _____.
   a. combines files with a common field
   b. can only be used with merged files
   c. is the opposite of the paste command
   d. formats output

3. Used with the awk command, the –F option specifies _____.
   a. an external file containing instructions
   b. that the input file has fixed-length records
   c. the output's form
   d. none of the above

4. The BEGIN script in the Awk program _____.
   a. executes only once during the program cycle
   b. is normally enclosed in curly braces if you issue more than one command
   c. executes when the program loads
   d. all of the above

5. Which option codes does the join command use to specify the list of output fields?
   a. –o
   b. –f
   c. –x
   d. –e

6. Which option does the join command use to specify the string to print when a line is unmatched?
   a. –e
   b. –o
   c. –f
   d. –x

7. Used with the join program, which of these displays the second field in the first file?
   a. –o 2.1
   b. –o 1.1
   c. –o 1.2
   d. none of the above

8. The join command is like a database program in that both _____.
   a. must work with a relational database file
   b. access tables instead of files
   c. use a relational join operation to connect files
   d. must be read by database-only programs

**E X E R C I S E S**

1. What is the advantage of using script files?

2. What is the difference between join and paste?

3. Why is the operation performed by the join command called a "relational join?"

4. What two ways do you use to specify patterns and actions to the awk command?

5. Create a join script for the vendors and products files showing which products do not have a matching vendor record.

6. Write a simple Awk program to print the phones1 file in Figure 4-3.

7. Write a script file to display the vendor file, and then run the script.

 **D I S C O V E R Y    E X E R C I S E S**

1. Use vi, Emacs, or the method of your choice to create the files cust_names, cust_ids, and cust_status. The files should have the following contents.

   Contents of cust_names:

   ```
   Smith Furniture Co.
   Wells Manufacturing
   Rose Department Store
   Haywood Resort
   ```

   Contents of cust_ids:

   ```
   101
   102
   114
   197
   ```

   Contents of cust_status:

   ```
   ACTIVE
   ACTIVE
   INACTIVE
   ACTIVE
   ```

2. Use the paste command to create a file named cust1. Combine the cust_ids and cust_names files to create cust1. Use the colon character as the field delimiter.

3. Use the paste command to create a file called cust2. Combine the cust_ids and cust_status files to create cust2. Use the colon character as the field delimiter.

4. Use the join command to join cust1 and cust2 and create the file cust_info. The key field is the first field of cust1 and cust2 (which lists the customer ID).

5. Write an awk command that reads the cust_info and displays the customer IDs followed by the customer names. The customer IDs should be printed in a right-justified field of 10 spaces.

# Advanced File Processing

**case ▶** Dominion Consulting is evaluating its programming staff and the staff's current workload. Management wants a Programmer Activity Status Report that shows programmers' names and the number of projects that each programmer is working on. Your assignment: to design and create the files necessary to obtain the data and then produce the report.

**After studying this lesson, you should be able to:**

- Use the pipe operator to redirect the output of one command to another command
- Use the grep command to search for a specified pattern in a file
- Use the uniq command to remove duplicate lines from a file
- Use the comm and diff commands to compare two files
- Use the wc command to count words, characters, and lines in a file
- Use the manipulate and format commands: sed, tr, and pr

# Selecting, Manipulating, and Formatting Information

Creating the Programmer Activity Status Report challenges you to make practical use of your UNIX file processing skills. You used many file processing commands in previous chapters. This lesson introduces new commands that let you complete advanced file processing tasks. Lesson B focuses on how to design a new application. You learn to design the application, create its files and shell scripts, and produce the final report.

## Advancing Your File Processing Skills

In Chapter 4 you learned to use several UNIX commands to extract and organize information from existing files and transform that information into a useful format. This chapter explains how to use other file processing commands, which are organized into two categories: select commands, and manipulation and transformation commands. Table 5-1 lists the select commands, which extract information.

| Command | Purpose |
| --- | --- |
| comm | Compare sorted files and show differences |
| cut | Select columns (fields) |
| diff | Compare and select differences in two files |
| grep | Select lines or rows |
| head | Select header lines |
| tail | Select trailing lines |
| uniq | Select unique lines or rows |
| wc | Count characters, words, or lines in a file |

**Table 5-1:** Select commands

The **manipulation and transformation commands** alter and transform extracted information into useful and appealing formats. Table 5-2 lists these commands.

| Command | Purpose |
| --- | --- |
| awk | Invoke Awk, a pattern-scanning and processing language |
| cat | Concatenate files |
| chmod | Change security mode of a file or directory |
| join | Join two files, matching row by row |
| paste | Paste multiple files, column by column |
| pr | Format and print |
| sort | Sort and merge multiple files |
| sed | Edit data streams |
| tr | Translate character by character |

**Table 5-2:** Manipulation and transformation commands

# Using the Select Commands

You used the head and tail commands in Chapter 1, and the cut command in Chapter 4. Now you can work with the grep, diff, uniq, comm, and wc commands, which also let you process files.

> Note: The command usage in this chapter demonstrates how commands generally work. Appendix B, "Syntax Guide to UNIX Commands," more completely describes these commands.

## Using Pipes

As you have seen, most UNIX commands take their input from stdin (the standard input device) and send their output to stdout (the standard output device). You have also used the > operator to redirect a command's output from the screen to a file, and the < operator to redirect a command's input from the keyboard to a file. The pipe operator (I) redirects the output of one command to the input of another command. The pipe operator is used in the following manner:

```
first_command | second_command
```

The pipe operator connects the output of the first command with the input of the second command. For example, the output of the ls command is commonly redirected to the more command. This technique allows you to scroll through a directory listing that does not fit on a single screen.

---

**To redirect the output of the ls command to the more command:**

**1**   Type **ls –l /etc** and press **Enter**. The output of the command scrolls quickly by.

**2**   Type **ls –l /etc | more**.

Notice the output fills the screen and pauses with the prompt "—More—" displayed on the bottom line. Each time you press the spacebar, the output advances to the next screen. Press the spacebar until the command has finished.

---

The pipe operator can connect several commands on the same command line, in the following manner:

```
first_command | second_command | third_command . . .
```

---

**To connect several commands with the pipe operator:**

■   Type **ls /etc | sort –r | more** and press **Enter**. This command redirects the directory listing of the /etc directory to the sort –r command. sort –r sorts the directory listing in reverse order. The sort command's output is redirected to the more command.

You see the directory listing of /etc in reverse order, one screen at a time.

---

## Using the grep Command

Use the grep command to search for a specified pattern in a file, such as a particular word or phrase. UNIX finds and then displays the line containing the pattern you specified. As you recall from Chapter 1, you can use the head command to retrieve the first 10 lines of a file. You can combine the grep and head commands to retrieve only the first 10 lines containing the word or phrase. For example, use grep with head to find the first 10 lines in /etc/termcap that contain the characters "IBM."

**To display lines in a file containing a particular word or phrase:**

**1** To see all the lines in the /etc/termcap file that contain the characters "IBM," type **grep IBM /etc/termcap** and press **Enter**. There are numerous lines and the output scrolls by quickly.

**2** Redirect the output of the grep command to the input of the more command. Type **grep IBM /etc/termcap | more** and press **Enter**.

**3** Press the **spacebar** until the command is finished.

**4** Redirect the output of the grep command to the head command. Type **grep IBM /etc/termcap | head** and press **Enter**.

This means "look for 'IBM' in the /etc/termcap file, and display the first 10 lines you find."

The grep command's options and wildcard support allow powerful search operations.

**To expand the grep command's search capabilities with its options and wildcard support:**

**1** To see each line in the /etc/termcap file that contains the word "Linux," type **grep Linux /etc/termcap** and press **Enter**. (Make sure to capitalize the L in Linux.)

**2** Some lines in the file contain the word "linux" (with a lowercase l). The search you performed in Step 1 only displayed the lines that contain "Linux." The –i option tells grep to ignore the case of the search characters. Type **grep –i linux /etc/termcap** and press **Enter**. You see the lines that contain either "Linux" or "linux."

**3** The grep command supports wildcard characters in the search string. To see all the lines of the /etc/termcap file that contain "lin" followed by any set of characters, type **grep –i' < lin' /etc/termcap** and press **Enter**.

**4** The grep command also supports wildcards in the filename. Type **grep linux /etc/*** and press **Enter**. You see the lines that contain "linux" from all the files in the /etc directory.

**5**    The –l (lowercase L) option instructs grep to display only the names of the files that contain the search string. Type **grep –l linux /etc/*** and press **Enter**. You see the names of the files in the /etc directory that contain "linux."

The grep command also searches files for phrases that contain spaces, as long as the phrase is specified on the command line inside quotation marks. For example, grep can search for the phrase "IBM PC," as demonstrated in the next set of steps.

**To search a file for a phrase:**

■    Type **grep "IBM PC" /etc/termcap** and press **Enter**.

You see all lines in the /etc/termcap file that contain the phrase "IBM PC."

In the previous examples, grep searches the file whose name is specified on the command line. grep can also take its input from another command, through the pipe operator.

**To redirect the output of a command to the grep comand:**

■    Type **ls /etc | grep magic** and press **Enter**. You see a list of the files whose names contain the word "magic."

Note: The shell programming chapters that follow describe the grep file search command in great detail.

## Using the uniq Command

The uniq command removes duplicate lines from a file. Because it compares only consecutive lines, the uniq command requires sorted input. The syntax of the uniq command is:

Syntax    **uniq** [options] *file1 file2*

In its simplest form, the uniq command removes identical lines or rows from a file. The following command creates the file inventory. It contains all the lines in the parts file, with duplicate lines eliminated.

```
uniq parts > inventory
```

The –u option instructs uniq to output only the lines of the source file that are not duplicated. (If a line is repeated, it is not output at all.) Here is an example:

```
uniq —u parts > single_items
```

The –d option instructs uniq to output one copy of each line that has a duplicate. Unduplicated lines are not output. Here is an example:

```
uniq —d parts > multi_items
```

The next steps illustrate common uses of the uniq command. To practice the uniq command, start by using the cat command with the output redirection operator to create a new file, zoo1, in your working directory. The file lists animal names, food descriptions, pounds eaten daily, and food costs. The duplicate records in Step 1 are not mistakes, so type them as shown. Then you'll use the uniq command to remove duplicate records.

**To remove duplicate lines with the uniq command:**

**1** After the $ command prompt, type the following text, pressing **Enter** at the end of each line:

```
cat > zoo1
Monkeys:Bananas:2000:850.00
Lions:Raw Meat:4000:1245.50
Lions:Raw Meat:4000:1245.50
Camels:Vegetables:2300:564.75
Elephants:Hay:120000:1105.75
Elephants:Hay:120000:1105.75
```

**2** Press **Ctrl+Z**.

**3** To use uniq to remove duplicate lines from the zoo1 file and use the output redirection operator to create the new file zoo2, type **uniq zoo1 > zoo2** and press **Enter**.

**4** To use the cat command to display the zoo2 file, type **cat zoo2** and press **Enter**.

**5** You see the contents of zoo2 as listed next. Notice that the uniq command removed the duplicate lines.

```
Monkeys:Bananas:2000:850.00
Lions:Raw Meat:4000:1245.50
Camels:Vegetables:2300:564.75
Elephants:Hay:120000:1105.75
```

## Using the comm Command

Like the uniq command, the **comm** command identifies duplicate lines. Unlike the uniq command, it doesn't delete duplicates and it works with two files rather than one. The comm command locates identical lines within two identically sorted files. It compares lines common to file1 and file2 and produces three-column output:

- The first column contains lines found only in file1.
- The second column contains lines found only file2.
- The third column contains lines found in both file1 and file2.

The syntax of comm is:

Syntax            comm [options] *file1 file2*

To practice using the comm command, start by creating the file my_list. Duplicate the file and then use the comm command to compare the two files.

**To use the comm command to compare files:**

**1** To create the file my_list, after the $ command prompt, type **cat > my_list** and press **Enter**.

**2** Type the following text, pressing **Enter** at the end of each line:

```
Football
Basketball
Skates
```

**3** Press **Ctrl+Z**.

**4** To copy my_list to a second file, your_list, type **cp my_list  your_list** and press **Enter**.

**5** Now use the comm command to compare my_list to your_list. Type **comm my_list your_list** and press **Enter**.

**6** You see the three-column output. Notice that the lines in the third column are those that both files contain. The files are identical.

```
Column 1        Column 2        Column 3
                                Football
                                Basketball
                                Skates
```

**7** Now add a new line to my_list. Type **cat >> my_list** and press **Enter**.

**8** Type **Books** and press **Enter**.

**9** Press **Ctrl+Z**.

**10** Use comm to compare my_list to your_list again. Type **comm my_list your_list** and press **Enter**.

**11** You see the three-column output, with the unique new line in my_list in column 1.

```
Column 1          Column 2          Column 3
                                    Football
                                    Basketball
                                    Skates

Books
```

## To find differences between two files:

**1** After the $ command prompt, type **diff zoo1 zoo2** and press **Enter**.

**2** You see this information:

```
3d2
< Lions:Raw Meat:4000:1245.50
5d3
< Elephants:Hay:120000:1105.75
```

This means that you need to delete the third and fifth lines from zoo1 so the file matches zoo2.

**3** To reverse the comparison order, type **diff zoo2 zoo1** and press **Enter**.

**4** You see this information:

```
2a3
> Lions:Raw Meat:4000:1245.50
3a5
> Elephants:Hay:120000:1105.75
```

This means that you need to add the two lines shown to zoo2, so the file matches zoo1.

## Using the diff Command

The diff command attempts to determine the minimal set of changes needed to convert file1 to file2. The command's output displays the line(s) that differ. The code 3d2 displayed above the line indicates that you need to delete the third line in file1, so file1 matches file2. The d means delete, the 3 means the third line from file1, and the 2 means that file1 and file2 will be the same up to but not including line 2. The code 2a3 indicates you need to add a line to file1, so file1 matches file2. The a means add a line or lines to file1. The 3 means line 3 is to be added from file2 to file1. The 2 indicates that the line must be added following line 2.

You can use the diff command to find the differences between zoo1 and zoo2.

## Using the wc Command

Use the wc command to count the number of lines (option –l), words (option –w), and bytes or characters (option –c) in text files. You may specify all three options in the command line, that is, -lwc. If you enter the command without options, you see counts of lines, words, and characters in that order. You can use the wc command to count the number of lines in a new file, counters.

---

**To create a file and count its lines:**

**1**  After the $ command prompt, type **cat > counters** and press **Enter**.

**2**  Type this text, pressing **Enter** at the end of each line:

```
Linux is a full featured UNIX clone.
Linux blends the best of BSD and Sys V.
```

**3**  Type **Ctrl+Z**.

**4**  To find the number of lines in counters, type **wc –l counters** and press **Enter**. UNIX reports that the file contains two lines.

**5**  To find the number of bytes in counters, type **wc –c counters** and press **Enter**. UNIX reports that the file contains 77 bytes.

**6**  To find the number of words in counters, type **wc –w counters** and press **Enter**. UNIX reports that the file contains 16 words.

**7**  To count words, characters, and lines in counters, type **wc –lwc counters** and press **Enter**. UNIX reports the counts for lines (2), bytes (77), and words (16).

---

# Using the Manipulate and Format Commands

In addition to the manipulate and format commands you used in Chapter 4, you can also use the sed, tr, and pr commands to edit and transform data's appearance before you display or print it.

## Introducing sed

When you want to make global changes to large files, you need a more powerful editor than interactive editors like vi and Emacs. Another UNIX editor, **sed,** is designed specifically for that purpose. The minimum requirements to run sed are an input file and a command that lets sed know what actions to apply to the file. sed commands have two general forms:

| Syntax | **sed** [options] *'command' file(s)* |
| --- | --- |
| | **sed** [options] *–f scriptfile file(s)* |

| Dissection | ■ The first form lets you specify an editing command on the command line, surrounded by single quotes. |
| --- | --- |
| | ■ The second form lets you specify a script file containing sed commands. |

You can use sed to work with a new file, unix_stuff, to display only certain lines and to replace text.

**To use sed to manipulate a file:**

**1** To create a new file, unix_stuff, in your working directory, type **cat > unix_stuff** and press **Enter**.

**2** Type this text, pressing **Enter** at the end of each line:

```
Although UNIX supports other database systems,
UNIX has never abandoned the idea of working with
flat files. Flat files are those that are based on pure
text with standard ASCII codes. Flat files
can be read by any operating system.
```

**3** Press **Ctrl+Z**.

**4** To display only lines 3 and 4, type **sed –n 3,4p unix_stuff** and press **Enter**. (The n option prevents sed from displaying any lines except those specified with the p command.)

This means "find lines numbered (-n) 3 and 4 in the file Unix_stuff and display them (p)."

You see lines 3 and 4:

```
flat files. Flat files are those that are based
on pure text with standard ASCII codes. Flat files
```

**5** In sed, you can place two commands on one line. If you want to delete lines 3 and 4 and then display the file, you must use sed's –e option to specify multiple commands on the same line.

**6** To delete lines 3 and 4 from unix_stuff and display the results, type **sed –n –e 3,4d –e p unix_stuff** and press **Enter**.

You see the text:

```
Although UNIX supports other database systems,
UNIX has never abandoned the idea of working with
can be read by any operating system.
```

Note: Lines 3 and 4 are not actually deleted from the file but simply filtered out so they are not displayed.

**7**   To display only lines containing the word, "Flat," type **sed –n /Flat/p unix_stuff** and press **Enter**.

You see the text:

```
flat files. Flat files are those that are based
on pure text with standard ASCII codes. Flat files
```

**8**   To replace all instances of the word "Flat" with "Text," type **sed –n s/Flat/Text/p unix_stuff** and press **Enter**. (The s command substitutes one string of characters for another.)

You see the text:

```
flat files. Text files are those that are based
on pure text with standard ASCII codes. Text files
```

To append new lines in sed, you must use the a\ command. This command appends lines after the specified line number. Like all other sed commands, it operates on all lines in the file if you do not specify a line number.

Next you can create a new script file, more_stuff. Include the append command, a\, in the file with the lines to be appended to the file unix_stuff. You must terminate each line, except for the last line of the file being added, with a backslash character. In the next steps, the $ preceding the a\ symbol tells sed to append more_stuff to unix_stuff after the last line in unix_stuff; without $, sed repeatedly adds all the lines in more_stuff after each line in unix_stuff.

**To create a script file to append lines to another file:**

**1**   To create the script file more_stuff, type **cat > more_stuff** and press **Enter**.

**2**   Type this text, pressing **Enter** at the end of each line:

```
$a\
Informix and Oracle, two major relational database\
companies have installed their RDBMS packages on UNIX\
systems for many years.
```

**3**   Press **Ctrl+Z**.

**4**   To use the sed command to run the script file, type **sed –f more_stuff unix_stuff** and press **Enter**.

You see this text:

```
Although UNIX supports other database systems,
UNIX has never abandoned the idea of working with
flat files. Flat files are those that are based
on pure text with standard ASCII codes. Flat files
can be read by any operating system.
Informix and Oracle, two major relational database
```

> companies have installed their RDBMS packages on UNIX
> systems for many years.

5  Use vi to create the file Stuff_replace. Insert the following sed commands into the file:

```
s/UNIX/Linux/
s/abandoned/given up/
s/standard/regular/
```

The lines in the file instruct sed to replace all occurrences of "UNIX" with "Linux," "abandoned" with "given up," and "standard" with "regular."

6  Execute sed, with the script file you created in Step 5, on the unix_stuff2 file. Redirect sed's output to the file unix_stuff2. Type **sed –f stuff_replace unix_stuff > unix_stuff2** and press **Enter**.

7  Type **cat unix_stuff2** and press **Enter**. You see the file with the changes specified by the stuff_replace script file.

### Translating Characters Using the tr Command

The tr command copies data from the standard input to the standard output, substituting or deleting characters specified by options and patterns. The patterns are strings and the strings are sets of characters.

| | |
|---|---|
| **Syntax** | **tr** [options] *string1 string2* |
| **Dissection** | ■ In its simplest form, tr translates each character in *string1* into the character in the corresponding position in *string2*. The strings are "quoted" with either single or double quotes. |
| | ■ Two options used most frequently are –d (delete character) and –s (substitute character). |

A popular use of tr is converting lowercase characters to uppercase characters. You can translate the file counters from lowercase to uppercase characters by specifying [a–z] as the lowercase characters and [A–Z] as the uppercase characters.

> **To translate lowercase characters to uppercase characters in the file counters:**
>
> ■ After the $ command prompt, type **tr [a-z] [A-Z] < counters** and press **Enter**.
>
> You see these lines:
>
> ```
> LINUX IS A FULL FEATURED UNIX CLONE.
> LINUX BLENDS THE BEST OF BSD AND SYS V.
> ```

You can also use the –d option with the tr command to delete input characters found in *string1* from the output. This is helpful when you need to remove an erroneous character from the file.

---

**To delete specified characters from the counters file:**

■ To delete the characters "full" from the output, type **tr –d "full" < counters** and press **Enter**.

You see this text:

```
Linx is a eatred UNIX cone.
Linx bends the best o BSD and Sys V.
```

Notice that the command deleted all characters in "full"—every f, u and l—from the output.

---

The –s option of the tr command checks for sequences of a *string1* character repeated several consecutive times. When this happens, tr replaces the sequence of repeated characters with one occurrence of the corresponding character from *string2*. For example, use the –s option when you need to change a field delimiter in a flat file from one character to another. For example, in the file zoo2, use tr to replace the field delimiter ":" with a space character, " ". First, use cat to display the file.

---

**To replace characters in the file counters:**

**1** After the $ command prompt, type **cat zoo2** and press **Enter**.

You see this text:

```
Monkeys:Bananas:2000:850.00
Lions:Raw Meat:4000:1245.50
Camels:Vegetables:2300:564.75
Elephants:Hay:120000:1105.75
```

**2** Type **tr –s ":" " " < zoo2** and press **Enter**.

You see this text:

```
Monkeys Bananas 2000 850.00
Lions Raw Meat 4000 1245.50
Camels Vegetables 2300 564.75
Elephants Hay 120000 1105.75
```

---

## Using the pr Command to Format Your Output

The pr command prints the specified files on the standard output in paginated form. If you do not specify any files or you specify a filename of "-", pr reads the standard input.

By default, pr formats the specified files into single-column pages of 66 lines. Each page has a five-line header, which, by default, contains the current file's name, its last modification date, current page, and a five-line trailer consisting of blank lines.

| | |
|---|---|
| **Syntax** | **pr** [options] [*file…*] |
| **Dissection** | ■ The three most frequently used options are –h (header-format), which lets you customize your header line; -d, which double-spaces output; and –l n, which sets the number of lines per page. |

Use pr to format and print the unix_stuff file. Use the pipe operator (|) to send the output to more, so the output screen does not flash by.

**To format a file:**

■ After the $ command prompt, type **pr –h "UNIX Files & Databases" <unix_stuff** (|) **more**, and press **Enter**.

You see this text:

```
99-11-22 02:35              UNIX Files & Databases
Page 1


Although UNIX supports other database systems,
UNIX has never abandoned the idea of working with
flat files. Flat files are those that are based
on pure text with standard ascii codes. Flat files
can be read by any operating system.
```

Now you can type the same command but add the –l 23 option to limit the number of lines per page to 23. Because the standard number of lines on most monitors is 24, you do not need to pipe the output to hold the screen.

**2** Type **pr –l 23 –h "UNIX Files & Databases" <unix_stuff**, and press **Enter**.

You see this text:

```
99-11-22 02:35              UNIX Files & Databases
Page 1


Although UNIX supports other database systems,
UNIX has never abandoned the idea of working with
flat files. Flat files are those that are based
on pure text with standard ascii codes. Flat files
can be read by any operating system.
```

# C O M M A N D   S U M M A R Y

| Chapter 5, Lesson A commands | | |
| --- | --- | --- |
| Command | Purpose | Options covered in this chapter |
| comm | Compare and output lines common to two files | |
| diff | Compare two files and determine which lines differ | |
| grep | Select lines or rows | -i ignores case<br>-l lists only filenames |
| pr | Format a specified file | -d double-spaces the output<br>-h customizes the header line<br>-l*n* sets the number of lines per page |
| sed | Specify an editing command or a script file containing sed commands | -a \ appends text after a line<br>-d deletes specified text<br>-e specifies multiple commands on one line<br>-n indicates line numbers<br>-p displays lines<br>-s substitutes specified text |
| tr | Translate characters | -d deletes input characters found in *string1* from the output<br>-s checks for sequences of *string1* repeated consecutive times |
| uniq | Remove duplicate lines to create unique output | |
| wc | Count the number of lines, bytes, or words in a file | -c counts the number of bytes or characters<br>-l counts the number of lines<br>-w counts the number of words |

# S U M M A R Y

- The UNIX file processing commands can be organized into two categories: select commands and manipulation and transformation commands. Select commands extract information. Manipulation and transformation commands alter and transform extracted information into useful and appealing formats.

■ The uniq command removes duplicate lines from the file. You must sort the file, because uniq compares only consecutive lines.

■ The comm command compares lines common to file1 and file2 and produces three-column output that reports variances between the files.

■ The diff command attempts to determine the minimal set of changes needed to convert file1 into file2.

■ The tr command copies data read from the standard input to the standard output, substituting or deleting the characters specified by options and patterns.

■ sed is a file editor designed to make global changes to large files. Minimum requirements to run sed are an input file and a command that tells sed what actions to apply to the file.

■ The pr command prints the standard output in pages.

# REVIEW QUESTIONS

1. Use select commands to _____.
   a. highlight text in a file
   b. format output
   c. extract information from a file
   d. redirect output to a file

2. Use manipulation and transformation commands to _____.
   a. change extracted information into a useful and appealing format
   b. change the file type
   c. extract information from a file
   d. redirect input

3. Which of these is a select command?
   a. cut
   b. cat
   c. sed
   d. uniq

4. Which of these is a manipulation and transformation command?
   a. cut
   b. cat
   c. sed
   d. uniq

5. Which of these commands processes two files simultaneously?
   a. comm
   b. diff
   c. sed
   d. uniq

**6.** The pr command produces _____.
   a. output just as cat does
   b. output just as less does
   c. paginated output to a line printer
   d. paginated output to the standard output

**7.** Which of these commands replaces colons in a file with blanks?
   a. sed ":" " " < filename
   b. tr –s ":" " " filename
   c. awk –F: '{ print " " }' filename
   d. tr –s ":" " " < filename

**8.** Which of these commands deletes characters from a file?
   a. sed –d ":" " " < filename
   b. tr –d ":" <filename
   c. tr –d: filename
   d. tr –d ":" " " filename

**9.** In sed, use the _____ option to append new lines.
   a. /a
   b. $/a
   c. add
   d. a\

**10.** Which of these commands converts lowercase characters in a file to uppercase characters?
   a. tr [a-z] [A-Z] filename
   b. tr "[a-z]" "[A-Z]" < filename
   c. tr "[A-Z]" "[a-z]" < filename
   d. tr a-z A-Z filename

**11.** The pipe (|) operator is used to _____.
   a. redirect output to a file
   b. redirect output to the screen
   c. redirect input from a file
   d. redirect one command's output to another command's input

**12.** What does the command grep Bob* /home/jill/members do?
   a. searches all files in the current directory whose names start with Bob for lines containing the string/home/jill/members. It displays the lines.
   b. searches the file /home/jill/members for lines that contain Bob followed by any other characters. It displays the lines.
   c. stores all the lines in all files that start with Bob in the /home/jill/members file.
   d. none of the above.

**13.** Which command displays on the screen the names of all files in the current directory with "jimmy" in their name?
   a. ls | grep jimmy
   b. ls | sort jimmy
   c. ls | tr jimmy
   d. sed jimmy | ls

**14.** The wc command counts _____ .
    a. words
    b. lines
    c. characters
    d. all of the above

# E X E R C I S E S

**1.** Use either the vi editor or cat >> to add lines to the your_list file. Use the comm command to compare your_list to my_list.

**2.** Convert the my_list file to all uppercase letters, and then run the comm command.

**3.** Remove all colon field separators from the zoo2 file.

# D I S C O V E R Y     E X E R C I S E S

**1.** Create a new file, their_list, and enter these lines in the file:

Radio

Camera

Boat

Use the sed command option to add these lines to the end of your_list:

Television

Computer

Stereo

**2.** Use the tr command to remove all colons from the /etc/passwd file and display the results on the screen.

**3.** Replace the word "Radio" with "Canoe" in the their_list file, and send the display to the standard output.

**4.** Use the cat command to create the file animals, containing the following lines:

```
Dog
Cat
Horse
Frog
```

Next, use the sed command to change the word "Cat" to "Kitten."

**5.** Write and run a sed script on the file you created in Discovery Exercise 4. The script should change "Dog" to "Puppy" and "Frog" to "Tadpole."

**After studying this lesson, you should be able to:**

- Design a new file processing application
- Design and create files to implement the application
- Use awk to generate formatted output
- Use cut, sort, and join to organize and transform selected file information
- Develop customized shell scripts to extract and combine file data
- Test individual shell scripts, and combine all scripts into a final shell program

# Using UNIX File Processing Tools to Create an Application

## Designing a New File Processing Application

The most important phase in developing a new application is creating a design. The design defines the information an application needs to produce. The design also defines how to organize this information into files, records, and fields, which are **logical structures,** because each represents a logical entity such as a payroll file, an employee pay record, or an employee social security field. Files consist of records and records consist of fields.

Now you're ready to create the Programmer Activity Status Report for Dominion Consulting. The report will show programmers' names and the number of projects that each programmer is working on. Start by designing and creating the files, including the records and fields, and then using advanced file processing commands to select, manipulate, and format information in the report.

### Designing Records

The first task in the design phase is to define the fields in the records. These definitions take the form of a **record layout** that identifies each field by name and data type (such as numeric or non-numeric). Design the file record to store only those fields relevant to the record's primary purpose. For example, you need two files for Dominion Consulting: one for programmer information and another for project information. Include a field for the programmer's name in the programmer file record and a field for the project description field in the project file record. Do not store a programmer's name in a project file, even though the programmer may be assigned to the project. Conversely, do not store project names in the programmer files.

Allocating only the space needed for the records' necessary fields keeps records brief and to the point. Short records, like short sentences, are easier to understand. Likewise, the simpler you make your application, the better it performs. However, make sure to include a field that uniquely identifies each record in the file. For example, the programmer file record includes a programmer number field to separate programmers who may have the same name.

Note: The programmer number field in the programmer file record should be numeric. Numeric fields are preferable to non-numeric fields for uniquely identifying records, because the computer interprets numbers faster than non-numeric fields. The project record can use a non-numeric project code to uniquely identify each project record, because Dominion project codes contain letters and numbers (EA-100).

## Linking Files

Multiple files are joined by a **link**—a common field that each of the linked files share. Another important task in the design phase is to plan a way to join files, if necessary. For example, the programmer-project application uses the programmer's number to link the programmer to the project file. Add the programmer's number field to the project record to link programmers to projects.

Note: The flexibility to gather information from multiple files, comprised of simple, short records, is the essence of a relational database system. UNIX includes several file processing commands that provide some of this relational database flexibility. You will implement some of these commands in this lesson.

Before you begin to create files for the application, review the record layouts for the programmer and project files illustrated in Figure 5-1.

```
Programmer File – Record Layout

Field Name                    Data Type         Example

programmer_number             Numeric           101

lname                         Alpha             Johnson

fname                         Alpha             John

midinit                       Alpha             K

salary                        Numeric           39000


Field Separator is a colon :

Sample Record:

101:Johnson:John:K:39000
```

```
Project File – Record Layout

Field Name                    Data Type         Example

project_code                  Alpha             EA-100

project_status                Numeric           1 (*See Note)

project_name                  Alpha             Reservation Plus

programmer_number             Numeric           110


Field Separator is a colon :

Sample Record:

EA-100:1:Reservation Plus:110

*Note: Project Status Codes 1=Unscheduled 2=Started 3=Completed 4=Cancelled
```

Figure 5-1: Programmer and project application record layouts

## Creating the Programmer and Project Files

Now that you have reviewed the basic elements of designing and linking records, you can begin to implement your application design. As you recall from Chapters 2 and 3, UNIX file processing predominantly uses flat files. Working with these files is easy, because you can create and manipulate them with text editors like vi and Emacs. The flowchart in Figure 5-2 provides an overview and analysis of programmer project assignments as derived from the programmer and project files.

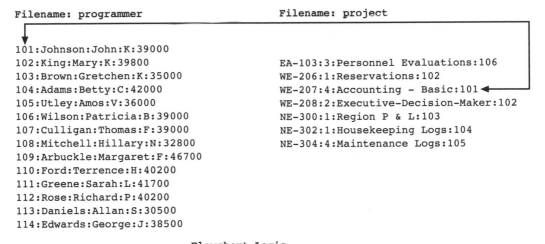

Filename: programmer

```
101:Johnson:John:K:39000
102:King:Mary:K:39800
103:Brown:Gretchen:K:35000
104:Adams:Betty:C:42000
105:Utley:Amos:V:36000
106:Wilson:Patricia:B:39000
107:Culligan:Thomas:F:39000
108:Mitchell:Hillary:N:32800
109:Arbuckle:Margaret:F:46700
110:Ford:Terrence:H:40200
111:Greene:Sarah:L:41700
112:Rose:Richard:P:40200
113:Daniels:Allan:S:30500
114:Edwards:George:J:38500
```

Filename: project

```
EA-103:3:Personnel Evaluations:106
WE-206:1:Reservations:102
WE-207:4:Accounting - Basic:101
WE-208:2:Executive-Decision-Maker:102
NE-300:1:Region P & L:103
NE-302:1:Housekeeping Logs:104
NE-304:4:Maintenance Logs:105
```

Flowchart Logic

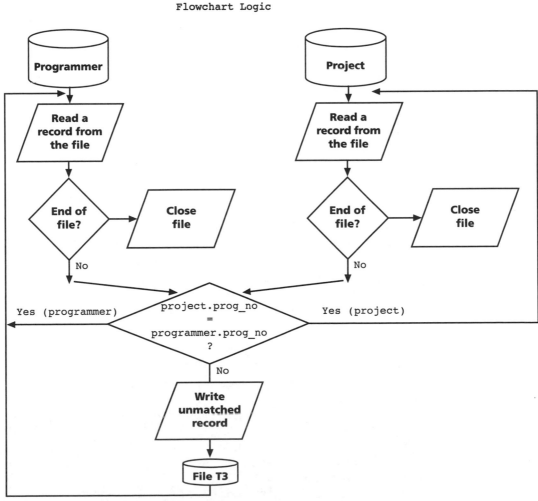

Figure 5-2: Overview and analysis of programmer assignments

Start by creating the programmer file in the vi editor.

---

### To create the programmer file:

**1**  After the $ command prompt, type **vi programmer** and press **Enter**.

**2**  Type **a** to switch to insert mode, and then type the following text, pressing **Enter** at the end of each line except for the last line:

```
101:Johnson:John:K:39000
102:King:Mary:K:39800
103:Brown:Gretchen:K:35000
104:Adams:Betty:C:42000
105:Utley:Amos:V:36000
106:Wilson:Patricia:B:39000
107:Culligan:Thomas:F:39000
108:Mitchell:Hillary:N:32800
109:Arbuckle:Margaret:F:46700
110:Ford:Terrence:H:44700
111:Greene:Sarah:L:41700
112:Rose:Richard:P:40200
113:Daniels:Allan:S:30500
114:Edwards:George:J:38500
```

**3**  Press **Esc** to switch to command mode.

**4**  Type **:wq** to write the file and exit from vi.

---

### To create the project file:

**1**  After the $ command prompt, type **vi project** and press **Enter**.

**2**  Type **a** to switch to insert mode, and type the following text, pressing **Enter** at the end of each line except for the last line:

```
EA-100:1:Reservation Plus:110
EA-100:1:Reservation Plus:103
EA-100:1:Reservation Plus:107
EA-100:1:Reservation Plus:109
EA-101:2:Accounting-Revenues Version 4:105
EA-101:2:Accounting-Revenues Version 4:112
EA-102:4:Purchasing System:110
EA-103:3:Personnel Evaluations:106
WE-206:1:Reservations:102
WE-207:4:Accounting - Basic:101
WE-208:2:Executive-Decision-Maker:102
NE-300:1:Region P & L:103
NE-302:1:Housekeeping Logs:104
NE-304:4:Maintenance Logs:105
```

**3** Press **Esc** to switch to command mode.

**4** Type **:wq** to write the file and exit from vi.

### Formatting Output

Chapter 4 introduced the awk command, which simplifies preparation of formatted output. Awk is actually a full-featured programming language and requires a chapter unto itself. The limited presentation here explains only the use of the printf action within the awk command, which formats output. The printf function has the syntax:

| | |
|---|---|
| **Syntax** | **printf** (*format, expr1, expr2, expr3 ...*) |
| **Dissection** | ■ *format* is always required. It is an expression whose string value contains literal text and specifications of how to format expressions in the argument list. Each specification begins with a percentage character (%), which identifies the code that follows as a modifier (- to left justify; width to set size; .prec to set maximum string width or digits to the right of decimal point; s for an array of characters (string); d for a decimal integer; f for a floating-point decimal number). Enclosed in double quotes (" "), format is often referred to as a "mask" that overlays the data fields (*expr's*) going into it. |
| | ■ $expr1, $expr2, $expr3 are awk expressions that represent data fields. These expressions typically take the form $1, $2, $3, etc. In the programmer file, the expression $1 indicates the programmer number (the first field), $2 indicates the programmer's last name (the second field), and $3 indicates the programmer's first name (the third field). |

You can use the awk command and printf function to print the programmer_number, programmer last name, and programmer first name, all left-justified.

**To print three fields:**

■ After the $ command prompt, type **awk –F: '{printf "%d %-12.12s %-10.10s\n",$1,$2,$3 }' programmer** and press **Enter**.

Each % symbol in the format string corresponds with a $ field: The %d specifies how to display the $1 field, the %-12.12s specifies how to display the $2 field, and the %-10.10s specifies how to display the $3 field. Here is a breakdown of each specifier:

■ %d indicates that field $1 is to appear in decimal digits.

- %-12.12s indicates that field $2 is to appear as a string. The minus sign (-) specifies the string is to be left-justified. The 12.12 indicates the string should appear in a field padded to 12 spaces, with a maximum size of 12 spaces.
- %-10.10s indicates that field $3 is to appear as a string. The minus sign (-) specifies the string is to be left-justified. The 10.10 indicates the string should appear in a field padded to 10 spaces, with a maximum size of 10 spaces.

The spaces that appear in the format string are printed exactly where they appear in relation to the fields (one is printed after $1, and another is printed after $2). The trailing \n tells awk to skip a line after displaying the three fields.

Awk provides a shortcut to other UNIX file processing commands when you need to extract and format data fields for output. For example, although it takes a few lines of code, you can use the cut, paste, and cat commands to extract and display the programmers' last names and salaries. Start by using the cut command to extract the last name (field 2) from the programmer file, and store the output in temp1. Next use the cut command to extract the salary (field 5) from the programmer file, and store the output in temp2. Then use the paste command to combine temp1 and temp2, and create the file Progsal. Finally use the more command to display the output. You can also accomplish the same task with one awk command.

**To extract and display information using cut, paste, and more:**

1   After the $ command prompt, type **cut –f2–d: programmer > temp1** and press **Enter.**

2   Type **cut –f5–d: programmer > temp2** and press **Enter.**

3   Type **paste temp1 temp2 > progsal** and press **Enter.**

4   To use the more command to display the output, type **more progsal** and press **Enter.**

You see output similar to the following excerpt:

```
Johnson     39000
King        39800
Brown       35000
Adams       42000
Utley       36000
. . .
```

**To accomplish the same task with one awk command:**

■ After the $ command prompt, type **awk –F: '{ printf "%-10.10s %7.0f\n", $2, $5 }' programmer** and press **Enter**.

You see output similar to the following excerpt:

```
Johnson      39000
King         39800
Brown        35000
Adams        42000
Utley        36000
. . .
```

## Cutting and Sorting

Now that you've created the programmer information file, you can select the programmer_number fields stored in the project file. These fields identify programmers who are currently assigned to projects. Refer to Figure 5-1 as you work through the next task.

Start by cutting the programmer_number fields from the project file (field 4) and piping (|) the output to a sort to place any duplicate numbers together. Pipe the sorted output to the uniq file to remove any duplicate programmer_numbers. Finally, redirect the output to a temporary file, t1. (The t1 file is a list of programmer numbers that identifies programmers who are assigned to projects.)

**To select fields from the project file:**

**1** After the $ command prompt, type **cut –d: -f4 project | sort | uniq > t1** and press **Enter**.

**2** To display the contents of t1, type **cat t1** and press **Enter**.

You see the list of programmer numbers:

```
101
102
103
104
105
106
107
109
110
```

The next step is to cut the programmer_number fields (field 1) from the programmer file and pipe the output as you did in Step 1. Call the new temporary file t2, which is a list of programmer numbers that identifies all programmers who work for Dominion.

**3**    Type **cut –d: -f1 programmer | sort | uniq > t2** and press **Enter**.

**4**    To display the contents of t2, type **cat t2** and press **Enter**.

You see this list of programmer numbers:

```
101
102
103
104
105
106
107
108
109
110
111
112
113
114
```

Now that t1 and t2 are sorted in the same order, you can match them. Use the comm command to select the lines from t1 that do not match lines in t2, and redirect the output to another file, t3, which lists programmer numbers of all programmers who are not assigned to projects.

**5**    Type **comm -13 t1 t2 > t3** and press **Enter**.

**6**    To display the programmer numbers for programmers who are not working on projects, type **cat t3** and press **Enter**.

You see this list of programmer numbers:

```
108
111
113
114
```

To display the names of unassigned programmers, you can now sort the programmer file in programmer_number order and write the output to t4.

**7**    Type **sort –t: +0 –1 –o t4 programmer** and press **Enter**.

Now use the join command to match programmer_numbers in t4 and t3, and redirect the output to t5, which contains the names of all programmers who are not assigned to a project.

**8**    Type **join –t: -j1 1 –j2 1 –o 1.2 –o 1.3 –o 1.4 t4 t3 > t5** and press **Enter**.

**9**  To display the contents of t5, type **cat t5** and press **Enter**.

You see the following list of programmer names:

```
Mitchell:Hillary:N
Greene:Sarah:L
Daniels:Allan:S
Edwards:George:J
```

Now you can transform the output using the sed editor to eliminate the colon field separators in t5.

**10**  Type **sed –n 's/:/ /g'p < t5** and press **Enter**.

You see this list of programmer names:

```
Mitchell Hillary N
Greene Sarah L
Daniels Allan S
Edwards George J
```

## Using a Shell Program to Implement the Application

Your application for Dominion Consulting currently consists of many separate commands that must run in a certain order. As you recall from Chapter 4, you can create a script file to simplify the application. Store your commands in a script file, which in effect becomes a program. (When you develop an application, you should usually test and debug each command before you place it in your script file.) You can use the vi editor to create the script files.

Note: Chapter 6 covers the subject of shell programming in detail.

Shell programs should contain not only the commands to execute but also comments to identify and explain the program. Use the pound (#) character in script files to mark comments. This tells the shell that the words following # are a comment, not a UNIX command. The next steps show how to add comments to your shell programs. Start by using the vi editor to create the script file, pact. Notice that you begin by inserting comments to identify and explain the program.

**To create a script and add comments:**

**1**  After the $ command prompt, type **vi pact** and press **Enter**.

**2**  Type **a** to switch to insert mode, and then type the text below, pressing **Enter** at the end of each line:

```
# ============================================================
# Script Name:    pact
# By:             Instructor
# Date:           November 1999
# Purpose:        Create temporary file, pnum, to hold the
#                  count of the number of projects each
#                  programmer is working on. The pnum file
#                  consists of
#                  prog_num and count fields
# ============================================================
cut -d: -f4 project | sort  | uniq -c |
awk '{printf "%s:%s\n",$2, $1}' > pnum
# cut prog_num, pipe output to sort to remove duplicates
# and get count for prog/projects.
# output file with prog_number followed by count
```

**3**  Press **Esc** to switch to command mode.

**4**  Type **:wq** to write the file and exit from vi.

Now you can run pact and use the less command to display the contents of pnum.

Note: The shell scripts in the following steps are executed using the sh command.

**To run the script:**

**1**  After the $ command prompt, type **sh pact** and press **Enter**.

**2**  Type **less pnum** and press **Enter**.

**3**  You see these programmer numbers and count fields:

```
101:1
102:2
103:2
104:1
105:2
106:1
107:1
109:1
110:2
112:1
```

You now have a file that contains programmer numbers and the number of projects that each programmer is working on. Next, create a script file, pnumname, to extract the programmer names and numbers from the programmer file and redirect the output to the file pnn.

### To create another script file:

1  After the $ command prompt, type **vi pnumname** and press **Enter**.

2  Type **a** to switch to insert mode, and then type the text below, pressing **Enter** at the end of each line:

```
# =======================================================
# Script Name:    pnumname
# By:        JQD
# Date:      Nov 1999
# Purpose: Extract Programmer Numbers and Names
# =======================================================
cut -d: -f1-4 programmer | sort -t: +0 -1 | uniq > pnn
# The above cuts out fields 1 through 4.
# The output is piped to a sort by programmer number.
# The sorted output is piped to uniq to remove duplicates.
# Uniq redirects the output to pnn.
```

3  Press **Esc** to switch to command mode.

4  Type **:wq** to write the file and exit from vi.

5  To run the shell program and use the less command to display the contents of pnn, type **sh pnumname** and press **Enter**.

6  Type **less pnn** and press **Enter**.

7  You see the programmer names and numbers, with duplicates eliminated:

```
101:Johnson:John:K
102:King:Mary:K
103:Brown:Gretchen:K
104:Adams:Betty:C
105:Utley:Amos:V
106:Wilson:Patricia:B
107:Culligan:Thomas:F
108:Mitchell:Hillary:N
109:Arbuckle:Margaret:F
110:Ford:Terrence:H
111:Greene:Sarah:L
112:Rose:Richard:P
113:Daniels:Allan:S
114:Edwards:George:J
```

Now you can create a script file, joinall, to join the files, pnn and pnumname, and redirect the output to pactrep.

---

### To create a script file that joins two files:

**1** After the $ command prompt, type **vi joinall** and press **Enter**.

**2** Type **a** to switch to insert mode, and then type the text below, pressing **Enter** at the end of each line:

```
# =========================================
# Script Name:  joinall
# By:           JQD
# Date:         Nov 1999
# Purpose:Join pnum and pnn to create a report file
# =======================================================
# join the files including the unassigned programmers
# You do this by placing the programmer names (pnn) file,
# first, in the join sequence.
join -t: -a1 -j1 1 -j2 1 pnn pnum  > pactrep
```

**3** Press **Esc** to switch to command mode.

**4** Type **:wq** to write the file and exit from vi.

**5** To run joinall and use less to display the contents of pactrep, type **sh joinall** and press **Enter**.

**6** Type **less pactrep** and press **Enter**.

**7** You see the programmer names, including unassigned programmers' names:

```
101:Johnson:John:K:1
102:King:Mary:K:2
103:Brown:Gretchen:K:2
104:Adams:Betty:C:1
105:Utley:Amos:V:2
106:Wilson:Patricia:B:1
107:Culligan:Thomas:F:1
108:Mitchell:Hillary:N
109:Arbuckle:Margaret:F:1
110:Ford:Terrence:H:2
111:Greene:Sarah:L
112:Rose:Richard:P:1
113:Daniels:Allan:S
114:Edwards:George:J
```

# Putting It All Together to Produce the Report

An effective way to develop applications is to combine small scripts in a larger script file. Because you have already executed the individual scripts and tested for accuracy, you can now place each in a script file in the proper sequence to produce the final programmer and project report for Dominion.

Start by using the vi editor to create the shell script practivity. Use the :r command to retrieve the pact, pnumname, and joinall scripts and place them in the practivity shell script. You can then use vi's dd command to remove the lines indicated in the comments.

**To create a final shell script:**

1   After the $ command prompt, type **vi practivity** and press **Enter**.

2   Type **a** to switch to insert mode, and then type the text below, pressing **Enter** at the end of each line:

```
# ==========================================================
# Script Name:  practivity
# By:           JQD
# Date:         Nov 1999
# Purpose:Generate Programmer Activity Status Report
# ==========================================================
```

3   Press **Esc** to switch to command mode.

4   To retrieve the three script files, type **:r pact** and press **Enter**. Move the cursor to the end of the file, type **:r pnumname** and press **Enter**. Move the cursor to the end of the file, type **:r joinall** and press **Enter**.

5   Use the **dd** command to delete the comments from the script. For example, you could move the cursor to each line that begins with a #, and then type dd. You could also move the cursor to the first line beginning with a #, and then type 9dd to delete the current line and the eight comment lines after it. Do the same for the remaining comment lines in the file.

Only these four lines should remain in the script:

```
cut -d: -f4 project | sort  | uniq -c |
awk '{printf "%s:%s\n",$2, $1}' > pnum
cut -d: -f1-4 programmer | sort -t: +0 -1 | uniq > pnn
join -t: -a1 -j1 1 -j2 1 pnn pnum  > pactrep
```

**6** Type the following in the script:

```
# Print the report
awk '
BEGIN {
  { FS = ":"}
  { print "\tProgrammer Activity Status Report" }
  { "date" | getline d }
  { printf "\t    %s\n",d }
  { print "Prog#\t  *——Name——-*  Projects" }
  { print
"=========================================================" }
  }
  { printf "%-s\t%12.12s %12.12s %s\t%d\n",
           $1, $2, $3, $4, $5 } ' pactrep
# remove all the temporary files
  rm pnum pnn pactrep
```

**7** Press **Esc** to switch to command mode.

**8** Type **:wq** to write the file and exit from vi.

**9** After the $ command prompt, type **sh practivity** and press **Enter**.

You see the report:

```
        Programmer Activity Status Report
           Tue Nov 23 11:16:43 EST 1999
        Prog#      *——Name——-*   Projects
        ========================================================
        101         Johnson      John K       1
        102         King         Mary K       2
        103         Brown        Gretchen K   2
        104         Adams        Betty C      1
        105         Utley        Amos V       2
        106         Wilson       Patricia B   1
        107         Culligan     Thomas F     1
        108         Mitchell     Hillary N    0
        109         Arbuckle     Margaret F   1
        110         Ford         Terrence H   2
        111         Greene       Sarah L      0
        112         Rose         Richard P    1
        113         Daniels      Allan S      0
        114         Edwards      George J     0
```

# C O M M A N D   S U M M A R Y

| Chapter 5, Lesson B commands | | |
| --- | --- | --- |
| Command | Purpose | Options covered in this chapter |
| printf | Tell the Awk program what action to take | none |
| sh | Execute a shell script | none |

# S U M M A R Y

- The design of a file processing application reflects what the application needs to produce. The design also defines how to organize information into files, records, and fields, which are logical structures.

- Use a record layout to identify each field by name and data type (numeric or non-numeric). Design file records to store only those fields relevant to each record's primary purpose.

- Shell programs should contain commands to execute and comments to identify and explain the program. The pound # character used in script files denotes comments.

- Write shell scripts in stages so you can test each part before combining them into one script. Using small shell scripts and combining them in a final shell script file is an effective way to develop applications.

# R E V I E W   Q U E S T I O N S

1. The first task of the design phase is to define the application's _____.
   a. records
   b. files
   c. shell programs
   d. logic

2. Used in script files, the ___ character denotes comments.
   a. *
   b. &
   c. ;
   d. #

3. What does %d indicate in an awk printf format string?
   a. Display the $ symbol.
   b. Display a field as a double-precision number.
   c. Display a field as a decimal digit.
   d. None of the above is correct.

4. What does %-10.10s indicate in an awk printf format string?
   a. Display a field as a left-justified string in a space padded to 10 characters, with a maximum of 10 characters displayed.
   b. Display a field as a right-justified string in a space padded to 10 characters, with a maximum of 10 characters displayed.
   c. Display a field as a single-precision number with 10 digits to the left and 10 digits to the right of the decimal point.
   d. None of the above is correct.

5. You can use the _____ command during a vi session to retrieve data from other files and insert it in a new vi file.
   a. :r
   b. :i
   c. :a
   d. :insert

6. Which of these awk commands outputs formatted fields?
   a. print
   b. display
   c. show
   d. printf

# EXERCISES

1. Write a one-line script file, lprog, using awk to print all fields in the programmer file. Use the sh command to execute lprog.

2. Write a one-line script file, lproj, using awk to print all fields in the project file. Use the sh command to execute lproj.

3. Use vi to create the script file lists, and then combine lprog and lproj into lists.

   Save lists and use the sh command to execute the lists script.

**DISCOVERY EXERCISES**

1.  Create the file called Software with the fields:

    ■ Project_number using the same numbers shown in the project file

    ■ Software Code using any three-digit number

    ■ Software Description such as Excel

2.  Write a small application joining software records to matching records in the project file, and use the Awk program to print a report describing the software for each project.

# CHAPTER 6

# Introduction to Shell Programming

**case ▶** Dominion Consulting needs a program to maintain its phone records file, which contains the following information about each employee: telephone number, name, department, job title, and date of hire. This program should let users add, change, delete, locate, and display specific employee information. You can meet these needs by creating a UNIX shell program. In this section, you learn the basic tools used to create UNIX shell programs. In Lesson B you create shell programs that let users view and add records to the phone database.

**In this lesson you will:**

- Understand the program development cycle using a high-level computer language and UNIX shell scripts
- Compare the shells to determine the best choice for programming
- Learn about shell variables, operators, and wildcard characters
- Write simple shell scripts to illustrate programming logic

# Using the UNIX Shell as a Programming Language

## Previewing the Application

The corp_phones file, which you create in this chapter, contains records with fields delimited by colons. Here is a sample record from the file:

```
219-432-4587:Mitchell:Barbara:C:4541:Admin Asst:12-14-1995
```

In Chapters 4 and 5 you learned several commands, such as grep, cut, paste, and awk, which you can use to manipulate, extract, and format information stored in files. Although these commands are powerful, they can be difficult for non-technical users. In addition, you must often use these commands together in long sequences to achieve the results you want. Repeatedly executing these command sequences can be cumbersome, even for the experienced technical user. UNIX shell scripts eliminate both of these problems. You can write shell scripts that present user-friendly screens and automatically issue commands like grep and awk to extract, format, and display information. This gives the non-technical user access to powerful features of UNIX. Shell scripts also save you time by automating long command sequences that you must perform often.

The shell script application you develop in this chapter and in Chapter 7 presents a menu of operations the user may choose from. Among other tasks, these operations automate the process of searching for, formatting, and displaying the phone number records in corp_phones. The application also provides data entry screens to ease the task of adding new records to the file.

To accomplish this chapter's case project, you will learn about these programming features of the UNIX shell:

- *Shell variables*: Your scripts often need to keep values in memory for later use. Shell variables are symbolic names that can access values stored in memory.
- *Operators*: Shell scripts support many operators, including those for performing mathematical operations.
- *Logic structures*: Shell scripts support sequential logic (for performing a series of commands), decision logic (for branching from one point in a script to another), looping logic (for repeating a command several times), and case logic (for choosing an action from several possible alternatives).

In addition, you will learn special commands for formatting screen output and positioning the cursor.

Before you begin writing shell scripts, you should understand the program development cycle.

## The Program Development Cycle

The process of developing an application is known as the **program development cycle**. The steps involved in the cycle are the same, whether you are writing shell scripts or high-level language programs.

The process begins by creating program specifications—the requirements the application must meet. The specifications determine what data the application takes as input, the processes that must be performed on the data, and the correct output.

After you determine the specifications, the design process begins. During this process, programmers create file formats, screen layouts, and logical algorithms (procedures) that the program will use. Programmers use a variety of tools to design complex applications. In the next chapter, you will study flowcharts and pseudocode, two important program design tools.

After the design process is complete, programmers begin writing the actual code, which they must then test and debug. When they find errors, they must correct them and begin the testing process again. This procedure continues until the application performs satisfactorily.

Figure 6-1 illustrates the program development cycle.

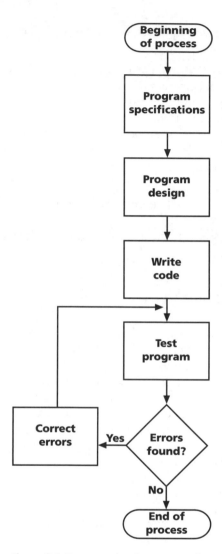

**Figure 6-1:** Program development cycle

## Using High-Level Languages

Computer programs are instructions often written using a high-level language like COBOL, C, or C++. A **high-level language** is a computer language that uses English-like expressions. For example, the following COBOL statement instructs the computer to add 1 to the variable COUNTER:

```
ADD 1 TO COUNTER.
```

Here is a similar statement, written in C++:

```
counter = counter + 1;
```

A program's high-level language statements are stored in a file called the **source file**. This is the file that the programmer creates with an editor such as vi or Emacs. The source file cannot execute, however, because the computer can only process instructions written in low-level **machine language**. As you recall from Chapter 3, machine-language instructions are cryptic codes expressed in binary numbers. Therefore, the high-level source file must be converted into a low-level machine language file, as described next.

The source file is converted into an executable machine-language file by a program called a **compiler**. The compiler reads the lines of code that the programmer wrote in the source file and converts them to the appropriate machine language instructions. For example, the Linux C++ compiler is named g++. The following command illustrates how it is executed:

```
g++ -o my_exe my_source.cpp
```

In this sample command, the –o option followed by my_exe instructs the compiler to create an executable file, my_exe. The source file is my_source.cpp. The command causes the compiler to translate the C++ program my_source.cpp into an executable machine-language program, which is stored in the file my_exe.

If a source file contains **syntax errors** (grammatical mistakes in language usage), it cannot be converted into an executable file. The compiler locates and reports any syntax errors, which the programmer must correct.

> Note: After compiling, the executable program may still contain fatal run errors or logic errors. Fatal run errors cause the program to abort due to an invalid memory location, for example. Logic errors cause the program to produce invalid results because of problems such as flawed mathematical statements.

Another way to accomplish programming tasks is to develop UNIX shell scripts.

## Using UNIX Shell Scripts

Introduced in Chapter 4, UNIX **shell scripts** are text files that contain sequences of UNIX commands. Like high-level source files, a programmer creates shell scripts with a text editor. Unlike high-level language programs, however, shell scripts do not have to be converted into machine language by a compiler. This is because the UNIX shell acts as an **interpreter** when reading script files. As an interpreter reads the statements in a program file, it immediately translates them into executable instructions, and causes them to run. No executable file is produced because the interpreter translates and executes the program statements in one step. If a syntax error is encountered, the program halts.

After you create a shell script, you simply tell the operating system that the file is a program that can be executed. This is accomplished by using the **chmod** ("change mode") command to change the file's mode. The mode determines how the file may be used. Recall that modes are denoted by single-letter codes, the most common being "r" (read), "w" (write), and "x" (execute). Further, the chmod command tells the computer who is allowed to use the file: the owner (u), the group (g), or all other users (o). For a complete description of the chmod command, see Appendix B, "Syntax Guide to UNIX Commands."

As you recall from Chapter 4, you can change the mode of a file so that UNIX recognizes it as an executable program that everyone (user, group, and others) can use. In the following example, the user is the owner of the file.

```
$ chmod ugo+x filename     <Enter>
```

By typing the filename after the system prompt, you can now run the shell program.

However, before any program can be run, it must be retrieved from a path identified in the **PATH variable,** which provides a list of directory locations where UNIX looks to find the executable programs. (See the section, "Variables," later in this chapter.) If the program resides in your current directory, which is not in the PATH variable, you can precede the program name with a dot slash (./) to tell UNIX to look in the current directory to find the program, as follows:

```
$ ./filename     <Enter>
```

Shell programs run less quickly than do compiled programs, because the shell must interpret each UNIX command inside the executable script file before it is executed. However, it generally takes less time to create a shell program than one written using a high-level language, because the process of invoking a compiler and producing an executable file is eliminated. Because it is usually faster and easier to write a program such as a shell script than a compiled language, many programmers prefer scripts.

### Prototyping an Application

A **prototype** is a running model of your application, which lets you review the final results before committing to the design. Using a shell program to create a prototype is often the quickest and most efficient method, because prototyping logic and design capabilities reside within UNIX.

After the working prototype is approved, the program can be rewritten to run faster using a compiled language such as C++. If the shell program performs well, however, you may not need to convert it to a compiled version.

Now that you better understand the program development cycle, you realize that it will be more efficient to maintain Dominion Consulting's phone records using a shell script. Your next step is to select the programming shell that will be most efficient for your application.

## The Programming Shell

All Linux versions use the Bash shell (Bourne Again Shell) as the default shell. Table 6-1 lists the three shells that come with most Linux distributions, their derivations, and distinguishing features.

| Shell Name | Original Shell It Is Derived From | Description |
|---|---|---|
| Bash | Bourne and Korn shells | Offers strong programming language features like shell variables, control structures, and logic/math expressions. Combines the best features of the other shells. |
| tsch | C Shell | Conforms to a programming language format. Shell expressions use operators like those found in the C programming language. |
| zsh | Korn shell | Reflects the Bash shell in many respects but also has C programming-like syntax. Useful if you are familiar with older Korn shell scripts. |

**Table 6-1:** Linux shells

The Bash shell offers improved features over the older Bourne and Korn shells and is fully backward-compatible with the Bourne shell. Additionally, the Bash shell, when compared to the other shells, has a more powerful programming interface. As a result, you should use the Bash shell (as contained in Red Hat's Linux version 5.2) to complete your assignment.

Now that you have selected the shell, you need to learn about what the shell scripts include, such as the variables, operators, and special characters.

## Variables

Variables are symbolic names that represent values stored in memory. The three types of variables discussed in this section are configuration variables, environment variables, and shell variables. Use **configuration variables** to store information about the setup of the operating system, and do not change them. You can set up **environment variables** with initial values that you can change as needed. These variables, which UNIX reads when you log in, determine many characteristics of your session. For example, you have already learned about the PS1 environment variable, which determines the way your prompt appears. Additionally, UNIX uses environment variables to determine such things as where it should look for programs, which shell to use, and the path of your home directory. **Shell variables** are those you create at the command line or in a shell script. They are very useful in shell scripts for temporarily storing information.

In this chapter you will learn several commands to create, access, and manipulate variables. For example, to see a list of your environment variables, use the **printenv** command.

## To see a list of your environment variables:

**1**    The list of environment variables probably spans more than one screen, so use the more command with printenv. Type **printenv | more** and press **Enter**.

You see a list of environment variables similar to the one shown in Figure 6-2.

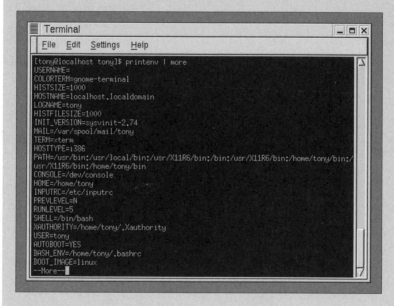

**Figure 6-2:** Output of printenv | more command

**2**    Press the **spacebar** until the output is complete.

Note: If you specify the name of a variable as an argument to the printenv command, it only displays the contents of that variable.

Environment and configuration variables bear standard names such as PS1, HOME, PATH, SHELL, USERNAME, and PWD. (Configuration and environment variables are capitalized to distinguish them from user variables). A script file sets the initial values of environment variables in your home directory. You can use these variables to set up and personalize your login sessions. For example, you can set your PATH variable to search for the location of commands that other users have created. Table 6-2 lists standard Bash shell variables.

| Name | Variable Contents | Determined by |
|------|-------------------|---------------|
| HOME | Path name for user's home directory | System |
| LOGNAME | Login name | System |
| TZ | Time zone used by system | System |
| SHELL | Path name of program for type of shell you are using | Redefinable |
| PATH | List of path names for directories searched for executable commands | Redefinable |
| PS1 | Primary shell prompt | Redefinable |
| PS2 | Secondary shell prompt | Redefinable |
| PS3 and PS4 | Holds prompts used by the set and select commands | Redefinable |
| IFS | Field delimiter symbol | Redefinable |
| MAIL | Name of mail file checked by mail utility for received messages | Redefinable |
| MAILCHECK | Interval for checking for received mail (example: 60) | Redefinable |
| MAILPATH | List of mail files to be checked by mail for received messages | User-defined |
| TERM | Terminal name | User-defined |
| MAILWARNING | If set and if a file in which Bash is checking for mail has been accessed since the last time it was checked, the message, "The mail in Mailfile has been read," appears | User-defined |
| CDPATH | Path names for directories searched by cd command for subdirectories | User-defined |
| EXINIT | Initialization commands for Ex/vi editor | User-defined |
| PWD | Current working directory | User-defined |

Table 6-2: Standard Bash Shell Environment and Configuration variables

| Name | Variable Contents | Determined by |
|------|-------------------|---------------|
| OLDPWD | Previous working directory as set by the cd command | User-defined |
| REPLY | Set to the line of input read by the read built-in command when no arguments are supplied | User-defined |
| UID | Expands to the user ID of the current user, initialized at shell startup | User-defined |
| EUID | Expands to the effective user ID of the current user, initialized at shell startup | User-defined |
| BASH | Full path name of Bash | User-defined |
| BASHVERSION | Version number of Bash | User-defined |
| SHLVL | Incremented by one each time an instance of Bash is started | User-defined |
| RANDOM | Generates a random integer when referenced. The sequence of random numbers may be initialized by assigning a value to RANDOM. | User-defined |
| HISTCMD | Index in the history list of the current command | User-defined |
| HISTSIZE | Number of commands the History command remembers. Default is 500. | User-defined |
| OPTARG | Value of the last option argument processed by the getopts built-in command | User-defined |
| OPTFIND | Index of the next argument to be processed by the getopts built-in command | User-defined |
| HOSTTYPE | Automatically set to a string that uniquely describes the type of machine on which Bash is executing | User-defined |
| HOSTFILE | Complete host name of the system. In the same format at /etc/hosts. | User-defined |

**Table 6-2:** Standard Bash Shell Environment and Configuration variables (*continued*)

| Name | Variable Contents | Determined by |
|------|-------------------|---------------|
| OSTYPE | Description of the operating system on which Bash is executing | User-defined |
| ENV | Filename containing commands to initialize the shell, as in .bashrc or .tcshrc | User-defined |
| HISTFILESIZE | Maximum number of lines contained in the history file. Causes the history file to be truncated when this size limit is reached. | User-defined |
| OPTERR | If set to the value 1, Bash displays error messages generated by getopts command | User-defined |
| PROMPTCOMMAND | Holds the command to be executed prior to displaying a primary prompt | User-defined |
| TMOUT | Number of seconds to wait for input after the primary prompt. Bash waits for that number of seconds and terminates if input does not arrive. | User-defined |
| FCEDIT | Default editor for the fc command | User-defined |
| FIGNORE | Colon-separated list of suffixes to ignore when performing filename completion | User-defined |
| INPUTRC | Filename for the Readline start-up file overriding the default of ~/.inputrc | User-defined |

**Table 6-2:** Standard Bash Shell Environment and Configuration variables (*continued*)

Operators are used to define and evaluate variables. Let's take a look at the various operators that UNIX uses.

## Shell Operators

The Bash shell operators are divided into three groups: defining and evaluating operators, arithmetic operators, and redirecting and piping operators.

## Defining and Evaluating Operators

Use the **equal sign (=) operator** to set a value in a variable, as follows:

`NAME=Becky`

This example sets the NAME variable to the value Becky. The variable names or values that appear to the left and right of an operator are its **operands**. The name of the variable you are setting must appear to the left of the = operator. The value of the variable you are setting must appear to the right.

**Note: Notice there are no spaces between the = operator and its operands.**

**To create a variable and assign it a value:**
- Type **DOG=Poodle** and press **Enter**.
  You created the variable DOG and set its value to Poodle.

The echo command is used to display the contents of a variable.

**To see the contents of a variable:**
**1**  Type **echo DOG** and press **Enter**.
   You see the word "DOG."
**2**  To see the contents of the DOG variable, you must precede the name of the variable with a $ operator. Type **echo $DOG** and press **Enter**.
   You see the word "Poodle."

Enclose the value in double quotes ("") if it contains spaces. The next command is an example.

**To set a variable to a string of characters containing spaces:**
**1**  Type **MEMO="Meeting will be at noon today"** and press **Enter**.
**2**  Type **echo $MEMO** and press **Enter**.
   You see the contents of the MEMO variable: Meeting will be at noon today.

You may also use single quotes. However, they suppress the evaluation of a variable like $HOME, whereas double quotes do not.

**To demonstrate the " and ' characters used with a variable name:**

**1** Type **echo '$HOME'** and press **Enter**.

You see $HOME on the screen.

**2** Type **echo "$HOME"** and press Enter.

You see the path of your home directory on the screen.

Finally, the **backquote (`) operator** is used to enclose UNIX commands whose output will become the contents of a variable.

**To demonstrate the backquote operator:**

**1** Type **TODAY=`date`** and press **Enter**. This command creates the variable TODAY, executes the date command, and stores the output of the date command in the variable TODAY. (No output appears on the screen.)

**2** Type **echo $TODAY** and press **Enter**. You see the output of the date command that was executed in Step 1.

## Exporting Shell Variables to the Environment

Shell scripts cannot automatically access variables created on the command line or by other shell scripts. To make a variable available to a shell script, you must use the export command to make it an environment variable.

**To demonstrate the export command:**

**1** Type **cat > testscript** and press **Enter**.

**2** Type **echo $MY_VAR** and press **Enter**.

**3** Type **Ctrl+D**. You have created a simple shell script named testscript. Its only function is to display the value of the MY_VAR variable.

**4** To make the script executable, type **chmod ugo+x testscript** and press **Enter**.

**5** After the $ prompt, type **MY_VAR=2** and press **Enter**.

**6** Type **echo $MY_VAR** and press **Enter** to confirm the operation above. You see "2" on the screen.

**7** Next look at the list of environment variables. Type **printenv | more** and press Enter.

Look carefully as you scroll through the output of the printenv command. You do not see the MY_VAR variable.

**8** Execute the shell script by typing **./testscript** and pressing **Enter**.

The script displays a blank line. This is because it does not have access to the shell variable MY_VAR.

> **9** Make the variable available to the script by typing **export MY_VAR** and pressing **Enter**.
>
> **10** Execute the script again by typing **./testscript** and pressing **Enter**. This time the value 2 appears.
>
> **11** Now look at your list of environment variables by typing **printenv | more** and pressing **Enter**. Again, look carefully as you scroll through the list. This time you see MY_VAR listed.

Notice that in the previous exercise you had to type the ./ characters before the name of the script file. This is because the shell looks for programs in the directories whose names are specified by the PATH variable.

> **To see the contents of the PATH variable:**
>
> ■ Type **echo $PATH** and press **Enter**.
>
> You see a list of directories. Notice that the path names are separated by colons (:).

Because new shell programs are most often kept in the current directory while they are being tested, you should add the current working directory to the PATH variable. Here is an example:

```
PATH=$PATH:.
```

Remember, the shell interprets $PATH as the contents of the PATH variable. The sample command sets the PATH variable to its current contents. The colon and dot (.) add the current directory to the search path so that the shell program can locate the new program.

> **To add the current working directory to the PATH variable:**
>
> **1** Type **PATH=$PATH:.** and press **Enter**.
>
> **2** Type **echo $PATH** and press **Enter**. The dot (.) is now appended to the list.
>
> **3** You can now run scripts in your current working directory without typing the ./ characters before their names. Test this by typing **testscript** and pressing **Enter**. You see testscript execute.

## Arithmetic Operators

**Arithmetic operators** consist of the familiar plus (+) for addition, minus (-) for subtraction, asterisk (*) for multiplication, and slash (/) for division. Table 6-3 explains other operators.

| Operator | Description | Example |
|----------|-------------|---------|
| -, + | Unary minus and plus | +R    (denotes positive R)<br>-R    (denotes negative R) |
| !, ~ | Logical and bitwise negation | !Y    (returns 0 if Y is non-zero, returns 1 if Y is zero.)<br>~X    (reverses the bits in X) |
| *, /, % | Multiplication, division, and remainder | A * B    (returns A times B)<br>A / B    (returns A divided by B)<br>A % B    (returns the remainder of A divided by B) |
| +, - | Addition, subtraction | X + Y    (returns X plus Y)<br>X – Y    (returns X minus Y) |
| >, < | Greater than and less than | M > N    (Is M greater than N?)<br>M < N    (Is M less than N?) |
| =, != | Equality and inequality | Q = R    (Is Q equal to R?)<br>Q != R    (Is Q not equal to R?) |

**Table 6-3:** Examples of the shell's arithmetic operators

When using arithmetic operators, the usual mathematical precedence rules apply: multiplication and division are performed before addition and subtraction. For example, the value of the expression 6 + 4 * 2 is 14, not 20. Precedence can be overridden, however, by using parentheses. For example, the value of the expression (6 + 4) * 2 is 20, not 14. Other mathematical rules also apply; for example, division by zero is treated as an error.

To store arithmetic values in a variable, use the let statement. For example, the following command stores 14 in the variable X:

```
let X=6+4*2
```

You can use shell variables as operands to arithmetic operators. Assuming the variable X has the value 14, the following command stores 18 in the variable Y:

```
let Y=X+4
```

**To practice using the arithmetic operators:**

**1**   Type **let X=10+2*7** and press **Enter**.

**2**   Type **echo $X** and press **Enter**. You see 24 on the screen.

**3**   Type **let Y=X+2*4** and press **Enter**.

**4**   Type **echo $Y** and press **Enter**. You see 32 on the screen.

Note: Constants beginning with 0 are interpreted as octal numbers. A preceding x denotes a hexadecimal number.

## Preventing Redirection from Overwriting Files

Recall that the > redirection operator overwrites an existing file. If you write a shell script that uses the > operator to create a file, you may want to prevent it from overwriting important information. You can use the set command with the **–o noclobber option** to prevent a file from being overwritten, as in the following example:

```
$ set —o noclobber      <Enter>
```

However, you can choose to overwrite a file anyway by placing an exclamation point after the redirection operator:

```
$ set —o noclobber      <Enter>
$ cat new_file > old_file
$ cat: file exists
$ cat: new_file >! old_file <Enter>
```

## More About Wildcard Characters

Shell scripts frequently use the asterisk (*) and other wildcard characters (such as ? and [), which help to locate information containing only a portion of a matching pattern. For example, to retrieve all program files whose names contain a ".c" extension, use the following command:

```
ls *.c
```

Wildcard characters are also known as **glob** characters. If an unquoted argument contains one or more glob characters, the shell processes the argument for filename generation. Glob characters are part of **glob patterns,** which are intended to match filenames and words. Special constructions that may appear in glob patterns follow:

- The question mark (?) matches exactly one character, except for the backslash and period.
- The asterisk (*) matches zero or more characters in a filename.
- [chars] defines a class of characters. The glob pattern matches any single character in the class. A class may contain a range of characters, as in [a-z].

For example, assume the working directory contains files chap1, chap2, and chap3. The following command displays the contents of all three files:

```
more chap[1-3]      <Enter>
```

Now that you understand some of the tools used to construct shell scripts, you'll see examples of how shell scripts are written to support the four basic logic structures needed for program development.

# Shell Logic Structures

The four basic logic structures needed for program development are sequential logic, decision logic, looping logic, and case logic.

## Sequential Logic

**Sequential logic** states that commands will be executed in the order in which they appear in the program. The only break in this sequence comes when a branch instruction changes the flow of execution. The following steps present a very simple example of a shell script using sequential logic. You create a simple shell script, seqtotal.

---

**To demonstrate sequential logic:**

**1**  Type **vi seqtotal** and press **Enter**.

**2**  Type **i** to switch to vi's insert mode.

**3**  Type the following lines:

```
let a=1
let b=2
let c=3
let total=a+b+c
echo $total
```

**4**  Press **Esc** to switch to vi's command mode.

**5**  Type **:wq** and press **Enter** to save the file and exit vi.

**6**  Next, test the new shell script, Seqtotal. (To save a few keystrokes, you use the sh command instead of the chmod command.) Type **sh seqtotal** and press **Enter**.

   You see the output of the program, which is 6.

---

Many programs are simple, straightforward command sequences. An example is the programmer activity report script you wrote in Chapter 5. The shell executes the script's commands in the order they appear in the file. You use sequential logic to write this type of application.

## Decision Logic

**Decision logic** enables your program to execute a statement or series of statements only if a certain condition exists. The **if statement** is the primary decision-making control structure in this type of logic. In the steps that follow, notice that the semicolon (;) separates commands on the same line.

Note: Throughout the sample scripts, variables are always enclosed in double quotes, as in "$choice," "$looptest," "$yesno," "$guess," and "$myfavorite," due to how the shell interprets variables. All shell variables, unless declared otherwise, are **strings**, which are arrays of characters. If you do not enter data in the string variables, the variables will be treated as blank strings, which result in an invalid test. The enclosing double quotes therefore maintain the validity of strings, with or without data, and the test is carried out without producing an error condition.

## To demonstrate decision logic:

**1** Type **vi os_choice** and press **Enter**.

**2** Type **i** to switch to vi's insert mode.

**3** Type the following lines:

```
echo -n "What is your favorite operating system? "
read OS_NAME
if [ "$OS_NAME" = "UNIX" ]
then
    echo "You will like Linux."
else
    echo "You should give Linux a try!"
fi
```

**4** Press **Esc** to switch to vi's command mode.

**5** Type **:wq** and press **Enter** to save the file and exit vi.

Before you run the program, let's examine its contents. The first statement uses the echo command to display a message on the screen. The –n option suppresses the line feed that normally appears after the message. The second statement uses the read command, which waits for the user to type a line of keyboard input. The input is stored in the variable specified as the read command's argument. The line in the program reads the user's input into the OS_NAME variable.

The next line begins an if statement. The word "if" is followed by an expression inside a set of brackets ([]). (The spaces that separate the [ and ] characters from the enclosed expression are necessary.) The expression, which is tested to determine if it is true or false, compares the contents of the OS_NAME variable with the string UNIX. (When you use the = operator in an if statement's test expression, it tests its two operands for equality. If the operands are equal, the expression is true. Otherwise, it is false.) If the contents of the OS_NAME variable is equal to UNIX, the statement that follows the word "then" is executed. In this program, it is an echo statement.

If the if statement's expression is false (if the contents of the OS_NAME variable does not equal UNIX), the statement that follows the word "else" is executed. In this program, it is a different echo statement.

Notice the last statement, which is the word fi. fi ("if" spelled backward) always marks the end of an if or an if...else statement.

**Now, test your code by executing it at least twice:**

**1** Run the program.

**2** When asked to enter the name of your favorite operating system, answer **UNIX**.

**3** Run the program again and respond with **MS-DOS** or some other operating system name.

**help**

Remember to use the chmod command first to make the script executable. Then type the script's name after the command prompt to execute it. Another way to run the script is to use the sh command, as you did with the seqtotal script.

**Nested Control Structures** You can nest a control structure, such as the if statement, inside another control structure. For example, a program may have an if statement inside another if statement. The first if statement controls when the second if statement is executed.

**To practice writing a nested if statement:**

**1** Open the os_choice file in vi or Emacs.

**2** Edit the file so it contains the following lines. (Code has been added to the else part of the original if statement.)

```
echo -n "What is your favorite operating system? "
read OS_NAME
if [ "$OS_NAME" = "UNIX" ]
then
   echo "You will like Linux."
else
   if [ "$OS_NAME" = "WINDOWS" ]
   then
        echo "A great OS for applications."
   else
        echo "You should give Linux a try!"
   fi
fi
```

**3** Execute the program and respond with **WINDOWS** when asked for your favorite operating system.

As you can see, the second if statement is located in the first if statement's else section. It is only executed when the first if statement's expression is false.

Decision logic structures, such as the if statement, are used in applications where different courses of action are required, depending on the result of a command or comparison.

## Looping Logic

In **looping logic,** a control structure (or loop) repeats until some condition exists or some action occurs. You will learn two looping mechanisms in this section: the for loop and the while loop.

You use the **for** command for looping through a range of values. It causes a variable to take on each value in a specified set, one at a time, and perform some action while the variable contains each individual value. The loop stops after the variable has taken on the last value in the set and has performed the specified action with that value.

### To demonstrate looping logic:

1   Create the file our_users with vi or Emacs.

2   Type the following lines into the file:

```
for USERS in john ellen tom becky eli jill
do
    echo $USERS
done
```

3   Save the file and exit the editor.

4   Give the file execute permission, and run it. Your screen appears similar to Figure 6-3.

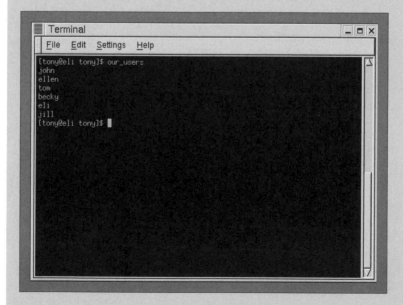

**Figure 6-3:** Output of Our_users script

The for statement you typed in Step 2 specifies that the variable USERS take on the values john, ellen, tom, becky, eli, and jill. Because there are six values in the set, the loop repeats six times. Each time it repeats, USERS contains a different value from the set, and the statement between the do and done statements is executed. The first value in the set is john, so the echo statement executes the first time with john stored in USERS. That is why john appears on the screen. The second time the loop executes, USERS contains ellen, so the echo statement displays ellen. This procedure repeats until no other names are left in the set.

**Executing Control Structures at the Command Line**  Most shell script control structures, such as the if and for statements, must be written across several lines. This does not prevent you from executing them directly on the command line, however.

**To demonstrate entering program control structures at the command line:**

■ Enter the following. Note you will type directly from the command line and not into a script file.

```
$ for myhobbies in tennis swimming movies travel <Enter>
> do                                              <Enter>
> echo $myhobbies                                 <Enter>
> done                                            <Enter>
```

After you finish typing you see results similar to Figure 6-4.

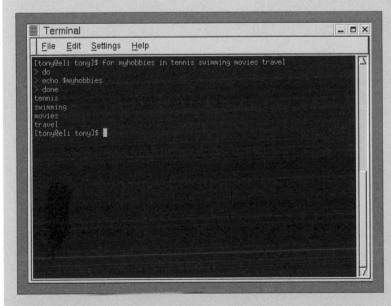

Figure 6-4: Results of for loop typed at command line

The shell knows more code will come after you type the first line. It displays the > prompt indicating it is ready for the control structure's continuation. The shell reads further input lines until you type the word "done," which marks the end of a for loop.

**Using Wildcard Characters in a Loop**  Now you can see how the for statement works with wildcard characters when you want to print a few chapters of a book.

**To create test data and use wildcards in a for loop:**

**1**  Type **cat > chap1** and press **Enter**.

**2**  Type **This is chapter 1** and press **Enter**.

**3**  Type **Ctrl+D**. The file chap1 is created.

**4**  Type **cat > chap2** and press **Enter**.

**5**  Type **This is chapter 2** and press **Enter**.

**6**  Type **Ctrl+D**. The file chap2 is created.

**7**  Type **cat > chap3** and press **Enter**.

**8**  Type **This is chapter 3**, and press **Enter**.

**9**  Type **Ctrl+D**. The file chap3 is created.

**10**  Use the vi or Emacs editor to create the shell program, chapters. The program should have these lines:

```
for file in chap[123]; do
   more $file
   done
```

**11**  Save the file and exit the editor.

**12**  Give the file execute permission, and test it. You see output similar to Figure 6-5.

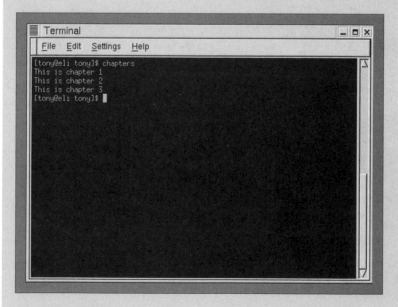

Figure 6-5: Results of chapters script

**The While Loop** A different pattern for looping is created using the while statement. The **while** statement best illustrates how to set up a loop to test repeatedly for a matching condition.

## To use the while statement:

**1** Use the vi or Emacs editor to create a shell script, colors.

**2** The script should contain these lines:

```
echo -n "Try to guess my favorite color "
read guess
while [ "$guess" != "red" ]; do
   echo "No, not that one. Try again. "; read guess
done
```

**3** Save the file and exit the editor.

**4** Give the file execute permission, and test it. You see output similar to Figure 6-6.

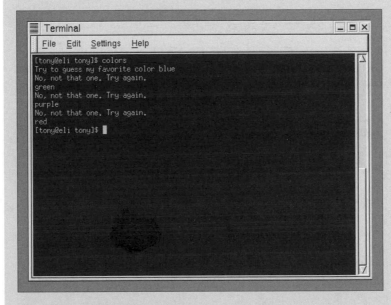

**Figure 6-6:** Results of colors script

The while loop tests an expression in a manner similar to the if statement. As long as the statement inside the brackets is true, the statements inside the do and done statements repeat.

Notice the use of the != symbol, which is the not-equal operator. It tests two operands and returns true if they are not equal. Otherwise, it returns false. In the steps you just completed, the echo and read statements inside the loop repeat until the user enters red.

Another example of the while loop is in a data entry form.

**To enter a while loop that will serve as a data entry form:**

**1**   Use vi or Emacs to create a script file, nameaddr.

**2**   Type these lines into the file:

```
looptest=y
 while [ "$looptest" = y ]
   do
      echo -n "Enter Name  : "; read name
      echo -n "Enter Street : "; read street
      echo -n "Enter City  : "; read city
      echo -n "Enter State  : "; read state
      echo -n "Enter Zip Code: "; read zip
      echo -n "Continue? (y)es or (n)o "; read looptest
   done
```

**3**   Save the file and exit the editor.

**4**   Give the file execute permission, and test it. You see output similar to Figure 6-7.

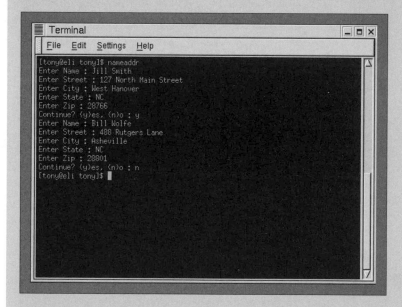

**Figure 6-7:** Output of nameaddr script

As you test the program, enter several names and addresses. When you finish, answer n (for no) when the program asks you, "Continue? (y)es or (n)o."

Use looping logic in applications where code must be repeated a determined or undetermined number of times.

## Case Logic

The **case logic** structure simplifies the selection of a match when you have a list of choices. It allows your program to perform one of many actions, depending upon the value of a variable. Note the use of two semicolons ( ;; ) that terminate the action(s) taken after the case matches to the test.

**To demonstrate case logic:**

**1**  Use the vi or Emacs editor to create the manycolors shell script.

**2**  Type these lines into the file:

```
echo -n "Enter your favorite color: "; read color
 case "$color" in
    "blue")  echo "As in My Blue Heaven.";;
    "yellow") echo "As in the Yellow Sunset.";;
    "red")   echo "As in Red Rover, Red Rover.";;
    "orange") echo "Autumn has shades of Orange.";;
    *    ) echo "Sorry, I do not know that color.";;
 esac
```

**3**  Save the file and exit the editor.

**4**  Give the file execute permission, and test it. You see output similar to that shown in Figure 6-8.

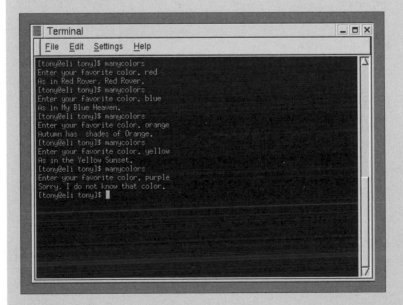

**Figure 6-8:** Output of manycolors script

In the Manycolors script, the case structure examines the contents of the color variable and searches for a match among the values listed. When a match is found, the statement that immediately follows the case value is executed. For example, if the color variable contains red, the echo statement that appears after "red") is executed. If the contents of the colors variable does not match any of the values listed, the statement that appears after *) is executed.

As you can see, case logic is designed to pick one course of action from a list of many, depending upon the contents of a variable. This control structure is ideal for menus, where the user chooses one of several values.

Note: The case structure is terminated by the word "esac," which is "case" spelled backwards.

In this section, you learned about shell variables, operators, and wildcard characters. You also learned about the four logic structures. In the next section, you'll use shell programming to create your application.

# SUMMARY

- A high-level language (such as C, C++, or COBOL) is a language that uses English-like expressions. A high-level language must be converted into a low-level (machine) language before the computer can execute it.

- The shell interprets UNIX shell scripts. They do not need to be converted to machine language because UNIX converts and executes them in one step.

- UNIX shell scripts, created with the vi or Emacs editor, contain instructions that do not need to be written from scratch, but rather can be selectively chosen from the operating system's inventory of executable commands.

- Linux shells are derived from the UNIX Bourne, Korn, and C shells. The three Linux shells are Bash, tcsh, and zsh; Bash is the most used Linux shell.

- UNIX keeps three types of variables: configuration, environment, and shell. Configuration variables contain set-up information for the operating system. Environment variables keep information about your login session. Shell variables are created in a shell script or at the command line. The export command is used to make a shell variable an environment variable.

- The shell supports numerous operators, including many for performing arithmetic operations.

- You can use wildcard characters in shell scripts, including the bracket ([]) characters. Brackets surround a set of values that can match an individual character in a name or string.

- The logic structures supported by the shell are sequential, decision, looping, and case.

**R E V I E W   Q U E S T I O N S**

**1.** Shell programs _____.
   a. can be developed faster than compiler programs
   b. run slower than their compiler counterparts
   c. serve as excellent prototypes
   d. All of the above

**2.** What is the difference between a configuration variable and an environment variable?
   a. The user sets configuration variables.
   b. The system sets environment variables.
   c. The system sets configuration variables.
   d. The user should never change environment variables.

**3.** Which of the following commands protect a file from being overwritten?
   a. set –o noclobber
   b. chmod 777 *filename*
   c. set –o clobber
   d. set !*filename*

**4.** The four basic logic structures are _____.
   a. sequence, decision, loop, and case
   b. sequence, iteration, loop, and case
   c. decision, iteration, case, and if-then
   d. for, next, while, and if

**5.** Which of these commands stores the output of the date command in the variable MYDATE?
   a. MYDATE=date
   b. date > MYDATE
   c. MYDATE=`date`
   d. date | MYDATE

**6.** The program development cycle can be described as _____.
   a. program design, program specifications, writing code, testing and debugging
   b. program specifications, program design, writing code, testing and debugging
   c. writing code, testing and debugging, program design, program specifications
   d. program design, writing code, testing and debugging, program specifications

**7.** The _____ command displays a list of environment variables.
   a. printenv
   b. envars
   c. ls –env
   d. cat envars

**8.** The _____ command makes a variable an environment variable.
   a. send
   b. port
   c. export
   d. import

9. Sequential logic can be described as _____.
   a. a logic structure for executing a statement or group of statements only if a certain condition exists
   b. a logic structure for executing a series of statements in the order they are written
   c. a logic structure for repeating a statement or series of statements
   d. a logic structure for performing one of many actions, depending upon the value of a variable

10. Decision logic can be described as _____.
   a. a logic structure for executing a statement or group of statements only if a certain condition exists
   b. a logic structure for executing a series of statements in the order they are written
   c. a logic structure for repeating a statement or series of statements
   d. a logic structure for performing one of many actions, depending upon the value of a variable

11. Looping logic can be described as _____.
   a. a logic structure for executing a statement or group of statements only if a certain condition exists
   b. a logic structure for executing a series of statements in the order they are written
   c. a logic structure for repeating a statement or series of statements
   d. a logic structure for performing one of many actions, depending upon the value of a variable

12. Case logic can be described as _____.
   a. a logic structure for executing a statement or group of statements only if a certain condition exists
   b. a logic structure for executing a series of statements in the order they are written
   c. a logic structure for repeating a statement or series of statements
   d. a logic structure for performing one of many actions, depending upon the value of a variable

13. The _____ command stores the user's input in a variable.
   a. input
   b. get
   c. read
   d. import

14. Shell programs are _____.
   a. compiled
   b. interpreted
   c. both compiled and interpreted
   d. neither compiled nor interpreted

# E X E R C I S E S

1. Create the file alphalist with the following entries:

   Alpha_romeo

   Chevrolet

   Buick

   Plymouth

   Dodge

   BMW

2. Sort the alphalist file and pipe it to a cat program to display a numbered list of cars.

3. Create a new file, myfile, in your home directory.
   a. Use the set –o noclobber. Create a second file, mynewfile.
   b. Enter this command: cat mynewfile > myfile <Enter>.
   c. Explain what happened.
   d. Now modify the redirection to make it work.

4. Fix this line of code to make it work:

   ```
   echo "Why don't you get a "van down by the river?"
   ```

5. If you do not have a bin directory in your home directory, create one. Look at the contents of the PATH variable. If it does not include the path to your bin directory, add it.

6. Create a variable, NAME. Store your full name in it.

7. Use the printenv command to display a list of environment variables. Is the NAME variable listed? Execute the command that makes NAME an environment variable.

 # D I S C O V E R Y    E X E R C I S E S

1. Use the sample menu as a guide, and create a new menu program that looks like this:

   Travel Menu

   ==========

   (L)ondon scenic tour

   (P)aris in the Spring

   (N)ew York Shopping Fantasy

   Make your selection ... (Q) to quit

2. Enter the command to store the output of the pwd command in a variable, PLACE. Display the contents of the PLACE variable on the screen.

3. Write a script named change_prompt. The script should change your prompt to display the date and the name of your working directory. Give the file execute permission, and test it.

4. Execute each of these commands:

```
let X=2+4*3
Y=2+4*3
```

Display the contents of each variable on the screen. How do you explain the difference?

5. Write a script file that performs the following steps:
   a. Stores 5 in variable A
   b. Stores 10 in variable B
   c. Stores the sum of A plus B in variable C
   d. Stores the difference of B minus A in variable D
   e. Stores the product of A times B in variable E
   f. Stores the quotient of B divided by A in variable F
   g. Displays the contents of all the variables

6. Write a script that asks the user to enter his or her first name. The script should include an if statement that compares the name the user entered with your name. If they are the same, the script should display the message, "That is my name too." Otherwise it should display the message, "That is a nice name."

7. Write a script file with a for loop that displays a list of your favorite music groups.

8. Repeat Discovery Exercise 7, but this time enter the for loop at the command line.

9. Write a script file that asks users to guess your name. If they guess incorrectly, the script should ask them to guess again. Repeat this until users correctly guess your name. (HINT: Use the while loop.)

10. Write a script file that asks the user to choose and enter the name of a country from the following list: America, Italy, France, Germany. The script then uses a case structure to display the name of a car made in the selected country. Use the cars listed in the table.

| Country | Car |
| --- | --- |
| America | Ford |
| Italy | Ferrari |
| France | Peugeot |
| Germany | Porsche |

In this lesson you will:

■ Create screen-management and cursor programs

■ Edit the .bashrc file to customize your personal working environment

■ Use the trap command

■ Enter and test shell programs to print the phone records, view the contents of the Corp_phones file, and add new phone records to the file

# Creating and Completing the Corporate Phones Application

## Using Shell Programming to Create a Menu

Before creating your corporate phone program, you first create a menu, which is a good example of a shell program that employs the four basic logic structures: sequence, decision, looping, and case. A significant feature of the menu program is the screen presentation, which you want be as appealing and user-friendly as possible. You can choose one of UNIX's lesser-known commands, tput, to make your screen place the prompt (cursor) at the user's data-entry point on the screen. The **tput command** initializes the terminal to respond to a setting that the user chooses. Some examples of this are:

■ tput cup 0 0: moves the cursor to row 0, column 0, the upper-left corner of screen
■ tput clear: clears the screen
■ tput cols: prints the number of columns for the current terminal
■ bold=`tput smso `offbold=`tput rmso`: sets boldfaced type

**To practice the tput command:**

■ Type the following command sequence, and press **Enter:**

```
tput clear ; tput cup 10 15 ; echo "Hello" ; tput cup 20 0
```

You see the results of the command sequence. The screen clears; the cursor is positioned at row 10, column 15, on the screen; the word "Hello" is printed; and the prompt's position is row 20, column 0.

Next, use the tput command to create a cursor utility. You can use this utility in other script files to position the cursor on the screen.

## To use the tput command to create a cursor utility:

**1**   Use the vi or Emacs editor to create a script file, cursor.

**2**   Enter the following lines in the program:

```
tput cup $1 $2
```

**3**   Save the file and exit the editor.

**4**   Make the cursor script executable with the chmod command.

**5**   Test the cursor script by typing **cursor 10 12** and pressing **Enter**. The cursor moves to the position 10, 12 on the screen.

Notice the script is passing $1 and $2 as arguments to the tput cup command. These are positional parameters: they reference arguments typed on the command line when the cursor script file is executed. For example, when you invoked the script with the command cursor 10 12, the $1 parameter holds the value 10, and the $2 parameter holds the value 12.

You will now use the tput command to create screen management and cursor programs for displaying menus and data entry screens.

## To use the tput command:

**1**   Use the vi or Emacs editor to enter a screen-management program, Scrmanage, containing the following lines:

```
tput cup $1 $2  # place cursor on row and col
tput clear     # clear the screen
bold=`tput smso` # set standout mode - bold
offbold=`tput rmso` # reset screen — turn bold off
echo $bold      # turn bold on
cursor 10 20; echo "Type Last Name:" # bold caption
cursor 12 20; echo "Type First Name:" # bold caption
echo $offbold   # turn bold off
cursor 10 41; read lastname # enter last name
cursor 12 41; read firstname # enter last name
```

**2**   Save the file and exit the editor.

**3**   Give the file execute permission, and test it.

You are now ready to enter the script to display the menu. (You will use this program as part of your application later in this section.)

**To enter the script:**

**1**    Use the vi or Emacs editor to enter the Phmenu program shown below.

```
#==============================================================
=
# Script Name:   phmenu
# By:            JQD (Your initial here)
# Date:          November 1999
# Purpose:       A menu for the Corporate Phone List
# Command Line: phmenu
#==============================================================
=
loop=y
while [ "$loop" = y ]
do
  clear
  cursor 3 12; echo "Corporate Phone Reporting Menu"
  cursor 4 12; echo "=============================="
  cursor 6 9; echo "P - Print Phone List  :"
  cursor 7 9; echo "A - Add New Phones    :"
  cursor 8 9; echo "S - Search for Phones :"
  cursor 10 9; echo "Q - Quit"
  cursor 11 32
  read choice || continue
done
```

**2**    Save the file and exit the editor.

**3**    Give the file execute permission, and test the program. (You will have to press **Ctrl+C** to exit the program, as the Quit option has not yet been programmed.)

Now that you have an idea of how to create a menu program, it will be helpful to learn some additional shell features and commands before creating your application. You will first learn how to customize your personal environment so that creating and testing a new program do not interfere with your other programs.

## Customizing Your Personal Environment

When your work requirements center on computer programming and shell scripting, consider customizing your environment by modifying the initial settings in the login scripts. For example, many programmers set up a personal bin directory where they can store and test their new programs without interfering with ongoing operations. ("Bin" is the traditional UNIX name for directories that hold executable files.) You can also modify the editors to make them automatically indent the text inside their programs in accordance with programmer usage.

An **alias** is a name that represents another command. You can use aliases to simplify and automate commands you use frequently. For example, the following command sets up an alias for the rm command.

```
alias rm="rm -i"
```

This command above causes the rm -i command to execute any time the user enters the rm command. This is a commonly used alias, as it ensures users are always prompted before the rm command deletes a file. Here are two other common aliases that help safeguard files:

```
alias mv="mv -i"
alias cp="cp -i"
```

**To practice creating an alias:**

**1**   To create an alias for the ls command, type **alias ls="ls -l"** and press **Enter**. Now, when you use the ls command, the ls -l command executes automatically.

**2**   Test the alias by typing **ls** and pressing **Enter**. You see a long directory listing.

The **.bashrc file** that resides in your home directory can be used to establish customizations that take effect for each login session. The .bashrc script is executed each time you generate a shell, such as when you run a shell script. Any time a subshell is created, the .bashrc is re-executed. The following .bashrc file is commented to explain how you can make your own changes.

```
.bashrc
# Source global definitions
if [ -f /etc/bashrc ]; then
      . /etc/bashrc # if any global definitions are
                    # run them first
alias rm 'rm -i'   # make sure user is prompted before
                   # removing files
alias mv 'mv -i'   # make sure user is prompted before
                   # overlaying files
set -o ignoreeof   # Do not allow Ctrl-D to logout

set -o noclobber   # Force user to enter >! To write
            # over existing files
PS1="\w \$"     # Set prompt to show working directory
```

In addition to knowing how to customize your work environment, you should also be familiar with the trap command.

# The trap Command

The trap command is useful when you want your shell program to automatically remove any temporary files that are created when the shell scripts runs. The **trap** command specifies that a command, listed as the argument to trap, is read and executed when the shell receives a specified system signal. Here is an example of the command:

```
trap "rm ~/tmp/* 2> /dev/null; exit" 0
```

This command has two arguments: a command to be executed, and a signal number from the operating system. The command, rm ~/tmp/* 2> /dev/null; exit, deletes everything in the user's tmp directory, redirects the error output of the rm command to the null device (so it does not appear on the screen), and issues an exit command to terminate the shell. The signal specified is 0, which is the operating system signal generated when a program exits. So, if this sample command is part of a script file, it causes the specified rm command to execute when signal 0 is sent by the operating system.

The programmer often sets up ~/tmp (a subdirectory of the user's home directory) to store temporary files. When the script file exits, any files placed in ~/tmp can be removed. This is called "good housekeeping" on the part of the programmer.

# Creating the Corp_phones File

The steps that follow require you to create the corp_phones file and place it in your /home/user/source directory.

**To create the corp_phones file:**

**1**  Use the vi or Emacs editor to create the corp_phones file.

**2**  Enter the following records in the file:

```
219-555-4567:Harrison:Joel:M:4540:Accountant:09-12-1985
219-555-4587:Mitchell:Barbara:C:4541:Admin Asst:12-14-1995
219-555-4589:Olson:Timothy:H:4544:Supervisor:06-30-1983
219-555-4591:Moore:Sarah:H:4500:Dept Manager:08-01-1978
219-555-4567:Polk:John:S:4520:Accountant:09-22-1998
219-555-4501:Robinson:Albert:J:4501:Secretary:08-12-1997
```

**3**  Save the file and exit the editor.

**4**  Use the following grep command to search the file for specific phone numbers. The output should look like:

```
$grep 219-555-4591 corp_phones  <Enter>
219-555-4591:Moore:Sarah:H:4500:Dept Manager:08-01-1978
```

**5**  Use a similar grep command to search the file for all Accountants. Your screen should look similar to Figure 6-9.

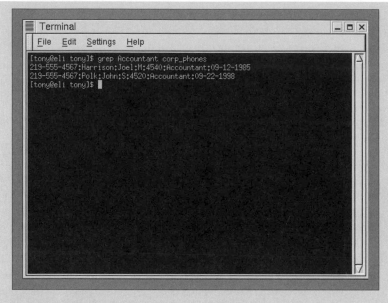

**Figure 6-9:** Results of grep command

Notice that you can extract information from the corp_phones file using grep, as well as other commands you learned in previous chapters. You will use such commands in building your script application.

You will now complete the menu program that you started at the beginning of this lesson.

**To complete the phone menu program:**

**1** Use the vi or Emacs editor, and retrieve phmenu. Add the boldfaced lines to the script.

```
#===============================================================
# Script Name:    phmenu
# By:             JQD
# Date:           March 1999
# Purpose:        A menu for the Corporate Phone List
# Command Line:   phmenu
#===============================================================
phonefile=~/source/corp_phones
loop=y
while [ "$loop" = y ]
do
  clear
  cursor 3 12; echo "Corporate Phone Reporting Menu"
  cursor 4 12; echo "=============================="
  cursor 6 9; echo "P - Print Phone List   :"
```

```
cursor 7 9; echo "A - Add Phone to List  :"
cursor 8 9; echo "S - Search for Phone   :"
cursor 10 9; echo "Q - Quit"
cursor 11 32;
read choice || continue
   case $choice in
     [Aa]) phoneadd ;;
     [Pp]) phlist1 ;;
     [Ss]) phonefind ;;
     [Vv]) less $phonefile;;
     [Qq]) exit ;;
     *)  cursor 14 4; echo "Invalid Code"; read prompt ;;
   esac
done
```

**2**  Save the file and exit the editor.

**3**  Give the file execute permission, and test it.

When you demonstrate your program to Dominion Consulting managers, they point out that some errors may occur when entering additional information. To locate errors quickly, you need to view unformatted records.

## Viewing Unformatted Records

It is often useful to have a program that displays unformatted file data, which means that the records appear exactly as they are stored on the disk. In the case of the phone records, the display shows the colon (:) characters that separate the variable-length fields. If problems develop, it is convenient to have a look at the raw data. To do this, you use the **less command** to display the records on the screen.

**To use the less command to view unformatted records:**

**1**  Open Phmenu in the editor of your choice, and add the boldfaced lines shown.

```
#=============================================================
# Script Name:    phmenu
# By:             JQD
# Date:           March 1999
# Purpose:        A menu for the Corporate Phone List
# Command Line:   phmenu
#=============================================================
phonefile=~/source/corp_phones
loop=y
while [ "$loop" = y ]
```

```
do
  clear
  cursor 3 12; echo "Corporate Phone Reporting Menu"
  cursor 4 12; echo "================================="
  cursor 6 9; echo "P - Print Phone List   :"
  cursor 7 9; echo "A - Add Phone to List  :"
  cursor 8 9; echo "S - Search for Phone   :"
  cursor 9 9; echo "V - View Phone List    :"
  cursor 10 9; echo "Q - Quit"
  cursor 11 32;
  read choice || continue
     case $choice in
       [Aa]) phoneadd ;;
       [Pp]) phlist1 ;;
       [Ss]) phonefind ;;
       [Qq]) exit ;;
       *)  cursor 14 4; echo "Invalid Code"; read prompt ;;
     esac
done
```

**2**  Save the file and exit the editor.

**3**  Test the script.

You are now ready to run a prototype of your program. To do this, you use the Awk program.

## Using Awk

The Awk program offers a good example of how the UNIX shell programmer can quickly create an application model. Using Awk accelerates development because a single awk command can select fields from many records and display them in a specified format on the screen. To run a prototype of your corporate phone program, combine the cursor program you wrote earlier with a line of Awk code.

### To use the Awk program:

**1**  Use the editor of your choice to create the **Phlist1** program. Use the following code as a guide.

```
#
===============================================================
# Script Name:   phlist1
# By:            JQD
# Date:          March 1999
```

```
# Purpose:       Use awk to format colon-separated fields
#                in a flat file and display to the screen
# Command line: phlist1
# ============================================================
clear
cursor 2 20; echo "Corporate Phone List"
cursor 3 20; echo "===================="
cursor 5 0;
awk -F: ' { printf "%-12s %-12s %s\t%s-%s-%s %s %10.10s
%s\n", $4, $5, $6, $1, $2, $3, $7, $8, $9 } ' Corp_phones
```

**2**   Save the file and exit the editor.

**3**   Give the file execute permission and run it. Your screen should look like Figure 6-10.

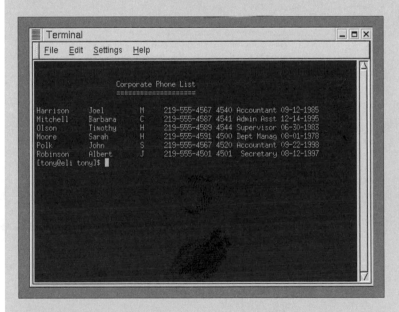

**Figure 6-10:** Output of Phlist1 script

You realize that names will be added to the corp_phones file, so you need to modify your shell script.

# Creating the Phoneadd Shell Program

The Phmenu program offers the option to add a phone record to the corp_phones file; that is, the user interacts with the program to enter a new employee's phone record. To do this, you can use a cursor program, similar to the one you wrote earlier, to design your data entry screen, display it, and place the cursor in the first data-entry field. You can subsequently position it for all the other entries.

## To create the phoneadd program to allow additions:

**1**  Use the editor of your choice to create the script phoneadd. Enter this code:

```
==========================================================
# Script Name: phoneadd
# By:          JQD
# Date:        March 1999
# Purpose:     A shell script that sets up a loop to add
#              new employees to the Corp_phones file.
#                  The code also prevents duplicate phone
#              numbers from being assigned.
# Command Syntax:  phoneadd
#

==========================================================
trap "rm ~/tmp/* 2> /dev/null; exit" 0 1 2 3
phonefile=~/corp_phones
looptest=y
while [ $looptest = y ]
do
   clear
   cursor 1 4; echo "Corporate Phone List Additions"
   cursor 2 4; echo "=============================="
   cursor 4 4; echo "Phone Number: "
   cursor 5 4; echo "Last Name   : "
   cursor 6 4; echo "First Name  : "
   cursor 7 4; echo "Middle Init : "
   cursor 8 4; echo "Dept #      : "
   cursor 9 4; echo "Job Title   : "
   cursor 10 4; echo "Date Hired  : "
   cursor 12 4; echo "Add Another? (Y)es or (Q)uit "
    cursor 4 18; read phonenum
   if [ "$phonenum" = 'q' ]
        then { clear; exit }
   fi
   cursor 5 18; read lname
   cursor 6 18; read fname
       cursor 7 18; read midinit
       cursor 8 18; read deptno
        cursor 9 18; read jobtitle
       cursor 10 18; read datehired
       # Check to see if last name is not a blank before you
       # write to disk
       if [ "$lname" > "            " ]
       then
echo $phonenum:$lname:$fname:$midinit:$deptno:$jobtitle: $date hired" >> $phonefile
       fi
```

```
   cursor 14 33; read looptest
   if [ "$looptest" = 'q' ]
      then { clear; exit }
   fi
done
```

**2**  Save the file and exit the editor. Give the file execute permission and run it. Test the program by adding the following employees:

**219-555-7175 Mullins  Allen L 7527 Sales Rep 09-12-2000**
**219-555-7176 Albertson Jeannette K 5547 DC Clerk**
**09-12-2000**

**3**  Now run the phmenu script and select **A** from the menu to execute the phone and script. Add another record to the file and then quit the program.

Your screen should look similar to Figure 6-11. (Note that the program shows only one person's information at a time.)

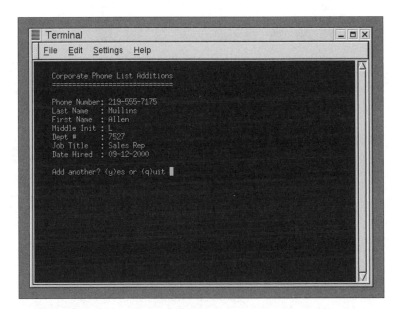

**Figure 6-11:** Phoneadd script screen

You created the shell script for the corporate phones application. However, you still need to address several deficiencies. For example, how can you return to a previous field as you enter the data? What happens when you enter the same employee twice? What happens if you assign a new employee a phone number that has already been assigned to someone else? Chapter 7, "Advanced Shell Programming," addresses these issues.

# SUMMARY

- You can use the tput command to create a simple cursor-placement program to enhance data entry functions.

- You can customize the .bashrc file that resides in the user's home directory to suit the needs of programmers and system administrators.

- You can create aliases and enter them into .bashrc to simplify often-used commands, such as ls –l and rm –i.

- Use the trap command inside a script file to remove temporary files after the script file has been run (exited).

- The grep command serves a key role in the development of shell programs by letting you search and retrieve information from files.

- The Awk program serves as an effective and easy-to-use tool for generating reports.

# COMMAND SUMMARY

| Chapter 6 Commands | |
| --- | --- |
| Command | Purpose |
| alias | Establishes an alias |
| case...in...esac | A programming structure that allows one action from a set of possible actions to be performed, depending upon the value of a variable |
| export | Makes a variable an environment variable |
| for; do...done | Causes a variable to take on each value in a set of values. An action is performed for each value. |
| if...then...else...fi | Causes one of two actions to be performed depending on a condition |
| let | Stores arithmetic values in a variable |
| printenv | Prints a list of environment variables |
| set –o noclobber | Prevents files from being overwritten by the > operator |
| tput cup | Moves the screen cursor to a specified row and column |
| tput clear | Clears the screen |
| tput cols | Prints the number of columns on the current terminal |
| tput smso | Enables boldfaced output |

---

**Chapter 6 Commands**

| | |
|---|---|
| tput rmso | Disables boldfaced output |
| trap | Executes a command when a specified signal is received from the operating system |
| while; do...done | Repeats an action while a condition exists |

---

(*continued*)

# R E V I E W    Q U E S T I O N S

1. A UNIX alias is _____.
   a. a name that replaces the standard UNIX command name
   b. an alternate name for a UNIX command
   c. always entered into the system-wide initialization file, /etc/profile
   d. preferably entered on the command line each time you log on

2. Use the trap command to _____.
   a. detect errors
   b. monitor for a system signal and take some action
   c. filter out bad data
   d. separate out corrupted information

3. Which of these would place the current directory in the PATH variable?
   a. PATH="$PATH:/~/
   b. PATH="$PATH:."
   c. PATH="$PATH:/home
   d. PATH="$PATH;."

4. You can use the tput command to _____.
   a. add data to the screen
   b. position the cursor on screen
   c. put a character in memory
   d. accept a character from the keyboard

5. You can use the grep command to _____.
   a. search a file for a matching pattern
   b. alter the text in a file
   c. create a mathematical formula
   d. create a pattern of words enclosed with brackets [ ]

6. A script program may access arguments passed to it with _____.
   a. positional parameters, such as $1, $2, etc.
   b. the variables $ARG1, $ARG2, etc.
   c. the argument command
   d. the script_param command

7. Many programmers create a directory in their home directory for storing executable programs. The traditional name for this directory is _____.
   a. programs
   b. executables
   c. prg
   d. bin

8. The file that is executed each time you log on is _____.
   a. .login
   b. autoexec
   c. .bashrc
   d. .welcome

9. The command tput cup is followed on the command line by _____.
   a. the word "clear"
   b. row and column numbers for subsequent screen output
   c. codes to make subsequent screen output old
   d. codes to disable bold output

10. Programmers often set up a directory for holding temporary files. The traditional name for this directory is _____.
    a. temporary
    b. temp
    c. etc
    d. tmp

11. The tput cols command _____.
    a. positions the cursor on the specified column
    b. sets the terminal to the specified number of columns
    c. prints the number of columns available on the current terminal
    d. enables boldfaced printing

12. The tput smso command _____.
    a. enables boldfaced printing
    b. disables boldfaced printing
    c. positions the cursor
    d. clears the screen

13. The tput rmso command _____.
    a. enables boldfaced printing
    b. disables boldfaced printing
    c. positions the cursor
    d. clears the screen

# EXERCISES

1. From the command line, issue a command that performs these steps: clears the screen; positions the cursor at row 5, column 30; displays your name; and positions the cursor at row 20, column 0.

2. Create the alias w that executes the command:

   `who −Hi`

3. Store the alias you created in Exercise 2 in the correct file, so it takes effect each time you log on.

4. Change the Phlist1 program to add a heading over the displayed fields when the file is viewed, for example:

   Last Name First Name MI Phone Number Dept# Title Date Hired

   ====================================================

# DISCOVERY EXERCISES

1. Remove the colon characters from the Phoneadd program's screen, and reposition the cursor to improve the appearance of the data entry.

2. Design and write a smaller version of the menu program.

3. Create a small shell program to display the employee phone records showing only their names and the date hired.

4. Create a script file that clears the screen, places two highlighted (boldfaced) lines on row 5, column 10, and row 6, column 12. Display two more, non-boldfaced lines on row 8, column 10, and row 10, column 10.

5. Create a file, music, that contains information on your CD collection. Each record in the file should have these fields:
   Artist Name
   CD Name
   Date Purchased
   Cost

6. Next, create a script file with a menu that lets you view the contents of the file, search for all CDs from a particular artist, and add new records to the file.

7. Design an Awk statement that formats and displays the records in the music file.

8. Describe how you would use the trap command to display the message, "That's all folks," when a script file exits.

# Advanced Shell Programming

**case** ▶ Dominion Consulting's managers are pleased with the new shell program that maintains the employee phone file. Based on the relatively small volume of transactions and file size, the programming supervisor agrees that the shell program will be a permanent solution for maintaining the corporate phone file. However, you need to enhance the program and incorporate new features, such as preventing the same phone number from being assigned to more than one person, re-entering data to correct errors, and sorting by employees' last names.

In this lesson you will:

■ Use flowcharting and pseudocode tools

■ Learn to write scripts that tell the system which shell to use as an interpreter

■ Use the test command to compare values and validate file existence

■ Use the translate command, tr, to display a record with duplicate fields

■ Use the sed command to delete a phone record

# Developing a Fully Featured Program

In the last chapter you began developing a program to automate the maintenance of the phone records in the corp_phones file. You developed a menu that presents several options and a data entry screen that allows records to be added to the file.

In this chapter you complete the program. You add code that deletes a specified record from the file, searches for a specified record, and sorts and displays all records in the file. You perform these tasks with the test, grep, sed, and tr commands. Before you begin adding this code, you learn about two standard program development tools: flowcharts and pseudocode.

## Analyzing the Program

A computer program is developed by analyzing the best way to achieve the desired results. Standard programming analysis tools help you do this. The two most popular and proven analysis tools are the program flowchart and pseudocode.

### Flowcharting

The **flowchart** is a logic diagram that uses a set of standard symbols that explain the program's sequence and each action it takes. For example, look at the flowchart in Figure 7-1.

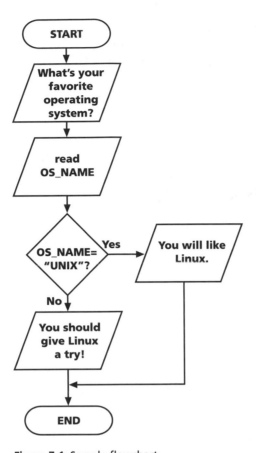

**Figure 7-1:** Sample flowchart

Figure 7-1 is a flowchart for the following program, which you wrote in Chapter 6.

```
echo -n "What is your favorite operating system? "
read OS_NAME
if [ "$OS_NAME" = "UNIX" ]
then
    echo "You will like Linux."
else
    echo "You should give Linux a try!"
fi
```

Each step in the program is represented by a symbol in the flowchart. The shape of the symbol indicates the type of operation being performed, such as input/output or a decision. Figure 7-2 shows standard flowcharting symbols and their meanings.

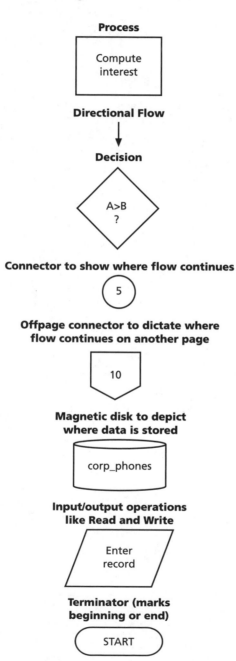

Figure 7-2: Standard flowchart symbols

The arrows that connect the symbols represent the direction in which the program flows from one symbol to the next. In the flowchart in Figure 7-1, the arrow after the START terminator shows the program flowing to an output operation that displays the message, "What is your favorite operating system?" Next, the program flows to an input operation that reads a value into OS_NAME. A decision structure (represented by a diamond-shaped symbol) is encountered next, which compares OS_NAME to "UNIX" to determine if the two are equal. If so, the program follows the "Yes" branch. This leads to an output operation that displays the message, "You will like Linux." If OS_NAME and "UNIX" are not equal, the program follows the "No" branch. This leads to an output operation that displays the message, "You should give Linux a try!" The two paths then converge and flow to the END terminator.

You manually create a flowchart using a drawing template. Flowchart templates provide the symbols that denote logical structures, input-output operations, processing operations, and the storage media that contain the files. (See Figure 7-2.) A variety of flowcharting software packages let you create flowcharts on your computer. Popular word-processing packages, such as Microsoft Word and WordPerfect, are also equipped with flowcharting tools.

## Writing Pseudocode

After creating a flowchart, the next step in designing a program is to write **pseudocode**. Pseudocode instructions are similar to actual programming statements. Use them to create a model that you can later use as a basis for a real program. For example, here are pseudocode statements for the os_choice program:

```
Display "What is your favorite operating system? " on the
screen.
Enter data into OS_NAME.
If OS_NAME is equal to "UNIX"
     then
     Display "You will like Linux." on the screen.
Else
     Display "You should give Linux a try!" on the screen.
End if.
```

Pseudocode is a design tool only, and never processed by the computer. Therefore, there are no strict rules to follow. The pseudocode should verbally match the symbolic representation of logic illustrated on the flowchart. For example, Figure 7-3 shows the flowchart and pseudocode that represent one change Dominion Consulting wants to make to its phone program (re-entering data in a field).

Before you can begin to work on the program, however, you need to do some preliminary work. First, you must ensure that everyone who runs the program does so with the correct shell. To do this, modify the program so it informs the operating system which shell to use while interpreting the statements in the script.

**Pseudocode:**

```
While entry = minus
    do
        Reposition cursor in previous field.
        Enter the data.
        Reposition cursor on field following the field that was
          just entered (re-entered data)
        Continue testing while loop.
    Done
```

**Flowchart:**

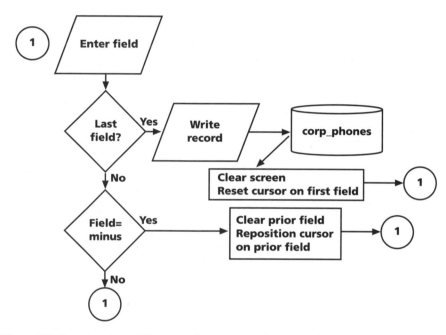

**Figure 7-3:** Pseudocode and flowchart for re-entry of previous fields

# Ensuring the Correct Shell Runs the Script

Each UNIX user has the freedom and capability of choosing which shell he or she prefers. When developing a shell script, you must be responsible for ensuring that the correct shell is used to interpret your script. This is because all shells do not support the same commands and programming statements.

You can instruct the system to run a script with a specific shell. You do so in the first line of the script. The line must start with the # character, followed by the

! character and the path of the shell. For example, this line tells the system to use the Bash shell:

```
#!/bin/bash
```

When the system reads this code line, it loads the Bash shell and uses it to interpret the statements in the script file. Since UNIX includes many shells, you should always begin your scripts with this statement.

Next, you need to make sure that the necessary directories and files are in place before you execute programs that depend on them. To do this, use the test command.

## Using the test Command

The **test** command makes preliminary checks of the UNIX internal environment and other useful comparisons (beyond those that the if command alone can perform). See Appendix B, "Syntax Guide to UNIX Commands," for a description of options available for the test command. You can place the test command inside your shell script or execute it directly from the command line. In this section you learn to use the test command at the command line. In the next section you use it in a script file.

The test command uses operators expressed as options to perform the evaluations. The command can be used to:

- Perform relational tests with integers (such as equal, greater than, less than, etc.)
- Test strings
- Determine if a file exists and what type of file it is
- Perform Boolean tests

Each type of test operation is discussed in more detail in the following sections.

### Relational Integer Tests with the test Command

The test command can determine if one integer is equal to, greater than, less than, greater than or equal to, less than or equal to, or not equal to another integer. Table 7-1 describes the integer testing options of the test command.

| Option | Meaning | Example Command |
|--------|---------|-----------------|
| -eq | equal to | test a –eq b |
| -gt | greater than | test a –gt b |
| -lt | less than | test a –lt b |
| -ge | greater than or equal to | test a –ge b |
| -le | less than or equal to | test a –le b |
| -ne | not equal to | test a –ne b |

**Table 7-1:** Integer testing options of test command

The test command returns a value known as an exit status. An **exit status** is a numeric value that the command returns to the operating system when it finishes. The value of the test command's exit status indicates the results of the test performed. If the exit status is 0 (zero), the test result is true. An exit status of 1 indicates the test result is false.

The exit status is normally detected in a script by the if statement or in a looping structure. You can view the last command's exit status by typing the command:

echo $?

## To demonstrate the test command with integer expressions:

**1**  Create the variable number with the value 20 by typing the command **number=20** and pressing **Enter**.

**2**  Type **test $number –eq 20** and press **Enter**.

**3**  Type **echo $?** and press **Enter**. Your screen looks similar to Figure 7-4.

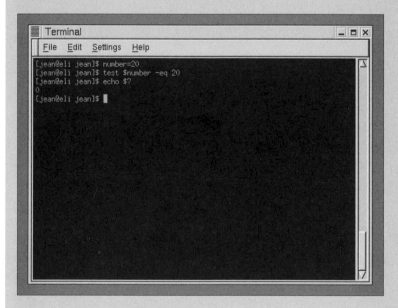

Figure 7-4: Testing an integer found true

The echo $? command displays the exit status of the last command that was executed. In this example, the test command returns the exit status 0, indicating the expression $number –eq 20 is true. This means $number is equal to 20.

**4** Type **value=10** and press **Enter**.

**5** Type **test $number –lt $value** and press **Enter**.

**6** Type **echo $?** and press **Enter**. Your screen looks similar to Figure 7-5.

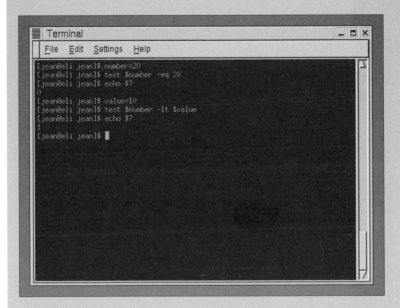

```
Terminal                                          _ □ ×
 File  Edit  Settings  Help
[jean@eli jean]$ number=20
[jean@eli jean]$ test $number -eq 20
[jean@eli jean]$ echo $?
0
[jean@eli jean]$ value=10
[jean@eli jean]$ test $number -lt $value
[jean@eli jean]$ echo $?
1
[jean@eli jean]$ █
```

**Figure 7-5:** Results of test command

In this example, the test command returns the exit status 1, indicating the expression $number –lt $value is false. This means $number is not less than $value.

## String Tests with the test Command

You can use the test command to determine if a string has a length of zero characters or a non-zero number of characters. It can also test two strings to determine if they are equal or not equal. Table 7-2 describes the string testing options of the test command.

| Option or Expression | Meaning | Example |
|---|---|---|
| -z | Tests for a zero-length string | test –z string |
| -n | Tests for a non-zero string length | test –n string |
| string1 = string2 | Tests two strings for equality | test string1 = string2 |
| string1 != string2 | Tests two strings for inequality | test string1 != string2 |
| string | Tests for a non-zero string length | test string |

**Table 7-2:** String testing options of test command

## To demonstrate the test command's string testing capabilities:

**1** Type **name="Bjorn"** and press **Enter**.

**2** Type **test $name = "Bjorn"** and press **Enter**.

**3** Type **echo $?** and press **Enter**. Your screen looks similar to Figure 7-6.

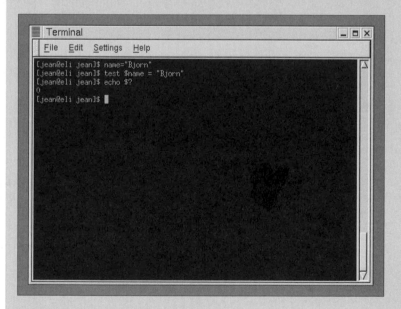

```
Terminal                                          _ □ ×
 File  Edit  Settings  Help
[jean@eli jean]$ name="Bjorn"
[jean@eli jean]$ test $name = "Bjorn"
[jean@eli jean]$ echo $?
0
[jean@eli jean]$ ▊
```

**Figure 7-6:** Testing a string found true

In the example above, the test command returns the exit status 0 indicating the expression $name = "Bjorn" is true. This means $name and "Bjorn" are equal.

**4** Type **test $name != "Barn"** and press **Enter**.

**5** Type **echo $?** and press **Enter**. Your screen looks similar to Figure 7-7.

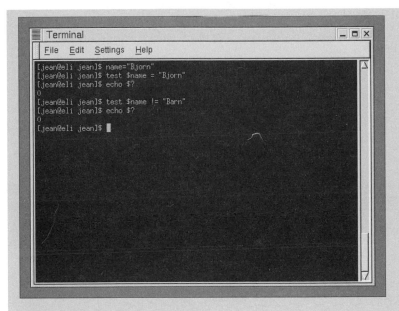

**Figure 7-7:** Testing unequal strings

In the example above, the test command returns the exit status 0 indicating the expression $name != "Barn" is true. This means $name and "Barn" are not equal.

**6**   Type **test –z $name** and press **Enter**.

**7**   Type **echo $?** and press **Enter**. Your screen looks similar to Figure 7-8.

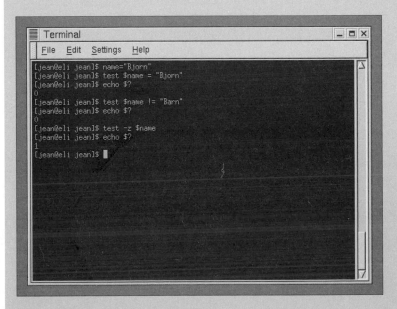

**Figure 7-8:** Testing a string found false

The last test command in the example above returns the exit status 1 indicating the expression –z $name is false. This means the string $name is not zero length.

## Testing Files with the test Command

The test command can determine if a file exists and if it has a specified permission or attribute (such as executable, readable, writeable, directory, etc.). Table 7-3 describes several of the command's file testing options.

| Option | Meaning | Example |
|--------|---------|---------|
| -e | True if a file exists | test –e file |
| -r | True if a file exists and is readable | test –r file |
| -w | True if a file exists and is writeable | test –w file |
| -x | True if a file exists and is executable | test –x file |
| -d | True if a file exists and is a directory | test –d file |
| -f | Tests if a file exists and is a regular file | test –f file |
| -s | True if a file exists and has a size greater than zero | test –s file |
| -c | Tests if a file exists and is a character special file (which is a character-oriented device, such as a terminal or printer) | test –c file |
| -b | Tests if a file exists and is a block special file (which is a block-oriented device, such as a disk or tape drive) | test –b file |

**Table 7-3:** File testing options of test command

**To demonstrate the test command's file testing capabilities:**

**1**  Use the touch command to create an empty file named test_file.

**2**  Use the **ls –l test_file** command to view the file's permissions. Your screen should look similar to Figure 7-9.

**3**  Note that the file has read and write permissions for you, the owner. Then type **test –x test_file** and press **Enter**.

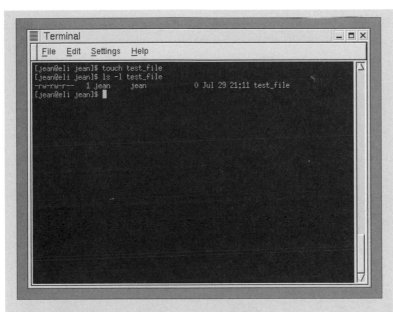

**Figure 7-9:** Creating test_file file

**4** Type **echo $?** and press **Enter**. Your screen looks similar to Figure 7-10.

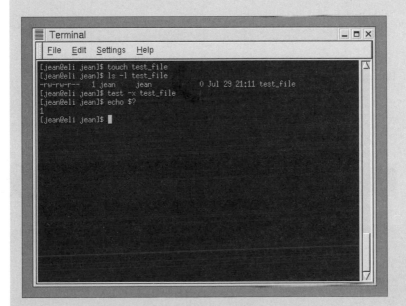

**Figure 7-10:** Testing a file to see if it's executable

The test command returns an exit status of 1, because test_file is not executable.

**5** Type **test –r test_file** and press **Enter**.

**6**  Type **echo $?** and press **Enter**. Your screen looks similar to Figure 7-11.

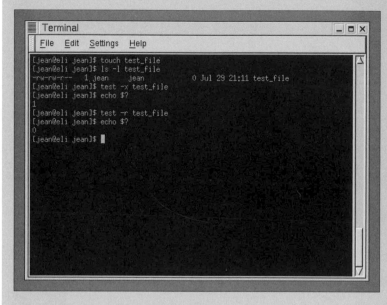

**Figure 7-11:** Testing a file to see if it's readable

The test command returns an exit status of 0 indicating test_file is readable.

## Performing Boolean Tests with the test Command

The test command's Boolean operators let you combine multiple expressions with AND and OR relationships. You can also use a Boolean negation operator. Table 7-4 describes Boolean operators.

| Option | Meaning | Example |
| --- | --- | --- |
| -a | Logical AND | test expression1 −a expression2 |
| -o | Logical OR | test expression1 −o expression2 |
| ! | Logical negation | test !expression |

**Table 7-4:** Test command's Boolean operators

The −a operator combines two expressions and tests a logical AND relationship between them. The form of the test command with the −a option is:

```
test expression1 —a expression2
```

If both expression1 and expression2 are true, the test command returns true (with a 0 exit status). However, if either expression1 or expression2 is false, the test command returns false (with an exit status of 1).

The −o operator also combines two expressions. It tests a logical OR relationship. The form of the test command with the −o option is:

```
test expression1 —o expression2
```

If either expression1 or expression2 is true, the test command returns true (with a 0 exit status). However, if neither of the expressions is true, the test command returns false (with an exit status of 1).

The ! operator negates the value of an expression. This means that if the expression normally causes test to return true, it returns false instead. Likewise, if the expression normally causes test to return false, it returns true instead. The form of the test command with the ! operator is:

```
test !expression
```

### To demonstrate the test command's Boolean operators:

**1**   Recall that the test_file file you created in the previous exercise has read and write permissions. Type **test –r test_file –a –w test_file** and press **Enter**.

This command tests two expressions using an AND relationship: -r test_file and −w test_file. If both expressions are true, the test command returns true.

**2**   Type **echo $?** and press **Enter**. Your screen looks similar to Figure 7-12.

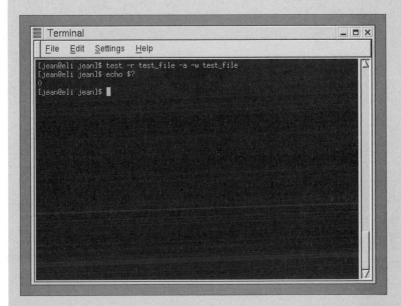

**Figure 7-12:** Using Boolean operators to test a file

The test command returns an exit status of 0 indicating that test_file is readable and writeable.

**3**    Type **test –x test_file –o –r test_file** and press **Enter**.

This command tests two expressions using an OR relationship: -x test_file and –r test_file. If either of these expressions is true, the test command returns true.

**4**    Type **echo $?** and press **Enter**. Your screen looks similar to Figure 7-13.

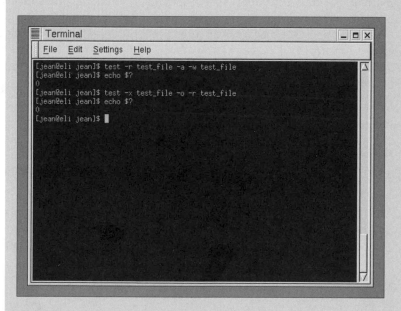

**Figure 7-13:** Testing with OR operator

The test command returns an exit status of 0 indicating that test_file is either executable OR readable.

**5**    Type **test ! –r test_file** and press **Enter**.

This command negates the result of the expression –r test_file. If the expression is true, the test command returns false. Likewise, if the expression is false, the test command returns true.

**6**    Type **echo $?** and press **Enter**. Your screen looks similar to Figure 7-14.

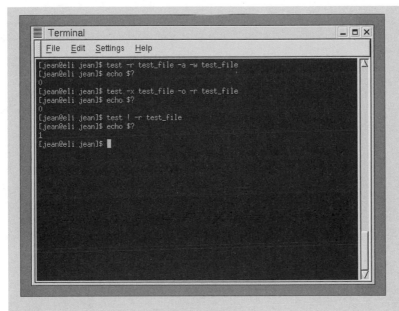

```
[jean@eli jean]$ test -r test_file -a -w test_file
[jean@eli jean]$ echo $?
0
[jean@eli jean]$ test -x test_file -o -r test_file
[jean@eli jean]$ echo $?
0
[jean@eli jean]$ test ! -r test_file
[jean@eli jean]$ echo $?
1
[jean@eli jean]$ ▮
```

**Figure 7-14:** Testing with negation operator

The test command returns an exit status of 1 indicating the expression ! –r test_file is false.

You next use the test command to determine if a directory exists. This lets you set up your environment properly to run the shell scripts you complete in Lesson B. In the following exercise you determine if you have a source directory in your home directory. If not, you create one and add it to the PATH variable. This enables you to run script files stored there without having to type **.** **/** before their names.

### To determine if a directory exists:

**1** Type **test –d source ; echo $?** and press **Enter**. This command determines if source exists and if it is a directory. Because the echo $? command is included on the same line, the exit status appears immediately after you press Enter.

If the exit status is 0, you already have a source directory. If this is so, skip to Step 3. Otherwise, continue to Step 2.

**2** If the command you entered in Step 1 results in exit status 1, you must create the /source directory. Type **mkdir source** and press **Enter**.

**3** In Chapter 6 you created the file corp_phones and the shell scripts phmenu and phoneadd. Determine if you have the corp_phones file by typing **test –e corp_phones ; echo $?** and pressing **Enter**. If you see the exit status 0, the file exists.

**4** Repeat the test command for the phmenu, phoneadd and phlist1 files. After you confirm that these files exist, copy them to the source directory.

**help**

> If you do not have the files from Chapter 6, see your instructor or technical support person for assistance.

**5** If you permanently add the /home/user-name/source (where user-name is your login name) directory to your PATH variable, it takes effect each time you log on. You should do this in your .bash_profile file. Load the file into the vi editor. Your screen looks similar to Figure 7-15.

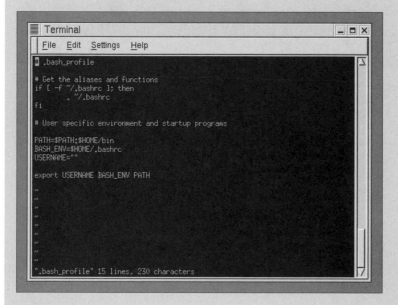

Figure 7-15: .bash_profile file

**6** Move the cursor to the line that reads:

`PATH=$PATH:$HOME/bin`

**7** Type **i** to switch to insert mode. Type **:$HOME/source** (include the colon) at the end of the line.

**8** Press **Esc,** then type **:wq** and press **Enter** to save the file and exit the editor.

**9** To make the new PATH value take effect, you must log off and then log back on. Do so now.

You created the source directory and added it to your PATH variable. You can store your script files there and execute them just by typing their names at the command line. In the next exercise, you validate the existence of the corp_phones file.

**To validate the existence of a file:**

1 Make sure you are in your source directory by typing $ **cd ~/source** and then pressing the **Enter** key.
2 Type **test –e corp_phones** and then press **Enter**.
3 Type **echo $?** and then press **Enter**. Your screen should show a "0," which indicates a true status.

To see a demonstration of a false status, repeat the test for the file phone_corp, which does not exist.

Next you practice using the test command in a script file. Once again, recall the os_choice script you wrote in Chapter 6:

```
echo -n "What is your favorite operating system? "
read OS_NAME
if [ "$OS_NAME" = "UNIX" ]
then
     echo "You will like Linux."
else
     echo "You should give Linux a try!"
fi
```

In the following exercise, you will modify the if statement so it uses the test command. When done, the program runs identically as it did before.

**To modify the if statement to use the test command:**

1 Make sure you are in your home directory. Load the os_choice file into vi or Emacs.
2 Change the line that reads:

```
if [ "$OS_NAME" = "UNIX" ]
```

So it reads:

```
if test $OS_NAME = "UNIX"
```

3 Save the file and exit the editor.
4 Test the script by executing it. Figure 7-16 shows sample output of the program.

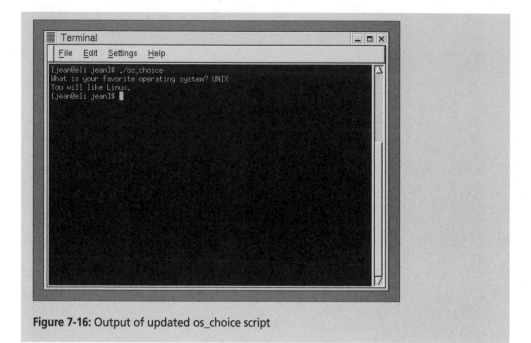

**Figure 7-16:** Output of updated os_choice script

In the next exercise, you modify a while loop so it uses the test command.

**To modify a while loop to use the test command:**

**1** Recall the script named colors, which you wrote in Chapter 6. It repeatedly asks the user to guess its favorite color, until the user guesses the color red.

```
echo -n "Try to guess my favorite color "
read guess
while [ "$guess" != "red" ]; do
    echo "No, not that one. Try again. "; read guess
done
```

**2** Load the file into vi or Emacs.

**3** Change the line that reads:

```
while [ "$guess" != "red" ]; do
```

So it reads:

```
while test $guess != "red" ; do
```

**4** Save the file and exit the editor.

**5**   Test the script. Figure 7-17 shows sample output of the program.

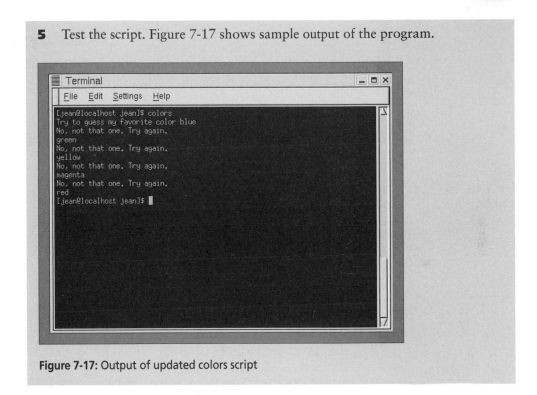

**Figure 7-17:** Output of updated colors script

So far, you used the test command from both the command line and from within script files. You also configured your home directory structure and your PATH variable so you can run your script files directly from the source directory. Your next step is to begin enhancing the corp_phones program by formatting record output.

## Formatting Record Output

To format record output, use the translate utility. The **translate utility (tr),** as you will recall from Chapter 5, changes the standard input (characters you type at the keyboard) character by character. The standard input can also be redirected with the < operator to come from a file rather than the keyboard. For example, the following command sends the contents of the counters file as input to the tr command. It converts lowercase characters to uppercase.

```
tr [a-z] [A-Z] < counters
```

By using the | operator, this command also works as a filter in cases where the input comes from the output of another UNIX command. For example, the following command sends the output of the cat command to tr:

```
cat names | tr -s ":" " "
```

This sample command sends the contents of the names file to tr. The tr utility replaces each occurrence of the : character with a space. The tr utility works like the sed command, except that sed changes the standard input string by string, not character by character.

You now use the tr utility to change lowercase characters to uppercase, as well as replace colon characters with spaces.

### To format using the grep and tr commands:

**1**  Use the grep command to retrieve a record from the corp_phones file that matches the phone number 219-555-4501, and then pipe the output to tr to replace the colon characters in the record with space characters. Type the following command and then press **Enter**:

```
$ grep 219-555-4501 corp_phones | tr ':' ' '
```

Your screen looks similar to Figure 7-18.

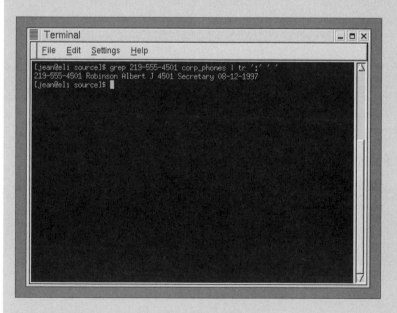

**Figure 7-18:** Output of grep and tr commands

**2** Change lowercase characters to uppercase in the corp_phones file by entering the following command and then pressing **Enter:**

```
$ cat corp_phones | tr '[a-z]' '[A-Z]'
```

Your screen looks similar to Figure 7-19.

**Figure 7-19:** Output of cat and tr commands

To search for phone numbers in the corp_phones file, your program can use techniques similar to those you executed in the steps above.

**To add record-searching capability to your program:**

**1** The phmenu program is already equipped to call the script phonefind when the user selects S from the menu. This command instructs the program to search for a phone number. Use the vi or Emacs editor to create the phonefind program. Type the code shown:

```
#!/bin/bash
#===========================================================
# Script Name: phonefind
# By:          TEG
# Date         November 2000
# Purpose:     Searches for a specified record in the
#              corp_phones file
#===========================================================
phonefile=~/corp_phones
clear
cursor 5 1
echo "Enter phone number to search for: "
cursor 5 35
read number
echo
grep $number corp_phones | tr ':' ' '
echo
echo "Press ENTER to continue..."
read continue
```

**2**  Save the file and exit the editor.

**3**  Use the **chmod** command to make the file executable, and then test the script by searching for the number 219-555-7175. Your screen should look similar to Figure 7-20.

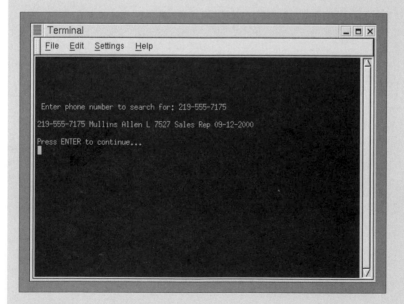

**Figure 7-20:** Output of phonefind script

You formatted the record output of the program; your next task is to delete phone records.

## Deleting Phone Records

In this section you review the sed command. Recall from Chapter 5 that sed takes the contents of an input file and applies actions, provided as options and arguments, to the file's contents. The results are sent to the standard output device. A simple way to delete a phone record using sed is with the d (delete) option. Here is a pseudocode representation of the necessary steps:

```
Enter phone number
Use sed -d to delete the matching phone number and output
to a temporary file, f
Confirm acceptance
If the output is accepted, copy the temporary file f back
to corp_phones (overlaying it)
```

Now you revise the phmenu script to include the delete option.

**To delete phone records by editing the phmenu program:**

**1** Make sure you are in the source directory. Using the vi or Emacs editor, retrieve the revised phmenu program and add the code shown in boldface.

```
#!/bin/bash
# ================================================================
# Script Name: phmenu
# By:              JQD
# Date:          November 1999
# Purpose:       A menu for the Corporate Phone List
# Command Line: phmenu
# ================================================================
phonefile=~/source/corp_phones
loop="y"
while test $loop = "y"
do
clear
cursor 3  12; echo "Corporate Phone Reporting Menu"
cursor 4  12; echo "==============================="
cursor 6   9; echo "V - View Phone List"
cursor 7   9; echo "P - Print Phone List"
cursor 8   9; echo "A - Add Phone to List"
cursor 9   9; echo "S - Search for Phone"
cursor 10  9; echo "D - Delete Phone"
cursor 12  9; echo "Q - Quit"
```

```
cursor 12 32;
read choice || continue
    case $choice in
      [Aa])    phoneadd ;;
      [Pp]) phlist1 ;;
      [Ss]) phonefind ;;
      [Vv]) clear ; less $phonefile ;;
       [Dd])    cursor 16 4; echo "Delete Phone Record"
                cursor 17 4; echo "Phone:"
                cursor 17 7; read number
                cursor 18 4; echo "Accept? (y)es or (n)o"
                cursor 18 26; read Accept
                if test $Accept = "y"
                  then
                    sed /$number/d$phonefile > f
                    cp f $phonefile
                fi
                ;;
      [Qq]) clear; exit ;;
      *) cursor 14 4; echo "Invalid Code"; read prompt ;;
    esac
done
```

**2**  Save the file and exit the editor. Later, when you test the program, the menu
will appear similar to Figure 7-21.

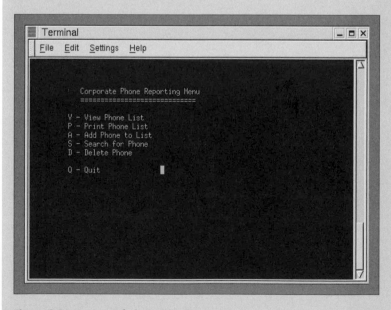

**Figure 7-21:** Output of phmenu script

**3** Use the more command to display the contents of the file before you delete a record. Your screen should be similar to Figure 7-22.

**Figure 7-22:** Contents of corp_phones file

**4** Run the phmenu program and test the delete option by removing phone number 219-555-4567. Figure 7-23 shows the Delete Phone Record screen.

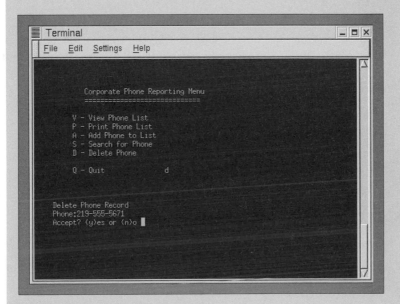

**Figure 7-23:** Delete Phone Record screen

**5**  Type **y** to confirm the deletion.

**6**  On the Main menu, select option **V** to view the phone file. Your screen looks similar to Figure 7-24.

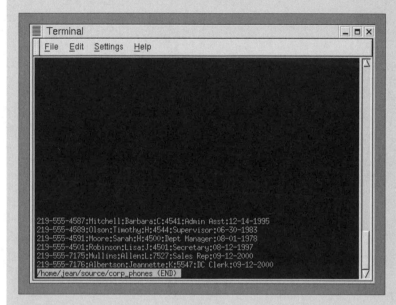

```
219-555-4587:Mitchell:Barbara:C:4541:Admin Asst:12-14-1995
219-555-4589:Olson:Timothy:H:4544:Supervisor:06-30-1983
219-555-4591:Moore:Sarah:H:4500:Dept Manager:08-01-1978
219-555-4501:Robinson:Lisa:J:4501:Secretary:08-12-1997
219-555-7175:Mullins:Allen:L:7527:Sales Rep:09-12-2000
219-555-7176:Albertson:Jeannette:K:5547:DC Clerk:09-12-2000
/home/jean/source/corp_phones (END)
```

**Figure 7-24:** View Phone List option

Notice the record for phone number 219-555-4567 is no longer in the file.

In this section you began to revise the shell phone program to meet Dominion Consulting's needs. You added code for the delete option to the phmenu script. In the next section you add code that prevents duplicate phone numbers from being entered in the file.

# SUMMARY

■  The two most popular and proven analysis tools are the program flowchart and pseudocode. The flowchart is a logic diagram drawn using a set of standard symbols that explain the flow and the action to be taken by the program.

■  Pseudocode is a model of a program. It is written in statements similar to actual code.

■  You can use the first line in a script file to tell the operating system which shell to use when interpreting the script.

- You can use the test command to validate the existence of directories and files as well as compare numeric and string values. You can place it inside your shell script or execute it directly from the command line.

- The translate utility (tr) changes the characters typed at the keyboard, character by character, and also works as a filter when the input comes from the output of another UNIX command. Standard input can also be redirected to come from a file rather than the keyboard.

- The sed command reads a file as its input and outputs the file's modified contents. You specify options and pass arguments to sed to control how the file's contents are modified.

# REVIEW QUESTIONS

1. Pseudocode is written to _____.
   a. guide the programmer in writing the program
   b. help eliminate the chance of omitting necessary instructions in the program
   c. match, verbally, the symbolic representation in the flowchart
   d. All of the above

2. To tell the system to use the Bash shell to interpret a script, use this code as the first line of the script file _____.
   a. !/bin/bash
   b. #/bin/bash
   c. #!/bin/bash
   d. #$/bin/bash

3. The test command compares two numeric values using the _____ option operator.
   a. =
   b. string
   c. ==
   d. -eq

4. The test command compares two string values using the _____ option operator.
   a. =
   b. string
   c. ==
   d. -eq

5. The test command's –a option is the _____ operator.
   a. logical AND
   b. absolute value
   c. test for hidden files
   d. logical negation

6. The test command's –o option is the _____ operator.
   a. logical AND
   b. logical OR
   c. overwrite
   d. logical negation

7. The tr command _____.
   a. translates only what is typed at the keyboard
   b. translates on a line basis like sed
   c. translates on a character-by-character basis
   d. translates characters originating from within files only

8. The tr command to change phone records to contain all lowercase characters is
   _____.
   a. tr upper lower corp_phones
   b. tr [a-z] [A-Z] corp_phones
   c. cat corp_phones | tr [a-z] [A-Z]
   d. tr [A-Z] [a-z] < corp_phones

9. The test command returns a value of _____ to indicate TRUE and
   _____ to indicate FALSE.
   a. 0, 1
   b. 1, 0
   c. blank err
   d. OK, !OK

10. The test command's return value appears when you type _____ at the
    command line.
    a. echo $$
    b. echo $?
    c. echo $-
    d. echo $.

 # EXERCISES

1. Use the tr command to translate the phone records file to contain a hyphen as the field
   separator instead of a colon (:). (Be sure to save the translated records to a different
   file.)

2. Set an environment variable, RHL, to the value "Red Hat Linux," and use the test and
   echo $? commands to determine if it matches "Red Hat Linux" and "RED HAT
   LINUX." How can you tell which one matches?

3. Set an environment variable called NUMVAL to 2000, and use the test and echo $?
   commands to determine if it matches the value 2000. What about 2020? How can you
   tell which one matches?

4. Write a flowchart for a program that tests your ability to perform simple arithmetic. The program should display two numbers that are to be added and ask the user to enter the sum. If the correct answer is given, the program should congratulate the user. If an incorrect answer is given, the program should show the user the correct answer.

5. Write pseudocode for the flowchart program you created in Exercise 4.

6. Write the actual code for the math-testing program you flowcharted in Exercise 4 and developed pseudocode for in Exercise 5. Figure 7-25 shows an example of the program's screen output.

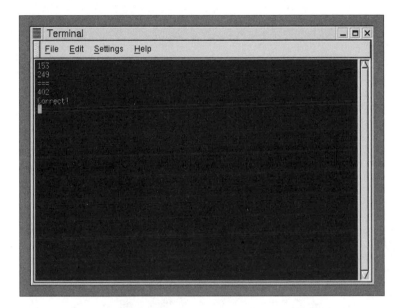

**Figure 7-25:** Math-testing program

7. Use vi or Emacs to create the file My_old_cars. The file should contain these records:

   1948:Ford:sedan
   1952:Chevrolet:coupe
   1960:Ford:Mustang
   1972:Chevrolet:Corvette
   1977:Plymouth:Roadrunner

   Next, write a shell script that displays a data entry screen. The script should allow additional records to be entered into the file.

8. Write a shell script that displays all records in the My_old_cars file. The colons should be converted to spaces before the output appears.

# DISCOVERY EXERCISES

1. Sort the corp_phones file by last name, and pipe the output to a tr command to convert all characters to uppercase and store output in a new file, Phoneupper.

2. Create a directory called Scripts in your source directory, and use the test command to validate that the directory exists.

3. Use your choice of the sed or tr command to convert all occurrences of the word "Accountant" in the corp_phones file to the word "Bookkeeper."

4. User Authentication Program: UNIX keeps users' login name stored in an environment variable named USER. Design a flowchart for a program that asks users who they are. Their response should be compared against the contents of the USER variable. If the two strings do not match, users should be asked again. This process should repeat until the correct user name is entered.

5. User Authentication Program: Write the pseudocode for the flowchart you designed in Discovery Exercise 4.

6. User Authentication Program: Write the actual code for the program you flowcharted in Discovery Exercise 4 and wrote pseudocode for in Discovery Exercise 5. Figure 7-26 shows a sample of the program's output.

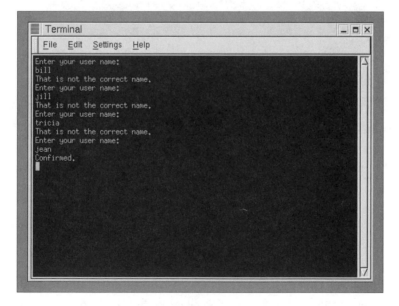

**Figure 7-26:** Output of User Authentication Program

**In this lesson you will:**

- Create a program algorithm to solve a problem
- Learn to create a quick screen-clearing technique
- Develop and test a program to re-enter fields during data entry
- Develop and test a program to eliminate duplicate records
- Develop and test a program to delete records from the file
- Create shell functions
- Load shell functions automatically from the command line when you log on

# Completing the Case Project

## Clearing the Screen

Before you begin to complete the programming tasks, you decide you want to clear screens more quickly. The **clear** command is a useful housekeeping utility for clearing the screen before new screens appear (which happens frequently in shell scripts), but you can use a faster method. You can store the output of the clear command in a shell variable. Recall from Chapter 6 that you can store the output of a command in a variable by enclosing the command in single back quotes. For example, this command stores the output of the date command in the variable TODAY:

```
TODAY='date'
```

The output of the clear command is a sequence of values that erases the contents of the screen. Storing these values in a variable and then echoing the contents of the variable on the screen accomplishes the same thing, but about ten times faster. This is because the system does not have to locate and execute the clear command, as it does when executing the clear command.

---

**To clear screens by setting a shell variable:**

**1** Set a shell variable, CLEAR, to the output of the clear command, by typing:

```
CLEAR='clear'
export CLEAR
```

**2** Use your new variable in your shell programs for a fast clear operation:

```
echo "$CLEAR"
```

**3** To make this fast clear always available, place these two lines of code at the end of your .bashrc file (or the equivalent login initialization file for your shell):

```
CLEAR='clear'
 export CLEAR
```

**4** Save the file, exit, and then log on again to activate the login script.

You are now ready to complete your first task: correcting entries. To do this, you need to manipulate the cursor.

## Moving the Cursor

The first task is to let the user return to a previously entered field and to correct data in that field before continuing. Recall that in Chapter 6 you created a script named cursor. The script accepts two arguments: the row and column number of a screen position. The cursor script then positions the cursor at the specified position using the tput command.

You want to allow users to return the cursor to a previous field on the screen when adding records to the corp_phones file. You decide that the minus character (-) will signal this. If the user enters a minus and presses the Enter key, the cursor is repositioned at the start of the previous field as shown on the screen. You will make this change by editing the phoneadd program (which provides the user with data-entry screens) that you already created. Your first step in editing the program is to create a program algorithm.

## Creating Program Algorithms

An **algorithm** is a sequence of commands or instructions that produces a desired result. The algorithm to solve a specific problem is frequently developed by following the logic shown in a flowchart and the expressed conditions necessary to carry out the logic described in the pseudocode.

Here is the pseudocode for repositioning the cursor at the previous field when the user enters the minus sign (-):

```
Read information into field2.
While field2 equals "-"
     Move cursor to position of previous field, field1.
     Clear current information displayed in field1.
     Read new information into field1.
     If field1 = "q"
     then
          Exit program.
```

```
        End if.
        Move cursor to position of field2.
        Read information into field2.
End While.
```

One code addition to the phoneadd program uses the algorithm for re-entering fields:

```
cursor 5 18; read lname
    while test "$lname" = "-"
        do    cursor 4 18; echo "                        "
              cursor 4 18; read phonenum
              cursor 5 18; read lname
        done
```

This code reads the last name into the variable lname. If lname contains a minus sign (-), the cursor moves to the previous field, which contains the phone number. The value displayed for the phone number is cleared from the screen, and a new value is entered into phonenum. The cursor is then moved back to the last name field, and the last name is entered. The while statement repeats this process as long as the user types a minus sign for the last name.

Note: Using the if statement instead of the while statement allows only one return to the prior field. Instead, you need a loop so the process repeats as long as the user enters a minus sign for the field.

Look at the while statement shown above:

```
while test "$lname" = "-"
```

The argument "$lname" is enclosed in quotation marks to prevent the command from producing an error, in the event the user types more than one word for the last name. For example, if the user enters Smith Williams for the last name, the statement above will be interpreted as:

```
while test "Smith Williams" = "-"
```

However, if the statement were written without the quotation marks around $lname, the statement would be interpreted as:

```
while test Smith Williams = "-"
```

This statement causes an error message, because it passes too many arguments to the test command.

You are now ready to edit the phoneadd program. You add the field re-entering algorithm to each part of the program that reads a value into a field.

**To allow re-entry of data:**

**1**    Make sure you are in the source directory. Load the Phoneadd program into the vi or Emacs editor.

**2** Add the boldfaced code shown below to the program. Notice that the revised code also includes your new, faster, screen clear feature. It also changes the existing if statements, so they use the test command.

```
#!/bin/bash
# ==============================================================
# Script Name: phoneadd
# By:          JQD
# Date:        March 1999
# Purpose:     A shell script that sets up a loop to add
#              new employees to the phonelist file.
#              The code also prevents duplicate phone
#              numbers
#              from being assigned.
# Command Line:       phoneadd
# ==============================================================
trap "rm ~/tmp/* 2> /dev/null; exit" 0 1 2 3
phonefile=~/source corp_phones
looptest="y"
while test "$looptest" = "y"
do
    clear
    cursor 1 4 ; echo "Corporate Phone List Additions"
    cursor 2 4 ; echo "=============================="
    cursor 4 4 ; echo "Phone Number: "
    cursor 5 4 ; echo "Last Name    : "
    cursor 6 4 ; echo "First Name   : "
    cursor 7 4 ; echo "Middle Init : "
    cursor 8 4 ; echo "Dept #       : "
    cursor 9 4 ; echo "Job Title    : "
    cursor 10 4; echo "Date Hired  : "
    cursor 12 4; echo "Add another? (y)es or (q)uit "
    cursor 4 18; read phonenum
    if  test $phonenum = "q"
    then
         clear ; exit
    fi
    cursor 5 18 ; read lname
    while test "$lname" = "-"
    do
         cursor 4 18 ; echo "               "
            cursor 4 18 ; read phonenumber
         if test "$phonenum" = "q"
         then
              clear ; exit
         fi
         cursor 5 18 ; read lname
    done
```

```
cursor 6 18 ; read fname
while test "$fname" = "-"
do
     cursor 5 18 ; echo "                    "
        cursor 5 18 ; read lname
     if test "$lname" = "q"
     then
           clear ; exit
     fi
     cursor 6 18 ; read fname
done
cursor 7 18 ; read midinit
while test "$midinit" = "-"
do
     cursor 6 18 ; echo "                 "
        cursor 6 18 ; read fname
     if test "$fname" = "q"
     then
           clear ; exit
     fi
     cursor 7 18 ; read midinit
done
cursor 8 18 ; read deptno
while test "$deptno" = "-"
do
     cursor 7 18 ; echo "                "
        cursor 7 18 ; read midinit
     if test "$midinit" = "q"
     then
           clear ; exit
     fi
     cursor 8 18 ; read deptno
done
cursor 9 18 ; read jobtitle
while test "$jobtitle" = "-"
do
     cursor 8 18 ; echo "                  "
        cursor 8 18 ; read deptno
     if test "$deptno" = "q"
     then
           clear ; exit
     fi
     cursor 9 18 ; read jobtitle
done
cursor 10 18; read datehired
while test "$datehired" = "-"
```

```
        do
             cursor 9 18 ; echo "              "
             cursor 9 18 ; read jobtitle
             if test "$jobtitle" = "q"
             then
                  clear ; exit
             fi
             cursor 10 18 ; read datehired
        done
        #Check to see if last name is not blank before you
        #write to disk
        if  test "$lname" != ""
        then
             echo "$phonenum:$lname:$fname:$midinit:$deptno:
$jobtitle:$datehired" >> $phonefile
        fi
        cursor 12 33 ; read looptest
        if  test "$looptest" = "q"
        then
             clear ; exit
        fi
done
```

**3**  Save the file and exit the editor.

**4**  Execute the phoneadd script. For the phone number, enter **219-555-4523** and press **Enter**. Your screen appears similar to Figure 7-27.

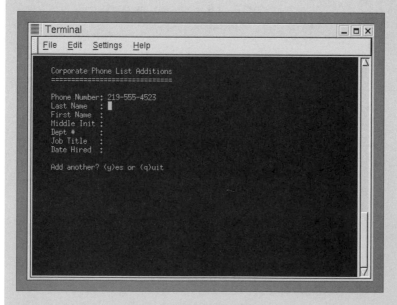

**Figure 7-27:** phoneadd screen

**5** In the Last Name field, type the **minus sign character** (-) and press **Enter**. Your cursor moves back the Phone Number field. Your screen looks like Figure 7-28.

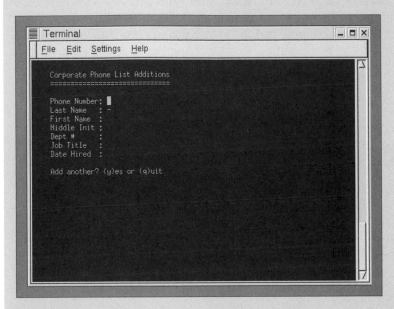

```
Terminal                                              _ □ ✕
  File   Edit   Settings   Help

   Corporate Phone List Additions
   =================================

   Phone Number: █
   Last Name   : -
   First Name  :
   Middle Init :
   Dept #      :
   Job Title   :
   Date Hired  :

   Add another? (y)es or (q)uit
```

**Figure 7-28:** Phoneadd screen ready for data re-entry

**6** Re-enter the phone number as **219-555-4511**, and press **Enter**.

**7** Complete the remaining fields with the information shown below. As the cursor moves to each field, test the program by typing the **minus sign** and pressing **Enter**. The cursor should move to the previous field each time.

**Last name: Brooks**
**First name: Sally**
**Middle initial: H**
**Department Number: 4540**
**Job Title: Programmer**
**Date Hired: 11-23-1999**

**8** After you enter all the information, quit the program. Use the cat command to display the contents of the corp_phones file. The new record should appear.

You completed the first task. You are now ready to work on the second task: protecting against duplicate phone numbers.

# Protecting Against Entering Duplicate Phone Numbers

Because users do not always enter valid data, a program should always check its input to ensure the user has entered acceptable information. This is known as **input validation**. Your next task is to create an input validation algorithm that prevents the user from adding a phone number that has already been assigned. The pseudocode and flowchart to accomplish this are shown in Figure 7-29.

**Pseudocode:**

```
If phone number is already on file
    then
        display message on the screen "This number has already been assigned to:"
        display the person's record who has the duplicate number.
        Clear the screen and prepare for another entry
End if
```

**Flowchart:**

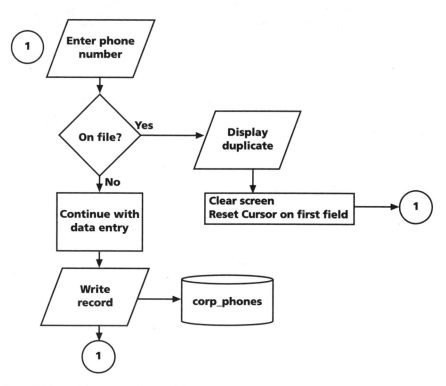

**Figure 7-29:** Revision #2 to phoneadd program script

In the following steps, you will add input validation code to the phoneadd script.

## To prevent phone number duplications:

1  Make sure you are in the source directory. Load the phoneadd script into vi or Emacs.

2  Add the boldfaced section of code to complete the revised script.

```
#!/bin/bash
#==========================================================
# Script Name: phoneadd
# By:          JQD
# Date:        March 1999
# Purpose:     A shell script that sets up a loop to add
#              new employees to the phonelist file.
#              The code also prevents duplicate phone
#              numbers
#              from being assigned.
# Command Line:     phoneadd
# ==========================================================
trap "rm ~/tmp/* 2> /dev/null; exit" 0 1 2 3
phonefile=~/corp_phones
looptest=y
while test "$looptest" = "y"
do
     clear
     cursor 1 4 ; echo "Corporate Phone List Additions"
     cursor 2 4 ; echo "==============================="
     cursor 4 4 ; echo "Phone Number: "
     cursor 5 4 ; echo "Last Name    : "
     cursor 6 4 ; echo "First Name   : "
     cursor 7 4 ; echo "Middle Init  : "
     cursor 8 4 ; echo "Dept #       : "
     cursor 9 4 ; echo "Job Title    : "
     cursor 10 4; echo "Date Hired   : "
     cursor 12 4; echo "Add another? (y)es or (q)uit "
     cursor 4 18; read phonenum
     if  test $phonenum = "q"
     then
             clear ; exit
     fi
```

```
        # Check to see if the phone number already exists
        while grep "$phonenum" $phonefile > ~/tmp/temp
        do
cursor 19 1 ; echo "This number has already been assigned to:"
        cursor 20 1 ; tr ':' ' ' < ~/tmp/temp
        cursor 21 1 ; echo "Press ENTER to continue... "
        read prompt
        cursor 4 18 ; echo "                    "
        cursor 4 18 ; read phonenum
    done
    cursor 5 18 ; read lname
    ... The remainder of the program is unchanged
```

**3** Save the file and exit the editor.

**4** If you have not already created a tmp directory under your home directory, do so now.

**5** Run the program. Test it by entering a phone number that already exists in the file, such as **219-555-4587**. Your screen should look like Figure 7-30.

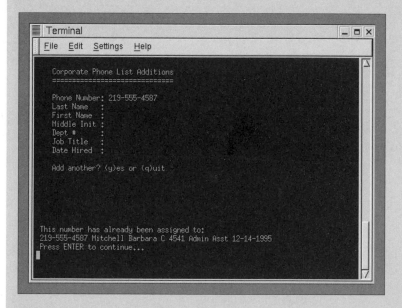

**Figure 7-30:** Revised phoneadd program

**6** Complete the data entry screen by entering a valid phone number.

Looking at the phoneadd program, you realize that it contains code that you may want to reuse for other programs. To do this, you use shell functions.

## Using Shell Functions

A **shell function** is a group of commands that is stored in memory and assigned a name. Shell scripts can use the function name to execute the commands. You can use shell functions to isolate reusable code sections, so that you do not have to duplicate algorithms throughout your program. For example, the phlist1 script can use several functions to sort the phone list in a variety of ways.

A function name differs from a variable name, because a function name is followed by a set of parentheses, and the commands that comprise the function are enclosed in curly braces. For example, look at the code for a function:

```
datenow()
{
date
}
```

The name of the function is "datenow." It has only one command inside its braces: the date command. When the datenow function is executed, it calls the date command.

Functions are usually stored in script files and loaded into memory when you log on. However, you can also enter them at the command line.

**To declare the simple datenow function:**

**1**  At the command line, type **datenow()** and press **Enter**. Notice the prompt changes to the > symbol. This indicates the shell is waiting for you to type more information to complete the command you started.

**2**  At the > prompt, type **{** and press **Enter**.

**3**  At the > prompt, type **date** and press **Enter**.

**4**  At the > prompt type **}** and press **Enter**. The normal prompt returns.

**5**  You created the datenow function and stored it in the shell's memory. Invoke it by typing **datenow** and pressing **Enter**. Your screen looks similar to Figure 7-31.

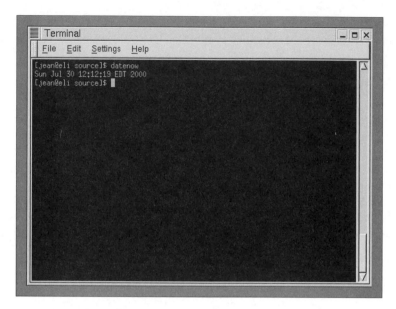

**Figure 7-31:** Output of datenow function

Arguments are passed to functions in the same manner as any other shell procedure. The function accesses the arguments using the positional variables $1 . . . $9. Simply type the arguments following the command name, placing a space between each argument. Now you redefine the datenow function so it accepts an argument.

**To redefine the datenow function to accept an argument:**

1   At the command line, type **datenow()** and press **Enter**. The commands you are about to type replace those currently stored in the datenow function.

2   At the > prompt, type **{** and press **Enter**.

3   At the > prompt, type **echo "$1"** and press **Enter**. When the function runs, this command displays the information passed to the function in the first argument.

4   At the > prompt, type **date** and press **Enter**.

5   At the > prompt type **}** and press **Enter**. The normal prompt returns.

6   Test the function by typing **datenow "Today is"** and pressing **Enter**. Your screen looks similar to Figure 7-32.

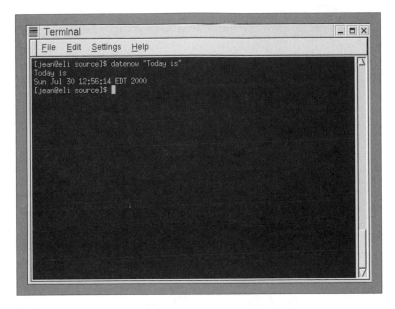

**Figure 7-32:** Results of revised datenow function

The exercises you just completed demonstrate how functions work in general. Typing functions at the command line is hardly productive, however, because they must be re-entered each time you log on. You will now learn how to use shell functions to reuse code and to make functions available each time you log in.

## Reusing Code

To improve your programming productivity, you should learn to reuse your code. This means that the functions and programs you develop should be shared with other programs and functions as much as possible, thereby helping to prevent duplications, save time, and reduce errors. A good illustration of this potential use of reusable functions can be demonstrated in the current phoneadd program. You can create several different sort functions and store them in memory. The phlist1 script can then call these functions to display the list of phone numbers, sorted in a variety of ways.

You can place multiple functions inside a shell script such as .myfuncs and execute them from your .bash_profile login script or simply run .myfuncs from the command line. This loads all your functions into memory just as you load environment variables.

**To place several functions inside a shell script:**

**1** Use the vi or Emacs editor to create the .myfuncs file inside your source directory.

**2** Enter the code for the following functions:

```
sort_name()
 {
  sort +1 -t: corp_phones
 }
 sort_date()
 {
  sort +6 -t: corp_phones
 }
 sort_dept()
 {
  sort +4 -t: corp_phones
 }
```

**3** Save the file and exit the editor.

Your next task is to load the .myfuncs file into memory so its functions may be executed. To do this, type a period (.) followed by a space, followed by the name of the file containing the functions.

**To load the .myfuncs file:**

**1** At the command line, type **. .myfuncs** and press **Enter**. Nothing appears, but the functions are loaded into memory.

**2** Test some functions. Type **sort_name** and press **Enter**. You see the phone records sorted by individuals' names.

**3** Type **sort_dept** and press **Enter**. You see the phone records sorted by department number.

You can load functions automatically by your .bash_profile or .bashrc files when you log on. This way, they are always available to any shell script that needs them.

**To modify your .bashrc file to load the .myfuncs script:**

**1** Load your .bashrc file into the vi or Emacs editor.

**2** At the end of the file, add the following command:

```
. ~/source/.myfuncs
```

3   Save the file and exit the editor.

4   Log out and log back on to load the functions.

5   Test the sort_name, sort_dept, and other functions.

Your last task is to display the phone listing in sorted order by employees' last names. You can do this by using your sort_name function, as stored in the .myfuncs file.

## Sorting the Phone List

To sort the phone list, make a minor revision to phlist1 to load the functions and then call sort_name to redirect the sorted output to a temporary file. The sorted temporary file serves as input to the Awk program that displays the records. The revised code will use the CLEAR variable also.

**To sort the phone listing:**

**1**   Make sure you are in the source directory. Use the vi or Emacs editor to add the code to the phlist1 script. The additions and revisions are in boldface.

```
#!/bin/bash
#==========================================================
# Script Name: phlist1
# By:      JQD
# Date:    March 1999
# Purpose:Use awk to format a colon-separated set of fields
#         in a flat file and display to the screen
# Command line:    bash phlist  <enter>
# ==========================================================
echo "$CLEAR"
cursor 2 20; echo "Corporate Phone List"
cursor 3 20; echo "===================="
cursor 5 0;
sort_name > sorted_phones
awk -F: ' { printf "%-12s %-12s %s\t%s%s%10.10s  %s\n",
        $2, $3, $4, $1, $5, $6, $7 } ' sorted_phones

cursor 23 1; echo "Review"
cursor 23 8; read prompt
```

**2**   This code assumes you have modified your .bashrc file so it loads the functions in .myfuncs when you log on. Save the file and exit the editor.

**3**   Test the file by typing **phlist1** and pressing **Enter**. Your screen looks similar to Figure 7-33. Press **Enter** when you finish observing the screen.

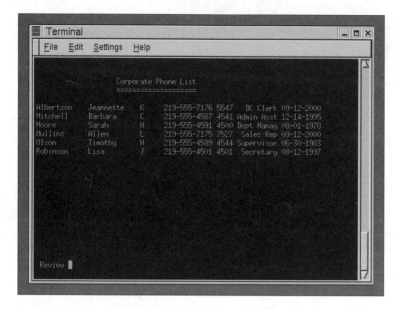

**Figure 7-33:** Output of revised phlist1 script

Adding code to call the other sort functions will be an exercise at the end of this chapter.

In this chapter you have learned to plan algorithms and programs using flow-charts and pseudocode. You have also learned to create complex decision expressions with the test command. You have furthered your use of the grep, tr, and sed commands to format output. In addition, you have learned advanced programming techniques, such as repositioning the cursor at a previous field in a data entry screen, and creating shell functions.

 # S U M M A R Y

- To speed clearing the screen, assign the clear command sequence to the shell variable CLEAR that can be set inside your login script, .bashrc. This clears your screen faster because it does not require a look-up sequence in a file every time it executes.

- An algorithm is a sequence of instructions or commands that produce a desired result. Following the logic flow expressed in flowcharts and pseudocode develops algorithms.

- Shell functions can simplify the program code by isolating code that can be reused throughout that program as well as others.

# COMMAND SUMMARY

Options and arguments of test command

| Option | Meaning | Example Command |
|--------|---------|-----------------|
| -eq | equal to | test a –eq b |
| -gt | greater than | test a –gt b |
| -lt | less than | test a –lt b |
| -ge | greater than or equal to | test a –ge b |
| -le | less than or equal to | test a –le b |
| -ne | not equal to | test a –ne b |
| -z | Tests for a zero-length string | test –z string |
| -n | Tests for a non-zero string length | test –n string |
| string1 = string2 | Tests two strings for equality | test string1 = string2 |
| string1 != string2 | Tests two strings for inequality | test string1 != string2 |
| string | Tests for a non-zero string length | test string |
| -e | True if a file exists | test –e file |
| -r | True if a file exists and is readable | test –r file |
| -w | True if a file exists and is writeable | test –w file |
| -x | True if a file exists and is executable | test –x file |
| -d | True if a file exists and is a directory | test –d file |
| -f | Tests if a file exists and is a regular file | test –f file |
| -s | True if a file exists and has a size greater than zero | test –s file |
| -c | Tests if a file exists and is a character special file (which is a character-oriented device, such as a terminal or printer) | test –c file |
| -b | Tests if a file exists and is a block special file (which is a block-oriented device, such as a disk or tape drive) | test –b file |
| -a | Logical AND | test expression1 –a expression2 |
| -o | Logical OR | test expression1 –o expression2 |
| ! | Logical negation | test !expression |

# REVIEW QUESTIONS

1. An algorithm is _____.
   a. a name that replaces the standard UNIX command name
   b. an alternate name for a UNIX command
   c. always entered into the system-wide initialization file, /etc/profile
   d. a derived formula made up of a sequence of commands that produce a desired result

2. A shell function can be recognized because it has _____ after the function name.
   a. curly braces
   b. parentheses
   c. brackets
   d. quotation marks

3. A shell function's commands are enclosed inside _____.
   a. curly braces
   b. parentheses
   c. brackets
   d. quotation marks

4. Shell functions are useful because _____.
   a. you can reuse the code in other programs
   b. it cuts down on re-entry of duplicate code inside shell programs
   c. increases your productivity as a shell programmer
   d. all of the above

5. What is the proper sequence for developing an algorithm?
   a. flowchart—algorithm—pseudocode
   b. flowchart—pseudocode—algorithm.
   c. algorithm—flowchart—pseudocode
   d. there is no one correct sequence

6. How do you pass arguments to a shell function?
   a. Enclose them inside the parentheses that follow the function name.
   b. Use the positional variables, $1, $2, $3 .. $9.
   c. Use the $? shell variable.
   d. Use $# shell variable.

7. The output of a command can be stored in a shell variable by enclosing the command in _____.
   a. parentheses
   b. double quotation marks
   c. single quotation marks
   d. back quote marks

8. Writing code to test and determine if user input is correct is known as
_____.
   a. algorithm design
   b. data validation
   c. flowcharting
   d. pseudocode design

9. If .numeric_functions is a script file of shell functions, the _____
command is used to load it into memory.
   a. numeric_functions
   b. load numeric_functions
   c. .numeric_functions
   d. install numeric_functions

10. True or false: shell functions may be executed from the command line.

 # E X E R C I S E S

1. From the command line create the function dir to execute this: ls –lq | more.

2. From the command line create the function simple_date to execute this: date +%D.

3. Create the executable script file .mystuff to contain the two functions created in
Exercises 1 and 2, and to call each function from the command line.

4. In the Lesson A exercises, you created the file my_old_cars. Write a shell script that
allows the user to enter a search string and displays all records in the file that contain a
string matching the search string. For example, if the user enters "Ford," the script displays all records that contain the word "Ford."

5. Write a shell script that allows the user to enter a search string and deletes all records
in the my_old_cars file that contain a string matching the search string. For example, if
the user enters "1948," the script deletes all records containing "1948."

6. Create shell functions that sort the records in the file my_old_cars. Your functions
should sort the records by year model (the first field), by make (the second field), and
by car model (the third field). Write a menu program that calls each sort function.

7. Write a Main menu program for the my_old_cars file and all the script files you have
created so far. Here is a list of the script files you should have:

   ■ Data entry screen
   ■ Script that displays all records in the file
   ■ Script that searches for and displays records containing a string
   ■ Script that deletes specified records from the file
   ■ Script that displays the records sorted in various ways

# DISCOVERY

1. Remove the colon characters from the phoneadd program and reposition the cursor to improve the appearance of the data entry screen.

2. Place the screen display from the phoneadd program in a function, called phscreen. Using the vi editor, type the function into .mystuff (from Exercise 3) and test the function by calling it from the command line.

3. Add menu items to phmenu that call the sort_date and sort_dept functions you created in the .myfuncs file. Test the program.

4. Create a shell function, average. Store it in a file, avgfunc. The function should accept three arguments. Assume the arguments are numbers. The function should calculate and output the average of the three numbers.

5. Create a script file, minmax. In the file, create a shell script, min. It should accept two arguments, assumed to be numbers. The function is to output the lesser of the two arguments. For example, if 5 and 10 are passed to the function, it should output 5.

6. Edit the minmax file you created in Discovery Exercise 6. Add a shell function named max. It should accept two arguments, assumed to be numbers. The function is to output the greater of the two arguments. For example, if 8 and 4 are passed to the function, it should output 8.

# Exploring the UNIX Utilities

**case ▶** Your supervisor at Dominion Consulting asks you to accomplish several computer tasks, including creating a bootable floppy disk, making backups on floppy disks, auditing system performance, analyzing hard disk storage, and removing unnecessary files. Further, you have been asked to create a man page to describe the Phmenu program that you wrote in Chapter 7.

**In this lesson you will:**

- Define the classifications of the UNIX utility programs
- Duplicate a floppy disk
- Create a "bootable floppy" to boot the system in case of emergency
- Determine hard disk usage and available free space
- Locate and remove unnecessary files from the hard disk
- Display the CPU status and internal memory usage

# Using the UNIX Utilities

In this chapter, you continue to explore UNIX utilities. Utilities are designed to provide basic services to UNIX users, just like your local utility companies provide basic services (e.g., electricity and running water) to your community. This chapter lets you practice using UNIX commands and utilities, such as using the man command with UNIX's text formatting utilities. Before you can begin to carry out your assigned tasks for Dominion Consulting, you need to learn more about UNIX utilities.

## Understanding UNIX Utilities

UNIX utilities let you create and manage files, run programs, produce reports, and generally interact with the system. Beyond these basics, the utility programs offer a full range of services that let you monitor and maintain the system and recover from a wide range of errors. UNIX utilities are classified into seven major function areas dictated by user needs: file processing, networking, communications, system status, programming, source code management, and miscellaneous. UNIX utilities are programs, but they are usually referred to as commands.

Note: For the sake of completeness, this chapter contains some references and commentary about all the utilities, but it concentrates on those utilities that relate to file processing, system status, and miscellaneous tasks.

Utility programs are distinguished from other operating system programs in that they are "add-ons" and not part of the UNIX shells or a component of the kernel. Utilities are also unique because they are exclusively dedicated to improving computer performance for the benefit of users. New utility programs are continually being added as developers find better and faster ways to make UNIX run more efficiently. Finally, most UNIX utilities are small programs that often consist of only one command.

## Classifying UNIX Utility Programs

Utilities can be classified in several categories, as some work exclusively with UNIX files, others handle network tasks, and still others are designed to help programmers. File processing utilities, listed in Table 8-1, is the largest category. These utilities display and manipulate files.

| Utility | Brief Description of Function |
|---------|------------------------------|
| afio | Creates an archive or restores files from archive |
| awk | Processes files |
| cat | Displays or joins files |
| cmp | Compares two files |
| comm | Compares sorted files and shows differences |
| cp | Copies files |
| cpio | Copies and backs up files to an archive |
| cut | Selects characters or fields from input lines |
| dd | Copies and converts input records |
| diff | Compares two text files and shows differences |
| fdformat | Formats a floppy disk at a low level |
| find | Finds files within file tree |
| fmt | Formats text very simply |
| grep | Matches patterns in a file |
| groff | Processes embedded text formatting codes |
| gzip | Compresses or decompresses files |
| head | Displays the first part of a file |
| ispell | Checks one or more files for spelling errors |
| less | Displays text files (pauses when screen is full) |
| ln | Creates a link to a file |
| lpr | Prints file (hard copy) |
| ls | Lists file and directory names and attributes |
| man | Displays documentation for commands |

**Table 8-1:** File processing utilities

| Utility | Brief Description of Function |
|---------|------------------------------|
| mkdir | Creates a new directory |
| mkfs | Builds a UNIX file system |
| mv | Renames and moves files and directories |
| od | Dumps formatted file |
| paste | Concatenates files horizontally |
| pr | Formats text files for printing and displays them |
| rdev | Queries or sets the root image device |
| rm | Removes files |
| rmdir | Removes directory |
| sed | Edits streams (non-interactive) |
| sort | Sorts or merges files |
| tail | Displays the last lines of files |
| tar | Copies and backs up files to a tape archive |
| touch | Changes file modification dates |
| uniq | Displays unique lines of sorted file |
| wc | Counts lines, words, and bytes |

**Table 8-1:** File processing utilities (*continued*)

System status utilities, listed in Table 8-2, is the second largest category. It includes utilities that display and alter the status of files, disks, and the overall system. These utilities let you know who is online, the names and status of running processes, the amount of hard disk space available, and where to find other commands you need to run.

| Utility | Brief Description of Function |
|---------|------------------------------|
| chgrp | Changes the group associated with a file |
| chmod | Changes the access permissions of a file |
| chown | Changes the owner of a file |
| date | Sets and displays date and time |

**Table 8-2:** System status utilities

| Utility | Brief Description of Function |
| --- | --- |
| df | Displays the amount of free space remaining on disk |
| du | Summarizes file space usage |
| file | Determines file type (e.g., shell script, executable, ASCII text, and others) |
| finger | Displays detailed information about users who are logged on |
| free | Displays amount of free and used memory in the system |
| kill | Terminates a running process |
| ps | Displays process status by process identification number and name |
| sleep | Suspends execution for a specified time |
| top | Dynamically displays process status, like ps, but in real time |
| w | Displays detailed information about the users who are logged on |
| who | Displays brief information about the users who are logged on |

**Table 8-2:** System status utilities (*continued*)

Network utilities, listed in Table 8-3, consist of the essential commands for communicating and sharing information on a network.

| Utility | Brief Description of Function |
| --- | --- |
| ftp | Transfers files over a network |
| rcp | Remotely copies a file from network computer |
| rlogin | Logs on to a remote computer |
| rsh | Executes commands on a remote computer |
| rwho | Displays the names of users attached to a network |
| telnet | Connects to remote computer on a network |

**Table 8-3:** Network utilities

The communication utilities, listed in Table 8-4, handle the mail and messaging tasks. These programs include some recent advanced features such as **Multipurpose Internet Mail Extensions (MIME)** support for sending and receiving binary files in mail messages.

| Utility | Brief Description of Function |
| --- | --- |
| mail | Sends electronic mail messages |
| mesg | Denies (mesg n) or accepts (mesg y) messages |
| pine | Sends and receives electronic mail and news |
| talk | Lets users simultaneously type messages to each other |
| write | Sends a message to another user |

**Table 8-4:** Communications utilities

Programming utilities, listed in Table 8-5, are designed to help users develop software projects written in C and C++ programs.

| Utility | Brief Description of Function |
| --- | --- |
| configure | Configures program source code automatically |
| gcc | Compiles C and C++ programs |
| make | Maintains program source code |
| patch | Updates source code |

**Table 8-5:** Programming utilities

As UNIX, and particularly Linux, gains market share, and applications continue to expand, use of the source code management utilities, listed in Table 8-6, should increase. These utilities have a proven track record in managing teamwork programming and are vital tools for scheduling and managing large-scale applications.

| Utility | Brief Description of Function |
|---------|------------------------------|
| ci | Creates changes in Revision Control Systems (RCS) |
| co | Retrieves an unencoded revision of an RCS file |
| cvs | Manages concurrent access to files in a hierarchy |
| rcs | Creates or changes the attributes of an RCS file |
| rlog | Prints a summary of the history of an RCS file |

**Table 8-6:** Source code management utilities

Finally, miscellaneous utilities include unique programs that perform very specific and special functions. As you can see from the functions descriptions in Table 8-7, these commands include providing a system calendar, scheduling events, and identifying terminals attached to the system.

| Utility | Brief Description of Function |
|---------|------------------------------|
| at | Executes a shell script at a specified time |
| cal | Displays a calendar for a month or year |
| crontab | Schedules a command to run at a preset time |
| expr | Evaluates expressions (used for arithmetic and string manipulations) |
| fsck | Checks and fixes problems on a file system (repairs damages) |
| tee | Clones output stream to one or more files |
| tr | Replaces specified characters, like a translation filter |
| tty | Displays terminal path name, like the built-in command, pwd |
| xargs | Converts standard output of one command into arguments for another |

**Table 8-7:** Miscellaneous utilities

Now that you understand that many diverse utilities are available, you are ready to use several of them to complete your tasks for Dominion Consulting.

# Using the File Processing Utilities

Recall that the file processing utilities help you display and manipulate files. You use several of these utilities to complete your tasks. First, you use the dd command to copy a file and change the format of the destination file at the same time.

## Using the dd Command

Files not only store information, but they also store it in a particular format. For example, most computers store text using ASCII codes. (IBM mainframes, however, use EBCDIC codes to store text.) In addition to the internal codes that computers use to store information, some files store text in all uppercase letters. Likewise, other files store text in all lowercase letters. Some files include only records, where each record consists of several fields. A special character, such as a colon, separates the fields, and each record ends with a new-line character. Different files have different internal formats, which depend upon how the file is used.

Whereas the standard UNIX copy utility, cp, duplicates a file, it cannot alter the format of the destination copy. Therefore, when you need to copy a file and change the format of the destination copy, use the dd command instead. Possessing a rich set of options that allow it to handle copies when other methods fail, the dd command can handle conversions to and from IBM's EBCDIC character types to the standard ASCII characters on non-IBM machines. The dd command is frequently used for devices such as tapes, which have discrete record sizes, or for fast multi-sector reads from disks.

> Note: For a more complete description of the options available for this command and others in this chapter, refer to Appendix B, "Syntax Guide to UNIX Commands."

The dd command has the general form:

**Syntax**    dd [*options*]

---

*Options* include if=*filename* and of=*filename*, which specify the input files and output files, respectively. Another frequently used option is bs=$n$, which specifies the block size, $n$, as an integer. You also have options to specify the input block size (*ibs=n*) and output block size (*obs=n*). Specifying block size, an optional requirement, speeds copying, especially when copying backups to tape.

Another advantage that the dd command has over cp is that all users, not just the system administrator, can copy files to and from the floppy drive. With cp, you must mount a floppy disk if you need to copy to or from the floppy disk. Usually, only the system administrator, who must be logged on as root, can issue the mount command. With the dd command there is no need to mount the floppy device to access it.

By duplicating a file with dd, you can learn the command's basic usage.

**To make a backup of a file using the dd command:**

**1** Use the cat command, or the editor of your choice, to create a file, datafile. The file should contain the following text:

`This is my data file.`

**2** Make a copy of the file by typing **dd if=datafile of=datafile.bak** and pressing **Enter**. Your screen looks similar to Figure 8-1.

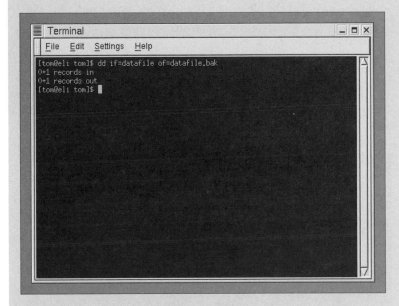

**Figure 8-1:** Results of dd command

# Making a Bootable Floppy Disk

It is a good idea to make a bootable floppy disk, because a computer problem (such as a crashed hard disk) may prevent you from starting UNIX from the system. To make a bootable floppy (in this case, for Red Hat Linux), you use four utility programs: the rdev, mkfs, fdformat, and dd commands. The rdev command queries and sets the **root device**, which is the hard disk partition that houses UNIX's root file system. The root file system, in turn, houses the UNIX kernel (core operating system), which is required to boot UNIX. (Under Red Hat Linux, the kernel is stored in a file whose name starts with vmlinuz. The file is usually stored in the /boot directory.) You can use the rdev command to set the root device with two arguments, where *image* is the name of the file holding the kernel and *root device* is the name of the UNIX partition that holds the root file system:

**Syntax**        rdev [*image*] [*root device*]

---

Use the mkfs command to build a UNIX or Linux file system on a device such as a floppy disk or a hard disk partition. The command is usually issued as follows, where *–t option* identifies the file system type and *filesystem* identifies the device name:

**Syntax**        mkfs [*-t option*] [*filesystem*]

---

The file system type, which determines how UNIX reads and writes information from or onto the device, is stored in the file /etc/fstab (file system table), as shown in Figure 8-2.

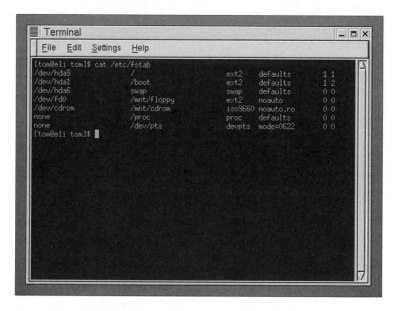

**Figure 8-2:** File system types as shown in /etc/fstab

The fdformat command formats a floppy at low levels to ensure that the media is clear of defects and is writeable. Unlike a high-level format that checks and verifies the disk's recording surface and sets up the file allocation tables (file system), as done on a Microsoft operating system, the low-level format prepares the recording surface but does not set up a file system. (The latter is the function of the mkfs utility, so the two programs, fdformat and mkfs, must work in tandem to prepare the floppy disk for use.) The low-level format checks the recording surface more thoroughly than the high-level format does. The command-line entry to format a floppy follows this usage, where the *–n* option disables the verification performed after the format. The *filesystem* is usually indicated as /dev/fd0 for drive A (the first floppy drive) and /dev/fd1 for drive B (the second floppy drive):

**Syntax**             fdformat [*-n*] [*filesystem*]

Note: The default format type is for 1.44 megabyte (high-density) floppies. The *filesystem* may also be indicated as /dev/fd0H1440 for a high-density floppy on drive A and /dev/fd1H1440 for a high-density floppy on drive B.

You are now ready to make a bootable disk.

Note: The next steps make the following assumptions:

- You have system-level privileges (are logged on under the root account).

- You are logged on to the host console. You cannot perform the steps if you are accessing a Linux computer via a telnet session.

**To make a bootable disk:**

**1**   Determine where vmlinuz, the file holding the Linux kernel, is located (most likely in /boot).

If you have trouble locating the file, use the find command: type **find / -name vmlinuz*** and press **Enter**.

**2**   Verify the /boot partition's location by typing **rdev** and then pressing **Enter**. Normally, the boot partition is located on the hda5 partition. Your screen should look similar to Figure 8-3.

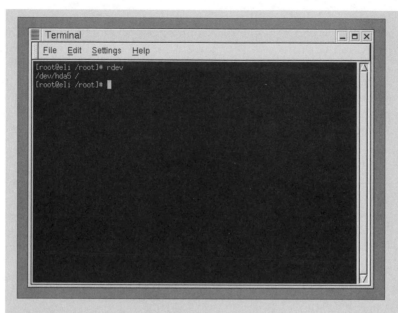

**Figure 8-3:** Results of rdev command

**3**  Insert a blank floppy disk in drive A.

**4**  Make a Linux file system on disk by typing **mkfs –t ext2 /dev/fd0 1440** and then pressing **Enter**. Your screen should now look similar to Figure 8-4.

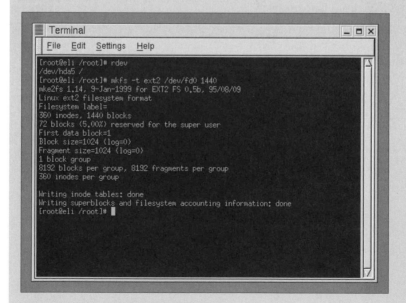

**Figure 8-4:** Results of mkfs command

**5**  Low-level format the disk by typing **fdformat /dev/fd0** and then pressing **Enter**. The utility displays its progress as it performs its operation. When the format is complete, your screen should look similar to Figure 8-5.

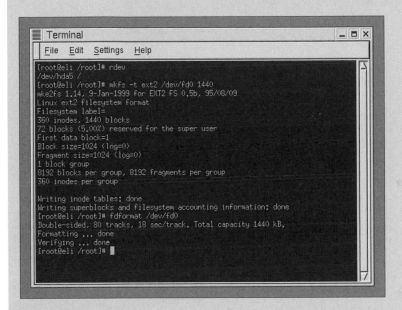

**Figure 8-5:** Results of fdformat command

**6**  Make the floppy disk bootable by typing **dd if=/boot/vmlinuz-2.2.5-15 of=/dev/fd0** and then pressing **Enter**.

Note: If you are not using Linux Red Hat Version 6, the kernel image (in this case, vmlinuz-2.2.5-15) will differ. Use the one you located in Step 1.

Note: After you create a bootable disk, you can use it to start the system. Place the bootable disk in drive A, and turn on the system. Linux then boots from the floppy disk instead of the hard drive.

You can also use the dd command to make a back-up copy of a floppy disk. You can copy the entire contents of a floppy to a single file on your hard drive. You can then copy the file onto a second floppy disk, thus making a back-up copy of the original disk. In the next exercise, you make a back-up copy of the bootable floppy disk you created in the previous exercise. You need a second blank disk, which has already been formatted.

**tip**

To format a second floppy disk, follow Steps 3 through 5 in the previous exercise.

Note: Like the steps in the previous exercise, the following steps can only be performed while you are logged on to the host console. The steps cannot be performed if you are accessing a Linux computer via a telnet session.

### To make a back-up copy of the bootable floppy disk:

**1** Insert the bootable floppy disk in the computer's floppy disk drive (commonly known as drive A).

**2** Copy the disk's contents into your current directory on the hard drive by typing **dd if=/dev/fd0 > duplicate.floppy** and then pressing **Enter**.

**3** Remove the floppy from drive A.

**4** Insert a formatted floppy disk in drive A.

**5** Copy the duplicate floppy disk image, duplicate.floppy, to the floppy by typing **dd if=./duplicate.floppy  of=/dev/fd0** and then pressing **Enter**. Make sure to use the dot (.) reference to the input file (if=./duplicate.floppy) to indicate that the input file is located in the current directory.

You have learned some useful utilities for preparing floppy disks and copying information to them. Next you learn to monitor the hard disk usage of your system.

## Checking Hard Disk Usage

UNIX system users, as well as the system itself, create and enlarge files. Eventually, unless files are removed, even the largest disk runs out of free space. To maintain adequate free space, you should use these basic strategies:

- Be vigilant against running dangerously low on free space by using the df command.
- Watch for conspicuous consumption by using the du command.
- Follow a routine schedule for "garbage" collection and removal by using the rm command.

Now you use each of these techniques to check hard disk usage.

## Using the df Utility

The df utility reports the number of 1024-byte blocks that are allocated, used, and available; the percentage used; and the mount point. The reports displayed are based on the command options entered.

### To use the df command to check hard disk usage:

**1**　Type **df** and then press **Enter**. (Note that you can enter the df utility without options.) Your screen looks similar to Figure 8-6.

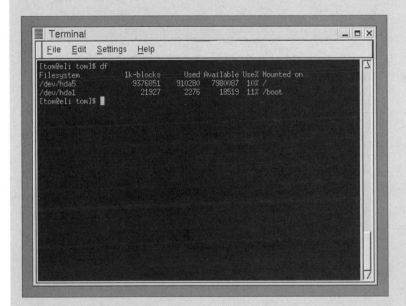

**Figure 8-6:** Output of df command

Of course, your file systems and their statistics will differ from those shown in Figure 8-6. In Figure 8-6, the df command reports that the /dev/hda5 file system has 9,376,851 blocks of 1 kilobyte each. There are 910,280 blocks in use, and 7,980,087 blocks available. Ten percent of the blocks are in use, and the file system is mounted on /.

**2**　You may specify a file system as an argument. The statistics for that file system alone appear on the screen. Type **df /dev/hda1** and press **Enter**. You see the disk statistics for the /dev/hda1 file system. Figure 8-7 shows an example.

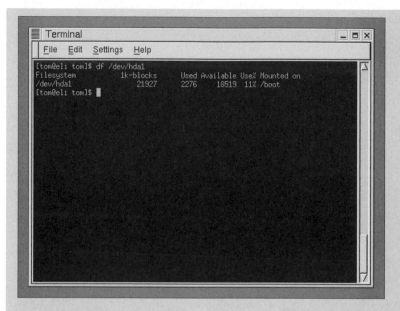

**Figure 8-7:** Results of df command

**3** The –h option causes the numbers to print in "human-readable" form. Instead of displaying raw numbers for size, amount of disk space used, and amount of space available, the statistics are printed in kilobyte, megabyte, or gigabyte format. Type **df –h** and press **Enter**. Figure 8-8 shows an example of the command's output.

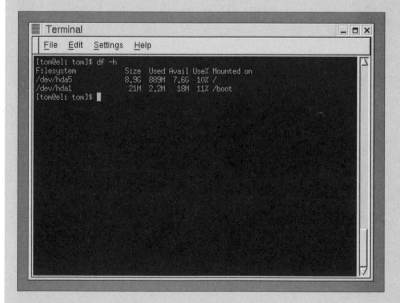

**Figure 8-8:** Output of df –h command

## Using the du Utility

The du utility summarizes disk usage. If you enter the command without options, you receive a report based on all file usage, starting at your current directory and progressing down through all subdirectories. File usage is expressed in number of 512-byte blocks (default) or by the number of bytes (the -b option).

### To report on disk usage:

**1** If you are still logged on as root, log out and then log on under your account.

**2** To receive a report on disk usage starting at your home directory, type **du | more** and then press **Enter.** (The results of the du command can be lengthy, so pipe its output to the more command.) Figure 8-9 shows an example of the command's output.

**Figure 8-9:** Output of du | more command

**3** The output shows the number of 512-byte blocks used in each subdirectory (including hidden subdirectories). Type **q** to exit the more command.

**4** To receive a report on disk usage by number of bytes starting at your home directory, type **du –b | more** and then press **Enter.** Figure 8-10 shows an example of the command's output.

**Figure 8-10:** Output of du –b | more command

**5**  Type **q** to exit the more command.

**6**  Like the df command, the du command supports the –h option to display statistics in human-readable format. Type **du –h | more** and press **Enter.** Figure 8-11 shows an example of the command's output.

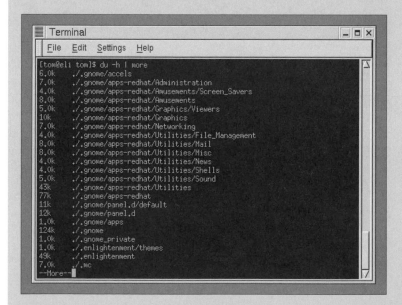

**Figure 8-11:** Output of du –h | more command

## Removing Garbage Files

An easy way to free space in your file systems is to remove garbage files. **Garbage files** are temporary files, such as a core file, that lose their usefulness after several days. A **core file** is created when an executing program attempts to do something illegal, like accessing another user's memory. The UNIX operating system detects the attempt and sends a signal to the program. The signal halts the offending program and creates a copy of the program and its environment in a file named core in the current directory. The programmer who wrote the program that "dumps core" (slang for this event) might be interested in dissecting the core file with a debugging tool. However, all too often the core file simply languishes unused in some branch of the directory hierarchy. All files created this way have the same name: core.

Another file with a generic name is a.out, the default for the output of program compilation procedures. Like core files, the true identity of these generically named files often gets lost over time. You can use a pipeline construction of the find command to retrieve these wasteful files and execute the rm command to remove them. You can also use the find command to search through the directory hierarchy and remove such files. You can write a find command so that it locates all files named core and a.out, and then remove each one. Here is such a command:

```
find . "(" —name a.out —o —name core ")" —exec rm {} \;
```

You have used the find command before to locate files. The command above locates every occurrence of the a.out and core files, and then deletes them with the rm command. The first argument, dot (.), tells find to start looking in the current directory. The argument "( —name a.out —o —name core ")" uses the —o (OR) operator. It tells find to search for files named a.out OR core. The —exec rm option instructs find to execute the rm command each time it locates a file with the name being searched for. The {} characters are replaced with the matching file name. For example, when the command locates an a.out file, the {} are replaced with a.out, so the command rm a.out is executed. The \; terminates the command.

Now you use the find command to search for and delete all occurrences of a.out and core.

> Note: The steps that follow assume you have a source directory in your home directory. The test files, a.out and core, are quickly created using the touch command, which, when followed by the filenames, creates empty files. The tilde (~) ensures that these files go into your home and source directories.

### To remove garbage files:

**1** Create some garbage files, core and a.out, and place them in your home directory and the subdirectory of home by typing **touch ~/core**, pressing **Enter**, typing **touch ~/a.out**, pressing **Enter**, typing **touch ~/source/core**, pressing **Enter**, typing **touch ~/source/a.out** and then pressing **Enter**.

**2**   Make sure you are in your home directory, then type **find . "( –name a.out –o –name core ")"** and press **Enter**. Your screen should resemble Figure 8-12.

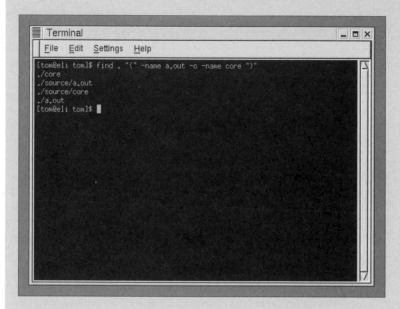

**Figure 8-12:** Results of find command

The results of the find command in Step 2 show the core and a.out files are in the current directory and in the source directory.

**3**   Remove the garbage files by typing **find . "( -name a.out –o –name core ")" –exec rm{} \;** and then pressing **Enter**.

**4**   Check that the files have been removed by repeating the find command you entered in Step 2. If the files have been removed correctly, there will be no output. If the files still exist, you didn't enter the find command in Step 3 correctly. Retype the command exactly as it appears in Step 3, and then repeat this step (4).

You can locate several other garbage files with the find command. For example, users often name files test, temp, or tmp to indicate temporary files that may be forgotten over time and should be removed.

You have now had an opportunity to use several file processing utilities. Next, you use some system status utilities.

## Applying System Status Utilities

As you see from the list of command descriptions in Table 8-2, the system status commands determine the system's performance. Although system engineers who assess the CPU's performance primarily use this data, you should at least know how to obtain this information. You can redirect the output of these commands to a file that you can then print and forward to the system administrator and system tune-up specialists.

One of the most effective utilities for auditing system performance is the top command. The top command displays a listing of the most CPU-intensive tasks, such as the processor state, in real time (the display is updated every 5 seconds by default). This means that you can actually see what is happening inside the computer as it progresses. The top command works with these options:

| | |
|---|---|
| **Syntax** | top [-] [d delay] [q] [S] [s] [i] [c] |
| **Dissection** | The d option specifies the delay between screen updates. The q option causes the top utility to refresh without delay. The S option specifies cumulative mode, where each process is listed with the CPU time that it has spent. The s option allows the top utility to run in secure mode, which disables the interactive commands (a good option for those not in charge of tuning the system). The i option causes the top utility to ignore any idle processes. Finally, the c option displays the command line instead of the command name only. While running, the top command supports interactive commands, such as k, which kills a running process. The top utility continues to produce output until you press q to terminate the execution of the program. |

The simplest way for most users to run the top utility is to simply issue the command without options.

**To use the top utility:**

1  Display the CPU activity by typing **top** and then pressing **Enter**. Your screen should look similar to Figure 8-13. (Don't forget this display changes dynamically while on screen.)

2  The processes are shown in the order of the amount of CPU time they use. After looking at the display for a short time, press **q** to exit from the top utility.

3  Run the top command again. Notice the leftmost column of information, labeled PID. This column lists the process ID of each process shown. Notice the PID of the top command. (In Figure 8-13, the top command's PID is 707. Yours will probably differ.)

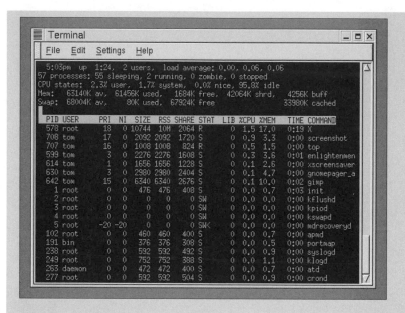

**Figure 8-13:** Output of top command

**4**  Press **k** to initiate the kill command. The top program asks you to enter the PID to kill. Enter the PID of the top command. Your screen should resemble Figure 8-14. Press **Enter** to kill the process. (You may have to press Enter a second time to return to a command prompt.) The top command is no longer running.

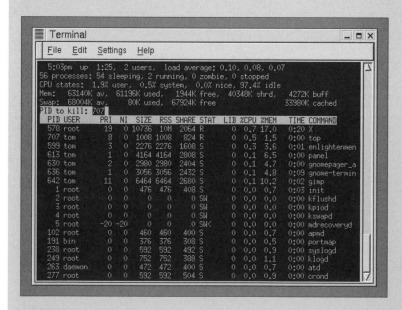

**Figure 8-14:** The k command

**5**  Run the top utility in secure mode by typing **top –s** and pressing **Enter**.

**6**  Press **k** to initiate the kill command. Because top is running in secure mode, it displays the message "Can't kill in secure mode," as shown in Figure 8-15.

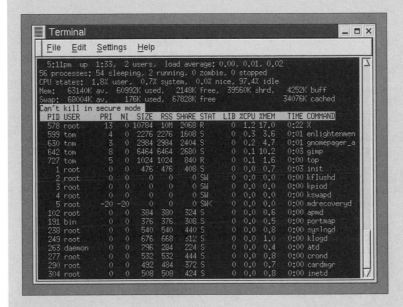

**Figure 8-15:** Top utility in secure mode

**7**  Press **q** to exit the top utility.

Table 8-8 summarizes several of the top command's options.

| Option | Description |
| --- | --- |
| -q | Causes the top command to display its output continually, with no delay between outputs |
| -s | Causes top command to run in secure mode, disabling its interactive commands, such as k (for kill) |
| -S | Runs top in cumulative mode. This mode displays the cumulative CPU time used by a process instead of the current CPU time used. |
| -I | Causes top to ignore any idle processes |
| -c | Causes top to display the command line that initiated each process, instead of only displaying the program name |

**Table 8-8:** Options for top command

Another useful, though static, display of memory usage is generated by the free command. The **free** command displays the amount of free and used memory in the system. Unlike top, the free utility runs and then automatically exits.

### To demonstrate the free command:

**1**    Type **free** and press **Enter**. Your screen looks similar to Figure 8-16.

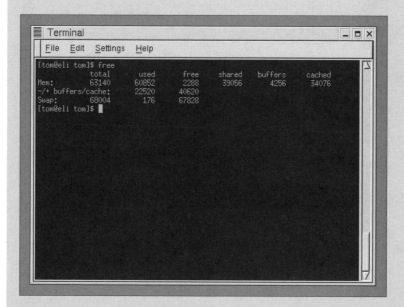

```
Terminal                                                      _ □ ×
 File   Edit   Settings   Help
[tom@eli tom]$ free                                                    △
               total      used      free    shared   buffers    cached
Mem:           63140     60852      2288     39056      4256     34076
-/+ buffers/cache:       22520     40620
Swap:          68004       176     67828
[tom@eli tom]$ ▌
```

**Figure 8-16:** Output of free command

**2**    The command displays the amount of total, used, and free memory. It also displays the amount of shared memory, buffer memory, and cached memory. In addition, the amount of total, used, and free swap memory is shown. By default, all amounts are shown in kilobytes.

**3**    Type **free –m** and press **Enter** to see the free command's output in megabytes.

**4**    Type **free –b** and press **Enter** to see the free command's output in bytes.

As mentioned earlier, you may want to forward these displays to the system administrator and tune-up specialists. You do this next.

### To forward displays generated by the top and free utilities:

**1**    Redirect the outputs of the top utility to a file in your current directory by typing **top > top_out** and then pressing **Enter**.

**2**  Wait about 10 seconds and then press **q** to exit the top utility.

**3**  Redirect the outputs of the top free to a file in your current directory by typing **free > free_out** and then pressing **Enter**.

**4**  Print the report for the system administrator and tune-up specialists by typing **lpr top_out**, pressing **Enter**, typing **lpr free_out**, and then pressing **Enter** again.

Because UNIX is a multitasking operating system, it allows you to run programs in the background while you continue to work with other programs. For example, if you have a program that prints a lengthy report, you can run it in the background and continue working with other programs while the report is printing. To run a program in the background, append the & character to the end of the command line.

### To run a program in the background:

**1**  Experiment by running the top utility in the background. Type **top &** and press **Enter**.

The system reports the PID of the program that you started in the background. In Figure 8-17, the PID is 797. The top utility runs, but because it runs in the background, you see no output.

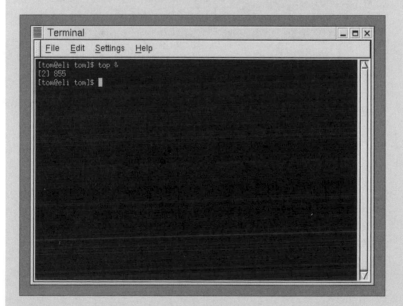

**Figure 8-17:** Running top utility in the background

**2** Continue to run the top utility in the background. The process is the subject of the next two exercises.

The ps command shows you a list of the processes currently running. When you use the command with no options, it shows a list of the processes associated with the current login session. When used with the –A option, it shows a very long list of all processes running on the system.

### To use the ps command:

**1** Type **ps** and press **Enter**. Your screen looks similar to Figure 8-18.

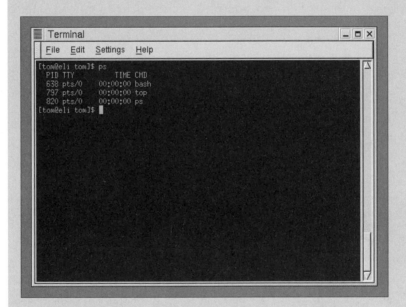

```
[tom@eli tom]$ ps
  PID TTY          TIME CMD
  638 pts/0    00:00:00 bash
  797 pts/0    00:00:00 top
  820 pts/0    00:00:00 ps
[tom@eli tom]$
```

**Figure 8-18:** ps command

**2** The output of the ps utility includes this information about each process:
- PID
- Name of the terminal where the process started
- Amount of time the process has been running
- Name of the process

Notice the top utility still runs in the background.

**3** To see a list of all processes running on the system, type **ps –A | more** and press **Enter**. Figure 8-19 shows an example of the command's output.

**Figure 8-19:** ps –A command

**4** Press the **spacebar** until the command finishes its output.

To force a process to terminate, use the kill command. Its two formats are:

**Syntax**

kill [process ID]
or...
kill %[process name]

When the kill command successfully executes, it terminates the process whose PID or name is passed as an argument.

**To use the kill command:**

**1** In this exercise you terminate the top utility that is still running in the background. Type **ps** and press **Enter**. Look at the list of process to find the top utility's PID.

**2** Type one of these commands (both perform the same operation):
**kill <*process id*>** and press **Enter**, or
**kill %top** and press **Enter**

**3**   Use the **ps** command again to see a list of the running processes. The top utility is no longer running.

Caution: Be very careful when using the kill command. If you kill a process that the
operating system needs, you can cause disastrous results!

In this section, you learned about several utilities to monitor and maintain the
system. You learned to use the dd command to copy files and duplicate floppy
disks. You used the mkfs command to create a file system on a floppy disk and used
the fdformat command to perform a low-level format on a floppy disk. You learned
to query the partition containing the root device with the rdev command. Also, you
learned to monitor disk, memory, and CPU usage with the df, du, top, and free
commands. Finally, you learned to run programs in the background with the &
operator, to list all running processes with the ps command, and to terminate
processes no longer needed with the kill command. In the next section you learn
about utilities that format text files.

# SUMMARY

- UNIX utilities are classified into seven major function areas dictated by user needs: file
  processing, networking, communications, system status, programming, source code
  management, and miscellaneous tasks.

- Utility programs are distinguished from other operating system programs, because they
  are "add-ons" and not a part of the UNIX shells, nor a component of the "kernel."

- Because utility programs are executed by entering their names on the command line,
  these programs are commonly referred to as commands.

- The dd command possesses a rich set of options that allow it to handle copies when
  other copying methods fail.

- To make a bootable floppy disk, you use four utility programs: rdev, mkfs, fdformat,
  and the dd commands.

- The rdev command queries and sets the root device. The root device is the hard disk
  partition that houses UNIX's root file system.

- The fdformat command low-level formats a floppy to ensure that the media is without
  defect and is writeable to set up a file system.

- The mkfs utility sets up a file system and works in tandem with fdformat to prepare
  the floppy disk for use.

- The df utility checks and reports on free disk space.

- The du command checks for disk usage (consumption).

- You can use a pipeline construction of the find command to retrieve wasteful files and then execute the rm command to remove them from the hard disk.

- The top and free utilities provide detailed views of the "internals" of the system that are invisible to the naked eye but directly related to the CPU's performance.

- You can redirect the output of the top and free commands to a disk file to use as input to print a report for the system administrator and system tune-up specialists.

- You run a program in the background by appending the & operator to the end of the command line.

- The ps command displays all processes currently running.

- The kill command terminates a specific process.

# R E V I E W   Q U E S T I O N S

1. UNIX utilities differ from other UNIX system programs in that _____.
   a. they are built into the shells
   b. they are an integral part of the kernel
   c. they handle file processing tasks
   d. they are external to the shells and the core operating system

2. The rdev command displays the _____.
   a. root directory
   b. root device
   c. floppy disk device
   d. user's home directory

3. The mkfs command _____.
   a. creates a file system type
   b. sets the root device
   c. makes a bootable floppy
   d. formats the floppy

4. Use the _____ command to make sure you are not running out of free space on the disk.
   a. dd
   b. du
   c. df
   d. rdev

5. Use the _____ command to determine how much file space is being consumed.
   a. dd
   b. du
   c. df
   d. rdev

6. Use the _____ command to summarize how disk space is being used.
   a. dd
   b. du
   c. df
   d. rdev

7. Display the CPU activity using the _____ command.
   a. top
   b. free
   c. test
   d. review

8. Which command locates and displays the a.out and core files recursively starting at the current directory?
   a. find . "(" -name a.out –o –name core ")"
   b. find / a.out –o –name core
   c. find / -name "a.out" –o –name "core"
   d. find ~/ -name "a.out" –o –name "core"

9. Which command terminates a running program or process?
   a. abort
   b. terminate
   c. end
   d. kill

10. Which option of the ps command displays all processes running in the system?
    a. –a
    b. –A
    c. –p
    d. –all

11. How do you terminate a process with the top utility?
    a. with the k command
    b. with the –a option
    c. with the a command
    d. with the –kill option

# E X E R C I S E S

1. Use the cat command or the editor of your choice to create a file, my_info. The file should contain your name and address. Use the dd command to copy the file to my_info.dup.

2. Insert a blank disk in the floppy drive of your computer. Use the mkfs command to create an ext2 file system on the disk.

3. Use the fdformat command to low-level format the disk in the floppy disk drive.

4. Use the dd command to copy the file my_info (the one you created in Exercise 1) to the floppy disk.

5. Use the dd command to make a duplicate of the floppy disk. Store the duplicate in a file dup.floppy in your home directory.

6. Use the dd command to copy the dup.floppy file (the one you created in Exercise 5) onto a second blank disk.

7. Use the redirection operator (>) to create test files test1, test2, and test3 in your home directory, and copy them into the source directory. Use the find command to display all the files.

8. Use the free command to determine the amount of free system memory.

9. Run the top program in the background.

10. Use the free command to check the amount of free system memory again. Has it changed because you are now running a program in the background?

11. Use the ps command to determine the top program's PID.

12. Use the kill command to terminate the top program, which is still running in the background.

# DISCOVERY EXERCISES

1. Use the df command with the correct option to display the number of gigabytes of disk space that are available on your system.

2. Use the du command to determine which subdirectory under your home directory holds the most information.

3. Use the du command again, but cause it to display its output in bytes rather than blocks.

4. Use the du command and specify the root directory (/) as its starting point. How many blocks does the /dev directory use?

5. In the section, "Removing Garbage Files," you entered a find command that locates and removes all files named a.out and core. Re-enter the same find command, but this time it should locate and remove the test1, test2, and test3 files you created in Exercise 7.

6. Run the man program with the argument du in the background.

7. Run the top program. Is the man program, which is currently running in the background, listed? Why or why not?

8. Use the ps command to see the currently running processes. What is the PID of the man command that is still running?

9. Use the kill command to terminate the man program.

In this lesson you will:

- Check the spelling of a file's contents
- Create your own man page
- Use the groff utility to format a man page document
- Use man to display your new man page

# Working with the Text Formatting File Utilities

## Spell-checking a Document

Sometimes, the simpler the command, the more useful it is. This is the case with the ispell utility. The **ispell utility** scans a text document, displays errors on the screen, and suggests other words with similar spellings as replacements for unrecognized words. A menu that appears on the bottom line of the screen shows corrective options and exit codes.

To become more familiar with the ispell utility, you next type a sample document.

**To see how the ispell utility works:**

**1** Use the vi or Emacs editor to create a file and name it **document1**.

**2** Enter the following text, with misspellings:

**This is a document that describes our newest
and fastest machineery. Take the time to lern
how to use each piece of equipment.**

**3** Save the file and exit the editor.

**4** Scan the file for spelling errors by typing **ispell document1** and then pressing **Enter**. Your screen should look similar to Figure 8-20.

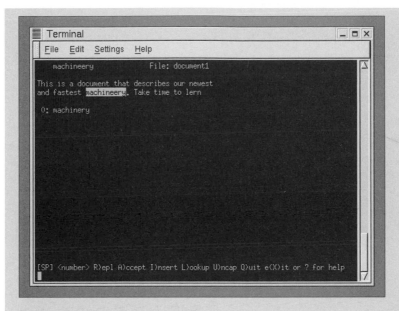

**Figure 8-20:** ispell utility

**5**  To correct the word "machineery," look at the menu options at the bottom of the screen, and then type **0** (zero) to replace it with the correctly spelled word.

**6**  On the next screen, the next misspelled word is block-highlighted, as shown in Figure 8-21. Type **05** to replace "lern" with "learn."

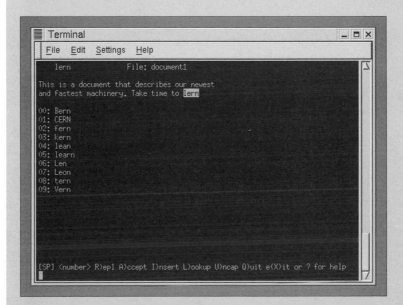

**Figure 8-21:** Correcting spelling mistakes with the ispell utility

Note: If the word "learn" appears next to a different number on your system, type that number.

**7**   The program exits and returns you to the command line. Type **cat document1** and press **Enter**.

**8**   The misspelled words have been corrected.

Now you learn about the cmp utility, which compares files and determines the first difference between them.

## Comparing Files

Suppose you have a file that you work with regularly. You make a back-up copy of the file for safekeeping. Later, you want to see if the original file has changed since you made the back-up copy. You can use the cmp utility to compare the contents of two files and report the first difference between them.

The general form of the cmp command is:

**Syntax**       cmp *file1 file2*

The cmp command displays the character position and line number of the first difference between the two files.

**To compare two files with the cmp command:**

**1**   Use the vi or Emacs editor to create the file file1, containing the text:

```
This is file 1.
I made it myself.
It belongs to me.
```

**2**   Save the file.

**3**   Use the editor to create the file file2, containing the text:

```
This is file 2.
I made it myself.
It belongs to you.
```

**4**   Save the file and exit the editor.

**5**   At the command line, type **cmp file1 file2** and press **Enter**. Your screen looks similar to Figure 8-22. The command reports that the two files differ at character position 14 on line 1.

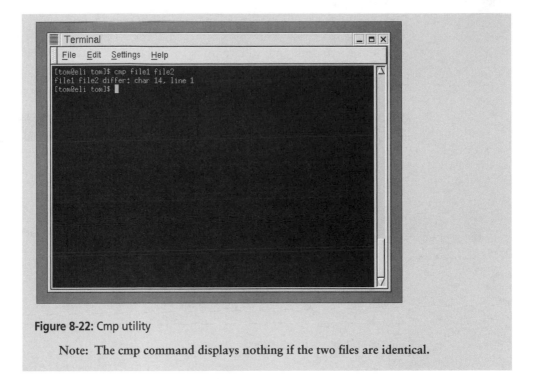

**Figure 8-22:** Cmp utility

Note:  The cmp command displays nothing if the two files are identical.

## Formatting Text in UNIX

Text formatting in UNIX involves preparing a text file with embedded typesetting commands and then processing the marked-up text file with a computer program. This program generates commands for the output device, such as a printer, a monitor, or some other typesetter. UNIX's nroff and troff commands are often used to process the embedded typesetting commands to format the output.

UNIX users have long used the nroff and troff commands to produce manuals, corporate reports, books, and newspapers. These programs evolved from an earlier program, RUNOFF (a utility created in the late 1970s), which read pure text with embedded codes to format and print a text-enriched report. An embedded code is a special sequence of characters that are included with the regular text in the file. The special codes are not printed, but interpreted as commands to perform text formatting operations. For example, there are codes to produce boldface print, center text, and underline certain lines.

Using embedded codes in text to produce enriched output provides the advantage of not needing additional word-processing programs to produce documents. You can use any editor that works with flat files, like vi or Notepad. In addition you can use added features, such as hyperlinks to cross-reference other documents from within your document. You do need, however, an HTML browser program like Netscape, or UNIX utilities such as nroff and troff, to translate and execute the embedded hyperlink codes.

Linux introduced groff, which implements the features of both nroff and troff. Table 8-9 lists some embedded codes supported by groff.

| Embedded Command | Meaning |
| --- | --- |
| .ce *n* | Center next *n* lines |
| .ds C | Center |
| .ds R | Right justify |
| .p *n* | Start a new paragraph indented *n* characters |
| .sa 0 | Turn off justification |
| .sa 1 | Turn on justification |
| .ul *n* | Underline the next *n* lines |

**Table 8-9:** Some groff embedded commands

The groff command's usage follows this format:

| | |
| --- | --- |
| **Syntax** | groff *[-Tdev]* |
| **Dissection** | The –T designates a device type, which specifies an output device such as ASCII to tell groff that the device is a typewriter-like device. In the format example, the device type *(dev)* is for the man pages. Some other device types include *ps* for postscript printers, *dvi* for TeX dvi format, and *lj4* for an HP LaserJet4-compatible printer. |

Your task for Dominion Consulting is to produce a man page that contains the standard man page sections. You are to use groff to produce the man page. The format codes consist of tags and font-change commands that control the formatting, which you type into your man page document. The tags and font-change commands consist of:

■ The .TH tag indicates the man page title, as well as the date and a version-number string. In the formatted man page, the version and date strings appear at the bottom of each page.

- The .SH tag indicates a section. (Section names usually appear in all upper-case characters on a man page.) Six common sections of a man page are:

  NAME: the name of the command or program
  SYNOPSIS: a brief description of the command or program
  DESCRIPTION: a detailed description of the command or program
  FILES: a list of files used by the command or program
  SEE ALSO: a list of other commands or programs that are related to this one.
  BUGS: a list of known bugs
- The .SS tag indicates the beginning of a subsection. For example, Options is a subsection of the DESCRIPTION section.
- The .TP tag indicates each item in the Options subsection.
- The \fB command changes the font to boldface, the \fI command changes the font to italic, the \fR command changes the font to roman, and the \fP command changes the font to its former setting.

You will now write a man page for the application, phmenu, that you completed in Chapter 7.

**To write and format a man page:**

**1**  Make sure you are in your ~/source directory. Recall that the ~ indicates your home directory.

**2**  Use the vi or Emacs editor to create the file phmenu.1. Type the following text into the file.

```
.TH PHMENU 1 "July 20, 2000" "phmenu Version 1.01"
.SH NAME
phmenu \- Menu for Dominion Employee Telephone Listings
.SH SYNOPSIS
\fB phmenu\fP
.SH DESCRIPTION
\fP Menu for maintaining employees' phones and job title
s\fP.
\fP Record includes phone number, name, dept, and date-
hired\fP.
.SS Options
.TP
\fB -v \fIView Phone List\fR
Display unformatted phone records.
.TP
\fD -p \fIPrint Phone List\fR
```

```
        Corporate Phones report sorted by Employee Name.
.TP
\fB -a \fIAdd Phone to List\fR
Add new phone record.
.TP
\fB -s \fISearch for Employee Phones\fR
Enter Name to search and retrieve phone record
.TP
\fB -d \fIDelete Phone\fR
Remove phone record
.SH FILES
.TP
\fC/home/dbadmin/source/corp_phones\fR
```

**3**  Save the file and exit the editor.

**4**  Test the man page by typing **groff –Tascii –man phmenu.1 | more** and then pressing **Enter**. Your screen should appear similar to Figure 8-23.

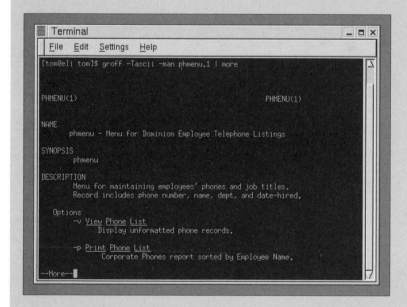

**Figure 8-23:** Phmenu man page

If you find any formatting discrepancies, check the dot commands and any embedded font changes against the code you typed in Step 2.

**5**  Press **q** to exit the more command, and then test your new man page by typing **man ./phmenu.1** and then pressing **Enter**. Your screen should be similar to Figure 8-24.

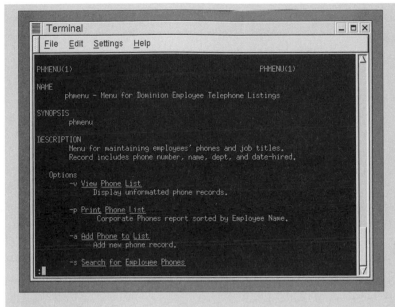

**Figure 8-24:** Phmenu man page viewed with the man program

When you are satisfied with the man page format, you can make it available to others by copying it (while logged on as root) to one of the /man directories. All man pages are stored in subdirectories of the /usr/man directory. These subdirectories have names such as man1, man2, man3, and man4. All man pages in man1 are identified with a common suffix, .1, so phmenu.1 is copied to /usr/man/man1. The suffix number represents the version number of the man page.

When you request a man page using the man program, you specify the version number you want to see by placing the number after the name. (If you type only the name, man looks recursively for the page through all the subdirectories, starting with /usr/man/man1, and then displays the first match.) For example, if you want man to print the second version of the break command, follow the man command with break 2.

Note: You need superuser privileges to copy phmenu.1 into the "root-owned" directory, /usr/man/man1. If you are not logged on to the root account, use the su command instead.

**To copy the man page into a /man directory:**

1  Type **su** and then press **Enter**.
2  Enter the root password and then press **Enter**.
3  Type **cp phmenu.1 /usr/man/man1** to copy the man page to the man directory, and then press **Enter**.

**4**  To exit from superuser mode, type **exit** and then press **Enter**.

**5**  Test that this file has been correctly copied by typing **man phmenu** and then pressing **Enter**.

In this lesson you learned to check the spelling of a document using the ispell utility. You learned to use the cmp command to check two files that seem similar, to determine any differences between them. Finally, you learned to create your own man page with the groff utility and test it with the man program.

# SUMMARY

■  The spell-checking utility, ispell, scans a text document for typing errors.

■  Text formatting in UNIX involves preparing a text file with embedded typesetting commands and then processing the marked-up text file with a computer program that generates commands for the output device.

■  The text containing the embedded typesetting commands is processed (read) by a program like UNIX's nroff and troff utility programs that formats the output.

■  Linux introduced groff, which implements the features of both nrofff and troff.

■  Those who have superuser (root) privileges, such as the system administrator, most often create man pages.

# REVIEW QUESTIONS

**1.**  The groff command is a(n) _____.
   a. text formatting utility
   b. man page utility
   c. search text utility
   d. editor

**2.**  True or false: The ispell utility only displays misspelled words. It does not allow you to change the misspelled words.

**3.**  The embedded commands used by groff to format a text file are placed in the
   _____.
   a. command line
   b. file itself
   c. same directory as the text file, in a special command file
   d. man1 directory

4. To produce the fourth version of the tty man page, type _____.
   a. man tty 4
   b. man 4 tty
   c. man tty.4
   d. man tty

5. Which of these commands gives an ordinary user the ability to print a man page from the current directory?
   a. man ./phmenu.1
   b. man phmenu
   c. man menu 1
   d. man –1 phmenu

6. The man page format codes consist of _____ and _____ _____ commands.
   a. tag, font change
   b. dot, dot dot
   c. header, footer line
   d. tag, sub header

7. The title of a man page is denoted by the _____ embedded command.
   a. .T
   b. .TITLE
   c. .NAME
   d. .TH

8. The \fB embedded command causes _____.
   a. the font to change to bold
   b. the text to appear in brackets
   c. the line to appear at the bottom of the screen
   d. the font to change back to the previous font

9. The man pages are normally copied into a subdirectory of _____ to make them available to all users.
   a. /etc
   b. /home
   c. /usr
   d. /usr/man

10. Which of these commands tests your man page?
    a. groff –T ascii phmenu.1 | more
    b. groff –T ascii –man phmenu.1 | more
    c. man –T ascii phmenu.1
    d. troff –T ascii phmenu.1

# EXERCISES

1. Use vi to create the document Spellcheck, and then type the following four lines, with spelling errors:

   ```
   Rosus are red,
   Vilets are blu,
   I luv Linux,
   and So should Yu.
   ```

2. Make a copy of the file called Spellcheck.bak. Run ispell and correct the original document, Spellcheck.

3. After you correct the Spellcheck file (created in Exercise 1), compare it to the Spellcheck.bak file with the cmp command.

4. Create a simple man page to describe a fictitious program, Movies, that searches a movie-rental database for movies using optional search-argument codes. The search-argument codes are S (enter star's name), M (enter movie name), and D (enter director's name).

   ● ● ● ● ● ● ● ● ● ● ● ● ● ● ● ● ● ● ● ● ● ● ● ● ● ● ● ● ● ● ● ● ● ● ● ● ● ● ● ● ● ● ● ● ● ● ● ● ● ● ● ●

   **Remember to enter a suffix (.1) to the man page document name and when you run man. As an ordinary user, you must enter the name plus the suffix.**

   ● ● ● ● ● ● ● ● ● ● ● ● ● ● ● ● ● ● ● ● ● ● ● ● ● ● ● ● ● ● ● ● ● ● ● ● ● ● ● ● ● ● ● ● ● ● ● ● ● ● ● ●

5. Run the Movies man page from your current directory by typing **$ groff –T ascii ./phmenu.1 | more** and then pressing **Enter**. What happened? Explain.

6. Now run the movies man page from your current directory by typing **$ groff –T ascii –man ./phmenu.1** and then pressing **Enter**. What happened? Explain. How would you fix the problem?

# DISCOVERY EXERCISES

1. Use the ispell utility on the Phmenu.1 man page you created in this chapter. Why must you be careful not to change all misspelled words the utility finds?

2. Edit the Phmenu.1 file and add a new section named SEE ALSO. Under this section, list the files:

   Phoneadd
   Phlist1

3. Save and test the revised file using the groff and man programs.

4. Edit the Phmenu.1 file and add a new section named BUGS. Under this section, list a line that reads:

   None Known

5. Save and test the revised file using the groff and man programs.

6. Edit the Phmenu.1 file and add a new section named AUTHOR. Under this section, list your name. Save and test the revised file using the groff and man programs.

# Perl and CGI Programming

**case** ▶ Dominion Consulting is offering a special promotion of software products. To give potential customers another method of responding to the promotion, the company's Sales Department asks you to create an interactive Web page. You can do so by creating scripts in Perl, a programming language similar to C that uses features from awk and shell programs.

# Learning to Use Perl

In this chapter, you learn how to use Perl to create effective, interactive Web pages. **Perl** (which stands for Practical Extraction and Report Language) was created in 1986 by Larry Wall as a simple report generator. Since then, the author and others have enhanced it so that it has become a powerful programming language. One of the most popular uses of Perl scripts today is to make interactive Web pages.

This chapter also expands on your previous knowledge of both awk and sed. You will learn more options and features of both by writing awk and sed scripts as problem-solving programs, not just as isolated commands within other programs.

Before you can begin to create your Web page, however, you first need to learn more about the structure and syntax of a Perl program.

## Introduction to Perl

Perl contains a blend of features found in other languages. It is very similar to the C language but also contains features found in awk and shell programs. You will begin learning Perl by examining a few simple programs, such as this one:

```
#!/usr/bin/perl
# Program name: example1.p
print("This is a simple\n");
print("Perl program.\n");
```

The first line in the program tells the operating system to use Perl to interpret the file. Recall from Chapter 7 that when the first line of a program begins with #!, the remainder of the line is assumed to give the path of the interpreter.

The second line in the sample program is a comment that lists the name of the file. Like shell scripts, Perl programs use the # character to mark the beginning of a comment. The third and fourth lines of the program display text on the screen. The program output is shown in Figure 9-1.

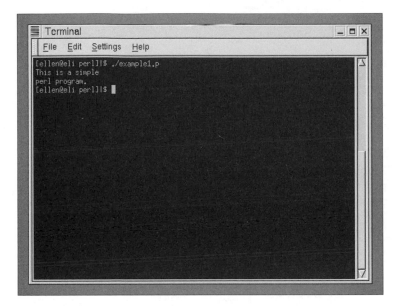

**Figure 9-1:** Output of example1.p

The print statements each have a single argument, which is displayed on the screen. The first print statement displays the string, "This is a simple." The \n characters display a new-line, which advances the cursor to the beginning of the next line. The second print statement is similar to the first. It displays the string, "Perl program," and then advances the cursor to the beginning of the next line. Notice that the two print statements end with a semicolon. All complete statements in Perl end with a semicolon.

> Note: The parentheses surrounding the print statement's argument are optional. For example, these two statements perform the same operation:

```
print ("Hello");
print "Hello";
```

Look at the next program, which uses a variable.

```
#!/usr/bin/perl
# Program name: example2.p
$name = "Charlie";
print("Greetings $name\n");
```

Figure 9-2 shows the program's output.

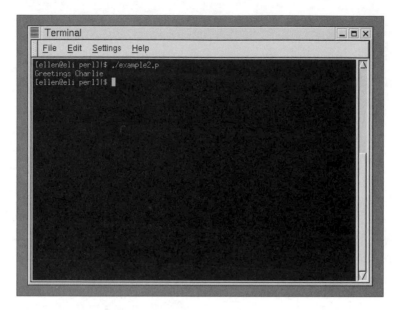

**Figure 9-2:** Output of example2.p

The example2.p program uses the variable $name. The variable is initialized with the string "Charlie." Notice that when $name is inserted in the print statement's argument, it displays the contents of the variable.

Perl can also read input from the keyboard. The next program is an example.

```
#!/usr/bin/perl
# Program name: example3.p
print ("Enter a number: ");
$number = <STDIN>;
print ("You entered $number\n");
```

The program's output is shown in Figure 9-3.

In Perl, <STDIN> reads input from the keyboard. The program uses this line to assign keyboard input to the variable $number:

```
$number = <STDIN>
```

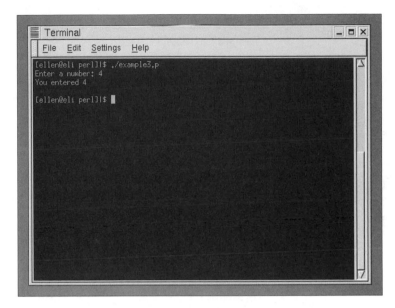

**Figure 9-3:** Output of example3.p

Like other languages, Perl offers the if-else statement as a decision structure. Here is an example:

```perl
#!/usr/bin/perl
# Program name: example4.p
print ("Enter a number: ");
$number = <STDIN>;
if ($number == 10)
{
    print ("That is the number I was thinking of.\n");
}
else
{
    print ("You entered $number\n");
}
```

The == operator tests two numeric values for equality. The if statement uses the == operator to determine if $number is equal to 10. If it is, the block (which consists of lines of code enclosed inside a set of curly braces) immediately following the if statement is executed. Otherwise, the block that follows the else statement is executed. Figure 9-4 shows the output of the program when the user enters 10.

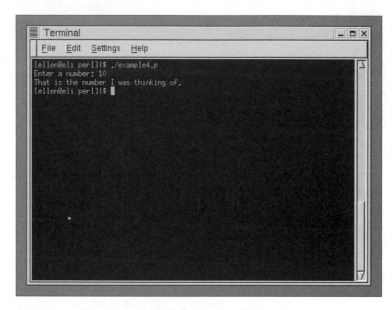

**Figure 9-4:** Output of example4.p when you enter 10

Figure 9-5 shows the output of the program when the user enters a value other than 10.

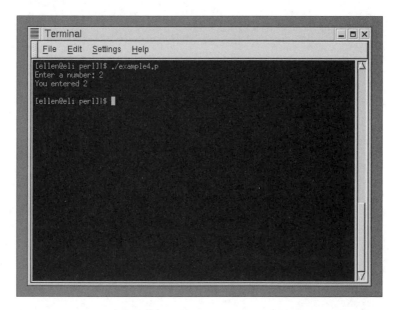

**Figure 9-5:** Output of example4.p when you enter a value other than 10

Perl also has operators that test for less than, greater than, less than or equal to, and greater than or equal to relationships. Table 9-1 shows each of Perl's numeric relational operators.

| Operator | Meaning |
|----------|---------|
| == | Equality |
| < | Less than |
| > | Greater than |
| <= | Less than or equal to |
| >= | Greater than or equal to |
| != | Not equal to |

**Table 9-1:** Perl's numeric relational operators

Perl can also perform relational tests on strings, which are sequences of characters. The string relational operators, however, are different from the numeric relational operators. The next program demonstrates how two strings, stored in variables, are compared for equality.

```perl
#!/usr/bin/perl
# Program name: example5.p
$my_name = "Ellen";
$your_name = "Charlie";
if ($my_name eq $your_name)
{
    print ("Your name is the same as mine.\n");
}
else
{
    print ("Hello. My name is $my_name\n");
}
```

The eq operator tests two strings to determine if they are equal. The output of the program is shown in Figure 9-6.

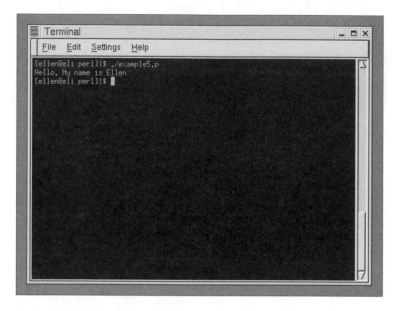

**Figure 9-6:** Output of example5.p

Table 9-2 lists Perl's string relational operators.

| Operator | Meaning |
| --- | --- |
| eq | Equality |
| lt | Less than |
| gt | Greater than |
| le | Less than or equal to |
| ge | Greater than or equal to |
| ne | Not equal to |

**Table 9-2:** Perl's string relational operators

Perl also provides standard arithmetic operators: + performs addition, - performs subtraction, * performs multiplication, and / performs division. The next program demonstrates a simple arithmetic operation.

```
#!/usr/bin/perl
# Program name: example6.p
$num1 = 10;
$num2 = 50;
$num3 = 12;
$average = ($num1 + $num2 + $num3) / 3;
print ("The average is $average\n");
```

Figure 9-7 shows the output of the program.

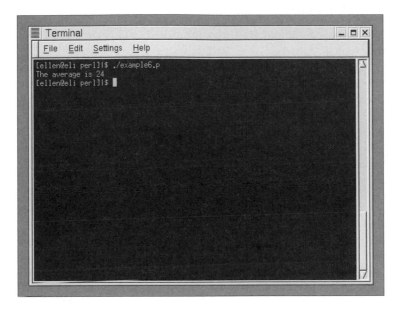

**Figure 9-7:** Output of example6.p

As you can see from the program above, Perl also lets you group operations within parentheses. Now that you have a general understanding of Perl, you will study its data types.

## Identifying Data Types

The computer programmer must understand not only what is contained in files, records, and fields, but also the format in which it is stored. Are the fields of information numeric or alphabetic? Are the fields made up of a combination of numbers and letters? How do you treat control characters such as tab and new-line? Although it may seem obvious that a data item such as a person's name cannot be added or multiplied, the programmer must write code that properly handles any and all data items that appear in a program. Otherwise, misidentified data generates processing errors. To do this, programmers need to identify data types.

Data may be represented in a Perl program in a variety of ways. You will learn about these types of data:

- Variables
- Constants
- Scalars
- Arrays
- Hashes

## Variables and Constants

**Variables** are symbolic names that represent values stored in memory. For example, the variable $x might hold the value 100, and $name might hold the sequence of characters, "Charlie." The value of a variable can change while the program runs. **Constants**, however, do not change value as the program runs. They are written into the program code itself. For example, this statement assigns the value of the constant 127.89 to the variable $num:

```
$num = 127.89
```

## Scalars

In the broadest sense, data is perceived as being either numeric or non-numeric. A non-numeric field of information is treated simply as a string of characters (hence the term *string*). Programmers associate strings with such items as a person's name, address, or license plate number. Numbers can also be used for logical analysis as well as for mathematical computations. A **scalar** is a simple variable that holds a number or a string. Scalar variable names begin with a dollar sign ($).

## Numbers

Numbers are stored inside the computer as either signed integers (as in 14321) or double-precision floating-point values (as in 23456.85). Numeric literals (constant values versus variable values) can be either integers or floating-point values. These numeric representations are consistent with all languages, but Perl also uses an additional convention with numeric literals to improve legibility: the underscore character, as in 5_456_678_901. (Perl uses the comma as a list separator.) The underscore only works within literal numbers specified in a program, not in strings functioning as numbers or in data read from elsewhere. Similarly, hexadecimal constants are expressed with the leading 0x prefix (as in 0xfff), and octal constants are expressed with the leading 0 prefix (as in 0256).

All of these are examples of statements that assign values to numeric scalar variables:

```
$x = 12;
$name = "Jill";
$pay = 12456.89;
```

## Strings

Strings are often used for logical analysis, sorts, or searches. **Strings** are sequences of any types of characters (including numbers that are treated as "characters" rather than digits). String literals are usually delimited by either single quotes (' ') or double quotes (" "). Single-quoted strings are not subject to interpolation (except for \' and \\, used to put single quotes and backslashes into a single-quoted string). Double quotes use the backslash (\) to precede a character that is to be treated as a control character. Table 9-3 lists the code and meaning for each string representation.

| Code | Meaning |
|------|---------|
| \n | New-line |
| \r | Carriage Return |
| \t | Horizontal Tab |
| \f | Form Feed |
| \b | Backspace |
| \a | Bell |
| \033 | ESC in octal |
| \x7f | Del in hexadecimal |
| \cC | Ctrl-C |
| \\ | Backslash |
| \" | Double quote |
| \u | Force next character to uppercase |
| \l | Force next character to lowercase |
| \U | Force all following characters to uppercase until \E is encountered |
| \L | Force all following characters to lowercase until \E is encountered |
| \Q | Backslash—quote all following non-alphanumeric characters until \E is encountered |
| \E | End \U, \L, \Q |

**Table 9-3:** Double-quoted string representation

For example, compare the use of special codes in the next program with those shown in Table 9-3.

```perl
#!/usr/bin/perl
# Program name: example7.p
print ("\\words\\separated\\by\\slashes\n");
print ("This is a \"quote\"\n");
print ("\Uupper case\n");
print ("\LLOWER CASE\n");
```

The program output is shown in Figure 9-8.

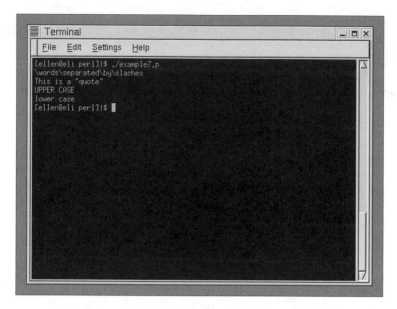

**Figure 9-8:** Output of example7.p

## Arrays

**Arrays** are variables that store an ordered list of scalar values that are accessed with numeric subscripts, starting at zero. An "at" sign (@) precedes the name of an array when assigning it values. When processing the individual elements of an array, however, use the $ character. For example, this program creates the array pets.

```
#!/usr/bin/perl
# Program name: example8.p
@pets = ("dog", "cat", "parrot", "hamster" );
print ("My pets are:\n");
print ("$pets[0]\n");
print ("$pets[1]\n");
print ("$pets[2]\n");
print ("$pets[3]\n");
```

Figure 9-9 shows the program output.

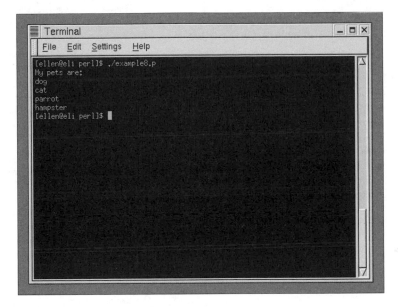

**Figure 9-9:** Output of example8.p

## Hashes

A **hash** is a variable that represents a set of key/value pairs. Hash variables are preceded by a percent sign (%) when they are assigned values. To refer to a single element of a hash, you use the hash variable name followed by the "key" associated with the value in curly braces. For example:

```
%animals = ('Tigers', 10, 'Lions', 20, 'Bears', 30);
$animals{'Bears'}
```

returns the value 30. Another, more readable way to define this is to use the ==> operator to define the key/value pairs:

```
%animals = (Tigers ==> 10, Lions ==> 20, Bears ==> 30);
```

Here is a program that demonstrates the use of a hash variable.

```
#!/usr/bin/perl
# Program name: example9.p
%animals = ('Tigers', 10, 'Lions', 20, 'Bears', 30);
print ("The animal values are:\n");
print ("$animals{'Tigers'}\n");
print ("$animals{'Lions'}\n");
print ("$animals{'Bears'}\n");
```

The program's output is shown in Figure 9-10.

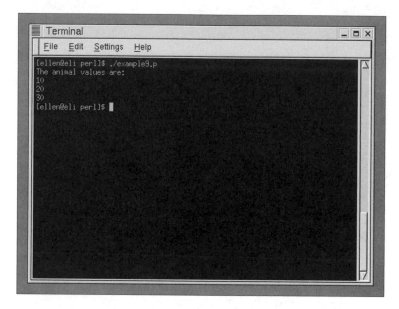

**Figure 9-10:** Output of example9.p

Now that you understand about data types, you are ready to learn more about programming using Perl. Perl's similarities and differences with other programming languages can be illustrated by comparing how the same program appears in awk and Perl.

## Perl versus Awk Programs

Awk does not require the programmer to explicitly set up looping structures as Perl does. Perl's while loop, on the other hand, is almost identical to the one found in C and C++. Awk, therefore, uses fewer lines of code to resolve pattern-matching extractions than Perl does. For example, look at the following awk program, awkcom.a, and its output. The program counts the number of comment lines that appear in the file specified on the command line.

```
#!/usr/bin/awk -f
# program name: awkcom.a
# purpose: Count the comment lines in a file
#          Enter the filename on the command line.

END {
     print "The file has ", line_count, " comment lines."
}
/^#/ && !/^#!/ { ++line_count }  # This occurs for every line.
```

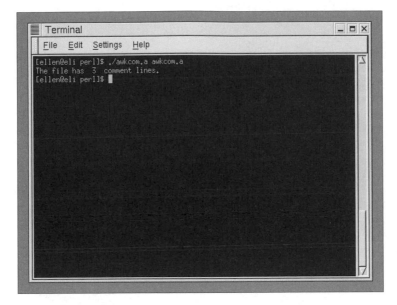

**Figure 9-11:** Output of awkcom.a

Now compare and contrast the awkcom.a program with this Perl program:

```perl
#!/usr/bin/perl
# program name: perlcom.p
# purpose: count the source file's comment lines

$filein = $ARGV[0];
while (<>)
{
    if (/^#/ && !/^#!/)
    {
        ++$line_count
    }
}
print ("File \"$filein\" has $line_count comment lines. \n"
);
```

Although the end results of both programs are very similar, you can see where the two programs differ. Awk uses an implicit while loop that automatically sends the entire contents of the file named on the command line to the pattern-matching and action part of the program. However, note that for the Perl program you need to build the while loop explicitly.

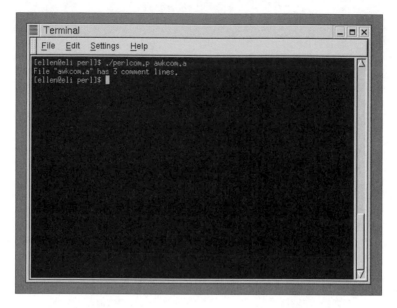

**Figure 9-12:** Output of perlcom.p

The first line of each program tells the shell program to run either the awk program or the Perl program and pass the statements in the file to the program for execution. Both programs also use the pound sign (#) to specify a comment line. Further, the pattern-matching code is the same in both programs. That is where the similarities end.

The –f option in the awk program tells the shell that the program is being called with a script file that contains the awk commands. Recall that awk contains more built-in commands to read lines from the file. All awk needs is the pattern-matching conditions to select the lines. The reading of the file, in awk, is implied as shown in this code.

```
/^#/&& !/^#!/ { ++line_count }
```

Awk also uses BEGIN and END to control when commands execute. All statements in a BEGIN block execute before the input file is read. All statements in an END block execute after all the contents of the input file have been read. This program only needs the END pattern.

In the Perl program, the code:

```
$filein = $ARGV[0];
```

takes the name of the file on the command line (ARGV[0]) and places it in a variable so it can be referenced later. The filename originally stored in ARGV[0] from the command line is destroyed during the while loop.

```
while (<>)
```

The <> symbol is called the **diamond operator.** Once the file is opened, you can access its data using the diamond operator. Each time it is called, it returns the next line from the file.

Curly braces open and close a block where you can place multiple statements:

```
if (/^#/ && !/^#!/)
{
    ++$line_count
}
```

This block tests to see if the line begins with the # character, but not with the #! characters. If true, the statement ++$line_count adds one to the $line_count variable and then closes the if block.

Whether awk or Perl is a good choice for you is a personal decision, but one should be part of your tool kit. There is no substitute for the kinds of work that either can perform very quickly, with minimal code preparation. For example, you probably would not want to write a C program for a task like scanning files for a matching pattern. Perl and awk are excellent when you are looking for a "needle in the haystack." Some say that the greater flexibility and power of Perl's expanded regular expressions give it a slight edge.

## How Perl Accesses Disk Files

Like most high-level programming languages, Perl uses filehandles to reference files. A **filehandle** is the name for an I/O connection between your Perl program and the operating system, and it can be used inside your program to open, read, write, and close the file. The convention is to use all uppercase letters for filehandles. In most instances, you must issue an open statement to open the file before you can access it. The exception to this occurs when you use the ARGV[0] variable to pass the filename to the program through the command line. In effect, you "open" it on the command line. As with other languages, every Perl program has three filehandles that are automatically opened: STDIN (the keyboard), STDOUT (the screen, to which the print and write functions are written by default), and STDERR (the screen, used to display error messages).

You will now learn common methods for opening and processing external files. The first program, perlread.p1, passes the filename on the command line, using the standard array variable that is reserved to do just that, ARGV[0]. This Perl program displays the contents of a file. (Recall that you can also use cat, less, and more for doing this.)

**To use Perl to display the contents of a file:**

**1** Use the cat command (or the editor of your choice) to create the test file students, containing the names Joseph, Alice, Mary, Zona, Aaron, Barbara, and Larry.

**2** Save the file.

**3** Use the editor of your choice to create the Perl program perlread.p1:

```
#!/usr/bin/perl
# program name: perlread.p1
# purpose: Display records in a file and count lines
$filein = $ARGV[0];
while (<>)
{
    print "$_";
    ++$line_count
}
print ("File \"$filein\" has $line_count lines. \n");
```

**4** Save the file and quit the editor.

**5** Give the file execute permission.

**6** Test the program by typing **./perlread.p1 students** and then pressing **Enter**. Your screen should now display the contents of the students file, shown in Figure 9-13.

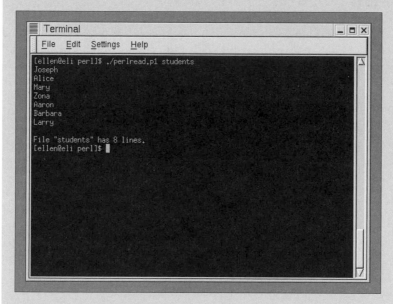

**Figure 9-13:** Output of perlread.p1

The first instruction ($filein = $ARGV[0];) saves the name of the file that is passed to the program and stores it in ARGV[0]. The while loop triggers the diamond operator (<>) that sequentially reads records from the file and places the value stored in ARGV[0] in the next record. This continues until the loop reaches the end of the file. When that happens, ARGV[0] contains a null (end-of-file character), so you cannot use ARGV[0] to reference the filename when the while loop terminates. Two commands inside the while loop are enclosed within curly braces: print "$_" displays each record that is read in, and ++$line_count increments (counts) the records in the file. The last command, print ("File \$filein\", has $line_count lines. \n") prints the name of the file (saved in $filein) and the number of lines in the file.

Next, you learn how to open the file from within your program, as opposed to passing it on the command line. All files opened inside programs must be closed before the program terminates.

**To use Perl to open a file from within a program:**

**1** Use the editor of your choice to create the file perlread.p2.

**2** Enter this Perl program:

```
#!/usr/bin/perl
# program name: perlread.p2
# purpose: Open disk file. Read and display the records in
#          the file. Count the number of records in the
#          file.

open (FILEIN, "students") || warn "Could not open students
file\n";
while (<FILEIN>)
{
     print "$_";
     ++$line_count;
}
print ("File \"students\" has $line_count lines. \n");
close (FILEIN);
```

**3** Save the file and quit the editor.

**4** Give the file execute permission.

**5** Test the program by typing **./perlread.p2** and then pressing **Enter**. Your screen should then display the contents of the students file, shown in Figure 9-14.

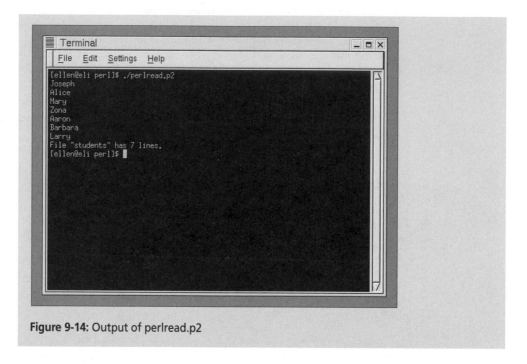

**Figure 9-14:** Output of perlread.p2

In the perlread.p2 program, the open function appears on line 5:

```
open (FILEIN, "students") || warn "Could not open students
file\n";
```

Nearly all program functions are written to return a value that indicates whether the function was carried out successfully. The values returned are considered true or false. A **true value** is usually represented with a 1, and sometimes any value greater than zero. A **false value** is represented with a 0 (zero). The open function returns true if the file is opened successfully and false if it failed to open. Opening a file can fail because the file is not found or because the file's permissions for reading and/or writing are not set. However, in Perl, a filehandle that has not been successfully opened can still be read, but you will get an immediate **EOF** (end-of-file signal), with no other noticeable effects. An EOF results in your program not letting you read from or write to the file, because the file is not available.

The two pipe characters "||" are the logical OR operator. When an expression on the left of a logical OR operator returns false, the expression on the right of the operator executes. The warn operator, on the right of the OR operator, displays an error message indicating the file did not open. Although displaying error conditions is not absolutely necessary in your programs, you should display them when it is obvious that the errors will cause subsequent problems if the program continues to run. This additional coding is especially essential in open statements.

After the file is open, access to the data is made through the diamond operator (<FILEIN>). When the diamond operator reaches the end of the file, it terminates the while loop. Except for the open and close statements and the use of the diamond operator, the perlread.p2 program is identical to perlread.p1.

# Using Perl to Sort

One of the most important tasks in managing data is organizing it into a useable format. Perl provides a powerful and flexible sort operator. It can sort string or numeric data in ascending or descending order. It even allows advanced sorting operations where you define your own sorting routine.

## Using Perl to Sort Alphanumeric Fields

You will now sort words in a Perl program into alphabetical order using the sort function.

**To use Perl's sort function:**

**1** Use the editor of your choice to create the program perlsort.p1. Enter the code:

```
#!/usr/bin/perl
# program name: perlsort.p1
# purpose: Sort a list of names contained inside an array
# Syntax: perlsort.p1 <Enter>
#=========================================================
@somelist = ( "Oranges", "Apples", "Tangerines",
              "Pears", "Bananas", "Pineapples"
            );
@sortedlist = sort @somelist;
print "@sortedlist";
print"\n";
```

**2** Save the file and exit the editor.

**3** Use the chmod command to grant the file execute permission.

**4** Run perlsort.p1. Your screen should look similar to Figure 9-15.

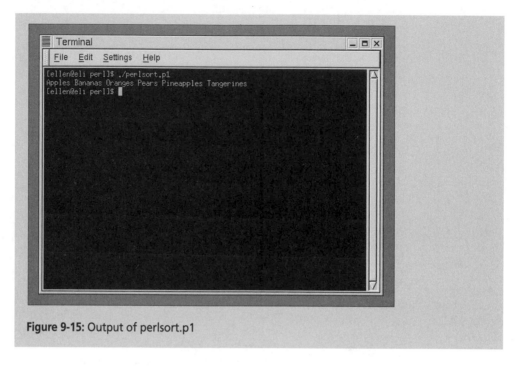

Figure 9-15: Output of perlsort.p1

Looking at the program, the statement:

```
@somelist = ( "Oranges", "Apples", "Tangerines",  "Pears",
"Bananas", "Pineapples");
```

puts the value of (Oranges, Apples, Tangerines, Pears, Bananas, Pineapples) into @somelist. The statement:

```
@sortedlist = sort @somelist;
```

calls the Perl sort function and returns the sorted output to the array variable, @sortedlist. The last two statements in the program print the sorted results and skip a line before the program terminates and returns to the command line.

Data is not always coded as part of the program or entered at the keyboard. Often, programs must read information from files. The next example demonstrates how Perl accesses a file by passing the filename on the command line.

**To use Perl to access a file by passing the filename on the command line:**

**1** Use the editor of your choice to create the program perlsort.p2. Enter the code:

```
#!/usr/bin/perl
# program name: perlsort.p2
# purpose: Sorts a text file alphabetically. Filename is
#          entered on the command line.
# Syntax: perlsort.p2 filename <Enter>
```

```
#============================================================
$x = 0;
while (<>)
{
  $somelist[$x] = $_;
  $x++;
}
@sortedlist = sort @somelist;
print @sortedlist;
```

2   Save the file and exit the editor.

3   Give the perlsort.p2 file execute permissions.

4   Run perlsort.p2, using students as the test file, by typing **./perlsort.p2 students** and then pressing **Enter**. Your screen should now display the list of student names, shown in Figure 9-16.

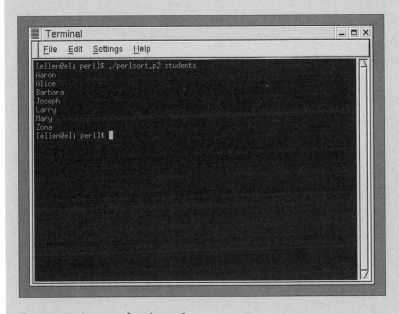

**Figure 9-16:** Output of perlsort.p2

The perlsort.p2 program uses the statement:

```
$x - 0;
```

to initialize a variable, $x, to contain an index to the array. The first element of every array is zero (0). In the while loop,

```
while (<>)
{
    $somelist[$x] = $_;
    $x++;
```

the next line in the file is automatically copied into the $_ variable. The assignment statement:

```
    $somelist[$x] = $_;
```

copies the contents of the $_ variable into an element of the array. The element is determined by the variable $x, which is used as a subscript. After the assignment operation occurs, the following statement executes:

```
    $x++;
```

The ++ operator adds one to its argument, so the statement increments the variable $x. As a result, the first name, Aaron, is placed in $somelist[0], Alice is placed in $somelist[1], and so on.

The statement:

```
@sortedlist = sort @somelist;
```

sorts the array, @somelist, placing the alphabetized names into @sortedlist, and the final instruction prints the alphabetized list of students' names.

## Using Perl to Sort Numeric Fields

Sorting numeric fields requires using a subroutine where you can define comparison conditions (e.g., greater than, less then, or equal to) between the data you are sorting. The sort routine is then called repeatedly, passing two elements to be compared on each call. The scalar variables $a and $b store the two values that are compared to select the larger value. Using the comparison operation, a return code of −1, 0, or +1 is returned, depending on whether $a is less than, equal to, or greater than $b, as in the demonstrated code:

```
sub numbers
{
    if ($a < $b) { -1; }
    elsif ($a == $b) { 0; }
    else { +1; }
}
```

When sorting numbers, you need to instruct Perl to use this sort subroutine as the comparison function, rather than the built-in ASCII ascending sort (the default). To do this, place the name of the subroutine between the keyword *sort* and the list of items to be sorted:

```
$sortednumbers = sort numbers 101, 87, 34, 12, 1, 76;
```

The statement instructs Perl to sort the values in the list but use the numbers subroutine to determine their order. The output is in numeric order, not ASCII order.

The numeric comparison of $a and $b is performed so frequently that Larry Wall, Perl's creator, developed a special Perl operator for numeric sorts, <=>. This sort operator, known as the **spaceship operator**, reduces coding requirements. To illustrate the code savings, compare the next sort subroutine using the spaceship operator with the previous one:

```
sub numbers
{
     $a <=> $b;
}
```

This numbers subroutine produces the same result as the first example, which uses an if-else statement. Perl allows an even more compact notation: the **inline sort block**, which looks like this:

```
@sortednumbers = sort { $a <=> $b; } @numberlist;
```

This statement uses the block { $a <=> $b; } as the sort routine. It eliminates the need for a separate subroutine. Let's examine how a Perl program sorts numeric data.

**To use Perl for numeric sorting:**

**1** Create the file numberlist, containing the data **130, 100, 121, 101, 120,** and **122.**

**2** Use the editor of your choice to create the perlsort.p3 program. Enter this code:

```
#!/usr/bin/perl
# program name: perlsort.p3
# purpose: Sorts numerically using a subroutine. Filename
#          is entered on the command line.
# Syntax: perlsort.p3 filename <Enter>
#=============================================================
$x = 0;
while (<>)
{
     $somelist[$x] = $_;
     $x++;
}
@sortedlist = sort numbers @somelist;
print @sortedlist;

sub numbers
{
     if ($a < $b)
          {-1; }
     elsif ($a == $b)
          { 0; }
     else
          {+1; }
}
```

**3** Save the file and exit the editor.

**4** Use the chmod command to grant the file execute permission.

**5** Test the program by typing **./Perlsort.p3 numberlist** and then press **Enter**. Your screen should appear similar to Figure 9-17.

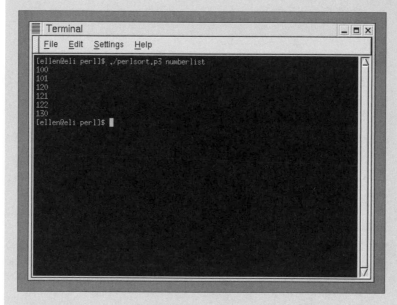

**Figure 9-17:** Output of perlsort.p3

The perlsort.p3 program uses a sort subroutine that compares $a and $b numerically rather than textually and initializes the array element index to start with the first element, 0. The while loop,

```
while (<>)
{
    $somelist[$x] = $_;
    $x++;
}
```

works the same as previously described, in that it reads records from a file and stores the lines inside an array.

The sort subroutine,

```
sub numbers
{
    if ($a < $b) { -1; }
    elsif ($a == $b) { 0; }
    else ( +1; }
}
```

compares the two numbers that are sequentially passed to it from the while loop. If the value in $a is less than the value in $b, the subroutine returns −1. If $a is equal to $b, the subroutine returns 0. Otherwise, the subroutine returns +1.

You will now see how using the spaceship operator can save you coding time.

**To use Perl's spaceship operator:**

**1** Use the editor of your choice to create the program perlsort.p4. Enter this code.

```perl
#!/usr/bin/perl
# program name: perlsort.p4
# purpose: Sort numerically using spaceship operator (<=>)
# syntax: perlsort.p4 filename <Enter>
#============================================================
$x = 0;
while (<>)
{
    $somelist[$x] = $_;
    $x++;
}
@sortedlist = sort numbers @somelist;
print @sortedlist;

sub numbers
{
    $a <=> $b;
}
```

**2** Save the file and exit the editor.

**3** Use the chmod command to grant the file execute permission.

**4** Test the program by typing **./perlsort.p4 numberlist** and then press **Enter**. Again, your screen should display the list of numbers sorted in ascending order, as shown in Figure 9-18.

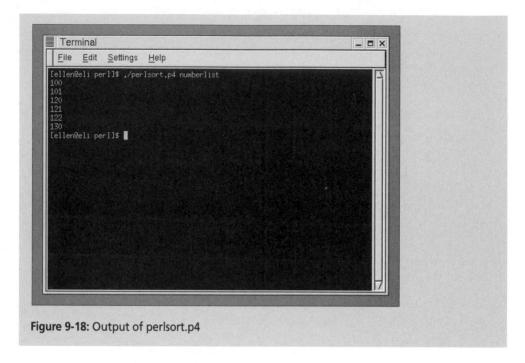

Figure 9-18: Output of perlsort.p4

In the perlsort.p4 program, notice that the only code changes to the perlsort.p3 program are those found in the shortened subroutine.

Now that you are more familiar with Perl, you will learn how to create a Web page. Then you will be ready to begin creating the Web page for Dominion Consulting.

 # SUMMARY

- Perl is being extensively used as a powerful text-manipulation tool similar to awk.

- Perl is written in scripts that are translated and executed by the Perl program.

- The programmer has to write process handling instructions for data items to prevent misidentification of data types and subsequent processing errors.

- Perl has three basic data types: scalars, arrays, and hashes. A scalar is a simple variable, such as a number or a name. Scalar variable names begin with $. Arrays are ordered lists of scalars that are accessed with numeric subscripts, staring at zero [0]. Array variable names are preceded with the at sign, @. Hashes are unordered sets of key/value pairs that you can access using the keys as subscripts. Hash variables begin with the percent sign, %.

- A list is an ordered group of simple variables or literals, separated by commas. For example, (101, 102, 103, 104) is an array of four values, 101 through 104.

- Anything besides a textual sort must be handled with a sort subroutine for which you can provide your own comparison function to determine greater-than, less-than, or equal-to conditions between the elements being sorted.

# REVIEW QUESTIONS

1. To read data from a file, Perl _____.
   a. works just like awk
   b. uses a while loop like C programs
   c. uses the spaceship operator
   d. always uses an array to store the records from the file

2. Perl scripts _____.
   a. begin with line indicating that /usr/bin/perl is the interpreter
   b. are not made executable
   c. do not support the use of if statements
   d. do not support the use of while loops

3. The spaceship operator refers to _____.
   a. CGI programming
   b. a shortcut for sorting names in Perl
   c. a shortcut for sorting numbers in Perl
   d. a Perl in-line sort

4. What does the statement $x = <STDIN>; perform?
   a. displays the contents of $x
   b. copies the string "STDIN" to $x
   c. copies the contents of the variable STDIN to $x
   d. reads keyboard input into $x

5. The == operator _____.
   a. tests two numbers for equality
   b. tests two strings for equality
   c. tests either numbers or strings for equality
   d. performs an assignment

6. The eq operator _____.
   a. tests two numbers for equality
   b. tests two strings for equality
   c. tests either numbers or strings for equality
   d. performs an assignment

7. The $ character precedes _____.
   a. array names
   b. scalar variable names
   c. hash names
   d. constants

8. The @ character precedes _____.
   a. array names
   b. scalar variable names
   c. hash names
   d. constants

9. The % character precedes _____.
   a. array names
   b. scalar variable names
   c. hash names
   d. constants

10. Assume that a program contains the code:

    ```
    @food = ("fruit", "steak", "bread", "vegetables" );
    ```
    What does the next statement print in the same program?

    ```
    print ("$food[2]");
    ```

    a. fruit
    b. steak
    c. bread
    d. vegetables

11. Assume that this code exists in a program:

    ```
    %food = ("fruit", 5, "steak", 10, "bread", 15, "vegetables",
    20 );
    ```
    What does the next statement print in the same program?

    ```
    print ("$food{'bread'}");
    ```

    a. 5
    b. 15
    c. steak
    d. bread

# EXERCISES

1. Write a Perl script to print "Hello Perl".
2. Write a Perl script to sort the numbers 1, 8, 15, 1000, 12, which are located in a memory array.
3. Create the file Ex2numbers using the numbers from Exercise 2. Write a Perl script using the spaceship operator to sort and display Ex2numbers.

4.  Write a Perl script with a hash variable. The hash variable should contain these names and telephone numbers:

Jean James          555-9898

Rhonda Smith        555-0982

Joe Milner          555-8944

Greg Jones          555-0716

The program should display the phone numbers of each individual.

 # DISCOVERY EXERCISES

1.  Modify the program perlcom.p (developed earlier in this chapter), so it counts all lines in the file that are not comments.

2.  Write a Perl program to count the number of records in the students file (created earlier in this chapter) that begin with the letter A.

3.  Write a Perl program that converts a value in inches to a value in centimeters and displays the result. (1 inch = 2.54 centimeters.)

4.  Write a Perl program that uses a while loop to display the values 1 through 12 and their squares.

5.  Write a Perl program that asks the user to enter two numeric values. Store the values in $x and $y. If $y is not zero, divide $x by $y and display the result. If $y is zero, display an error message indicating that division by zero is not possible.

**In this lesson you will:**

- Create an HTML document for the World Wide Web
- Use Perl and CGI scripts to make your Web pages interactive
- Use X-Window and Netscape to retrieve Web pages

# Creating an Interactive Web Page

## Setting Up a Web Page

You can create a Web page using **HTML (Hyper Text Markup Language)**. HTML is a format for creating documents with embedded codes known as **tags**. When the document is viewed in a Web browser, such as Netscape Navigator or Internet Explorer, the tags give the document special properties. Examples of properties include foreground and background colors, font size and color, and the placement of graphic images. In addition, HTML tags let you place **hyperlinks** in a document. A hyperlink is text or an object that, when clicked, loads another document and displays it in the browser.

After you use HTML to create a Web page, you then publish the page on a Web server. A **Web server** is a system connected to the Internet running Web server software, such as Apache. The Web server software lets other users access the HTML document via the Internet.

You may experiment with and test HTML documents using a UNIX or Linux system's localhost networking feature. The **localhost** feature allows your UNIX or Linux system to access its own internal network configuration instead of an external network. To use the localhost, you do not need to be connected to the Internet. More importantly, the localhost can emulate a real-world Web site, so you can carry out the testing and development of your new Web pages. Stand-alone testing of new Web pages is recommended: after fully testing your work, you can then later transfer your documents to any Web server, knowing that they are ready to perform.

**tip**

To run the Web pages and CGI programs in this lesson, you must have the Apache Web Server program installed on your Linux Computer. (See Appendix C for instructions on installing Apache.)

# Creating Web Pages

You may use a visual HTML editor, such as Netscape Composer or Microsoft FrontPage, to create Web pages. These programs let you graphically construct a Web page in a "what you see is what you get" fashion. If you have no visual HTML editor, all you need is a text editor. You create the HTML document by typing its text and the desired embedded tags. Here is a sample HTML file.

```
<HTML>
<HEAD><TITLE>My Simple Web Page</TITLE></HEAD>
<BODY>
<H1>Just a Simple Web Page</H1>
This is a Web page with no frills!
</BODY>
</HTML>
```

All special codes contained inside angled brackets <> are tags. The first tag, <HTML>, identifies the file as an HTML document. Notice the corresponding </HTML> tag at the end of the file. Everything between the <HTML> and </HTML> tags are considered text with HTML tags. In general, most tags are used this way. One tag marks the beginning of a section, while a corresponding tag marks the end of the section.

Note that there are two parts to the code: a head and a body. The **head** contains the title, which appears on the top bar of your browser window. The **body** defines what appears within the browser window. All other tags refine the Web page's appearance. Figure 9-19 shows the Web page's appearance in the Netscape Web browser.

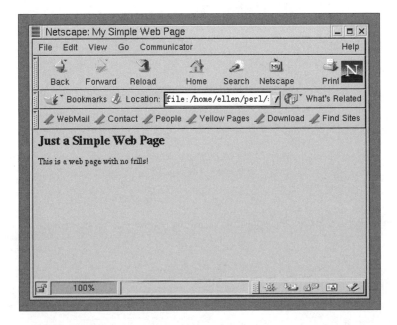

**Figure 9-19:** Simple Web page

You can use tags to set background and foreground colors and to manipulate text with such tags as <FONT SIZE=n>(*insert text here*). You can change text sizes with the heading tags, where <H1> is the largest and <H6> is the smallest. (However, note that users' browsers may also automatically change the actual text size.)

Because standard HTML ignores multiple spaces, tabs, and carriage returns, you can enclose text within <PRE></PRE>(preformatted text) tag pairs. Otherwise, any consecutive spaces, tabs, carriage returns, or combinations produce a single space. You can also use the <P> tag, which creates two line breaks, or the <BR> tag, which creates one line break. Neither tag requires a closing tag.

Browsers automatically wrap text so you don't need to worry about page widths. To center text, however, use <CENTER>(*text here*)</CENTER>. To indent from both margins, use <BLOCKQUOTE>(*text here*)</BLOCKQUOTE>. To change color, use <FONT COLOR="RGB"(*text here*)</FONT>, where RGB is the RGB color code. An **RGB color code** is a set of three numbers that specify a color's red, green, and blue components. For example, the code 512218 specifies a red component of 51, a green component of 22, and a blue component of 18. The higher the number, the more intense the color component.

Here is another example of an HTML file.

```
<HTML>
<HEAD><TITLE>UNIX Programming Tools</TITLE></HEAD>
<BODY>
<H1><CENTER>My UNIX Programming Tools</CENTER></H1>
<H2>Languages</H2>
<P>Perl</P>
<P>Shell Scripts</P>
<P>C and C++</P>
<H2>Editors</H2>
<P>vi</P>
<P>Emacs</P>
<H2>Other Tools</H2>
<P>awk</P>
<P>sed</P>
</BODY>
</HTML>
```

Figure 9-20 shows the file as it appears in a Web browser.

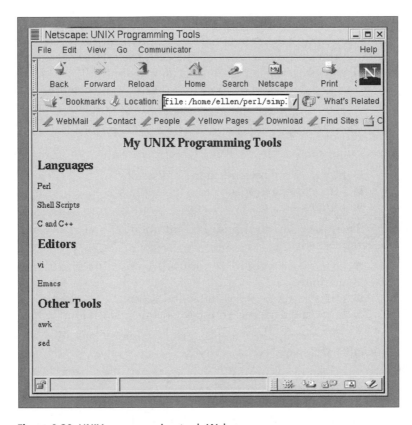

**Figure 9-20:** UNIX programming tools Web page

Now that you have general knowledge of creating Web pages, you need to learn how to use Perl and CGI to make them interactive.

## CGI Overview

Perl is the most commonly used language for **CGI (Common Gateway Interface) programming.** CGI is a protocol, or set of rules, governing how browsers and servers communicate. Any script that sends or receives information from a server needs to follow the standards specified by CGI. Thus, scripts written in Perl follow the CGI protocol. CGI Perl scripts are specifically written to get, process, and return information through your Web pages, that is, they make your Web pages interactive.

To allow your HTML document to accept input, especially where CGI rules apply, precede the input area with a description of what you want users to enter. For example, if you want users to enter cost, you would use this code:

```
Total Cost? <INPUT TYPE=text NAME=cost SIZE=10>
```

In addition, consistent with transmitting information to and from Web sites, you can use the special code INPUT TYPE=submit, which sends the data out when a user clicks the Submit button. The destination that you wish to receive the submitted information is coded into the FORM tag. The **FORM tag** specifies how to obtain the information to be transferred. There are two methods, GET and POST. The **GET** method transfers the data within the URL itself. **POST** uses the body portion of the HTTP request to pass parameters. (You will use the POST method in this chapter.)

You can download hundreds of already written scripts and use them in your own Web page applications. Some of these scripts are free, such as subparseform.lib, which is used in these demonstrations. It was downloaded from http://www.cook-wood.com/perl.

Other sources for free Perl CGI scripts are:

- http://www.worldwidemart.com/scripts
- http://www.extropia.com
- http://www.awsd.com/scripts

These sites provide useful Perl information and answers to FAQs (frequently asked questions):

- http://www.perl.com (a huge site that is a home to a vast collection of information)
- http://language.perl.com/faq/index.html
- http://language.perl.com/info/documentation.html

Before creating the Web page for Dominion Consulting, you will first see how a sample Web page works in UNIX.

**To see a sample Web page:**

**1** To make a subdirectory to store your HTML, CGI scripts, and Perl scripts, type **cd /home/httpd/cgi-bin**, press **Enter**, type **mkdir <your user name>**, and then press **Enter**. For example, if you are the user Ellen, you will create the directory /home/httpd/cgi-bin/ellen.

Note: Make sure that the /home/httpd/cgi-bin directory is given full access permissions (usually done by the System Administrator). To do this on your own PC, log on as superuser, type **chmod 777 /home/httpd/cgi-bin** and then press **Enter**.

**2** Change your working directory to the new directory you created in Step 1.

**3** See your instructor or technical support person for instructions for copying the following programs and scripts to the new directory:

projest.html

projest.cgi

subparseform.lib

**4** Start the X-Window system (the UNIX equivalent of Microsoft Windows) to run the Netscape browser. To do so, type **startx** and then press **Enter**. Your screen should look similar to Figure 9-21.

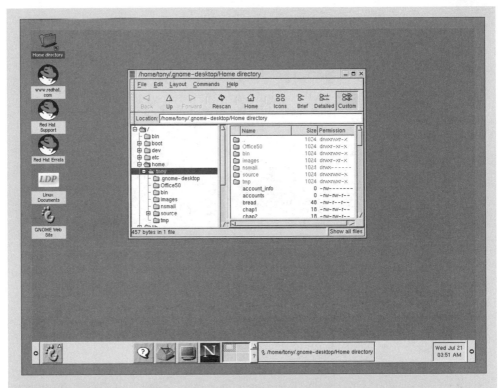

**Figure 9-21:** X-Window system

**5** Within X-Window, you can execute Netscape from a command line. You can access the command line in a Terminal window. To open a Terminal window, click the **Terminal** icon, illustrated in Figure 9-22.

**Figure 9-22:** Terminal icon

**6** The Terminal window appears, as shown in Figure 9-23. Click inside the Terminal window to make it active.

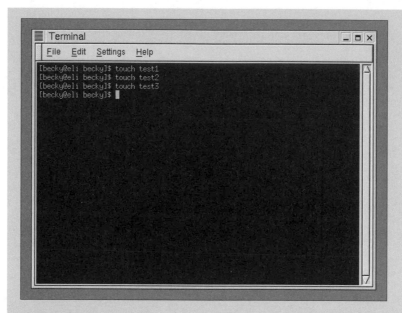

**Figure 9-23:** Terminal window

**7** You will view the file projest.html in the web browser, but first you must modify the file so it will know where its CGI script is located. Load the file projest.html into the editor of your choice. The contents of the file are shown below.

```
<!- Program Name: projest.html ->

<HTML><HEAD><TITLE>Dominion Project
Analysis</TITLE></HEAD>
<BODY>

<H2>Average Profit per Project Calculation</H@>
<FORM METHOD=POST ACTION="http://localhost/cgi-
  bin/ellen/projest.cgi">
Total cost of projects last year? <INPUT TYPE=text
NAME=projcost SIZE=10>
Number of Projects? <INPUT TYPE=text NAME=projects
  SIZE=10>
Project revenue received? <INPUT TYPE=text NAME=revenue
  SIZE=10>
<HR><INPUT TYPE=submit NAME=submit VALUE=Submit>
<INPUT TYPE=reset NAME=reset VALUE="Start over">
</FORM></BODY></HTML>
```

The line in boldface must be modified. Change the name "ellen" to your logon name. For example, if your logon name is sam, you will modify the line to read:

```
<FORM METHOD=POST ACTION="http://localhost/cgi-
bin/sam/projest.cgi">
```

Save the file and exit the editor.

**8** You must now execute the Netscape browser to see the sample Web page. To open Netscape Communicator, type netscape and then press Enter. The Netscape opening screen appears, as shown in Figure 9-24.

Note: If this is the first time that you have accessed Netscape, you may have to click the Accept button at the lower right of the opening screen.

**9** Click in the **Location** text box, press **Del** to delete the current text, and then type **file:/home/httpd/cgi-bin/<your user name>/projest.html** as the location of your Web page. For example, if you are the user Ellen, type file:/home/httpd/cgi-bin/ellen/projest.html.

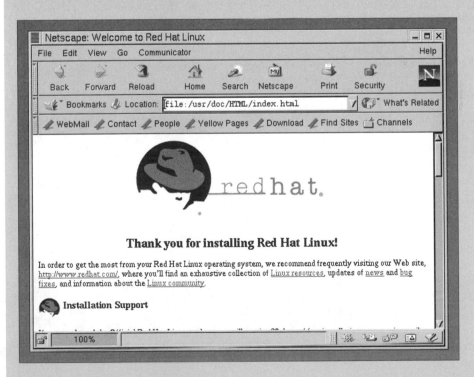

**Figure 9-24:** Netscape opening screen

**10** Press **Enter**. The opening screen for the projest.html Web page appears, as illustrated in Figure 9-25.

Here is the source code for the projest.html file.

**Click on the Submit button to ask Apache to use the Common Gateway Interface to retrieve and run the projest.cgi script**

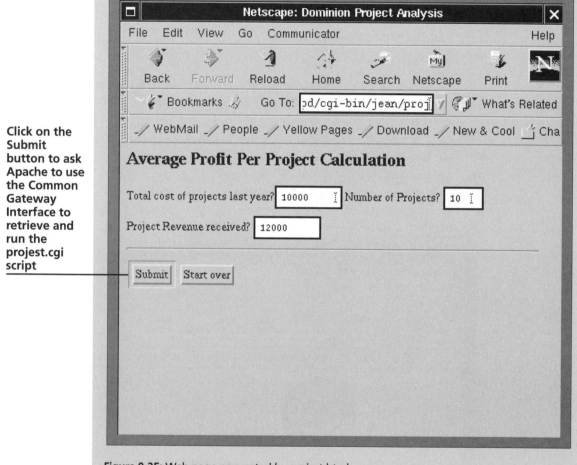

Figure 9-25: Web page generated by projest.html

**11** To confirm that you want to use the Common Gateway Interface connection, click the **Submit** button in the Confirmation screen. (You can avoid the Confirmation screen in the future if you click the Show the Alert Next Time button.) Perl executes the program and the Apache server then passes the Web page response back to the Netscape browser for display. Your screen, the final screen that is part of the Perl/cgi script response, should now look similar to Figure 9-26.

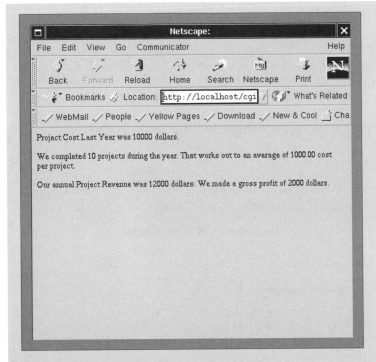

**Figure 9-26:** Final Perl/CGI script response screen

Here is the source code used to generate this Web page.

```
#!/usr/bin/perl
# Program name: projest.cgi
require "subparseform.lib;"

&Parse_Form;
$projcost = $formdata{'projcost'};
$projects = $formdata{'projects'};
$revenue = $formdata{'revenue'};

$average = $projcost / $projects;
$average = sprintf("%.2f", $average);
$grossprofit = $revenue - $projcost;

print "Content-type: text/html\n\n";
print "<P>Project Cost Last Year was $projcost dollars.";
print "<P>We completed $projects projects during the year.
That works out to an average of $average cost per
project.";
print "<P>Our annual Project Revenue was $revenue dollars.
We made a gross profit of $grossprofit dollars";
```

Now that you have seen a demonstration of how Web pages work using UNIX, you are ready to create your own Web page.

## Creating the Dominion Consulting Web Page

Dominion Consulting is currently offering all its hotel management customers a special promotional price for three customized applications. The company wants to present a Web page that offers customers an opportunity to order the promotional items over the Internet. The planned Web page is shown in Figure 9-27. You will now create that page.

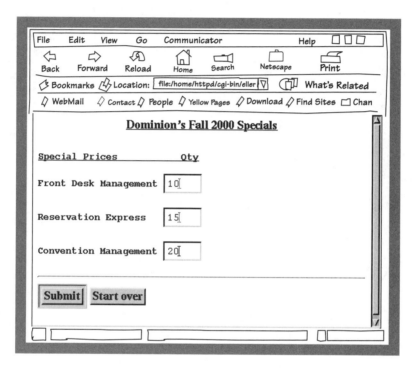

**Figure 9-27:** Planned Dominion Consulting sales promotion Web page

### To create a Web page:

**1**  Use the editor of your choice to create the HTML document software.html. Enter this HTML code:

```
<!- Program Name: software.html->
<HTML><HEAD><TITLE>Dominion Consulting</TITLE></HEAD>
<BODY BGCOLOR=WHITE>
<CENTER><H1><U>Dominion's Fall 2000 Specials</H1></CENTER>
<FORM METHOD=POST ACTION="http://localhost/cgi-bin/<your
user name>/software.cgi">
<BR>
<H2><U><PRE>Special Prices                    Qty</PRE></U></H2>
<FONT SIZE=5>
<PRE>Front Desk Management <INPUT TYPE=text NAME=frontdk
Size=5></PRE>
<PRE>Reservation Express    <INPUT TYPE=text NAME=reserve
```

```
SIZE=5></PRE>
<PRE>Convention Management <INPUT TYPE=text NAME=convmgt
SIZE=5></PRE>
<HR><INPUT TYPE=submit NAME=submit VALUE=Submit>
<INPUT TYPE=reset NAME=reset VALUE="Start over">
</FORM></BODY></HTML>
```

**2**  Save the file in your cgi-bin/<your user name> directory, and exit the editor.

**3**  Now use the editor to create the CGI Perl script software.cgi. Enter this code:

```perl
#!/usr/bin/perl
# Program name: software.cgi

require "subparseform.lib";&Parse_Form;
$frontdk = $formdata{'frontdk'};
$reserve = $formdata{'reserve'};
$convmgt = $formdata{'convmgt'};

$qtotal = $frontdk+$reserve+$convmgt;
$tfrontdk = $frontdk*200;
$treserve = $reserve*150;
$tconvmgt = $convmgt*180;
$total = $tfrontdk+$treserve+$tconvmgt;

print "Content-type: text/html\n\n";
print "";
print "</FONT><FONT  SIZE=6 PTSIZE=20>

</P><P ALIGN=CENTER><B><CENTER>Dominion Special</CENTER>

</P><P ALIGN=LEFT></FONT><FONT  SIZE=3 PTSIZE=10>
";
print "<CENTER></FONT><FONT  SIZE=5 PTSIZE=16>

<U>
Thank you for your order.</U>

</FONT><FONT  SIZE=3 PTSIZE=10></CENTER>";
print "
";
print "<TABLE BORDER=1 BGCOLOR=CYAN ALIGN=CENTER
WIDTH=300 CELLSPACING=5>";
print "<TR><TH ALIGN=CENTER>Qty</TH>";
print "<TH ALIGN=CENTER>Software</TH>";
print "<TH ALIGN=CENTER>Total</TH></TR>";
print "<TR><TD ALIGN=CENTER>$frontdk</TD>";
print "<TD ALIGN=CENTER>Front Desk Management</TD>";
print "<TD ALIGN=CENTER>\$$tfrontdk</TD></TR>";
print "<TR><TD ALIGN=CENTER>$reserve</TD>";
print "<TD ALIGN=CENTER>Reservation Express</TD>";
print "<TD ALIGN=CENTER>\$$treserve</TD></TR>";
print "<TR><TD ALIGN=CENTER>$convmgt</TD>";
print "<TD ALIGN=CENTER>Convention Management</TD>";
```

```
print "<TD ALIGN=CENTER>\$$tconvmgt</TD></TR>";
print "<TR><TD ALIGN=CENTER>$qtotal</TD>";
print "<TD ALIGN=CENTER>Total:</TD>";
print "<TD ALIGN=CENTER>\$$total</TD></TR></TABLE>";
</XMP></FONT><FONT  COLOR="#0f0f0f" BACK="#fffffe"
SIZE=3 PTSIZE=10>
```

**4** Save the file in your cgi-bin/<your user name> directory, and exit the editor.

**5** Use the chmod command to grant the file execute permission.

Now that you have entered both the code for the Web page and CGI script, you should test your work. Recall that with Linux Red Hat 6.0, you can use the local-host to carry out the testing and development of your new Web page.

### To test a Web page:

**1** Within X-Window, start Netscape Communicator by opening a Terminal window, typing **netscape** at the command line, and then pressing **Enter**.

**2** In the location box, type **file:/home/httpd/cgi-bin/<your user name>/soft-ware.html**. Press **Enter**.

**3** Enter quantities of **10, 15,** and **20** for the products, and then click the **Submit** button. Your screen should now look similar to Figure 9-28.

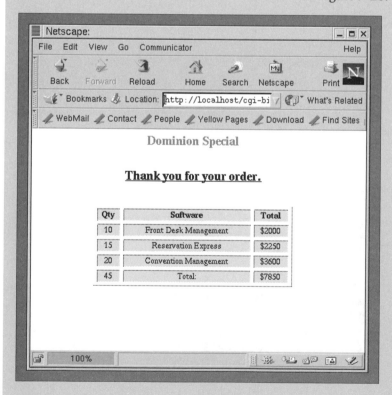

**Figure 9-28:** Web page returned to the browser from software.cgi

You have successfully created the Web page for Dominion Consulting by using your knowledge of Perl programming.

# SUMMARY

- An HTML document contains two parts: a head and a body. The head contains the title, which appears on the top bar of your browser window. The body defines what appears within the browser window.

- CGI (Common Gateway Interface) is a protocol or set of rules governing how browsers and servers communicate. Any script that sends or receives information from a server needs to follow the standards specified by CGI.

- To run your Web pages, you need to be in X-Window and have access to a Web browser such as Netscape Communicator and a Web server such as Apache. Using UNIX, you can also test your Web pages using the localhost feature.

# REVIEW QUESTIONS

1. True or False: HTML tags are special codes enclosed in square brackets ([]).

2. True or False: Most tags are used in pairs: one marks the beginning of a section while a corresponding tag marks the end of a section.

3. Which section of an HTML document contains the title?
   a. HEAD
   b. BODY
   c. PARAGRAPH
   d. BLOCKQUOTE

4. Text between the _____ tags appears centered.
   a. [CENTER] and [/CENTER]
   b. <CENTER> and </CENTER>
   c. <ALIGN=center> and </ALIGN>
   d. <JUSTIFY=center> and </JUSTIFY>

5. To run Netscape in UNIX or Linux, you _____.
   a. need not be in X-Window
   b. should be in X-Window
   c. must be in X-Window
   d. must have the Apache server installed

6. A basic HTML document has a _____.
   a. head and a body
   b. title and a body
   c. set of tags
   d. link to other Web pages

7. The _____ button in an HTML script is used to transfer the data to a Web server that passes it to a CGI script.
   a. Transfer
   b. Accept
   c. Go
   d. Submit

8. Which of the following is not true?
   a. Perl is the most commonly used CGI programming language.
   b. Perl is the only language used for CGI programming.
   c. CGI scripts do not require any language other than .cgi scripts.
   d. Perl CGI scripts are invoked by Web pages.

9. In Perl, the _____ character precedes an array variable name.
   a. $
   b. #
   c. %
   d. @

# EXERCISES

1. Create a personal Web page with your name, address, telephone number, and a brief paragraph describing your hobbies and interests. Your name should be centered in a large heading.

2. Design a Web page that allows the user to enter his or her age. The page should have a Submit button that, when clicked, invokes a CGI script. The script should display the user's age in days. (Don't worry about leap years.)

3. Design a Web page that allows the user to enter the width and length of a rectangle. The page should have a Submit button that, when clicked, invokes a CGI script. The script should display the area of the rectangle (width × length).

# DISCOVERY EXERCISES

1. Create an HTML and CGI Perl script to create an interactive Web page to accept your first and last name in the HTML file and pass it to the CGI Perl script, where it displays, "Hello," followed by your first and last name.

2. Create a Perl program to read both the students file and the number list file. Display the students' names in alphabetical order. Display the numbers in the order in which they were read.

3. Design a Web page that is a simple addition calculator. It should allow the user to enter two values. When the user clicks a Submit button, a CGI script returns the sum of the two numbers.

# CHAPTER

# 10

# Developing UNIX Applications in C and C++

**case ▶** Dominion Consulting's customers are becoming more conscious of computer security. The programming staff is answering an increasing number of questions about data privacy and protection. Your supervisor asks you to write a simple program that can demonstrate how file encryption and decryption works. (**File encryption** is an operation that scrambles a file's contents into a secret code. A **decryption operation** restores the file to its original state.)

**In this lesson you will:**

- Create simple C programs
- Use the make utility to revise and maintain source files
- Identify program errors and fix them
- Create a complete C programming application

# C Language Programming

In this chapter, you learn not only how to write C programs, but also how to use other software development tools, such as the make utility. The **make utility** is a UNIX program that controls changes and additions to the programs as they are being developed. Finally, you also write simple C++ programs, so you can understand how C++ programming differs from C programming.

## Introducing C Programming

C is the language in which UNIX was developed and refined. The original UNIX operating system was written in assembly language. **Assembly language** is a low-level language that provides maximum access to all the computer's devices, both internal and external. However, assembly language requires more coding and a greater in-depth treatment of all internal control items. The C language was partly developed to resolve the more lengthy requirements of assembly language. It has drastically reduced these requirements to a high-level set of easy-to-understand instructions. Dennis Ritchie and Brian Kernighan, two Bell Lab employees, rewrote most of UNIX using C in the early 1970s.

> Note: Ken Thompson, another Bell Lab employee, also deserves credit for his influence on the development of C. He wrote a forerunner of C, called B, in 1970 for the first UNIX system to run on the DEC PDP-7 mini-computer.

Since its inception, the C language has evolved from its original design as an operating system language to its current status as a major tool in the development of any high-performance application for general use. Since C is native to UNIX, it works best as a UNIX application development tool, where the operating system views the application as an extension of its core functionality. For example, daemons (specialized system process that run in the background) are written in C. They access the UNIX system code just as any other part of the operating system.

C programming may be described, in a nutshell, as a language that uses relatively small, isolated functions to break down large complex tasks into small and easily resolved subtasks. This function-oriented design allows programmers to create their own program functions to interact with the predefined system functions to create powerful and comprehensive solutions to the largest of applications.

Using C to write a program for Dominion's security demonstration is a good choice. Because C is a compiled language, the program source code cannot be viewed. This is an important consideration, because the source code of a security program reveals how the program works. Before you begin to write this program, however, you first need to learn the basics of C programming.

## Creating a C Program

A C program consists of separate bodies of code, known as **functions**. In other languages, bodies of code have different names, such as subroutines or procedures. Each of these bodies of code is designed so it contributes to the execution of a single task. You put together a collection of these functions, and they become a program. Within the program the functions call each other as needed and work to solve the problem for which the program was originally designed.

Creating a program is never done in a single step. As a programmer, you complete many phases before the program is ready to run. The first phase is to create the source code of the program. As with shell scripts and Perl programs, you use a text editor, such as vi or Emacs, to create C programs.

The next phase is to execute the preprocessor and compiler. The **preprocessor** makes modifications to your program, such as including the contents of other files and creating constant values. After the preprocessor prepares your program, the **compiler** executes. The compiler is a program that translates the source code into **object code**, which consists of binary instructions. If you made errors, the compiler locates many of them. When this happens, you use the text editor to correct the errors and recompile the program.

Many compilers translate source code into assembly code. This requires that an **assembler** be invoked to translate the assembly code into object code. The compiler usually invokes the assembler automatically, so you do not need to enter additional commands. Some compilers translate directly from source code into object code, skipping the assembly step. Whatever type of compiler you use, the outcome of this phase is the creation of a file that contains object code.

The final phase requires the use of another tool called a **linker**. This program links all the object files that belong to the program, along with any library functions the program may use. The result is an **executable file**. The entire process is depicted in Figure 10-1.

## C Key Words

The C language, like all programming languages, includes **key words**. These key words have special meanings, so you cannot use them as names for variables or functions. Table 10-1 lists C key words.

**Source File**

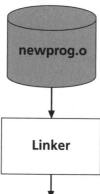

newprog.c

Preprocessor

Compiler

The compiler actually puts out an assembly
language version here that is then
translated into object code (binary).

**Object File**

newprog.o

Linker

**Executable Program**

newprog.

**Figure 10-1:** C program compilation process

## The C Library

As you can see from Table 10-1, the C language is very small. It has no input or output facilities as part of the language. All I/O is performed through the C library. The **C library** consists of functions that perform file, screen, and keyboard operations, as well as many other tasks. For example, certain functions perform string operations, memory allocation and control, math operations, and much more. When you need to perform one of these operations in your program, you place a **function call** at the desired point. The linker joins the code of the library function with your program's object code to create the executable file.

| | | | |
|---|---|---|---|
| auto | double | int | struct |
| break | else | long | switch |
| case | enum | register | typedef |
| char | extern | return | union |
| const | float | short | unsigned |
| continue | for | signed | void |
| default | goto | sizeof | volatile |
| do | if | static | while |

**Table 10-1:** C key words

## Program Format

As mentioned earlier, C programs are made up of one or more functions. Every function must have a name, and every C program must have a function called **main**. Here is a very simple C program:

```
int main()
{
}
```

This program does absolutely nothing, yet it contains all the elements necessary for a valid C program. The next two paragraphs examine the bare essentials.

Note the word "main" followed by a set of parentheses. (A following section, "Specifying Data Types," defines the first item—int.) This is the name of a function. As mentioned earlier, all C programs must have a function called main. The parentheses denote that this is a function name.

On the next line is an opening brace. In a C program this denotes the beginning of a block of code. The closing brace on the next line denotes the end of the block of code. All functions must have an opening and a closing brace. The statements that normally make up the function appear between the two braces. In the sample program there are no statements; therefore, the function does nothing. The braces are still required.

## Including Comments

The /* symbol denotes the beginning of a comment, and the */ symbol denotes the end of a comment. The compiler ignores everything in between. This example shows a C program comment:

```
/* Here is a program that does nothing. */
int main()
{
}
```

In the example, the comment "Here is a program that does nothing" appears at the top of the program. The beginning of the comment is marked with /* and the end with */. The compiler sees this program as being no different than the earlier version that had no comment.

## Using the Preprocessor #include Directive

Here is a sample program that performs output:

```
/* A simple C program */
#include <stdio.h>
int main()
{
    printf("Hello from the Linux World!\n");
}
```

Figure 10-2 shows the program's output.

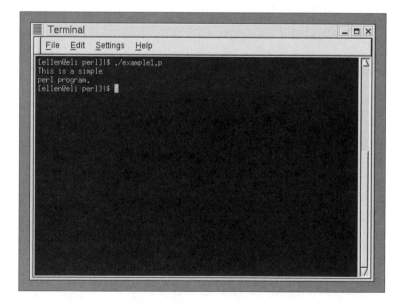

**Figure 10-2:** C program output

In the program above, you see the statement:

```
#include <stdio.h>
```

This is called a **preprocessor directive**. As mentioned earlier, the preprocessor processes your program before the compiler translates it into object code. It reads your program, looking for statements that begin with the # symbol. These statements are considered preprocessor directives and cause the preprocessor to modify your source code in some way. For example, the #include directive causes the preprocessor to include another file in your program, at the point where the #include directive appears.

The file **stdio.h** is called a **header file** and is part of your C development system. This file contains information the compiler needs to process standard input or output statements. Any program that performs standard input or output must include the stdio header file. Because the sample program uses the printf statement (which performs standard output), it must include stdio.h.

The C development system includes a number of header files. All library functions require that you include a particular header file.

## Specifying Data Types

Variables and constants represent data used in a C program. You must declare variables and state the type of data that the variable will hold. A variable's data type determines the upper and lower limits of its range of values. Data types with wider ranges of values occupy more memory than those with narrower ranges. The exact limits of the ranges vary among compilers and hardware platforms.

Table 10-2 shows a list of the basic data types that may be used in a C program.

| Data Type | Description |
| --- | --- |
| char | Occupies a single byte. Designed to hold one character from the character set used by the running machine. |
| int | Holds integer values. The size of an int variable should be the natural size of an integer on the running machine, but it is not always. |
| float | A single-precision, floating-point value. |
| double | A double-precision, floating-point value. |

Table 10-2: C data types

As mentioned earlier, the exact upper and lower limits of each of the range of values for data types depends on the compiler and hardware platform being used. You can use three modifiers with int data types: short, long, and unsigned. The short and long modifiers make an integer variable smaller or larger than its natural size. Typically, a long int occupies twice as many bits as an int. On some machines a short int occupies half the number of bits as an int, but in many cases there is no difference between a short int and an int.

Table 10-3 shows typical limits and memory requirements of C data types.

| Data Type | Bytes | Minimum Value | Maximum Value |
|---|---|---|---|
| char | 1 | -128 | 127 |
| unsigned char | 1 | 0 | 255 |
| short int | 2 | -32,768 | 32,767 |
| unsigned short | 2 | 0 | 65,535 |
| int | 4 | -2,147,483,648 | 2,147,483,647 |
| long int | 4 | -2,147,483,648 | 2,147,483,647 |
| unsigned long | 4 | 0 | 4,294,967,295 |
| float | 4 | -3.4028E+38 | 3.4028E+38 |
| double | 8 | -1.79769E308 | 1.79769E+308 |

**Table 10-3:** Typical C data type limits and memory requirements

## Character Constants

Characters are represented internally in a single byte of the computer's memory. When a character is stored in the byte, it is set to the character's code in the host character set. For example, if the machine uses ASCII codes, the letter A is stored in memory as the number 65. This is because the ASCII code for A is 65.

When you represent character data in a program as a character constant, you enclose the character in single quote marks. Here are some examples:

'A'
'C'
'a'
'z'

## Using Strings

A string is a group of characters, like a name. Strings are stored in memory in consecutive memory locations. When you use string constants in your C program, they must be enclosed in double quote marks. Here are some examples:

"Linux is a great operating system."
"Good Morning!"
"Enter your name and age."

Unlike higher level languages, C does not provide a specific data type for character strings. C requires that you view strings the same way the computer does, as an array of characters. Here is how you might declare a character array to store a string:

```
char name[20];
```

This is just like declaring a char variable, except for the [20] appended to the variable name. It indicates that name should be an array of 20 characters. It is large enough to hold a string of up to 19 characters. This is because in C all strings are terminated with a null character. A **null character** is a single byte where all bits are set to zero.

## Including Identifiers

**Identifiers** are names given to variables and functions. When naming variables and functions, resist the temptation to use short names that do not convey the meaning of the item. Using meaningful identifiers greatly enhances the style of your program. There are only a few rules to remember:

- The first character must be a letter or an underscore (the _ character).
- After the first character you may use letters, underscores, or digits.
- Variable names may be limited to 31 characters, and some compilers require the first 8 characters of variable names to be unique.
- Uppercase and lowercase characters are distinct.

These are all examples of legal identifiers:

```
radius
customer_name
earnings_for_2000
_my_name
```

## Declaring Variables

You must declare all variables before you use them in a program. A declaration begins with a data type and is followed by one or more variable names. Here is an example:

```
int days;
```

This example declares a variable named days. Its data type is int, so days is large enough to hold any value that fits within the range of an int. Notice that the declaration ends with a semicolon, as do all complete C statements.

You can declare multiple variables of the same type on the same line. Here is an example:

```
int days, months, years;
```

This example declares three variables, each of type int, named days, months, and years. Notice that commas separate the names.

You can initialize variables with values at the time they are declared by placing an equal sign after the variable name and then a constant value. Here is an example:

```
int days = 5, months = 2, years = 10;
```

## Understanding the Scope of Variables

The **scope** of a variable is the part of the program in which the variable is defined and therefore accessible. You can declare a variable either inside a function or any place that is not inside a function.

Variables that are declared inside a function are called **automatic variables**. These variables are local to the function in which they are declared. Here is an example:

```
/* This program declares a local variable
   in function main. The program does nothing
   else.  */
int main()
{
int days;
}
```

Here, the variable days is an automatic variable and is local to the function main.

You can also declare a variable outside of any function, as in the following example:

```
/* This program declares a global variable
   The program does nothing else.  */

int days;
int main()
{
}
```

In the program above, the variable is external, or global. The scope of a global variable is the entire program, beginning at the point where the declaration was made. The scope of an automatic, or local, variable is the body of the function in which it is declared.

The only place inside a function where local variables may be declared is at the beginning of the body of the function—after the opening brace and before any statement. You can declare global variables anywhere in a program except inside a function.

## Using Math Operators

Table 10-4 lists the C arithmetic operators.

| Operator | Meaning |
|---|---|
| + | addition |
| - | subtraction |
| * | multiplication |
| / | division |
| % | modulus |
| ++ | increment |
| -- | decrement |

**Table 10-4:** C arithmetic operators

You can use these operators to create regular math expressions, as in the following examples:

```
x = y + 3;
num = num * 3;
days = months * 30;
```

These examples introduce the assignment operator (the equal sign). It works by taking the value of the expression on its right and assigning that value to the variable whose name is on its left. In the example days = months * 30, the value in the variable months is multiplied by 30 and the product is stored in the variable days.

**Increment and Decrement Operators** The last two operators shown in Table 10-4 are the **increment** (++) and **decrement** (--) operators. These are unary operators, meaning they work with one operand. The following example shows the variable count being incremented:

```
count++;
```

Likewise, this variable can be decremented by the following statement:

```
count--;
```

The first two examples of the count variable show these operators in their post-fix form, which means they come after the variable. You can also use them as prefix operators:

```
++ count;
-- count;
```

The operators behave differently depending on which form is used. Assume the variable j is set to 4. In this statement,

```
x = j++;
```

the ++ operator is used in postfix form. This means the assignment operator (=) uses the value of j before it is incremented. In effect, it says "set x equal to j, then increment j." After the operation, x will be equal to 4 and j will be equal to 5.

If the prefix form of the operator is used, you get different results:

```
x = ++j;
```

This statement says "increment j, then set x equal to j." Both x and j will be equal to 5 after the statement executes.

## Generating Formatted Output with printf

One of the most commonly used screen output library functions is printf. The f stands for "formatted," as the function allows you to format and print several arguments of differing data types. The printf function is used in the following manner:

**Syntax**    printf (control string, expression, expression,...)

---

The first argument is called the **control string**. It specifies the way formatting should occur. Following the control string may be a variable number of arguments. Each of these will be an expression whose value is to be printed. Here is perhaps the most simple example of a printf statement:

```
printf("Hello");
```

The example only uses a control string. The word Hello will be printed as is on the screen. Here is another example.

```
printf("Your age is %d", 30);
```

The %d that appears in the control string is called a format specifier. It will not be printed as part of the message, but tells printf to substitute a decimal integer in its place. The decimal integer is the very next argument, the number 30. This printf statement prints the following message on the screen:

```
Your age is 30
```

Although this example illustrates the usage of the %d format specifier, it is not very realistic. You are more likely to use it in the following manner:

```
printf("Your age is %d", age);
```

Here, printf substitutes the value in the integer variable age for the %d. The next example prints the values of three int variables:

```
printf("The values are %d %d %d", num1, num2, num3);
```

This message will contain the values of num1, num2, and num3, in that order. You can also pass arithmetic expressions to printf:

```
printf("You have worked %d minutes", hours*60);
```

In fact, you can pass any valid C expression to printf. However, be sure you use an appropriate format specifier. Table 10-5 shows a list of valid format specifiers.

| Format Specifier | Meaning |
| --- | --- |
| %c | Single character |
| %d | Signed decimal integer |
| %e | Floating-point number, e notation |
| %E | Floating-point number, E notation |
| %f | Floating-point number, decimal notation |
| %g | Causes %f or %e to be used, whichever is shorter |
| %G | Causes %f or %E to be used, whichever is shorter |
| %i | Signed decimal integer |
| %o | Unsigned octal integer |
| %p | Pointer |
| %s | Character string |
| %u | Unsigned decimal integer |
| %x | Unsigned hex integer using digits  0-f |
| %X | Unsigned hex integer using digits 0-F |
| %% | Print a percent sign |

**Table 10-5:** Format specifiers

You have learned enough C programming basics to write a simple program.

**To write a simple C program:**

**1**  Use the editor of your choice to create the file **inches.c**. Enter the code:

```
/* This program converts 10 feet to inches. */

#include <stdio.h>

int main()
{
     int inches, feet;
     feet = 10;
     inches = feet * 12;
     printf("There are %d inches in %d feet.\n", inches,
feet);
}
```

**2**  Save the program and exit the editor.

**3**  The C compiler is executed by the gcc command. Type **gcc inches.c** and press **Enter**. If you typed the program correctly, you see no messages. If you see error messages, load the program into the editor and correct the mistake.

**4**  By default, the compiler stores the executable program in a file named a.out. Execute a.out by typing **./a.out** and pressing **Enter**. Your screen looks similar to Figure 10-3.

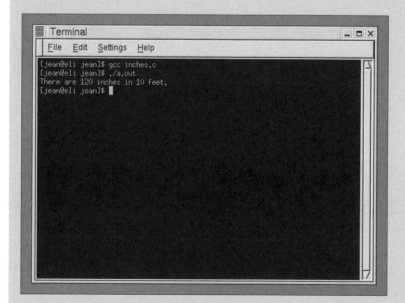

**Figure 10-3:** Output of a.out

**5**  You can specify the name of the executable file with the –o option. Type **gcc –o inches inches.c,** and press **Enter.** The command compiles the Inches.c file and stores the executable code in a file named Inches.

**6**  Run the inches program by typing **./inches** and pressing **Enter.**

## Using the if Statement

The if statement allows your program to make decisions depending upon whether a condition is true or false. The general form of the if statement is:

**Syntax**                 if (condition) statement;

---

If the condition is true, statement will be performed. Here is an example:

```
if (weight > 1000) printf("You have exceeded the limit.");
```

If the variable weight contains a value greater than 1000, the printf statement executes.

Sometimes you may need to execute more than one line of code if a condition is true. C allows you to substitute a block of code for the single statement, when necessary. Here is an example:

```
if (weight > 1000)
{
    printf("Warning!\n");
    printf("You have exceeded the limit.\n");
    printf("Just thought you\'d like to know.");
}
```

The program segment above causes the three printf statements to execute if weight is greater than 1000.

The if-else construct allows your program to do one thing if a condition is true and another if it is false. Here is an example:

```
if (hours > 40)
    printf("You can go home now");
else printf("Keep working.");
```

The "keep working" message prints only when the condition (hours > 40) is false. Here is an example using blocks of code:

```
if(hours>40)
{
    printf("Go home.\n");
    printf("You deserve it.");
}
else
{
    printf("Keep working.\n");
    printf("Stop playing with the computer.");
}
```

### To practice the C if-else statement:

**1** Create the file **radius.c** with your choice of editor. Enter the following C code:

```
/* This program calculates the area of a circle */
#include <stdio.h>
int main()
{
    float radius = 50, area;
    area = 3.14159 * radius * radius;
    if (area > 100)
        printf("The area, %f,  is too large.\n", area);
    else
        printf("The area, %f, is within limits.\n",
area);
}
```

**2** Save the file and exit the editor.

**3** Compile the program by typing **gcc –o radius radius.c** and pressing **Enter**. If you see error messages, edit the file and correct your mistakes.

**4** Execute the program by typing **./radius** and pressing **Enter**.

## Using C Loops

Loops in C are similar to those you have used in shell scripts and Perl programs. C provides three looping mechanisms: the for loop, the while loop, and the do while loop. Using the for loop is best when you know how to control the number of times that the loop is to perform. If it is unclear how many times the loop should perform, then use the while or do-while loop.

Here is an example of the for loop:

```
for (count = 0; count < 100; count++)
    printf("Hello\n");
```

This loop means the message "Hello" will print 100 times. Following the word "for" is a set of parentheses containing three arguments. The arguments are separated by semicolons.

The first argument is the initialization. The variable count is being used to track the number of times the loop has run. The initialization is a statement that is executed before the first time through. In the example above, the initialization stores the number 0 in count.

The second argument is the test condition. The for loop executes as long as the test condition is true. It is evaluated before each iteration of the loop. If the condition is true, the iteration is performed. Otherwise, the loop terminates. In the example, the loop performs as long as count is less than 100.

The third argument is the update. It is performed at the end of each iteration. In the example, the loop increments the variable count.

This program segment shows an example of the while loop:

```
x=0;
while (x++ < 100)
    printf("x is equal to %d\n", x);
```

This loop repeats while x is less than 100. The next example illustrates a do-while loop, which is very similar to the while loop.

```
x=0;
do
    printf("x is equal to %d\n", x);
while (x++ < 100);
```

The difference between the while loop and the do-while loop is that the while loop tests its condition before each iteration, and the do-while loop tests after each iteration.

**To practice using a C loop:**

**1** Use the editor of your choice to create the file **rain.c**. Enter this C code:

```
/* rain.c   */
#include <stdio.h>
int main()
{
    int rain, total_rain = 0;
    for (rain = 0; rain < 10; rain++)
    {
        printf("We have had %d inches of rain.\n", rain);
        total_rain = total_rain + rain;
    }
    printf("We have had a total/#");
    printf("/of %d inches of rain.\n", total_rain);
}
```

**2** Save the file and exit the editor.

**3**   Compile the program and store the executable code in a file named rain.

**4**   Run the program. Your screen should look similar to Figure 10-4.

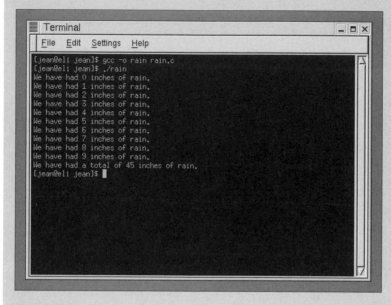

```
[jean@eli jean]$ gcc -o rain rain.c
[jean@eli jean]$ ./rain
We have had 0 inches of rain.
We have had 1 inches of rain.
We have had 2 inches of rain.
We have had 3 inches of rain.
We have had 4 inches of rain.
We have had 5 inches of rain.
We have had 6 inches of rain.
We have had 7 inches of rain.
We have had 8 inches of rain.
We have had 9 inches of rain.
We have had a total of 45 inches of rain.
[jean@eli jean]$
```

**Figure 10-4:** Output of rain

## Defining Functions

When you define a function, you declare the function's name and create the lines of code that make up the function's block of code. You also state what data type is returned from the function (if any). Here is an example.

```
void message()
{
    printf("Greetings from the function message.");
    printf("Have a nice day.");
}
```

The word "void" indicates that this function does not return a value. The name of the function is message. A set of parentheses follows the name. There are only two statements in this function, both printfs. The function might appear in a complete program as

```
#include <stdio.h>

void message();

int main()
{
    message();
}
```

```
void message()
{
    printf("Greetings from the function message.\n");
    printf("Have a nice day.\n");
}
```

The line under the include statement that reads,

```
void message();
```

is called a function prototype. It tells the compiler about the function in advance. The word "void" means that this function returns no data. Void functions in C are like subroutines in Fortran or procedures in Pascal. They are merely modules of code that perform some task.

After the function prototype comes the function main. Main includes only one line, which reads:

```
message();
```

This is a function call. You call functions by placing their name, followed by a set of parentheses and a semicolon, at the desired place in the program. This causes the program's control to pass to the function. When the program returns from the function, it resumes execution at the very next line after the function call.

After main is the definition of the function message. The output of the program is shown in Figure 10-5.

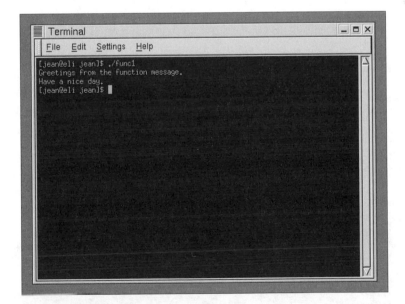

**Figure 10-5:** Demonstration of a function

## Using Function Arguments

Sometimes it is necessary to pass information to a function. A value passed to a function is called an argument. Arguments are stored in special automatic variables.

Here is an example.

```
void print_square(int val)
{
        printf("\nThe square is %d", val*val);
}
```

This function takes an int argument. When it receives the argument, the function stores the argument in the variable val. The printf statement causes the value of the expression val*val to print. Here is a complete program that uses the function:

```
#include <stdio.h>

        void print_square(int val);

main()
{
        int num = 5;
        print_square(num);
}


void print_square(int val)
{
        printf("\nThe square is %d\n", val*val);
}
```

The output of the program is shown in Figure 10-6.

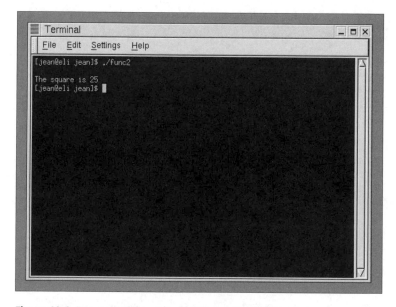

**Figure 10-6:** Demonstration of a function argument

## Using Function Return Values

In addition to accepting arguments, functions may also return a value. This means you can make function calls part of arithmetic operations and assignments. For example, suppose you have a function called triple. It is designed to take an int argument and return that value multiplied by three. You could use the function call in a manner such as:

```
y = triple(x);
```

The function receives the value in x, triples it, and then returns this value. The statement above stores the return value in a variable called y. Here is what the triple function might look like:

```
int triple(int num)
{
        return(num * 3);
}
```

The function is defined as an int function. This means that it returns an int value. You may place a call to this function anywhere in your program where an int is expected. The function takes a single argument, which is also an int. In the function the argument is stored in the variable num. There is only one line in the function's block of code:

```
return(num*3);
```

This is the return statement. It is used to return a value back to the calling part of the program. In this example the value of num * 3 is returned. The next sample program demonstrates the function:

```
#include <stdio.h>

int triple(int num);

int main()
{
    int x = 6, y;
    y = triple(x);
    printf("%d tripled is %d\n.", x, y);
}

int triple(int num)
{
        return (num * 3);
}
```

The program output is shown in Figure 10-7.

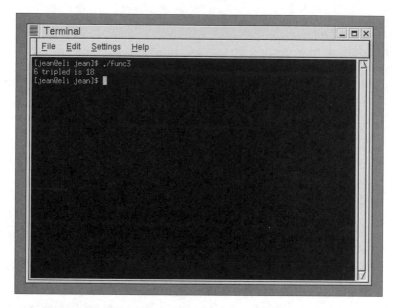

**Figure 10-7:** Demonstration of a program's return value

## To practice writing functions that accept arguments and return a value:

**1** Use the editor of your choice to create the file **absolute.c**. Enter the following code:

```c
#include <stdio.h>

int absolute(int num);
int main()
{
    int x = -12, y;
    y = absolute(x);
    printf("The absolute value of %d is %d\n", x, y);
}

int absolute(int num)
{
    if (num < 0)
        return (-num);
    else
        return (num);
}
```

**2** Save the file and exit the editor.

**3** Compile the program and save the executable code in a file named **absolute**.

**4** Run the program. Your screen should look similar to Figure 10-8.

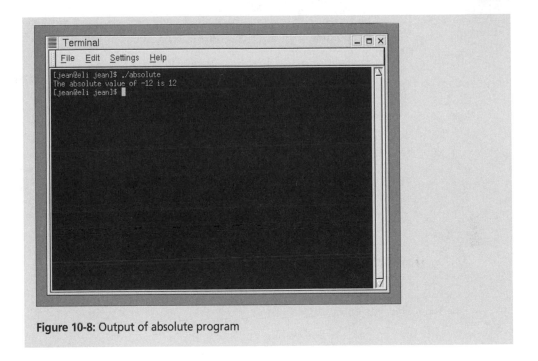

**Figure 10-8:** Output of absolute program

## Working with Files in C

Files are continuous streams of data. They are typically stored on disk. Many file operations are sequential, meaning they work from the beginning of the file to the end. When the file is opened, you are working with the beginning of the file. Every time a byte is read from or written to the file, your current position in the file is moved forward by one byte.

**File Pointers**  C file input/output is designed to use file pointers, which point to a predefined structure that contains information about the file. The structure template is found in stdio.h. You must declare a file pointer in order to use the I/O package. Here is an example:

```
FILE *fp;
```

This declares fp as a FILE pointer. It will be used with various file access functions.

**Opening and Closing Files**  Before you can use a file, it must be opened. The library function for opening a file is fopen. Here is an example.

```
fp = fopen("myfile.dat", "r");
```

The fopen function takes two arguments: the filename and the access mode. This example opens a file named myfile.dat. The "r" means that the file will be opened for reading. The following statement uses the "w" access mode for writing:

```
fp = fopen("myfile.dat", "w");
```

The fopen function returns a file pointer. If the file cannot be opened, it returns a NULL pointer (a pointer to address zero). Here is one way you can test to see if the file was opened:

```
if ((fp = fopen("myfile.dat", "r")) == NULL)
{
        printf("Error opening myfile.dat\n");
        exit(0);
}
```

The opposite of opening a file is closing it. When a file is closed, its buffers will be flushed, ensuring that all data was properly written to it. The fclose function is used to close files that were opened by fopen. Here is an example:

```
fclose(fp);
```

**Performing File Input/Output**   C provides many functions for reading and writing files. For the case project, you concentrate on two: fgetc and fputc.

The two functions, fgetc and fputc, perform character input/output on files. Here is an example of fgetc:

```
ch = fgetc(fp);
```

fgetc reads a single character from the file and points to it. The character will be read from the current position. Character output is performed with fputc. Here is an example:

```
fputc(ch, fp);
```

The character stored in ch is written to the current position of the file referenced by fp.

**Testing for the End of File**   Use the feof function to determine if the end of file has been encountered during an input operation. Here is an example:

```
if (feof(fp))
        fclose(fp);
```

The feof function returns a non-zero value if the end of file was encountered. Otherwise, it returns 0.

Now that you have a basic understanding of file operations in C, you are ready to practice writing a program that performs file input/output:

## To perform file input/output:

**1**   Use the editor of your choice to create the file **buildfile.c**. Enter this code in the file:

```
#include <stdio.h>
```

```
int main()
{
    FILE *out_file;
    int count = 0;
    char msg[] = "This was created by a C program.\n";

    if ((out_file = fopen("testfile", "w")) == NULL)
    {
        printf("Error opening file.\n");
        exit(1);
    }
    while (count < 33)
    {
        fputc(msg[count], out_file);
        count++;
    }
    fclose(out_file);
}
```

**2**  Save the program and exit the editor.

**3**  Compile the program and save the executable in a file named **buildfile**.

**4**  Run the **buildfile** program. The program creates another file, testfile.

**5**  To see the contents of testfile, use the **cat** command.

## Using the Make Utility to Maintain Program Source Files

You may often work with a program that has many source-code files. For example, the absolute program you created in the previous exercise can be divided into two files: one that holds the function main and another that holds the function absolute. The two files are then compiled and linked together, as demonstrated in the following steps.

### To compile and link two files:

**1**  Use the editor of your choice to create the file **abs_func.c**. Enter this code:

```
int absolute(int num)
{
    if (num < 0)
        return (-num);
    else
        return (num);
}
```

**2** Save the file.

**3** Create the file **abs_main.c**. Enter this code:

```
#include <stdio.h>

int absolute(int num);
int main()
{
    int x = -12, y;
    y = absolute(x);
    printf("The absolute value of %d is %d\n", x, y);
}
```

**4** Save the file and exit the editor.

**5** Compile and link the two programs by typing **gcc abs_main.c abs_func.c –o abs** and pressing **Enter**. The compiler separately compiles abs_main.c and abs_func.c. Their object files are linked together, and the executable code is stored in the file abs.

**6** Run the abs program. Your screen should look similar to Figure 10-9.

**Figure 10-9:** Output of abs program

As you develop multi-module programs and make changes, you must compile the program repeatedly. However, with multi-module source files, you only need to compile those source files in which you made changes. The linker then links the newly generated object-code files with previously compiled object-code, thereby creating a new executable file. However, keeping track of what needs to be recompiled and what does not can become an overwhelming task when the program involves dozens of source-code files. This is where the make utility helps.

The **make utility** tracks what needs to be recompiled by using the time stamp field, which is stored in all the source files. All you have to do is create a control file, called the **makefile** (which is actually a file named makefile), for the make utility to use. The control file lists all your source files and their relationships to each other. These relationships are expressed in the form of targets and dependencies. A **target file** depends on another file to determine if any action needs to be taken to rebuild the target file. (The ultimate target file is, of course, the executable file that results from linking all the object files together.) The **dependent files** are source files, such as the .c source files, or .h files that serve as headers to be included within the source files.

The makefile must exist in the current directory. It feeds the make utility all it needs to know to first examine and recompile any changed modules and then relink the objects to produce a new executable program. You can also give the makefile another name, such as make_abs. To do this, you need to enter an −f option followed by the name of the makefile. This is useful when you are developing more than one application from within the same directory.

The contents of make_abs, an example of a makefile, follow:

```
abs_main.o: abs_main.c
    gcc −c abs_main.c
abs_func.o: abs_func.c
    gcc −c abs_func.c
abs2: abs_main.o abs_func.o
    gcc abs_main.o abs_func.o −o abs2
```

Two types of lines are shown in the file: dependencies and commands. The first line is a dependency, and the second line is a command:

```
abs_main.o: abs_main.c
    gcc −c abs_main.c
```

The first line establishes a dependency between abs_main.o and abs_main.c. If abs_main.c is newer than abs_main.o, the command on the second line executes (rebuilding abs_main.o).

The third and fourth lines, as well as the fifth and sixth lines, establish similar dependencies and commands.

The command line entry to build the abs2 program using the makefile is:

```
make −f make_abs abs2
```

The −f option instructs make to read the file make_abs instead of makefile. After executing the command, you can run the abs2 program. Figure 10-10 shows the output of the make command and the abs2 program.

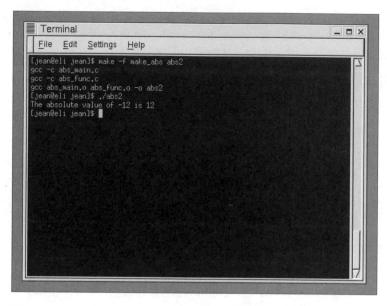

**Figure 10-10:** Making and running abs2 program

If you forget whether you have made changes since the last time you ran the program, you can use make to check the source files' time stamps and rebuild the program if necessary. The make utility will not recompile if the program is current. For example, Figure 10-11 shows the output of the make command when all modules of the abs2 program are up to date.

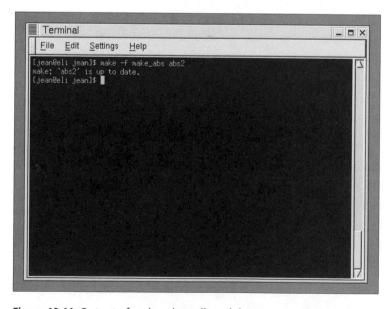

**Figure 10-11:** Output of make when all modules are up to date

The make utility follows a set of rules, both defaults and user-defined. In general, a make rule has:

- A target, the name of the file you want to make (in the example above, the target is Abs2)
- One or more dependencies, the files upon which the target depends
- An action, a shell command that creates the target.

Now that you have learned the structure of a makefile, you can create a simple multi-module C project.

**To create a simple multi-module C project:**

**1** Use the editor of your choice to create the file **square_func.c**. Enter this code in the file:

```
int square(int number)
{
        return (number * number);
}
```

**2** Save the file.

**3** Next create the file **square_main.c**. Enter this code:

```
#include <stdio.h>
int square(int number);

int main()
{
    int count, sq;
    for (count = 1; count < 11; count++)
    {
        sq = square(count);
        printf("The square of %d is %d\n", count, sq);
    }
}
```

**4** Save the file.

**5** Next, create a makefile named **make_square**. Enter the following text:

```
square_func.o: square_func.c
        gcc -c square_func.c
square_main.o: square_main.c
        gcc -c square_main.c
square: square_func.o square_main.o
        gcc square_func.o square_main.o -o square
```

**6** Save the file and exit the editor.

**7**  Build the program by typing **make –f make_square square** and pressing **Enter**. (If you have errors, load the incorrect module into the editor and correct your mistakes.)

**8**  Run the square program. Your screen should look similar to Figure 10-12.

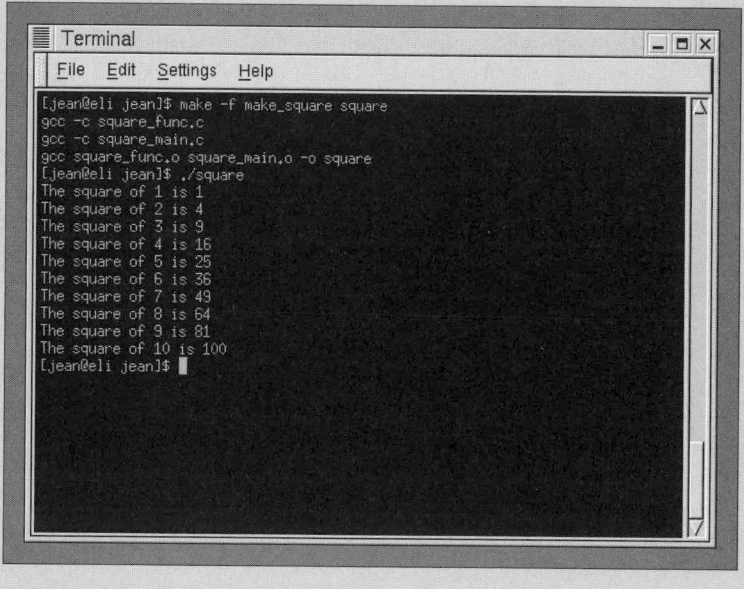

```
[jean@eli jean]$ make -f make_square square
gcc -c square_func.c
gcc -c square_main.c
gcc square_func.o square_main.o -o square
[jean@eli jean]$ ./square
The square of 1 is 1
The square of 2 is 4
The square of 3 is 9
The square of 4 is 16
The square of 5 is 25
The square of 6 is 36
The square of 7 is 49
The square of 8 is 64
The square of 9 is 81
The square of 10 is 100
[jean@eli jean]$
```

**Figure 10-12:** Building and running the square program

Now that you understand the basics of writing a program in C, you'll learn how to debug a program.

## Debugging Your Program

Typical errors for new C programmers include using incorrect syntax, such as forgetting to terminate a statement with a semicolon. Or, because almost everything you type into a C program is in lowercase, your program may have a case-sensitive error. Here is an example of what you might see on the screen if you omit a closing quote inside a printf command:

```
simple.c:10: unterminated string or character constant
simple.c:10: possible real start of unterminated constant
```

The compiler generally produces more error lines than the number of mistakes it finds in the code. The compiler reports the error lines and any surrounding lines affected by the mistake(s).

Note: Remember that every time you modify (correct or add text to) your program source file, you must recompile the program to create a new executable program.

To correct syntax errors within your programs, you must therefore perform the following steps:

1. Write down the line number of each error and a brief description.
2. Edit your source file, moving your cursor to the first line number the compiler reports.
3. Within the source file, correct the error and then move the cursor to the next line number. Most editors display the current line number to help you locate specific lines within the file.
4. After correcting all the errors, save and re-compile the file.

Now that you understand how to write and debug simple C programs, you are ready to create interactive programs that read input from the keyboard.

## Creating a C Program to Accept Input

You can draw from many standard library functions to accept input; that is, enter characters using the keyboard. Some like getchar() are character-oriented, while others like scanf() are field-oriented. This section concentrates on scanf().

Unlike many other library input functions, scanf can be used to input values of a variety of data types. You use it like this:

**Syntax**      scanf(control string, address, address,...);

---

The scanf() function uses a control string with format specifiers in a manner similar to printf. The arguments that follow the control string are the addresses of variables where the input is to be stored. Consider the following example.

```
scanf("%d", &age);
```

The %d format specifier works just like it does for printf. Here it indicates that scanf() should interpret the input value as a decimal integer.

The &age argument tells scanf to store the input value in the variable age. The & is the address operator. When used with a general variable, it returns the memory address where this variable is located. The scanf() function needs the address of a variable to store an input value there. The next example shows how scanf() can be used to input a string.

```
scanf("%s", city);
```

Notice that this example does not use the & operator. Anytime you use the name of an array, it resolves to the address of the first element. It would be an error to use the & operator with the name of an array.

The format specifiers for scanf() are generally the same as those used with printf(). Table 10-6 shows the format specifiers for scanf().

| Format Specifier | Interpretation |
|---|---|
| %c | Single character |
| %d | Signed decimal integer |
| %e, %f, %g | Floating-point number |
| %E, %G | Floating-point number |
| %I | Signed decimal integer |
| %o | Signed octal integer |
| %p | Pointer |
| %s | String. Ignores leading white-space characters, then reads until it encounters another white-space character. |
| %u | Unsigned decimal integer |
| %x, %X | Signed hex integer |

**Table 10-6:** scanf() format specifiers

Table 10-7 shows a list of modifiers you can use with scanf format specifiers.

| Modifier | Meaning |
|---|---|
| h | Used to indicate a short int or short unsigned int. Example: "%hd" |
| l | Used to indicate a long int or long unsigned int. Example: "%ld" <br> Also used to indicate a double. Example: "%lf" |
| L | Used to indicate a long double. Example: "%Lf" |

**Table 10-7:** Modifiers for scanf() format specifiers

Although it rarely contributes to a program's user-friendliness, the scanf statement can accept multiple inputs. Here is an example:

```
scanf("%d %f %d", &x, &y, &z);
```

The statement above accepts values in the variables x, y, and z which are int, float, and int, respectively. While typing values, the user must separate the three values with white-space characters. White-space characters are spaces, tabs, and new-lines.

You'll now write a C program to accept input from a keyboard.

**To use C to accept keyboard input:**

**1** Use the editor of your choice to create a file named **keyboard.c**. Enter this code and then save the file:

```
/*===========================================================
Program Name: keyboard.c
Purpose:     Enter data using the keyboard

=========================================================== */

#include <stdio.h> /* the standard input/output library */
int main()
  {
  char string[50]; /* a string field */
  float my_money; /* a floating decimal field */
  int weight; /* an integer field */
  printf("\nEnter your First Name: ");
  scanf("%s", string);
  printf("\nEnter your Desired Monthly Income: ");
  scanf("%f",&my_money);
  printf("\nEnter your friend's weight: ");
  scanf("%d",&weight);
  printf("\n\n Recap\n");
  printf("I am %s and I wish to have %8.2f per month",
      string, my_money);
  printf("\nI never would have guessed you weigh %d",
     weight);
  printf("\n\n");
  }
```

**2** Compile the program by typing **gcc keyboard.c –o keyboard** and then pressing **Enter**.

**3** Execute the program by typing **./keyboard** and then pressing **Enter**. Your screen should now look similar to Figure 10-13. Note that your screen will appear differently depending on what you have input.

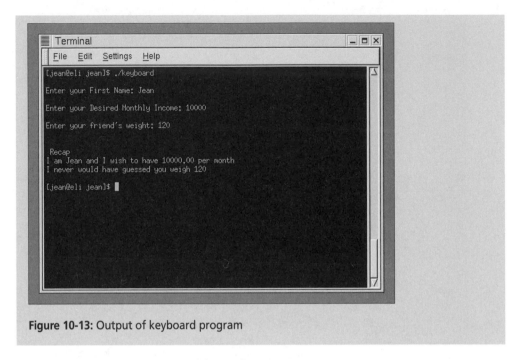

**Figure 10-13:** Output of keyboard program

Now that you have created C programs that perform keyboard and file I/O, you are ready to write the security demonstration programs.

## Encoding and Decoding Programs

If a file contains sensitive information, you may wish to encrypt it so others cannot read its contents. When a file is **encrypted**, its contents are encoded or modified in such a way that the original contents are not distinguishable. A formula is used to perform the encryption, so that an alternative **decryption** algorithm can restore the file to its original contents.

The program you have been asked to write for Dominion Consulting's programming staff will be simple in design. It will open a file, read a character from the file, add 10 to the character's ASCII value, and then write the character to a second file. This procedure repeats until all characters in the file have been read, modified, and written to the second file. The second file will be an encoded version of the first file.

The decoding program will work opposite of the way the encoding program works. It will read a character from the encrypted file, subtract 10 from its ASCII code, and write the character out to another file. This procedure repeats until all encrypted characters have been converted to their original state and stored in the second file.

**To create the encoding program:**

**1**   Use the editor of your choice to create the file **encode.c**. Enter this code in the file:

```c
#include <stdio.h>

void encode(FILE *, FILE *);

int main()
{
    FILE *in_file, *out_file;
    char infile_name[81], outfile_name[81], input;

    printf("Enter the name of the file to encode: ");
    scanf("%s", infile_name);
    if ((in_file = fopen(infile_name, "r") ) == NULL)
    {
        printf("Error opening %s\n", infile_name);
        exit(0);
    }
    printf("Enter the output file name: ");
    scanf("%s", outfile_name);
    if ((out_file = fopen(outfile_name, "w") ) == NULL)
    {
        printf("Error opening %s\n", outfile_name);
        exit(0);
    }
    encode_file(in_file, out_file);
    printf("The file has been encoded.\n");
    fclose(in_file);
    fclose(out_file);
}
```

**2**   Save the file.

**3**   Create the file **encode_file.c** and enter this code:

```c
#include <stdio.h>

void encode_file(FILE *in_file, FILE *out_file)
{
    char input;

    while (!feof(in_file))
    {
      input = fgetc(in_file);
            input += 10;
                fputc(input, out_file);

    }
}
```

**4**   Save the file.

**5**   Create the file **decode.c**. Enter this code:

```
#include <stdio.h>

void decode_file(FILE *, FILE *);

int main()
{
   FILE *in_file, *out_file;
   char infile_name[81], outfile_name[81], input;

   printf("Enter the name of the file to decode: ");
   scanf("%s", infile_name);
   if ((in_file = fopen(infile_name, "r") ) == NULL)
   {
           printf("Error opening %s\n", infile_name);
           exit(0);
   }
   printf("Enter the output file name: ");
   scanf("%s", outfile_name);
   if ((out_file = fopen(outfile_name, "w") ) == NULL)
   {
           printf("Error opening %s\n", outfile_name);
           exit(0);
   }
   decode_file(in_file, out_file);
   printf("The file has been decoded.\n");
   fclose(in_file);
   fclose(out_file);
}
```

**6**   Save the file.

**7**   Create the file **decode_file.c**. Enter this code:

```
#include <stdio.h>

void decode_file(FILE *in_file, FILE *out_file)
{
   while (!feof(in_file))
   {
     char input;

     input = fgetc(in_file);
     input -= 10;
        fputc(input, out_file);
   }
}
```

**8**   Save the file. You are now ready to create the makefiles for both the encode and decode programs.

**9**   Enter the following code in the editor, and save it in the file **encode_make**:

```
encode: encode.o encode_file.o
    gcc encode.o encode_file.o -o encode

encode.o: encode.c
    gcc -c encode.c

encode_file.o: encode_file.c
    gcc -c encode_file.c
```

**10**  Create a file named **decode_make**, and enter this code:

```
decode: decode.o decode_file.o
    gcc decode.o decode_file.o -o decode

decode.o: decode.c
    gcc -c decode.c

decode_file.o: decode_file.c
    gcc -c decode_file.c
```

**11**  Save the file. You are ready to build the programs.

**12**  Type **make -f encode_make** and press **Enter**.

**13**  Type **make -f decode_make** and press **Enter**. Your screen should resemble Figure 10-14.

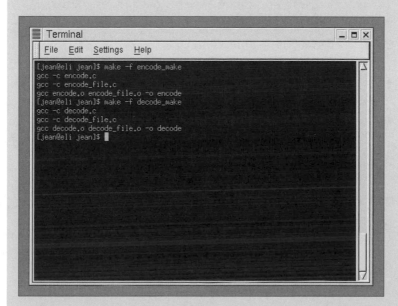

**Figure 10-14:** Output of make commands

You will test the encode program by encrypting the testfile that you created in file I/O exercise. The file contains the string "This was created by a C program."

**14** Type **./encode** and press **Enter**. Your screen appears similar to Figure 10-15.

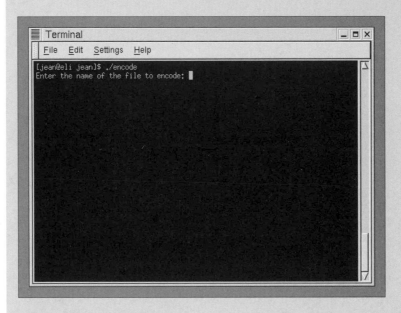

**Figure 10-15:** Encode program

**15** In response to the prompt, type **testfile** and press **Enter**.

**16** The program now asks for the name of the output file.

**17** Type **secret_file** and press **Enter**.

The contents of testfile have been encoded and stored in secret_file.

**18** Use the **cat** command to look at the contents of secret_file. Your screen looks similar to Figure 10-16.

**19** Run the decode program by typing **./decode** and pressing **Enter**.

The program asks you to enter the name of the file to decode.

**20** Type **secret_file** and press **Enter**.

Next the program asks you to enter the output file name.

**21** Type **normal_file** and press **Enter**.

The contents of secret_file have been decoded and stored in normal_file.

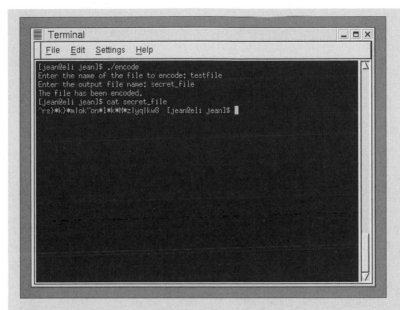

**Figure 10-16:** Results of encode program

**22** Use the **cat** command to look at the contents of normal_file. Your screen should look similar to Figure 10-17.

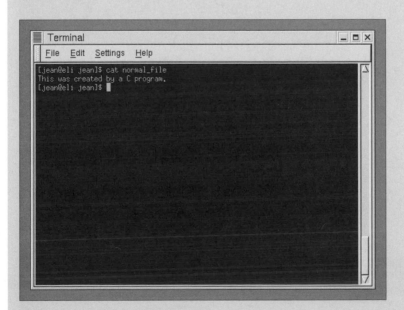

**Figure 10-17:** Contents of normal_file

You have now learned some fundamentals of programming in C, including working with files, using the make utility to maintain program source files, debugging your program, and using the encoding and decoding programs.

# S U M M A R Y

- The C language concentrates on how best to create commands and expressions that can be elegantly formed from operators and operands.

- C programs often consist of separate source files called program modules that are compiled separately into object code and linked to the other object codes that make up the program.

- The C program structure begins with the execution of instructions located inside a main function that calls other functions that contain more instructions.

- The make utility is used to maintain the application's source files and the default make control file is called makefile.

# R E V I E W   Q U E S T I O N S

1. In general a make rule has a _____.
   a. target, dependencies, and an action
   b. source, object, and executable
   c. header, a body, and a footer
   d. target and an action

2. The name of a C function can be recognized because it is followed by _____.
   a. < >
   b. ( )
   c. ( );
   d. { }

3. In C, a block of instructions is enclosed inside _____.
   a. < >
   b. ( )
   c. [ ]
   d. { }

4. The preprocessor reads the contents of a C source file, looking for statements that begin with _____.
   a. $
   b. %
   c. #
   d. !

5.  In an #include directive, the name of the standard library header files are enclosed with _____.
    a.  the less-than "<" and greater-than ">"
    b.  double quotation marks " "
    c.  left and right brackets [ ]
    d.  left and right parentheses ( )

6.  The unsigned and short modifiers may be applied to the _____ data type(s).
    a.  float and double
    b.  int
    c.  double
    d.  int and char

7.  In a C program, character constants are enclosed in _____.
    a.  " "
    b.  #
    c.  ()
    d.  []

8.  The ampersand (&) that precedes a variable name is called the _____ operator.
    a.  declarative-pointer
    b.  address-of
    c.  reference
    d.  fixed-pointer

9.  The C programming development tool used to facilitate compiling and maintaining the source code is called the _____.
    a.  precompiler
    b.  preprocessor
    c.  make utility
    d.  memory manager

10. When you compile a C program, the compiler creates a binary file called the _____ file.
    a.  source
    b.  executable
    c.  link
    d.  object

# EXERCISES

1.  Write a C program named myname.c that displays your name on the screen.
2.  Write a C program named calc.c that allows you to enter seven numbers. The program should calculate and display the sum and average of the numbers.

3.  Write a program named condays.c that asks you to enter a number of days. The program should convert the number of days to a number of weeks and a number of months. Display the values.

4.  Write a program named num_table.c that displays a table of the numbers 1 through 20, with the squares and cubes of the numbers.

 # DISCOVERY EXERCISES

1.  Rewrite your solution to Exercise 4 so a function named display_table() displays the table of numbers.

2.  Rewrite your solution to Discovery Exercise 1 so the display_table() function accepts an argument. The argument is the starting value of the table. For example, if 5 is passed to the function as an argument, the function displays the values 5–25, along with their squares and cubes.

3.  Rewrite your solution to Discovery Exercise 2 so the display_table() function is in a separate file from function main. Compile and link the files.

4.  Create a makefile to compile and create a program for the calc.c program you created in Exercise 2.

5.  Create a makefile to compile and execute your solution to Discovery Exercise 3.

# C++ Programming in a UNIX environment

## Introducing C++ Programming

C++ is a programming language developed by Bjarne Stroustrup at AT&T Bell Labs. It builds on the C language to add object-oriented capabilities. As a result, C++ is best learned after you have been programming in C for a while. With C++ you can do "more with less" after you learn its nuances. Functions, the building blocks of C programming, are incorporated in C++ with added dimensions such as **function overloading**, which makes the functions respond to more than one set of criteria and conditions.

C and C++ share many similarities. For example, programs in both languages start with the main() function and call other functions that include blocks of instructions enclosed within curly braces. Both languages also have similar source files. The C++ compiler readily accepts C language syntax and coding structures. For example, you can take the file encryption and decryption programs you created in Lesson A and fully compile them using the C++ compiler. Both languages fully support compiler directives such as #include and #define. The C++ compiler's name is **CC** for most UNIX versions and **g++** for Linux versions.

Note: One important distinction should be made about C++ programs. You can place your variable declarations anywhere inside the program, before or after the instructions. This is not true of C programs, in which program variables must precede all the instructions.

The major differences between the two languages become evident when you start using the C++ enhancements and class structures, which depart dramatically from standard C procedures. C follows procedural principles, whereas C++ primarily follows object-oriented programming principles while still allowing procedural programming methods. Procedural programming follows long-standing traditions that separate the data to be processed from the procedures that process. Procedural techniques require that the data fields be named and defined by data types (integers, characters, strings, floating decimals, and a variety of structures and arrays) before any processing begins. Object-oriented programming, on the other hand, allows the data to be described by name and type anywhere in the program. More significantly, C++ programs introduce objects as a new data class. **Objects** are a collection of data and a set of operations, called **methods**, that manipulate the data. Unlike standard C functions, C++ methods are part of the object they belong to, not the program.

Other more minor differences between C and C++ concern the name of the compiler (Linux calls the C++ compiler **g++**) and the suffix attached to a C++ source file, often **.C** or **.cpp**.

## Creating a Simple C++ Program

To illustrate the similarity between C and C++, you will create a short program, simple.C, which displays a message on the screen exactly as the program simple.c does. The differences between the two languages start with the #include <iostream.h> instead of #include <stdio.h>. The only other difference is the use of the cout I/O stream object instead of printf.

**To write a C++ program:**

**1**  Use the editor of your choice to create **simple.C**. Enter this code:

```
//============================================================
// Program Name: simple.C
// By:           JQD
//Purpose:       First program in C++ showing how to
//               produce output.

//============================================================

#include <iostream.h>

void main(void)
{
    cout << "Welcome to C++ Programming\n";
}
```

**2**  Use the C++ compiler to create a program called **sim_plus** by typing **g++ simple.C –o sim_plus** and pressing **Enter**.

**3**  Run sim_plus. Your screen looks similar to Figure 10-18.

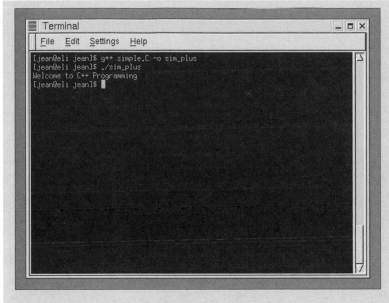

**Figure 10-18:** Output of sim_plus program

Looking at the program, notice that C++ uses // to denote a comment line. (You can also use C's /* and */ to enclose comments in your C++ program.) Recall that comments help to identify and describe the program for all who need to review the program. Comments are ignored by the compiler and do not cause the computer to perform any action when the program runs.

Further, note that the standard library functions for I/O are found in the iostream.h instead of stdio.h as in the C program. The only other difference between the C and C++ programs is the use of cout in the C++ program.

To continue the comparison between C and C++, you'll next see how a C++ program reads and displays the information in a file.

## Creating a C++ Program That Reads a Text File

You will learn further differences between C and C++ by entering the next C++ program, which reads a text file.

**To create a C++ program that reads a text file:**

**1** Use the editor of your choice to create the file **fileread.C**. Enter this code:

```
// A C++ file that reads the contents of a file.

#include <fstream.h>
```

```
void main(void)
{

    ifstream file("testfile");
    char record_in[256];

    if (file.fail())
        cout << "Error opening file.\n";
    else
    {
        while (!file.eof())
        {
            file.getline(record_in, sizeof(record_in));
            if (file.good())
                cout << record_in << endl;
        }
    }
}
```

**2**   Save the file and exit the editor.

**3**   Compile the program and save the executable code in fileread.

**4**   Test the fileread program. Your screen should appear similar to Figure 10-19.

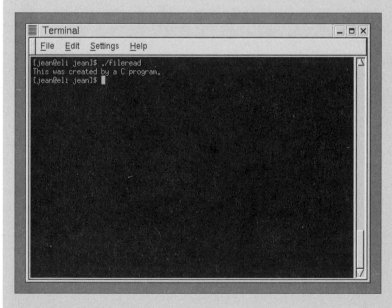

**Figure 10-19:** Output of fileread program

There are several differences in the way C and C++ handle file operations. For example, the code:

```
ifstream file ("testfile");
```

tells the compiler to use the ifstream class to perform file input and output operations. The identifier *file* follows the class name. This statement is similar to the following C statement:

```
FILE *file;
```

Further, the file.fail() function is a part of the ifstream class and reports an invalid condition with the file access. The endl stream manipulator causes the screen output to skip a line.

The file.getline() function reads in a line from the file and stores it in the buffer record_in for subsequent processing. The file.good flag is a component of ifstream class and is used to determine if the record accessed contains data.

Now that you have an understanding of how C++ is similar to C, next you'll see how C++ provides additional enhancements.

## How C++ Enhances C Functions

C++ created a way to define a function so that it can handle multiple sets of criteria, called **function overloading**. Whereas C functions are quite flexible, function overloading adds considerably to their overall use by expanding the function definition to accept varying kinds and numbers of parameters. During compilation, the C++ compiler determines which function to call based on the number and types of parameters the calling statement passes to the function. For example, in the next exercise you overload a function to access the system date in two different ways.

**To use function overloading:**

**1**   Use the editor of your choice to type the contents of datestuf.C:

```
// Program name: datestuf.C
// Purpose: shows you two ways to access the system date.

#include <iostream.h>
#include <time.h>

void display_time(const struct tm *tim)
{
    cout << "1. It is now " << asctime(tim);
}

void display_time(const time_t *tim)
{
    cout << "2. It is now " << ctime(tim);
}
```

```
void main(void)
{
    time_t tim = time(NULL);
    struct tm *ltim = localtime(&tim);
    display_time(ltim);
    display_time(&tim);
}
```

**2**   Save the file and then exit editor.

**3**   Compile datestuff.C by typing **g++ datestuf.C -o datestuf** and pressing **Enter**.

**4**   Test the program. Your screen should be similar to Figure 10-20.

**Figure 10-20:** Output of datestuf program

Notice how the same function name is used for the different calls to the two different date types that are contained in <time.h>. One is a structure; the other is not.

```
void display_time (const struct tm *tim)
void display_time (const time_t *tim)
```

The program is able to distinguish which function to use based on the type being passed to it.

```
Display_time(ltim);       Uses the structure type
Display_time(&tim);       Uses the time_t type
```

Now that you have learned the basic structure of a C++ program, you will learn to create object-oriented programs with the C++ class construct.

## Setting Up a Class

One of the more difficult concepts to grasp is the use of the C++ class data structure. A data structure lets you create abstract data types. An **abstract data type** is one defined by the programmer for a specific programming task.

You might begin by thinking of the class as made up of members that interrelate to make the class perform like an object rather than just a normal structure. Its methods (which are like C functions) are part of the class and considered behaviors of the class. The similarity between a class and a structure is that both store related data. You can use structures in C++ just as you do in C. However, in C++ you can and should use a class when your program performs specific operations on the data. For example, you can create a class for an object called cube when you want to compute the volume of any size cube:

```
//=========================================================

// Program Name: cube.C
// Purpose: Show how to set up a class. The class is called
//          cube, and computes the volume of a cube.

//=========================================================

#include <iostream.h>

//---- cube class
class Cube
{
     int height, width, depth; // private data members
public:
     // ----- constructor
     Cube(int ht, int wd, int dp)
          { height = ht; width = wd; depth = dp; }
     // ----- member function
     int volume()
          { return height * width * depth; }
};

void main(void)
{
     Cube thiscube(7, 8, 9);  // declare a Cube
     cout << thiscube.volume() << "\n";  // Compute &
display volume
}
```

**To compute the volume of any size cube:**

**1**    Use an editor to type in cube.C shown above, and then save the file.

**2**    Compile cube.C and store the executable code in the file cube.

**3**    Test cube. Your screen should look similar to Figure 10-21.

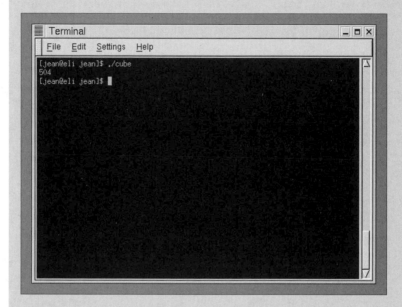

**Figure 10-21:** Output of cube program

In looking at the program, the line class cube tells the compiler that you are declaring a new class called cube. The variables within the class are called private data members and can only be accessed by members of this class. If you create objects in your program of type cube, then they can access the cube's private data members: height, width, and depth variables.

Constructors and other member functions can be defined outside, as well as inside, of a class definition. Unlike a structure, whose members are all accessible to a program, a class can have members that the program can directly access using the dot (.) operator (public members) and other members that the program cannot access directly (private members). To access the private data and methods, the program must call the public methods.

In this lesson you have learned the basic differences between C and C++ programs. You have written C++ programs that perform screen and keyboard I/O, as well as file operations. In addition, you have created simple programs with class objects.

# SUMMARY

- The major difference between C and C++ is that C follows procedural principles and C++ primarily follows object-oriented programming.

- The standard stream library used by C++ is iostream.h.

- C++ provides two statements for standard input and standard output: cin and cout respectively. These are defined in the class libraries contained in <iostream.h>.

- C++ offers a way to define a function so that it can handle multiple sets of criteria. This function is called overloading.

- endl skips a line like "\n" does in the C language.

- A C++ class is made up of members that interrelate to make it perform like an object rather than just a normal structure.

- You should use a class in C++ when your program performs specific operations on the data.

# REVIEW QUESTIONS

1. C++ introduces a stream object for displaying output, which is called _____.
   a. cout
   b. cin
   c. cerr
   d. printf

2. C++'s stream object that interacts between the user and computer to handle keyboard input is _____.
   a. cin
   b. cout
   c. cerr
   d. getchar

3. In C++, what do you call the structure that consists of data members and methods?
   a. stream
   b. class
   c. object
   d. array

4. A class can have members that the program can directly access using the dot (.) operator. These accessible members are identified with the _____ access specifier.
   a. private
   b. public
   c. inline
   d. offline

5. You can enter comments in the C++ source code by using _____.
   a. two slashes "//" preceding the comment
   b. the C /* and */ enclosures
   c. preceding the comment with ##
   d. both a and b

6. Which of these contains incorrect syntax?
   a. cout << "My Name is: "; // prompt for name
   b. cout >> "My Name is: "; // prompt for name
   c. cout << "My Name is: " << endl; // prompt for name
   d. cout << "My Name is:\n"; // prompt for name

7. Which of these is using incorrect syntax?
   a. cin >> integer1;  // read an integer
   b. cin >> name; // read a string field
   c. cin << integer1; // read an integer
   d. cin >> letter; // read a char

8. The _____ initializes object members automatically every time the program creates a class instance.
   a. static function
   b. constructor function
   c. private variables
   d. object assignment

# E X E R C I S E S

1. Write a small C++ program called nameaddr.C to display your name and address.

2. Refer to the C program, keyboard.c, presented in Lesson A, and write the equivalent program, called keyboard.C, in C++. Compile and test it.

3. Write a C++ program that does the following:

   Asks the user for values to be stored in the variables E and R.
   Multiplies E times R and stores the result in the variable I.
   If I is greater than 10, prints the message, "Value exceeds upper limit." If I is less than 1, prints the message, "Value does not meet the lower limit."

# DISCOVERY EXERCISES

1. Create a C++ version of the num_table.c program you created in Exercise 4 of Lesson A.

2. Modify the program you wrote for Discovery Exercise 1 so it uses a different type of loop. For example, if the program now uses a for loop, rewrite it so it uses a while loop.

3. Create a C++ program with a class named circle. The class should have the following member variables: radius, diameter, and area.

   The constructor should accept one argument: the circle's radius. The constructor should calculate the diameter of the circle as radius * 2, and the area as 3.1416 * radius * radius. These values should be stored in the class's member variables. In addition, the class should have a member function that returns the circle's area, a member function that returns the circle's diameter, and a member function that returns the circle's area. Demonstrate the class in a simple program.

# CHAPTER

# 11

# The X Window System

case ▶ Traditionally, the programmers and staff at Dominion Consulting have used the UNIX Bash shell as their sole interface with the systems they operate. Management has now decided to use the X Window system, in addition to the Bash shell, on all in-house systems. Your supervisor asks you to instruct each staff member on how to:

- Configure a computer to launch the X Window system when you start the computer, and instruct each staff member on how to implement the configuration
- Interact with the X Window system
- Personalize the desktop environment, and set up a password-protected screen saver
- Add a program to the X Window menu, and add an icon that invokes a program to the X Window desktop
- Use the File Manager, Spreadsheet, Calendar, and gEdit applications

In this lesson you will:

- Describe the X Window system and its client/server model
- Understand the role of the Window Manager
- Start the X Window system
- Navigate within the X Window system and use its components

# Starting and Navigating an X Window Session

## What Is the X Window System?

The X Window system is a **graphical user interface** (GUI) that runs on Linux and many UNIX operating systems. Like Windows and the Macintosh operating systems, it provides an easy-to-use, graphical method of operating the computer. Programmers may also develop applications that run on the X Window system and support GUI components, such as windows, dialog boxes, buttons, and pull-down menus. Figure 11-1 shows a typical X Window screen.

The X Window system was originally developed at the Massachusetts Institute of Technology (MIT). It was created so different brands of hardware, running different variations of UNIX, would all look and feel the same to the user. It was also designed to run applications across a network consisting of different types of computers. The system developed at MIT, currently in its eleventh version, is appropriately called **X11**. **XFree86** is a version of X11 that was ported to the PC and runs on Linux.

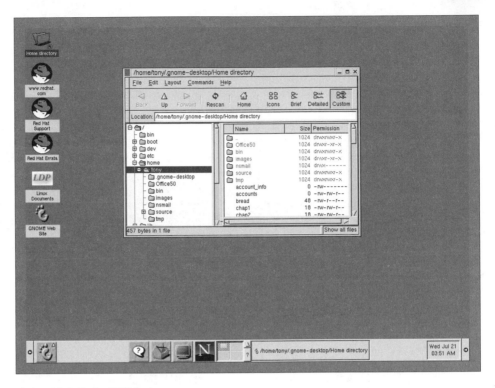

**Figure 11-1:** Typical X Window screen

## X Window Clients and Servers

Although you can easily use the X Window system to run programs stored on your local computer, you can also run applications over a network. X Window uses a client/server model where a program can run on one computer but display its output on another. For example, suppose you have a network with two computers: system A and system B. The user on system A can invoke and run a program that resides on system B. Although the user of system A sees the program running in a window on his or her computer, it might actually be executing on system B. This interaction is transparent to the user of system A, who may not know the program is actually running on a different computer. Additionally, systems A and B can be different types of computers, each running a different variation of UNIX.

In X Window network terminology, the desktop system that the user runs a program from is called the **X server**. The system that hosts and executes the program is called the **X client**.

> Note: In normal network terminology, the server is the system that hosts a program, and the client is the system run by the user. In X Window jargon, the terms client and server mean the opposite. The terms are reversed because the X Window server (on the desktop) performs operations requested by the client (on the host system). For example, the client might request that the server display a window or ask the server to move a window to a different position on the screen.

# Window Managers

Like the UNIX operating system itself, the X Window system is layered and built from components. At the top layer is the **Window Manager**. The Window Manager controls how windows appear and how users control them. In many regards, the Window Manager is to the X Window system as the shell is to UNIX: each provides the user an interface to the underlying components.

Many Window Managers have been developed, and most of them are available for free. Linux supports over 50 different ones. Table 11-1 lists some common Window Managers currently in use.

| Window Manager | Description |
|---|---|
| AnotherLevel | Based on the fvwm Window Manager and commonly used with Red Hat Linux |
| CDE | Common Desktop Environment |
| Enlightenment | Popular Window Manager sometimes called E. Also commonly used with Red Hat Linux. |
| fvwm | Virtual Window Manager |
| fvwm95 | Version of fvwm with a Windows 95 look and feel |
| KDE | K Desktop environment |
| olwm | Open Look Window Manager |
| mwm | Motif Window Manager |
| twm | Tab Window Manager or Tom's Window Manager |

**Table 11-1:** Common Window Managers

## Using GNOME

The **GNU Network Object Model Environment (GNOME)**, a product of the GNU project, is not a Window Manager, but a desktop environment that must be used along with a Window Manager. By default, Red Hat 6 installs the Enlightenment Window Manager with GNOME (pronounced "guh-nome"). All examples in this chapter use Enlightenment and GNOME.

> Note: The GNU project is an organization with the stated purpose of developing a free, UNIX-like, operating system named GNU. The Linux kernel is used in many GNU distributions. The project's Web site is www.gnu.org.

# Starting the X Window System

If your system does not start the X Window system automatically, you may invoke it by using the startx command.

**To start the X Window System (if your system does not automatically start it):**

■ Type **startx** and press **Enter**.

You see a display similar to Figure 11-2.

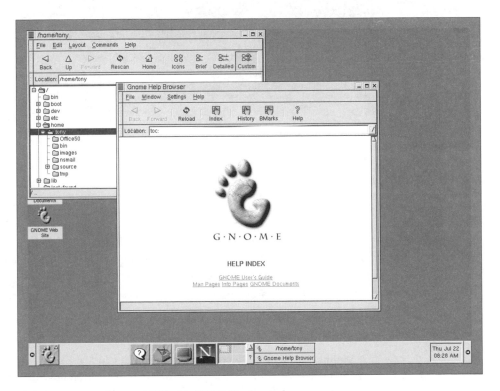

**Figure 11-2:** Introductory X Window/GNOME screen

## Configuring Linux to Automatically Start the X Window System

If your system does not automatically start the X Window system, you may configure it to do so. This is accomplished by modifying a line in the file /etc/inittab.

**To view the contents of /etc/inittab:**

**1** Type **more /etc/inittab** and press **Enter.** Your screen looks similar to Figure 11-3.

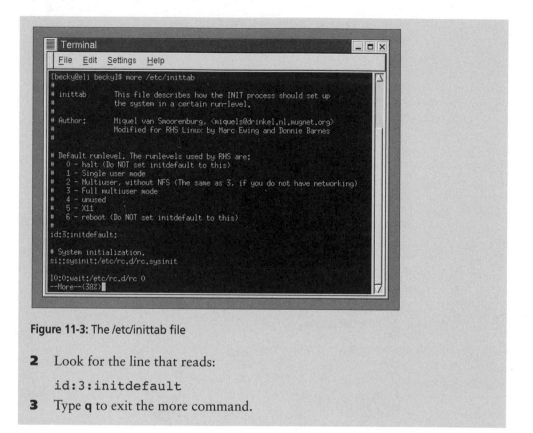

```
[becky@eli becky]$ more /etc/inittab
#
# inittab        This file describes how the INIT process should set up
#                the system in a certain run-level.
#
# Author:        Miquel van Smoorenburg, <miquels@drinkel.nl.mugnet.org>
#                Modified for RHS Linux by Marc Ewing and Donnie Barnes
#
# Default runlevel. The runlevels used by RHS are:
#    0 - halt (Do NOT set initdefault to this)
#    1 - Single user mode
#    2 - Multiuser, without NFS (The same as 3, if you do not have networking)
#    3 - Full multiuser mode
#    4 - unused
#    5 - X11
#    6 - reboot (Do NOT set initdefault to this)
id:3:initdefault:

# System initialization.
si::sysinit:/etc/rc.d/rc.sysinit

l0:0:wait:/etc/rc.d/rc 0
--More--(38%)
```

**Figure 11-3:** The /etc/inittab file

**2**   Look for the line that reads:

   id:3:initdefault

**3**   Type **q** to exit the more command.

The code shown above establishes the operating system's default **run level**, or mode of operation, at 3. Run level 3 is full multi-user mode. By raising the run level to 5, the system starts in X11 mode, which automatically starts the X Window system.

Note: Configuring your system requires superuser privileges. You must be able to log on as root to complete the following exercise.

Caution: You should be very careful any time you log on as root. Because the root user has privileges to alter any part of the system configuration and delete any file, you could accidentally corrupt the operating system.

The next exercise is optional and assumes you have been given permission to log on as root. Because it requires you to shut down and reboot the system, you should perform it only if you are the sole user on a PC running Linux. You need to know the password for the root account.

**To configure your system to start the X Window system automatically:**

**1**   Log out of the system, and log back on as root.

**2**   Change your current working directory to /etc.

**3** Make a back-up copy of the inittab file. Use a command such as **cp inittab inittab.safe**, and press **Enter**. You could restore the back-up copy if you accidentally corrupt the inittab file.

**4** Open the inittab file in vi or Emacs.

**5** Change the line:

```
id:3:initdefault
```

to

```
id:5:initdefault
```

**6** Save the file and exit the editor.

**7** Reboot the system by typing **shutdown –r now** and pressing **Enter**. The –r option causes the system to reboot. The now argument tells the shutdown command to start shutting down immediately.

**8** When the system starts again, you will be greeted by the X Window Login screen. Log on with your normal user name and password.

Now that you know how to start the X Window system, you are ready to learn to navigate it and control its common components.

## Interacting with the X Window System

You interact with the X Window environment through its many components. Figure 11-4 shows the opening GNOME screen, with its major components labeled.

Here is a description of the components in Figure 11-4.

- Icons: There are a number of **icons,** or small images, on the screen. Each causes an action to take place when activated. You activate an icon by positioning the mouse pointer over it and clicking the left mouse button.
- GNOME Panel: This component is a strip that runs across the bottom of the screen, and includes a number of icons. Each icon invokes an **applet** when activated. An applet is a small application written specifically to be placed on the panel.
- Windows: Every program, application, or applet that runs under the X Window system runs in a window. Windows have many of their own components, which you will learn about in this chapter.
- Desktop Area: This is the background area that holds the windows and icons you are working with during your X Window session.

Now that you can identify the major components of the GNOME screen, you will learn to interact with each one.

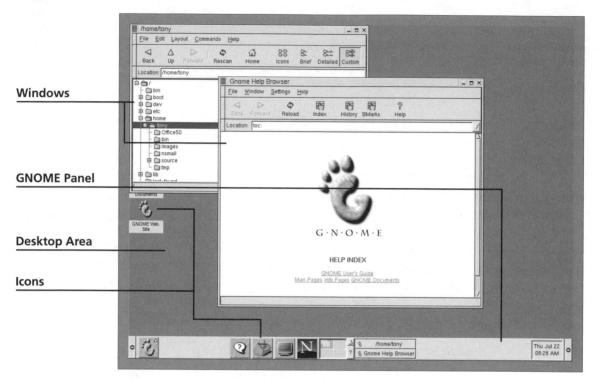

**Windows**

**GNOME Panel**

**Desktop Area**

**Icons**

**Figure 11-4:** Major GNOME components

## Interacting with Windows

Windows have their own components, as shown in Figure 11-5.

Here is a description of the window components.

- Border: Each window is outlined with a border.
- Title Bar: At the top of the window border is a title bar. The title bar lists the name of the window or the application running in the window.
- Window Options button: Click this button to see a menu offering several useful window operations.
- Iconify button: Click this button to collapse the window into a small icon. The icon appears in a section of the panel known as the Pager. The program in the window is still running but is hidden from sight.
- Minimize/Maximize button: Click this button to alternately expand the window to fill the screen and reduce the window to its original size.
- Close button: Click this button to close the window and terminate the application running in it.
- Scroll bar: If a window contains more information than it can display, you see a scroll bar. The scroll bar lets you scroll through all the window's content.

**Window Options Button**

**Title Bar**

**Iconify Button**

**Minimize/ Maximize Button**

**Close Button**

**Border**

**Scroll Bar**

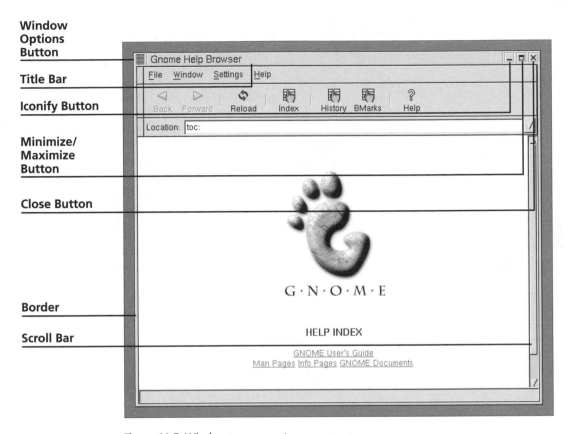

**Figure 11-5:** Window components

**tip**

**Many GNOME window components appear and function exactly like their counterparts in Windows 98. If you are already comfortable with Windows 98, you will be comfortable with most window operations in GNOME.**

One of the basic window operations is resizing.

### To practice resizing a window:

**1** If you do not see a window titled "Gnome Help Browser" on your screen, invoke it by clicking the large question mark icon on the panel, shown in Figure 11-6. If you do see the Help Browser window, skip to Step 2.

**GNOME Help Browser icon**

**Figure 11-6:** Gnome Help Browser icon

**2** Move the mouse pointer to the right edge of the window border. The pointer becomes a horizontal double-headed arrow. Click and hold the left mouse button while dragging the mouse pointer to the right. You see the window expand horizontally. Drag the mouse pointer back to the left, and the window shrinks horizontally. Release the mouse pointer to stop resizing the window.

**3** Move the mouse pointer to the bottom edge of the screen. The pointer becomes a vertical double-headed arrow. Click and hold the left mouse button as you move the pointer, first up and then down. The window shrinks and expands vertically.

**4** Move the mouse pointer to the lower-right corner of the window. The pointer becomes a slanted double-headed arrow. Click and hold the left mouse button while dragging the mouse pointer toward the lower-right corner of the screen. The window expands both horizontally and vertically. Drag the pointer back toward the upper-left corner of the screen, and the window shrinks horizontally and vertically.

**5** Release the mouse pointer to stop resizing the window.

**tip**

The Help Browser contains useful information on using GNOME. Its contents are hyperlinked in a manner similar to a Web page.

Other basic window operations are moving, shading, and unshading a window.

**To practice moving, shading, and unshading a window:**

**1** Move the mouse pointer to the window's title bar. The pointer becomes a four-way arrow.

**2** Click and hold the left mouse button as you drag the mouse pointer across the screen. The window moves to follow the mouse pointer.

**3** Release the mouse button to stop moving the window.

**4** Shading a window means to collapse it, or "draw it up" into its title bar. Double-click the title bar to shade the window.

**5** Double-click the title bar again to unshade the window.

Most window components offer context-sensitive pop-up Help boxes. These are useful for discovering the purpose of a button or another component.

**To practice using the pop-up Help boxes:**

**1**   Position the mouse pointer on the window's title bar.

**2**   After a brief moment, a box describing how to use the title bar pops up.

**3**   Perform this action with other buttons on the window, and discover their use.

By now you have probably realized that pointing to an object on the screen and clicking the left button carries out most mouse operations. From this point forward, this action is called "clicking." Actions that require you to click the right mouse button are called "right-clicking."

The Iconify, Minimize/Maximize, and Close buttons are at the top right corner of the window. Use these to adjust the window's size and to terminate the window's application.

Refer to Figure 11-5 to review each button's location.

**To practice using the Minimize, Maximize, and Close buttons:**

**1**   Click the **Iconify** button. The window shrinks to an icon.

**2**   The Help Browser is still running, however. Look at the panel (located at the bottom of the screen). In a section known as the Pager, illustrated in Figure 11-7, you see a button for the Gnome Help Browser.

**Pager**

Figure 11-7: The Pager

**3**   Click the **Gnome Help Browser** button in the Pager. You see the window reappear.

**4**   Click the **Minimize/Maximize** button. The window expands to fill the entire screen.

**5**   Click the **Minimize/Maximize** button again. The window shrinks back to its previous size.

**6**   Click the **Close** button. The application terminates and its window disappears from the screen.

Finally, the Windows Options button displays a menu of basic and advanced window operations:

- Close terminates the application and closes the window.
- Annihilate also closes the window but can be used in cases where the application is malfunctioning, when it will not let you close the window.
- Iconify reduces the window to an icon in the GNOME Pager.
- Raise brings the window on top of all other windows.
- Lower puts the window beneath all other windows.
- Shade/Unshade collapses or expands a window.
- Stick/Unstick makes a window visible on all desktops. (Desktops are covered later in this chapter.)
- Desktop displays a menu that allows you to move the window to specific desktops.
- Window Size displays a menu that allows you to change the width and height of the window.

Note: You can customize the items in the Windows Options menu, which may be different on your system.

**To practice using the Windows Options menu:**

**1** Click the **large question mark** icon on the panel to open the Help Browser window.

**2** Click the **Windows Option** button in the upper-left corner of the window.

**3** Experiment with several options on the menu.

**4** When finished, close the **Help Browser** and any other open windows.

## Interacting with the Panel

The panel, which appears at the bottom of the GNOME screen, features the Pager (which you used in the previous section), a clock, and several icons. The icon at the left end of the panel, shown in Figure 11-8, is the Main menu button.

**Figure 11-8:** Main menu button

Clicking the Main menu button reveals the Main menu, which offers icons of its own and several submenus.

**To practice using the Main menu:**

**1**    Click the **Main menu** button. You see the Main menu, illustrated in Figure 11-9.

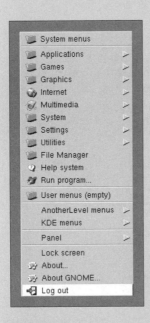

System menus
Applications
Games
Graphics
Internet
Multimedia
System
Settings
Utilities
File Manager
Help system
Run program...
User menus (empty)
AnotherLevel menus
KDE menus
Panel
Lock screen
About...
About GNOME...
Log out

**Figure 11-9:** Main menu

**2**    Items followed by an arrow contain submenus. Position the mouse pointer over any of these to see the submenu appear.

**3**    Click the **File Manager** item. You see the File Manager window open.

**4**    Click the **Close** button on the File Manager window to close the application. (Note that depending on your computer's configuration, a File Manager window may open automatically when you start the X Window System.)

To the right of the Main menu button another set of icons typically appear, as shown in Figure 11-10.

**Figure 11-10:** Panel icons

You have already used the large question mark icon, which opens the Help Browser. The toolbox icon opens the Control Center, a program for configuring the GNOME environment. The icon displaying an image of a computer screen executes a terminal emulation program, which allows you to use the command line within a window. The last icon in the figure displays the Netscape logo. It executes the Netscape Communicator Web browser and e-mail client.

**To practice launching the terminal emulation program and Netscape Communicator:**

1   Click the **Terminal Emulator** icon, which displays an image of a computer screen. A terminal window appears with a command prompt.

2   You cannot use the window until it is active. Click anywhere in the window to make it active. You see the title bar change color.

3   Practice shell commands such as ls-l, date, and who in the window. Leave the window open. (Note that depending on your computer's configuration, a terminal window may open automatically when you start the X Window System.)

The next area on the panel is the GNOME Pager, shown in Figure 11-11.

Desktop View

Applications View

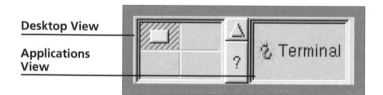

**Figure 11-11:** GNOME Pager

The GNOME Pager is an **applet,** a small application designed to run on the panel. As shown in Figure 11-11, the left section of the Pager is the Desktop View. The Desktop View is divided into four areas. These are virtual desktops that you may switch to at any time. Currently, you are using the first desktop area, which is represented by the upper-left quadrant of the Desktop View.

**To practice using the Desktop View:**

1   Make sure the Terminal Emulation program is running on your current desktop.

2   Your current desktop is represented by the upper-left square of the Desktop View. Click each of the other quadrants of the Desktop View. Notice that each appears as a clear desktop, with no windows open.

3   Click the lower-right quadrant of the Desktop View.

**4**  Click the **large question mark** icon on the panel to open the Help Browser. Notice a small square in the lower-right quadrant of the Desktop view, approximating the position of the Help Browser window.

**5**  Click the upper-left quadrant of the Desktop view to return to your original desktop. You see the Terminal Emulation window.

The second area of the Pager is the Applications View. It holds an icon for each application that is running in the current desktop area. As you have already learned, an application that is represented by an icon may be restored to the desktop by clicking its icon in the Applications View. Between the Desktop View and Application View areas are two small icons: one with an up arrow and one with a small question mark. The up-arrow icon displays a list of all running applications. The small question-mark icon opens the GNOME Pager Settings window, which allows you to customize the Pager.

Near the right edge of the panel is the Clock applet shown in Figure 11-12.

**Figure 11-12:** Clock applet

By default, the clock displays the date and time. You can modify its properties, however, by right-clicking it.

**To modify the Clock applet properties:**

**1**  Position the mouse pointer over the Clock applet's display, and click the right mouse button. You see a small shortcut menu.

**2**  Click **Properties**. You see the Clock Properties window, shown in Figure 11-13.

**3**  The Time Format buttons allow you to choose from a 12- or 24-hour display. The Show date check box toggles the date display on or off. The Unix time check box toggles the time display between hours and minutes, and the internal UNIX time format. Click the **24 hour** button, and the **Show date** button.

**4**  Click **OK**. The date no longer appears, and the time appears in 24-hour format.

Clock properties                                           ☒

Clock

Time Format            ☐ Show date
  ⌃ 12 hour
  ⌄ 24 hour           ☐ Unix time

    🖰 OK        ✔ Apply        ✗ Close        ? Help

**Figure 11-13:** Clock Properties window

**5**  Repeat the procedure in Steps 1 and 2 to open the Clock Properties window again.

**6**  Reset the Clock applet to display the time in a 12-hour format and show the date.

If an application's window is very large or if you are using a low resolution display, you may want to remove the panel from the screen. The Hide button, shown in Figure 11-14, is at the left edge of the panel. (Note that depending on you computer's configuration, the arrow may not appear on the Hide button.)

**Figure 11-14:** Hide button

A similar button, with an arrow pointing to the right, is at the right edge of the panel. When you click either of these buttons, you hide the panel.

**To practice hiding the panel:**

**1**  Click the **Hide** button at the left edge of the panel (next to the Main menu button). You see the panel slide out of view.

**2**  The right Hide button is still visible. Click it to bring the panel back into view.

Now that you have learned the basic techniques of interacting with the X Window system, and the GNOME environment in particular, you are ready for more advanced operations. In the next lesson you will learn to run built-in X Window applications and configure your desktop.

# S U M M A R Y

- The X Window system is a graphical user interface, or GUI, that runs on many UNIX and Linux systems. It allows users to run applications transparently across a network.

- The X Window system is built in layers. The top layer, with which the user interacts, is called the Window Manager. By default, Red Hat 6 uses the Enlightenment Window Manager with the GNOME environment.

- Use the startx command at the command line to start the X Window system. A line in the /etc/inittab file directs Linux to start the X Window system automatically.

- The GNOME environment consists of icons, a panel, windows, and the desktop area.

- You resize, move, minimize, maximize, and close a window by interacting with its border, title bar, and buttons.

- The GNOME Panel provides access to the Main menu and icons for applets. One applet is the Pager, which shows the virtual desktops and buttons for all the running applications. The panel provides a button that hides and shows it.

- You can configure the Clock applet to display the date and the time in 12-hour, 24-hour, or the internal UNIX format.

# R E V I E W   Q U E S T I O N S

1. In the X Window client/server model, the system that hosts and executes the application is the _____.
   a. client
   b. server
   c. workstation
   d. host

2. The top layer of the X Window system is the _____.
   a. X Window kernel
   b. network manager
   c. Window Manager
   d. window shell

3. The command that starts the X Window system is _____.
   a. start
   b. startx
   c. runx
   d. start x

4. The _____ file directs UNIX to automatically start the X Window system.
   a. /usr/xwindow
   b. /etc/xwindow
   c. /etc/inittab
   d. /root/inittab

5. Clicking the Iconify button on a window causes the window to _____.
   a. collapse into a small icon in the Pager
   b. close
   c. shrink to a smaller size
   d. expand to fill the screen

6. The Minimize/Maximize button on a window causes the window to _____.
   a. collapse into a small icon in the Pager
   b. close
   c. shrink to a smaller size
   d. alternately expand to fill the screen and shrink to its original size

7. A(n) _____ is a small application written to be placed on the panel.
   a. smallapp
   b. applet
   c. GNOME program
   d. script

8. The Pager's desktop view shows _____.
   a. the desktops of other systems on the network
   b. different background colors that may be placed on the desktop
   c. the virtual desktop in four quadrants
   d. the name of the application running on the desktop

9. The Pager's application view shows _____.
   a. a history of recently run applications
   b. button icons for all applications currently running
   c. a list of all available applications on the system disk
   d. how to execute an application

10. A button that hides the panel from view is located at _____.
    a. the left end of the panel
    b. the right end of the panel
    c. the center of the panel
    d. both a and b

 # E X E R C I S E S

1. Start the X Window system on your computer. Open the GNOME Help Browser, and perform these window operations:
   a. Shade and unshade the window
   b. Maximize the window
   c. Minimize the window
   d. Iconify the window
   e. Restore the window from the Pager
   f. Close the window

2. Open the GNOME Help Browser while the upper-left quadrant of the Pager's virtual desktop view is active. Describe how the icon for the current desktop changes.

3. Activate the upper-right quadrant of the Pager's desktop view, and open a terminal window. Practice a shell command, such as ls.

4. Activate the lower-left quadrant of the Pager's desktop view, and open another terminal. Use the who command to see a list of current users. Note how many times you are listed.

5. Change the Clock applet so the time appears in 24-hour format and the date does not appear.

6. What is the difference between closing a window and using the Annihilate command on the Window Options menu?

 # D I S C O V E R Y   E X E R C I S E S

1. Open a terminal window in the current desktop. Next, open a Gnome Help Browser window in the same desktop. How does the icon for the current desktop indicate that two windows are open?

2. With the terminal window and the Gnome Help Browser still open, note the button icons in the Pager's application view. Change your current desktop by selecting the lower-right quadrant of the Pager's desktop view. Describe the contents of the application view now.

3. With the Help Browser open, use the mouse to resize the window as small as possible. Next, use the Minimize/Maximize button to expand the window to full screen. Click the Minimize/Maximize button again. To what size did the window shrink?

4. Display the contents of the /etc/inittab file. What comments describe the available run levels?

5. The Help Browser offers an interface similar to a Web browser. Open it and practice looking up some topics you have studied in this section.

# Running Applications and Customizing the Desktop

## Running Built-in Applications

The staff at Dominion Consulting frequently needs programs for calendar, text editing, and spreadsheet operations. They could also benefit from a graphical file management utility. Your next task is to find built-in applications for all these needs. After reading this section and completing its exercises, you will be able to:

■ Use the File Manager application to navigate the file system, and to copy, move, and delete files

■ Use the Calendar application to keep appointments and a to-do list

■ Start the Spreadsheet application and the gEdit application

■ Copy text from one window and paste it in another

■ Change your desktop background and your screen saver

■ Move icons on the panel and add other applets to the panel

■ Add new icons that launch your own programs on the panel

■ Add your own programs to the Main menu

Management has asked you to instruct the other staff members on how to locate and execute programs that will help them do their job more productively. They also ask you to investigate using a graphical file management tool. You decide to consult the Gnome Help Browser and find references to a program called File Manager. You've also read about a calendar program. Both programs are executed from the Main menu.

## To run the File Manager program:

**1**  Click the **Main menu** button. The Main menu appears.

**2**  Click the **File Manager** entry. The File Manager application appears, as shown in Figure 11-15.

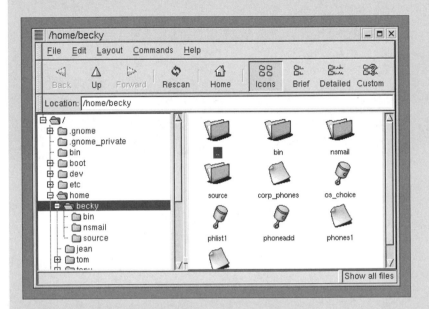

**Figure 11-15:** File Manager

**3**  The left area of the window is a tree view of the file system, as shown in Figure 11-16.

The directories appear with folder icons. Notice that some directories have plus signs (+) next to their entry and others have minus signs (-). The plus and minus signs indicate that the directory has subdirectories.

**4**  Click the **plus sign** that appears before the etc directory. (If you do not see the plus sign, click the etc directory's folder.) The tree display expands to show all subdirectories that are immediately below the etc directory. Also, the plus sign has become a minus sign, indicating the directory view is expanded.

**5**  Click the **minus sign** that now appears before the etc directory. The view of the etc subdirectories collapses, and the minus sign once again becomes a plus sign.

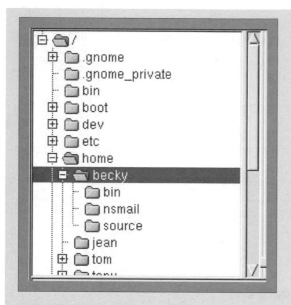

**Figure 11-16:** Directory tree

**6**    The current working directory appears highlighted in the directory tree diagram. The right area of the window, which is similar to Figure 11-17, shows the files and subdirectories in the current working directory.

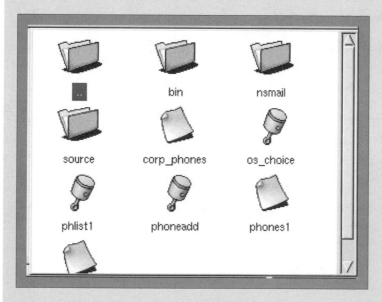

**Figure 11-17:** File view

**7** Click the entry for the **dev** directory. (Click the name dev, or click the folder icon next to the name.) /dev is now your current working directory. You see the files and subdirectories in dev in the right window. Experiment by clicking several directories shown in the tree diagram. Notice that the File Manager will not allow you to enter a directory you do not have permission to enter.

The button bar, just below the menu bar, appears similar to Figure 11-18.

**Figure 11-18:** File Manager button bar

**8** Click the **Home** button. The File Manager returns you to your home directory.

**9** By default, file listings appear in Icon view (as shown in Figure 11-17). You may also display them in Brief view, Detailed view, and Custom view. Click the **Brief** button on the button bar. Your file display becomes a brief list, similar to that shown in Figure 11-19.

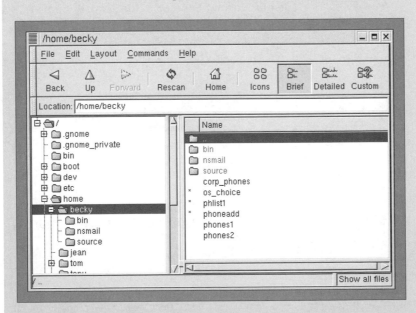

**Figure 11-19:** Brief view

**10** Click the **Detailed** button. Your file display becomes a detailed listing, similar to that shown in Figure 11-20.

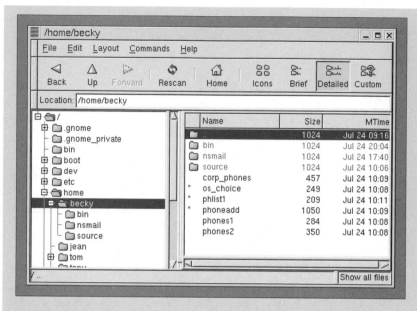

**Figure 11-20:** Detailed view

**11** Click the **Custom** button. You see a file display similar to that shown in Figure 11-21.

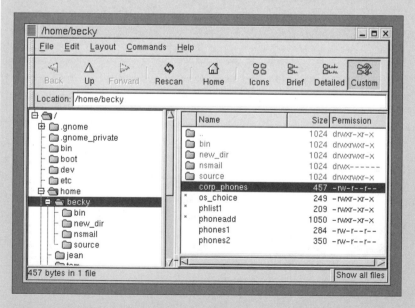

**Figure 11-21:** Custom file display

**12** The Custom display is called "custom," because it displays the file attributes you can modify. Click the word **Edit** on the menu bar. The Edit menu appears.

**13** Click **Preferences** on the Edit menu bar. The Preferences window, similar to Figure 11-22, appears.

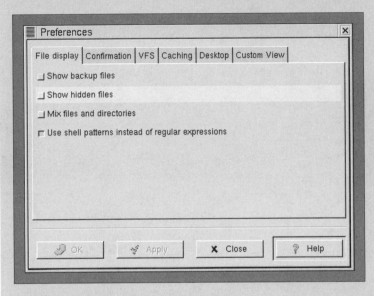

**Figure 11-22:** Preferences window

**14** Click the **Custom View** tab. You see the Custom View section, similar to that shown in Figure 11-23.

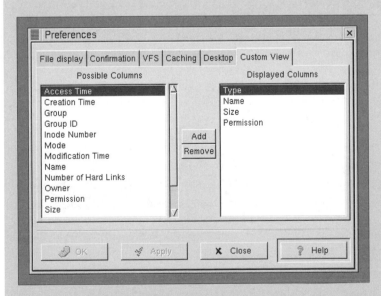

**Figure 11-23:** Custom view section of Preferences window

**15** The items listed under Possible Columns may be included in the custom display. The items under Displayed Columns are those currently included. In the Possible Columns section, click **Owner**.

**16** Next, click the **Add** button. Owner is now added to the Displayed Columns section.

**17** Click the OK button. The Custom View is updated to include the owner of each file and directory. The display is similar to Figure 11-24.

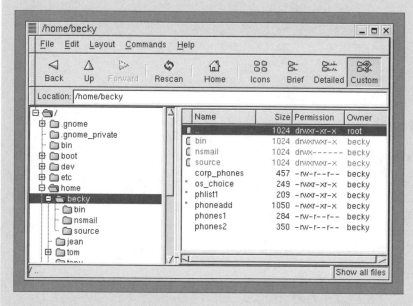

**Figure 11-24:** Updated Custom view

The File Manager also provides convenient methods for copying, renaming, and deleting files. These procedures must be part of your instruction to the other staff at Dominion Consulting.

### To copy, rename, and delete files:

**1** Make sure the File Manager is still running. Before experimenting with file operations, create a set of empty files. Click the **Terminal Emulation** icon on the panel, as shown in Figure 11-25.

**Figure 11-25:** Terminal Emulation icon

**2**   A terminal window appears with a command prompt. Click in the window to activate it.

**3**   Create the files test1, test2, and test3 with the touch command. Your screen appears similar to Figure 11-26.

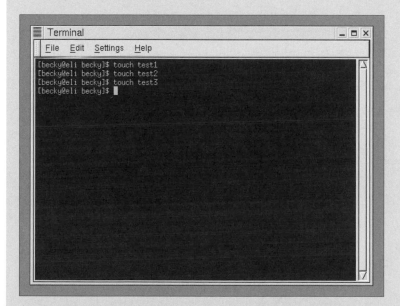

**Figure 11-26:** Terminal window

**4**   Close the **Terminal** window.

**5**   The File Manager display should be updated because new files were created. Click the **Rescan** button. Listings for the test1, test2, and test3 files appear in the File view.

**6**   Switch back to Icon view by clicking the **Icons** button.

**7**   Right-click the **test1** file icon.

**8**   On the shortcut menu, click **Copy**. The Copy window appears, as shown in Figure 11-27.

**9**   You will now copy the file to test4 in your home directory. In the text box, type the pathname **/home/*username*/test4** (where *username* is your user name). Click the **OK** button.

**10**   The test4 file appears in the File view. Again, right-click the **test1** icon.

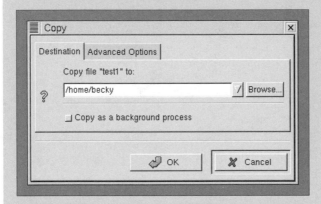

**Figure 11-27:** Copy window

**11**   On the shortcut menu, click **Delete**. The Delete Confirmation window appears, as shown in Figure 11-28.

**Figure 11-28:** Delete Confirmation window

**12**   Click the **Yes** button to delete the file.

**13**   Right-click the **test2** file icon, and then click **Move** on the shortcut menu. The Move window, as shown in Figure 11-29, appears.

**14**   You will now rename (move) the file to Test5, in your home directory. In the text box, type the pathname **/home/*username*/test5** (where *username* is your user name). Click the **OK** button. The file is renamed test5.

**15**   The File Manager also lets you perform operations on multiple files at once. Switch to Brief view by clicking the **Brief** button.

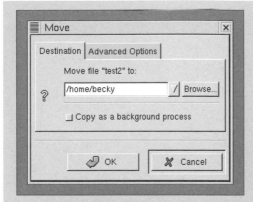

**Figure 11-29:** Move window

**16** Click the **test3** file to select it.

**17** Hold down the **Shift** key, and click the **test5** file. You see test3, test4, and test5 highlighted.

**18** Right-click any of the selected files.

**19** On the shortcut menu, click **Delete**.

**20** The Delete Confirmation window appears. Click **Yes**.

The three files are deleted.

When you select a file and then hold down the Shift key while selecting another file, you also select all the files whose names appear between the two selected files. You can hold down the Ctrl key while selecting files to add them to your selection one at a time.

The File Manager also allows you to create new directories.

**To create a directory with the File Manager:**

**1** With File Manager running, click **File** on the menu bar. The File menu appears.

**2** Point to **New** on the File menu. A submenu appears.

**3** Click **Directory**. The Create a new Directory window appears, as shown in Figure 11-30.

**Figure 11-30:** Create a New Directory window

**4**  You will now create the new_dir directory in your home directory. In the text box, type the pathname **/home/*username*/new_dir** (where *username* is your user name). Click **OK**.

The File view is updated with the new_dir directory listing.

**5**  Close the File Manager application.

In this section you have learned the basic operations of the File Manager, which will prove very helpful to the staff at Dominion Consulting as they learn to use the X Window system. In the next section you explore the Calendar application.

## Using the Calendar Application

The GNOME calendar application is easy to use and offers several helpful features. It allows you to set up appointments, create to-do lists, and view your calendar by the day, week, month, or year. This will be a useful program for the rest of the staff at Dominion Consulting.

**To use the Calendar application:**

**1**  Open the **Main menu** and point to **Applications**. A submenu appears.

**2**  Click **Calendar**. The Calendar window appears, as shown in Figure 11-31.

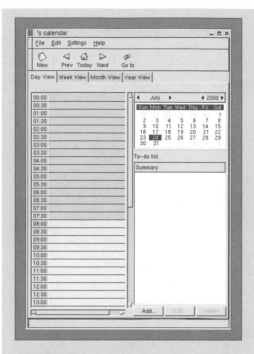

**Figure 11-31:** Calendar application

**3** By default, the calendar appears in Day view. On the left, the day's hours appear in 30-minute increments. On the right, a calendar for the month appears, with today's date highlighted. Beneath the month's calendar is an empty to-do list. Click the **Week View** tab to see the display change to a weekly view, as shown in Figure 11-32.

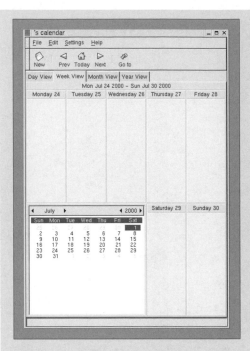

**Figure 11-32:** Week view

**4** Next, click the **Month View** tab. The calendar looks like Figure 11-33.

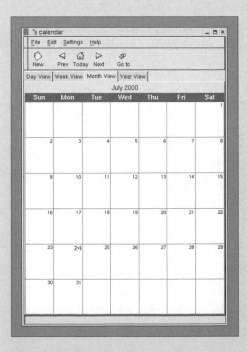

**Figure 11-33:** Month view

**5** Next, click the **Year View** tab. The calendar changes to a year view, as shown in Figure 11-34.

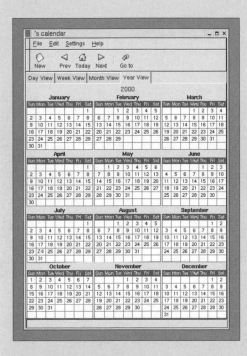

**Figure 11-34:** Year view

**6** Click the **Day View** tab to return to the Day view.

**7** Before entering appointments in the calendar, you notice the times appear in 24-hour format. You need to change them to regular 12-hour format. Click **Settings** on the menu bar. A menu appears.

**8** Click **Preferences**. The Preferences window appears, as shown in Figure 11-35.

**9** Notice that the 24-hour button is pushed down. Click the **12-hour (AM/PM)** button.

**10** Click **OK**. The times now appear in 12-hour format.

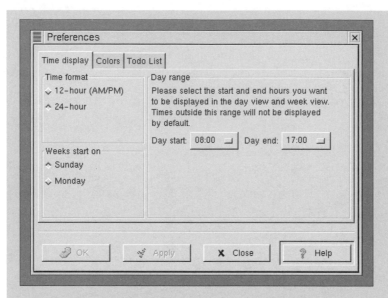

**Figure 11-35:** Calendar Preferences window

**11**   You need to enter an appointment you have with Carmen Scott later today. Click the **New** button on the button bar. The Create new appointment window appears, as shown in Figure 11-36.

**12**   In the Summary text box, type **Meeting with Carmen Scott to discuss projected staff development needs**.

**13**   You need to specify a starting time, which is 2:00 PM. Click the blank button next to the start time. A menu pops up. Position the mouse pointer over 2:00 PM, and then click **2:00 PM** on the submenu.

**14**   The meeting is scheduled to last until 3:30 PM. Click the blank button next to the end time. A menu pops up. Position the mouse pointer over 3:00 PM, and then click **3:30 PM** on the submenu.

**15**   Click the **OK** button. If a window appears informing you that the file has changed since it has loaded and asks if you want to continue, click the **Yes** button.

**16**   At 4:00 PM today, the sales team is scheduled to make a presentation. Click the **New** button on the button bar. The Create new appointment window appears. Type **Sales Team Presentation** in the Summary box.

**17**   Schedule the presentation to last from **4:00 PM** until **5:00 PM**. Click **OK**.

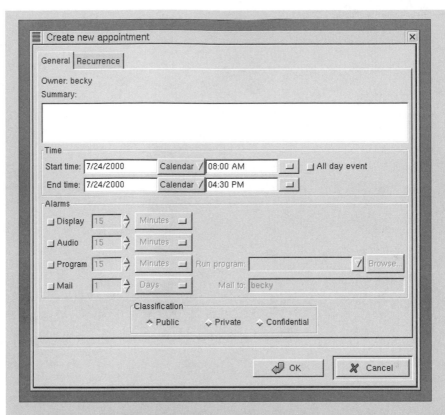

**Figure 11-36:** Create New Appointment window

**18** Scroll the Day view down to see the afternoon appointments. A window appears similar to the one shown in Figure 11-37.

**19** Click the **Week View** and then click the **Month View** tabs to see how the appointments appear in each of those views. (No appointments are visible in the Year view.)

**20** You remember that Jean asked you to help her troubleshoot a printer problem. Add that to the to-do list by clicking the **Day View** tab and then clicking the **Add** button at the bottom of the window. The Create to-do item window appears.

**21** In the Summary text box, type **Troubleshoot printer.**

**22** In the Due Date box, type tomorrow's date.

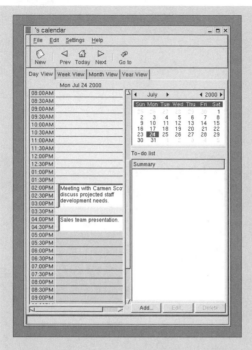

**Figure 11-37:** Day view with afternoon appointments

**23** In the Item Comments box, type **Help Jean with her printer.** The Create to-do item window appears as shown in Figure 11-38.

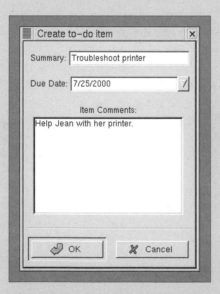

**Figure 11-38:** Create to-do item window

**24**   Click the **OK** button. The item is added to the to-do list.

**25**   Click the **Close** button to close the Calendar window.

When you started the Calendar application, you noticed an entry on the Applications menu named Gnumeric spreadsheet. You know the staff at Dominion consulting will need a spreadsheet program, so you decide to experiment briefly with it.

## Using the Spreadsheet Application

The Gnumeric spreadsheet application offers many functions that anyone with spreadsheet experience will find familiar. It supports a large set of math functions and comes with extensive online documentation. You decide to test a simple sum function to see if the spreadsheet works like other well-known spreadsheets.

**To become familiar with the Gnumeric spreadsheet:**

**1**   Open the **Main menu** and then the **Applications menu**.

**2**   Click **Gnumeric spreadsheet**. You see a window similar to Figure 11-39.

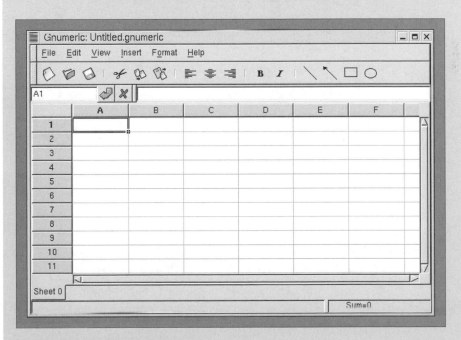

**Figure 11-39:** Gnumeric spreadsheet

**3** Enter the following values in the indicated cells:

**Cell A1: 147.90**

**Cell A2: 459.20**

**Cell A3: 712.35**

**Cell A4: 923.88**

**4** In cell A5, enter the function **=sum(a1:a4)** and press **Enter**. The window now appears like Figure 11-40.

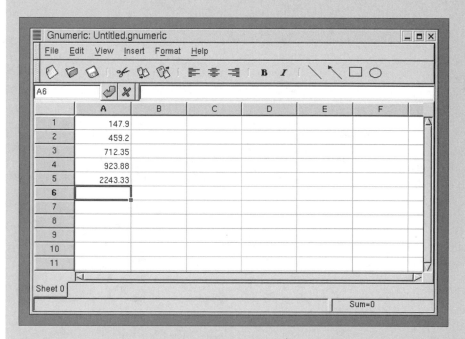

**Figure 11-40:** Updated spreadsheet window

**5** Next, you decide to test the program's numeric formatting capabilities. Place the mouse pointer in cell A1.

**6** Hold down the left mouse button, and drag the cursor to cell A5.

**7** Release the mouse pointer. Cells A1 through A5 are now selected.

**8** Click **Format** on the menu bar. A menu appears.

**9** Click **Cells**. The window in Figure 11-41 appears.

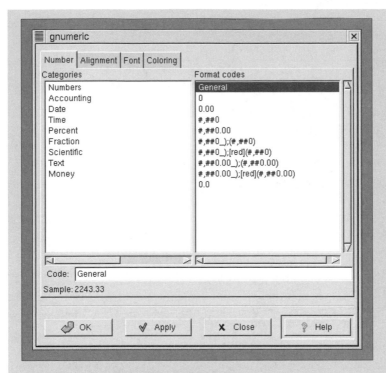

**Figure 11-41:** Cell Formatting window

**10** In the Categories list, click **Money.**

**11** In the Format Codes list, you see a list of number formats. Click **$#,##0.00_);[red]($#,##0.00).**

**12** Click the **OK** button. The spreadsheet now appears like Figure 11-42.

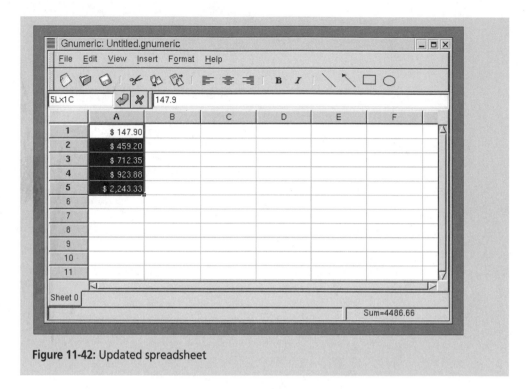

**Figure 11-42:** Updated spreadsheet

You have determined that the Gnumeric spreadsheet application will be useful to the staff at Dominion, and you plan to include it in your training. Before you close the application, you decide to test the X Window system's ability to cut and paste text and objects. You recall seeing an editor named gEdit, listed under the Applications menu. You decide to perform a simple cut and paste operation between the editor and the spreadsheet.

**To demonstrate cut and paste:**

**1**   Open the **Main menu** and then the **Applications menu**.

**2**   Click **gEdit**. You see a window similar to Figure 11-43.

**3**   In the editor, type **Daily Revenue Figures**.

**4**   Press the **Home** key to move the cursor to the beginning of the line of text you just entered.

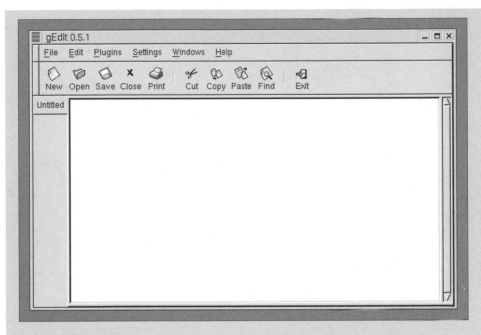

**Figure 11-43:** gEdit editor

**5** Press **Shift+End** to highlight the entire line of text. The gEdit window should look similar to Figure 11-44.

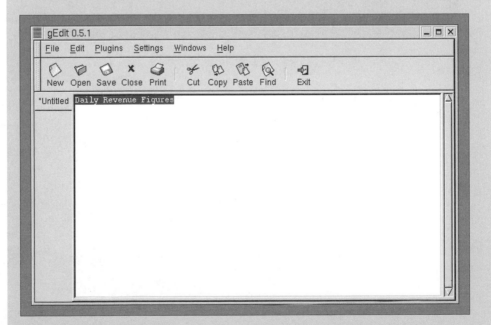

**Figure 11-44:** Highlighted text

**6** Click the **Copy** button on the button bar. The text is now copied into the clipboard.

**7** Activate the spreadsheet application by clicking any visible part of its window or clicking its icon in the Pager.

**8** Click **cell B1**.

**9** Click **Edit** on the menu bar, and then click **Paste**. Your spreadsheet looks like Figure 11-45.

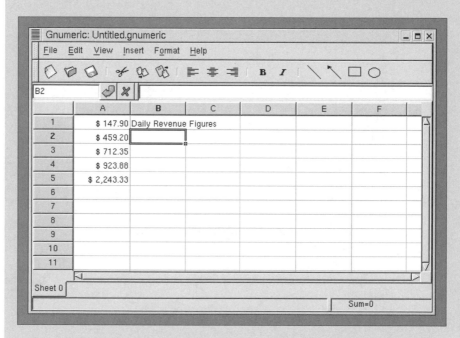

**Figure 11-45:** Spreadsheet with pasted text

**10** Save the spreadsheet you have created as **Revenue** and then exit the application. Close the gEdit editor without saving the file.

One benefit the X Window system offers is the ability to work in multiple windows at the same time. For example, in the previous exercise you worked with the gEdit application in one window while using the spreadsheet application in another window. You can also work in multiple terminal windows at once. For example, you can edit a C program in one window, compile it in another window, and execute it in third window.

**To use multiple terminal windows in a production environment:**

**1** Click the **Terminal Emulation** icon on the panel. A terminal window opens. Click in the **terminal window** to activate it.

**2** Use the vi editor to open the **encode.c source** file you created in Chapter 10. Your screen appears similar to Figure 11-46.

**Figure 11-46:** One terminal window

**3** Click the **Terminal Emulation** icon on the panel again. A second terminal window opens. Click in the new terminal window to activate it. Type **./encode** and press **Enter** to execute the encode program. Your screen should look similar to Figure 11-47.

**4** Viewing a program's source code while it is executing is a helpful debugging technique. Click the **first terminal window** again to activate it, and then move the window to a position on the screen so both terminal windows are visible. (You may need to move both windows to see them adequately.) By viewing both the program source code and the running program's output, you can see that the encode program is currently executing a scanf statement.

**5** The encode program, which is running in the second terminal window, asks you to enter a filename. To determine which file you will encode, you will now open a third terminal window and view a directory listing. Click the **Terminal icon** on the panel to open the third terminal window. Click in the **new terminal window** to activate it.

**Figure 11-47:** Two terminal windows

**6** Type **ls** and press **Enter**. Your screen should look similar to Figure 11-48.

**7** Look at the list of files in the window, and decide which one you will encrypt with the encode program. Click in the window in which the encode program is running, and type the filename.

**8** The program next asks you to enter an output filename. Type **scrambled** and press **Enter**. The program ends and returns to a command line.

**9** Close the three terminal windows.

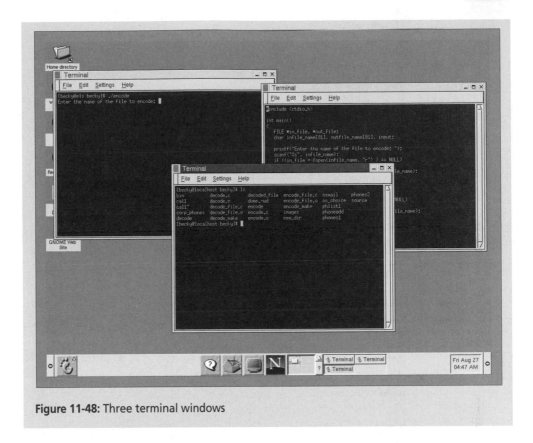

**Figure 11-48:** Three terminal windows

You have learned the primary operations of the File Manager and the Calendar, and confirmed that the X Window system has spreadsheet and editor applications. You have also learned to work in multiple windows at once. Now, you are ready to conduct your first training session with the staff at Dominion consulting.

# Configuring the Desktop

You may customize many aspects of the X Window system. In this section you will learn to personalize your desktop environment by changing the background image and specifying a screen saver. Then you will learn to configure the items on the panel and add new applets to it. Finally, you will learn to add your own items to the Main menu.

## Changing the Background and Screen Saver

The background is the desktop area behind all windows and icons. You can change the color of the desktop or specify a graphic image (known as **wallpaper**) to be used as a background. You change the background by clicking the Configuration Tool icon on the panel, shown in Figure 11-49.

**Figure 11-49:** Control Center icon

## To change the background:

**1**   Click the **Configuration Tool** icon. You see the Control Center window, shown in Figure 11-50.

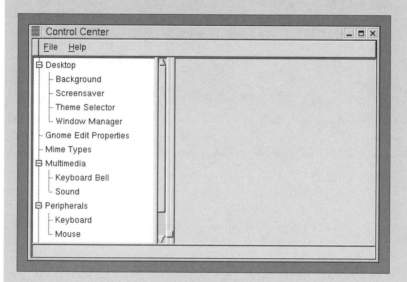

**Figure 11-50:** Control Center window

**2**   Click the word **Background,** which appears under Desktop in the left frame of the window. You see the Background Properties window shown in Figure 11-51.

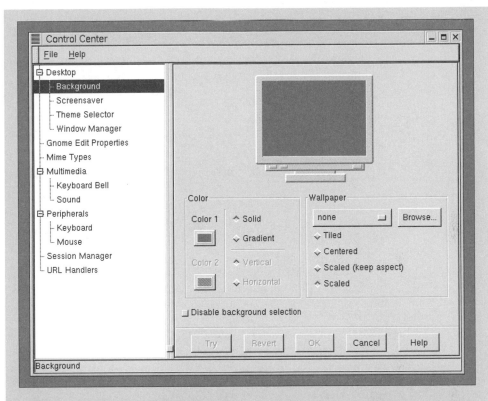

**Figure 11-51:** Background Properties window

**3**   You can choose a solid color, a gradient color, or an image to fill the background. First, set your background to a solid color. Make sure the **Solid** button is pressed, then click the **Color 1** button. You see the Pick a color window shown in Figure 11-52.

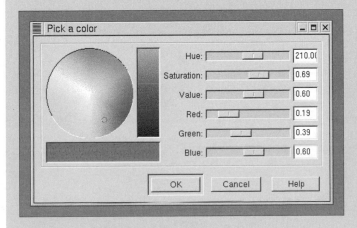

**Figure 11-52:** Pick a color window

**4**  Look at the color wheel, and find a color you would like for your background. Click the area containing that color.

**5**  Click **OK**. You return to the Background Properties window. Click the **Try** button to see how the color looks in your background.

**6**  Next, try a gradient color. A gradient color gradually fades, or blends, from one color to another. Click the **Gradient** button.

**7**  Click the **Color 2** button. You see the Pick a Color window again.

**8**  Click another color in the color wheel, and click **OK**.

**9**  On the Background Properties window, click the **Try** button. The gradient color selection appears on the screen.

**10**  Next, try a wallpaper image. Click the **Browse** button under the Wallpaper section. You see the Wallpaper Selection window, which is similar to Figure 11-53.

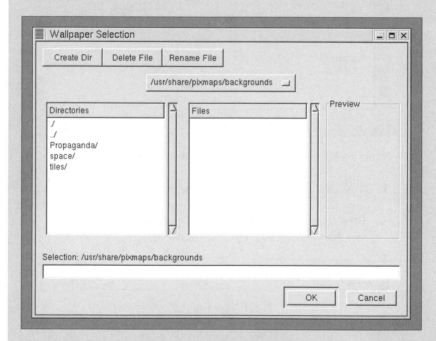

**Figure 11-53:** Wallpaper Selection window

Note:The directories you see listed may differ from the ones shown in the figure. The selections available to you depends on how Linux is installed on your system.

**11**  Double-click one of the directories listed in the Wallpaper Selection window. You see a list of filenames in the Files pane.

**12**  Click one of the listed filenames. A preview of the image appears in the preview pane. Each time you click a filename, you see a preview of the file.

**13**  Select an image you like, and click **OK**.

**14** On the Background Properties window, click the **Try** button to apply the wallpaper image to the background.

**15** Repeat the steps above until you find a color, gradient color, or wallpaper image you like. In the Background Properties window, click **OK**.

**Changing the Screen Saver** You can use the X Window screen saver to deter unauthorized use of a terminal or workstation by requiring a password. When the screen saver is active, it will not deactivate until the user enters his or her login password. You use the Control Center window to activate and configure the screen saver.

**To select and configure a screen saver:**

**1** Click the **Configuration Tools** icon. On the Control Center window, click the word **Screensaver**. You see the Screensaver Properties window shown in Figure 11-54.

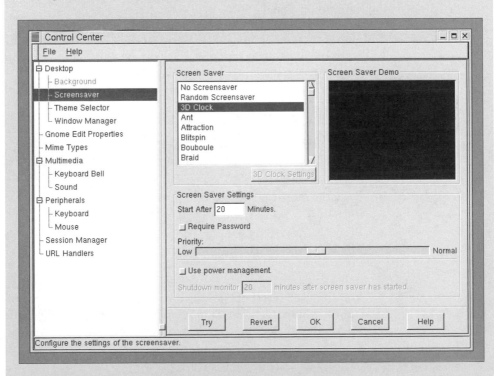

**Figure 11-54:** Screensaver Properties window

**2**  From the Screen Saver list, click a screen saver, such as 3D Clock. You see a preview of the screen saver in the Screen Saver Demo area.

**3**  In the Screen Saver Settings area, you can set the number of minutes that must elapse before the screen saver activates. Click in the **Start After** text box, and type **1**.

**4**  Click the **Require Password** button.

**5**  Click **OK** on the Screensaver Properties window.

**6**  Do not type or move the mouse for one minute. When the screen saver activates, deactivate it by pressing a key or moving the mouse. A window appears requesting your password. Type your password and press **Enter**.

**7**  Open the Screensaver Properties window, and adjust the screen saver time to **10** minutes.

**8**  Exit the Screensaver Properties window, and close the Control Center window.

## Configuring the Panel

You may configure almost every aspect of the GNOME panel. In this section you will learn to adjust the position of icons on the panel, add new applets to the panel, and add your own icon that launches a program.

### To adjust the position of icons on the panel:

**1**  Right-click an applet icon on the panel.

**2**  On the shortcut menu, click **Move applet**. The mouse pointer becomes a four-way arrow.

**3**  Drag the mouse pointer to the left or right. As you do, the icon moves along the panel.

**4**  When you decide where you would like to move the icon, click the mouse. The icon stays in its current place.

You can use several other applets in addition to those that appear on the panel by default. Management at Dominion Consulting has asked you to instruct the other staff how to add these applets to their panels:

■ The CPULoad applet displays an animated bar graph that indicates the usage of your machine's CPU.

■ The Disk Usage applet displays a pie chart indicating the system's used and free disk space.

**To add the CPULoad and Disk Usage applets to the panel:**

**1**  Position the mouse pointer over any part of the panel not occupied by an icon, and right-click.

**2**  On the shortcut menu, point to the **Add applet** item. A submenu appears.

**3**  Point to the **Monitors** item on the submenu. Another submenu appears.

**4**  Click **CPULoad**. A small square appears on the panel. This is where the CPULoad animated bar graph will appear as you use your system.

**5**  Right-click an unoccupied area of the panel again.

**6**  On the shortcut menu, point to **Add applet**.

**7**  On the submenu, point to **Monitors**.

**8**  Click **Disk Usage**.

A rectangular area appears on the panel. This is where the disk usage pie chart appears, showing the system's used and free space.

**9**  To determine which color indicates used space and which indicates free space, right-click the area containing the pie chart.

**10**  On the shortcut menu, click **Properties**.

The Diskusage Settings window appears, as shown in Figure 11-55.

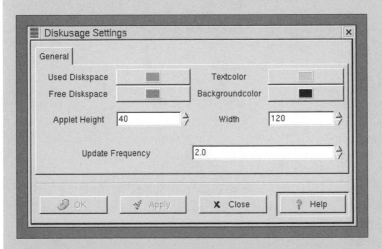

**Figure 11-55:** Diskusage Settings window

**11**  This window shows which colors indicate used and free disk space. Change the color settings by clicking the color buttons and selecting a new color from the color wheel. When you're finished, click the **Close** button.

In addition to the available applets, you may also add your own programs as applets to the panel. Management at Dominion Consulting has asked you to add the phoneadd script to the panel. (You developed the phoneadd script in Chapters 6 and 7.)

**To add the phoneadd script to the panel as an applet:**

**1**   Position the mouse pointer over an unoccupied area of the panel, and right-click. The shortcut menu appears.

**2**   You need to add a launcher applet to the panel. A launcher executes another program when you click its icon. Click **Add new launcher** on the shortcut menu. You see the Create launcher applet window, as shown in Figure 11-56.

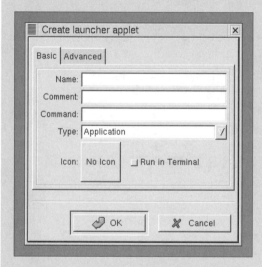

Figure 11-56: Create Launcher Applet window

**3**   In the Name text box, type **phoneadd Script**.

**4**   In the Comment text box, type **Adds a phone number to the corp_phones file**.

**5**   In the Command text box, type **./phoneadd**.

**6**   Leave the Type text box set to **Application**.

**7**   Click the **Run in Terminal** button.

**8**   Click the **Icon** button. The Choose an icon window appears, similar to Figure 11-57.

**Figure 11-57:** Choose an icon window

**9**  Scroll through the set of icons. When you see one you would like to use for the phoneadd script, click it. Then click **OK**.

**10**  On the Create launcher applet window, click **OK**. The icon you selected appears on the panel.

**11**  Position the mouse pointer over the phoneadd icon, but do not click it yet. After a moment, a Help box appears with the text you entered in the launcher applet Comment box.

**12**  Click the icon. The script file executes in a terminal window. The window looks similar to Figure 11-58.

**13**  Test the application by entering your own name and false information for department number, job title, and date hired.

**14**  Finally, type **q** to quit the program. The terminal window closes.

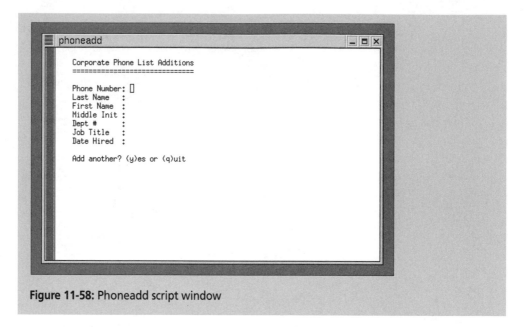

**Figure 11-58:** Phoneadd script window

In this section you learned to customize the panel by moving icons and adding applets and icons for your own programs. This makes your work easier, because the panel displays frequently needed information (such as the amount of free disk space) and automates the execution of programs you run often. Next you will learn to further customize the desktop environment by adding your own programs to the Main menu.

## Adding Programs to the Main Menu

Management at Dominion Consulting is pleased that you have learned to add applications to the panel. Now they ask you to instruct the staff to add applications to the Main menu as well. You decide to show them how to add the phoneadd script, so it will be accessible from both the panel and the Main menu.

**To add the phoneadd script to the Main menu:**

**1** Click the **Main menu** button. The Main menu appears. Notice that in the middle of the menu, a section appears labeled User menus. This is where you want to add an entry for the phoneadd application.

**2** Position the mouse pointer over the **Settings** entry. A submenu appears.

**3** On the submenu, click **Menu editor**. The GNOME menu editor window appears, as shown in Figure 11-59.

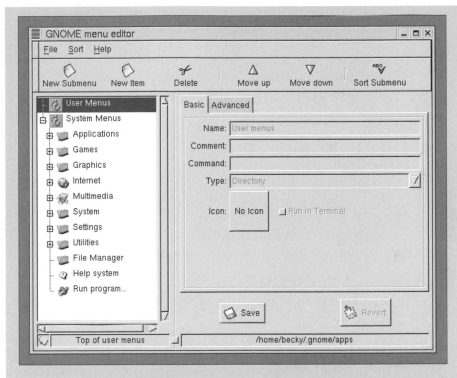

**Figure 11-59:** GNOME Menu Editor window

**4**   Be sure that User Menus is selected in the left area of the window, and then click the **New Item** button near the top of the window.

**5**   In the Name text box, type **Add a Phone Number.**

**6**   In the Comment text box, type **Adds a phone number to the corp_phones file.**

**7**   In the Command text box, type **./phoneadd.**

**8**   Leave the Type text box set to **Application.**

**9**   Click the **Run in Terminal** button.

**10**   Click the **Icon** button. The Choose an icon window appears (shown in Figure 11-57).

**11**   Select the same icon you selected when adding the phoneadd script to the panel. Click **OK** to return to the Menu Editor window.

**12**   Click the **Save** button.

**13**   Close the Menu Editor window.

**14**   Click the **Main menu** button. The Main menu appears.

**15**   Under the User menus entry, click **Add a Phone Number.**

**16**   The phoneadd script executes in a terminal window. Close the terminal window.

The staff and management at Dominion Consulting are delighted to know how to customize their X Window system environment and add programs to the panel and Main menu. Executing frequently used applications from menu entries or icons is usually faster than using long commands. It also eliminates typing errors, such as misspelling a command or program name. These benefits will certainly increase productivity and make the staff's daily work easier.

# SUMMARY

- The File Manager is a graphical application for managing your directories and files and for navigating the file system.

- In addition to the File Manager, the X Window system has several other built-in applications. Examples are a calendar program, a spreadsheet, and an editor.

- You can copy text from one window and paste it into another.

- You can customize the background of your display with a color or with a graphic image known as wallpaper.

- You may choose from a number of screen savers, which activate when there has been no keyboard or mouse activity after a specified period of time. The screen saver may be password protected, requiring the user to enter his or her password to deactivate it.

- You can customize the panel by adding and moving applet icons. You can even add icons that launch your own programs.

- You can customize the Main menu by adding entries that execute your own programs.

# COMMAND SUMMARY

| Chapter 11 commands | | |
| --- | --- | --- |
| Command | Purpose | Options covered in this chapter |
| shutdown | Shuts the system down | -r specifies that the system should shut down, then restart |
| startx | Starts the X Window System | |

# REVIEW QUESTIONS

1. The + sign next to directories in the File Manager's directory tree view indicates _____.
   a. more than one directory has this name
   b. the directory is empty
   c. the directory is full and no more files may be stored in it
   d. the directory contains subdirectories

2. The term "wallpaper" refers to _____.
   a. an image placed on the desktop
   b. a computer game
   c. the gradient color of the background
   d. the amount of video memory in the system

3. You can move an applet icon on the panel by _____.
   a. clicking the icon and using the arrow keys
   b. clicking the icon, pressing Ctrl+M, and then using the arrow keys
   c. right-clicking the icon and selecting Move applet from the menu
   d. selecting Move Icon from the File Manager's Edit menu

4. Use the Launcher applet to _____.
   a. start the X Window system
   b. start your own program from the panel
   c. play a space computer game
   d. display the Main menu

5. When you select a file and then hold down the _____ key while selecting another file, all the files whose names appear between the two selected files are also selected.
   a. Shift
   b. Ctrl
   c. Alt
   d. M

6. The _____ application lets you create a to-do list.
   a. gEdit
   b. Calendar
   c. Gnumeric Spreadsheet
   d. File Manager

7. True or false: The Gnumeric Spreadsheet Application performs mathematical functions, such as adding a column of numbers.

8. A gradient background color is _____.
   a. made of shades of gray
   b. one solid color
   c. a color that gradually fades, or blends, into another color
   d. transparent

9.  True or false: Your screen saver password is different from your login password.

10. To add your own program to the panel as an applet, right-click an unoccupied area of the panel and select _____ from the shortcut menu.
    a. Add new launcher
    b. Add new program
    c. Add new applet
    d. Add new program

# E X E R C I S E S

1.  Launch the File Manager and create these directories under your home directory:
    new_files
    old_files

2.  Open a Terminal window and create these empty files in your home directory:
    file1
    file2
    file3

3.  Use the File Manager to copy the files you created in Exercise 2 into the old_files directory.

4.  Use the File Manager to move the files that are in the old_files directory into the new_files directory.

5.  Use the File Manager to delete file1, file2, and file3 in your home directory.

6.  Change the File Manager's custom view so it shows this file information:
    Name
    Permission
    Creation Time
    Access Time

7.  Reconfigure the background so it has a gradient color.

8.  Make sure the Diskusage applet is added to the panel. Reconfigure the colors it uses to represent free and used disk space.

9.  Open the Calendar application and add these appointments:
    Meeting with insurance agent, today at 4:30 PM
    Meeting with VP of Sales tomorrow at 10:00 AM
    Meeting with Jim today at 11:00 AM
    Meeting with Sally tomorrow at 2:00 PM

10. After you enter the appointments listed in Exercise 9, look at them in the Day, Week, and Month views.

# D I S C O V E R Y   E X E R C I S E S

1. Use vi or Emacs to create the script file list. The file should contain the command: ls –l

2. Create an icon on the panel that launches the list script file you created in Discovery Exercise 1.

3. Run the list script file from the icon you created on the panel in Discovery Exercise 2. Does the directory listing scroll by too fast to see? Modify the script file so the user must press Enter after the list is displayed. This will pause the output, so you have time to see it.

4. Add an entry to the Main menu for the list script file.

5. In this chapter you added the CPULoad and Diskusage applets to the panel. You can also choose other applets. Experiment by adding several of them to the panel.

6. Open the Gnumeric Spreadsheet, create a spreadsheet named ss_practice, and enter the values:
575.9 in cell A1
901.2 in cell A2
1047.09 in cell A3
89.7 in cell A4
1124.5 in cell A5
In cell B1 enter the function that sums cells A1 through A5.

**If you cannot remember how to use the function for summing cells, refer to the spreadsheet exercise earlier in this chapter, or use the spreadsheet's online help system.**

7. After you enter the spreadsheet values listed in Discovery Exercise 6, experiment with the Accounting, Fraction, Money, and Scientific formats.

8. Scroll through all available screen savers in the Control Center's Screensaver Properties window, looking at a preview of each one. Select a new screensaver and test it.

# How to Access a UNIX/Linux Operating System

This appendix explains your options for accessing a computer running UNIX or Linux as its operating system. Typically, you access a UNIX/Linux system in one of these circumstances:

- You use a dumb terminal directly connected to a communications port on the UNIX/Linux system.
- You use your school's local area network to connect to a remote UNIX/Linux system.
- You use a dial-up connection to your Internet Service Provider (ISP) or school server, and then access a remote UNIX/Linux system.

If you use a dumb terminal to access a UNIX/Linux system, you only need to turn on the terminal and press a key on the keyboard. You then see a UNIX/Linux login prompt, where you can enter your user name and password and begin working immediately. If you use your school's local area network to access a remote system, you must first establish a Telnet session to the system. See "Using Telnet to Access a Remote System" for complete instructions. If you are using a dial-up connection to access a remote system through your ISP or school server, continue to the next section.

## Using a Dial-Up Connection to Access a Remote System

This section gives detailed instructions on setting up a dial-up connection. If you are already dialing into an ISP or your school server, you can skip the next sections, dial into your ISP or school server, and then proceed to "Using Telnet to Access a Remote System."

### Setting Up a Dial-Up Network Connection in Windows 95 and 98

This section lists the steps typically necessary for setting up a dial-up network connection in Windows 95 or Windows 98. After you configure the dial-up connection on your system, you may use your modem to dial into your Internet Service Provider (ISP) or your college account. If your ISP or college has provided you with different instructions, follow them instead of the steps listed here.

Note: These instructions assume that your modem is already installed in your computer.

**Information You Need** Before starting these steps, make sure you have the following information:

- The telephone number for the server to which you are connecting
- The user name your ISP or school assigned to you
- Your ISP or school account password
- The IP address of the server to which you are connecting
- The IP address of your DNS server
- The domain of the server to which you are connecting

If you do not know one or more of the items listed, contact your ISP or school technical support staff for assistance.

You may also need your Windows 95 or 98 CD.

## Configuring Your System for Dial-Up Networking

The following steps are necessary to set up your system for dial-up networking.

### To set up dial-up networking:

**1** Click the **Start** button, point to **Settings**, and then click **Control Panel.**

**2** In the Control Panel window, double-click the **Network** icon. You see a dialog box similar to Figure A-1. Make sure the Configuration tab is selected, as shown in the figure.

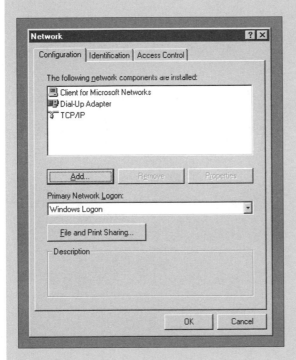

**Figure A-1:** Network dialog box

**3** The Network dialog box lists the network components installed on your system. Network components are software, hardware, protocols, and services necessary to establish a network connection. You should see each of these components: Client for Microsoft Networks, Dial-Up Adapter, and TCP/IP. If all these components are listed, skip to the "Configuring Your System's Network Connection." If any are missing, you must install them by continuing to the next steps.

**4** To install the client for Microsoft networks, click the **Add** button in the Network dialog box. You see the Select Network Component Type dialog box, shown in Figure A-2.

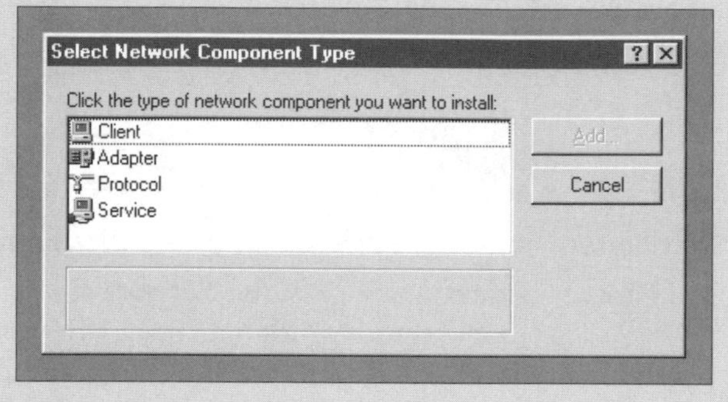

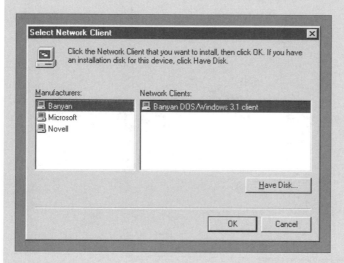

**Figure A-2:** Select Network Component Type dialog box

**5**  Double-click **Client**. You see the Select Network Client dialog box shown in Figure A-3.

**Figure A-3:** Select Network Client dialog box

**6**  In the Manufacturers List, click **Microsoft**.

**7**  In the Network Clients list, click **Client for Microsoft Networks**.

**8**  Click the **OK** button. You return to the Network dialog box and see the Client for Microsoft Networks component listed.

**9**  To install the Dial-Up Adapter, click the **Add** button in the Network dialog box. You see the Select Network Component Type dialog box, illustrated in Figure A-2.

**10**  Double-click **Adapter**. You see the Select Network Adapters dialog box, similar to Figure A-4.

**11**  In the Manufacturers List, click **Microsoft**.

**12**  In the Network Adapters list, click **Dial-Up Adapter**.

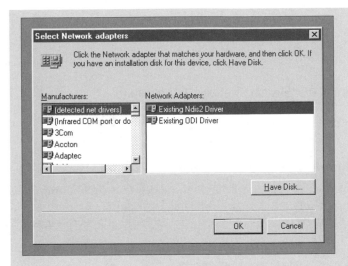

**Figure A-4:** Select Network Adapters dialog box

**13**   Click the **OK** button. You return to the Network dialog box and see the Dial-Up Adapter component listed.

**14**   To install TCP/IP, click the **Add** button in the Network dialog box. You see the Select Network Component Type dialog box illustrated in Figure A-2.

**15**   Double-click **Protocol**. You see the Select Network Protocol dialog box, similar to Figure A-5.

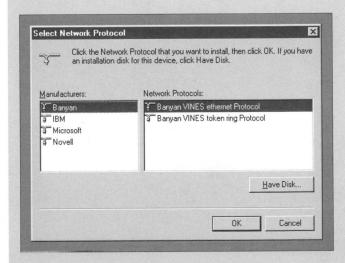

**Figure A-5:** Select Network Protocol dialog box

**16**   In the Manufacturers List, click **Microsoft**.

**17**   In the Network Protocols list, click **TCP/IP**. (You may have to scroll down the list to find it.)

**18** Click the **OK** button. You return to the Network dialog box and see the TCP/IP component listed.

## Configuring Your System's Network Connection

The following steps are necessary to configure your system's network connection.

### To configure your system's network connection:

**1** In the Network dialog box, double-click **Dial-Up Adapter** under the Network Components list. You see the Dial-Up Adapter Properties dialog box. Click the **Bindings** tab. The window should look similar to Figure A-6.

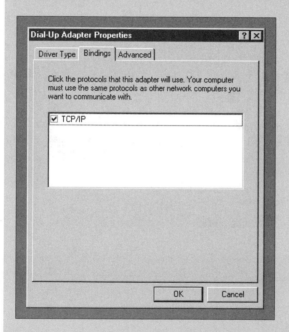

**Figure A-6:** Dial-up Adapter Properties dialog box, Bindings tab

**2** Click the **TCP/IP** box to check it, if necessary. If you see other protocols listed, make sure they have no check marks next to them. If they do, click them to remove the check marks.

**3** Click the **OK** button. You return to the Network dialog box.

**4** In the Network dialog box, double-click **TCP/IP** under the Network Components list. If you see the TCP/IP Properties dialog box, click the **OK** button. Click the **IP Address** tab. The window should look similar to Figure A-7.

**5** Confirm that the **Obtain an IP address automatically** option is selected. If not, click it to select it.

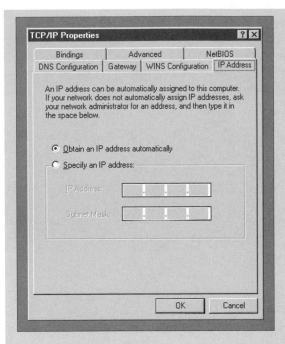

**Figure A-7:** TCP/IP Properties dialog box, IP Address tab

**6** Click the **Gateway** tab. The dialog box looks similar to Figure A-8.

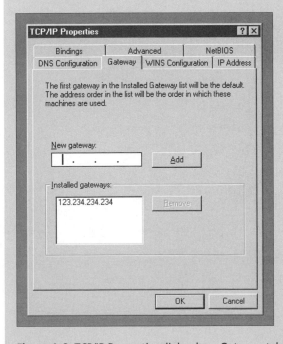

**Figure A-8:** TCP/IP Properties dialog box, Gateway tab

**7**  Click in the **New Gateway** text box, and type the IP address of the server you are connecting to. (Your ISP or school technical support staff must provide you with this address.) Click the **Add** button. The IP address you entered appears in the list of Installed Gateways.

**8**  Click the **WINS Configuration** tab. The dialog box looks similar to Figure A-9.

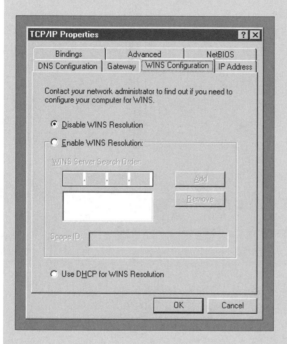

**Figure A-9:** TCP/IP Properties dialog box, WINS Configuration tab

**9**  Click the **Disable WINS Resolution** button to select it, if necessary.

**10** Click the **DNS Configuration** tab. The dialog box looks similar to Figure A-10.

**11** Click the **Enable DNS** option to select it.

**12** If the **host** text box is empty, click it and type any name you want to give your local machine. (Usually, the name is unimportant.) In the **Domain** text box, enter the domain name of the server you are connecting to. This name will be similar to *campus.edu* or *course.com*. Your ISP or school technical support staff must provide you with the name.

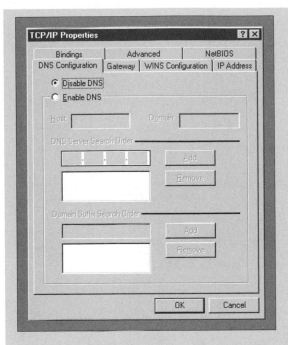

**Figure A-10:** TCP/IP Properties dialog box, DNS Configuration tab

**13** Click in the **DNS Server Search Order** box, and type the IP address of the DNS Server you will use. Your ISP or school technical support staff must provide you with this information. Click the **Add** button next to the address you just entered.

**14** Click in the **Domain Suffix Search Order** box, and enter the same domain name that you entered in the Step 12. Click the **Add** button next to the domain name.

**15** Click the **OK** button. You return to the Network dialog box.

**16** The **OK** button again. If you are asked for your Windows 95 or 98 CD, insert it in the CD-ROM drive and click the **OK** button.

**17** After Windows installs the network drivers, you are asked if you want to restart your computer. Click the **Yes** button. Your computer restarts.

## Installing Dial-Up Networking

The following steps are necessary to install dial-up networking.

## To install dial-up networking:

**1**   After your computer restarts, click the **Start** button, point to **Programs**, and then point to **Accessories**.

**2**   If you see a **Communications** menu, point to it. If you see **Dial-Up Networking** on the Accessories or Communications menu, skip to the steps beginning with, "To set up a new connection." Otherwise, you will need to install the connection from your Windows 95 or 98 CD. Continue to Step 3.

**3**   To install Dial-Up Networking, click the **Start** button, point to **Settings**, and then click **Control Panel**.

**4**   In the Control Panel window, double-click the **Add/Remove Programs** icon. When the Add/Remove Programs Properties dialog box appears, click the **Windows Setup** tab. A window appears similar to Figure A-11.

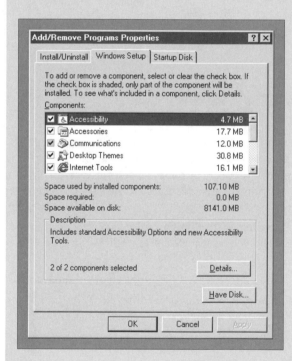

**Figure A-11:** Add/Remove Programs Properties dialog box, Windows Setup tab

**5**   In the Components list, click **Communications**. Then click the **Details** button. The Communications dialog box that appears is similar to Figure A-12.

**Figure A-12:** Communications dialog box

**6**   Click the **Dial-Up Networking** box to check it, if necessary.

**7**   Click the **OK** button. You see the Add/Remove Programs Properties dialog box. Click the **OK** button. If you are prompted for your Windows 95 or 98 CD, insert it into the CD-ROM drive and click the **OK** button. Windows will complete the installation of dial-up networking.

## Setting Up a New Connection

The following steps are necessary for setting up a new connection.

**To set up a new connection:**

**1**   Click the **Start** button, point to **Programs**, and then point to **Accessories**. Click Dial-Up Networking, if possible. If not, point to the **Communications** menu, and then click **Dial-Up Networking**.

**2**   Double-click the **Make New Connection** icon. The Make New Connection wizard opens, and you see a dialog box similar to Figure A-13.

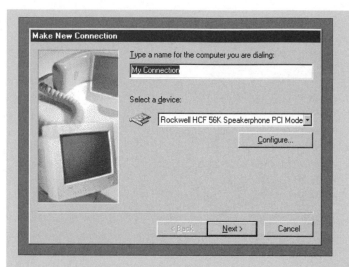

**Figure A-13:** Make New Connection wizard

**3** Click in the box labeled **Type a name for the computer you are dialing**, and then type a description such as **My ISP Connection** or **My University Account**.

**4** Be sure that your modem is selected in the **Select a Modem** text box. If not, click the **list** arrow, and then click the name of your modem.

**5** Click the **Next** button.

**6** In the **Area Code** and **Telephone Number** text boxes, type the area code and telephone number for the server you are connecting to. Be sure that the country you are in is selected in the **Country Code** text box. If not, click the list arrow and then select your country from the drop-down list. Click the **Next** button.

**7** In the next dialog box, click the **Finish** button. You return to the Dial-Up Networking dialog box and see an icon for the new connection you just created.

**8** Right-click the new icon and select **Properties** from the shortcut menu. The Connection Properties dialog box appears.

**9** Click the **Server Types** tab. The dialog box looks similar to the one in Figure A-14.

**10** Click the **Type of Dial-up Server** list arrow, and then click **PPP: Internet, Windows NT Server, Windows 98.** (If you are running Windows 95, click **PPP: Windows 95, Windows NT 3.5, Internet.**)

**11** In the **Allowed network protocols** section, click the **TCP/IP** box to check it, if necessary. No other choices in this section should be checked.

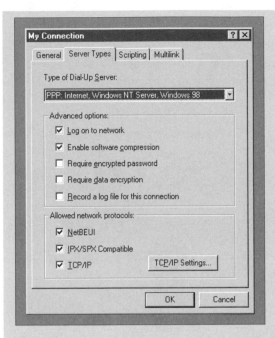

**Figure A-14:** Connection Properties dialog box, Server Types tab

**12** Click the **TCP/IP Settings** button. The TCP/IP Settings dialog box, shown in Figure A-15, appears.

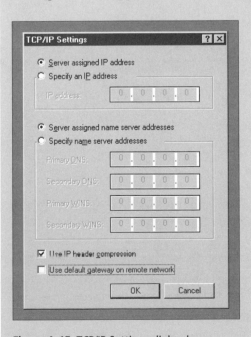

**Figure A-15:** TCP/IP Settings dialog box

**13**   Click the **Server assigned IP address** option button to select it, if necessary.

**14**   Click the **Specify name server addresses** option button to select it, if necessary.

**15**   In the **Primary DNS** text box, type the IP address of the DNS server you will use. Your ISP or school technical support staff must give you this information. The Secondary DNS, Primary WINS, and Secondary WINS text boxes should read 0.0.0.0.

**16**   Click to check the **Use IP header compression** and **Use default gateway on remote network** boxes, if necessary.

**17**   Click the **OK** button to close the TCP/IP Settings dialog box. When you return to the Connection Properties dialog box, click the **OK** button.

**18**   You are now ready to connect. Double-click the connection icon you created in Step 7. The Connect To dialog box, similar to Figure A-16, appears.

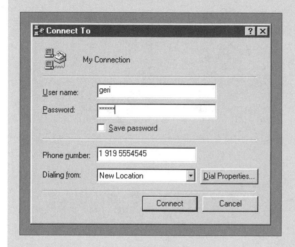

**Figure A-16:** Connect To dialog box

**19**   Enter your user name in the User name text box. In the Password text box, type your password, and then click the **Connect** button. The connection process begins, which may take a minute or more.

After you connect to the remote server, you can use your Telnet client to log on to a UNIX/Linux system. Continue to the next section, "Using Telnet to Access a Remote System," and follow the steps to establish a Telnet session.

## Using Telnet to Access a Remote System

After your computer is connected to your school's local area network or has a dial-up connection to a remote server, you can use the Telnet program to log on to a UNIX/Linux system.

## Information You Need

Before starting these steps, make sure you have the following information:

- The server and domain name of the UNIX/Linux system you want to log on to or the system's IP address
- Your user name and password on the UNIX/Linux system

### To establish a Telnet connection:

**1**  Click the **Start** button and then click **Run**.

**2**  In the Run dialog box, type **telnet** and click **OK**. The Telnet window appears, as shown in Figure A-17.

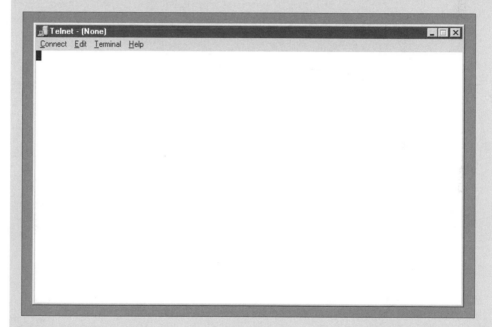

**Figure A-17:** Telnet window

**3**  Click **Connect** on the menu bar, and then click **Remote System**. The Connect dialog box appears, as shown in Figure A-18.

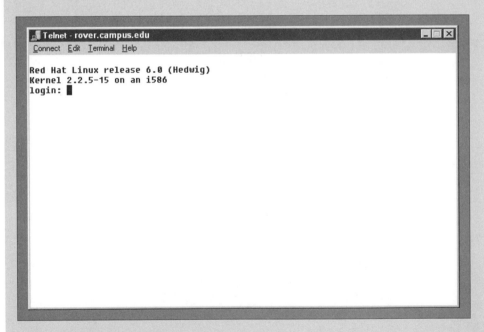

**Figure A-18:** Connect dialog box

**4**  In the Host Name text box, type the server and domain names. For example, *zeus.campus.edu* specifies the server *zeus* in the domain *campus.edu*. As an alternative, you can type the server's IP address in the host name box.

**5**  Click the **Connect** button. You see a login prompt, similar to Figure A-19.

```
Telnet - rover.campus.edu                              _ □ ×
Connect  Edit  Terminal  Help

Red Hat Linux release 6.0 (Hedwig)
Kernel 2.2.5-15 on an i586
login: █
```

**Figure A-19:** Remote login prompt

**6**  Type your user name and password to log on to the system.

**7**  When you finish your session, click **Connect** on the menu bar, then click **Exit**. The Telnet program ends your session and closes.

# Syntax Guide to UNIX Commands

This appendix provides a quick reference to the UNIX commands and utilities covered in this text. Table B-1 lists the commands alphabetically, including the command name, its purpose, and any useful options. Table B-2 lists the UNIX utilities by category. Table B-3 summarizes the vi editor commands, while Table B-4 summarizes the emacs editor commands. The UNIX command syntax uses the format diagrammed in Figure B-1.

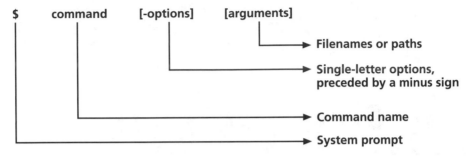

**Figure B-1:** Command syntax format

| Command | Purpose | Useful Options |
|---------|---------|----------------|
| alias | Create an alias for a command | |
| awk | Invoke a pattern-scanning and processing language | –f indicates code is coming from a disk file, not the keyboard. -F specifies the field separator. |
| cal | Show the system calendar for a specified year or month | -j displays the Julian date format. |
| cat | Concatenate or display files | -n displays line numbers. |
| cd | Change directories | |
| chmod | Change security mode of a file or directory (r: read, w: write, x: executable) Set file permissions for specified users (u: user, g: group, o: others, a: all) | |
| clear | Clear the screen | |
| comm | Compare sorted files and show differences | |
| cp | Copy files from one directory to another | -i requests confirmation if the target file already exists. -r copies directories to a new directory. |
| cut | Select and extract columns or fields from a file | -c specifies the character position. -d specifies the field separator. -f specifies the field position. |

| Command | Purpose | Useful Options |
|---------|---------|----------------|
| **date** | Display the system date | **-u** displays the time in Greenwich Mean Time. |
| **diff** | Compare and select differences in two files | |
| **. (dot)** | Run a process in the current directory | |
| **.. (dot dot)** | Run a process in the parent directory | |
| **echo** | Display the specified arguments on the output device | |
| **emacs** | Start the emacs editor | |
| **exit or logout** | Exit UNIX | |
| **export** | Export a specified list of variables to other shells Make a variable an environment variable | |
| **find** | Locate files that match a specified criteria | **-name** *filename* finds files with the *filename.* **-print** prints the pathname for each file found. **-type** *file type* finds files with the specified access type. |
| **grep** | Select lines or rows that match a specified pattern | **-c** displays the count of matching lines. **-i** ignores case. **-l** lists only filenames. **-n** displays line numbers. **-v** displays lines that do not match the specified pattern. |
| **head** | Display the first few lines of a file. | **-n** *n* displays the first *n* lines of the specified file. |
| **history** | List all commands you enter during a UNIX session | |

**Table B-1**
(continued)

| Command | Purpose | Useful Options |
|---------|---------|----------------|
| **join** | Join two files, matching row by row | **-a** *n* produces a line for each unpairable line in file *n*, where *n* = 1 or 2.<br>**-e** *str* replaces the empty fields for the unpairable line with the string specified by *str*.<br>**-j** specifies the common fields on which the join is to be made.<br>**-o** specifies a list of fields to be output. The list contains blank-separated field specifiers in the form *m.n*, where *m* is the file number and *n* is the position of the field in the file. Thus –o 1.2 means output the second field in the first file.<br>**-t** specifies the field separator character. By default this is a blank, tab, or new-line character. Multiple blanks and tabs count as one field separator. |
| **kill** | End a process | |
| **less** | Display a long file one screen at a time, and scroll up and down | |
| **let** | Store arithmetic values in a variable | |
| **ln** | Create a link between files, thereby allowing more than one name for a file | |
| **lp** | Print a file | **-d** prints on a specified printer.<br>**-n** prints a specified number of copies of the file. |

**Table B-1**
(continued)

| Command | Purpose | Useful Options |
|---------|---------|----------------|
| ls | List a directory's contents, including its files and subdirectories | **-a** lists the hidden files.<br>**-l** lists files in long format, showing detailed information.<br>**-r** lists files in reverse alphabetic order.<br>**-s** shows the size of each file. |
| man | Display the online manual for the specified command | |
| mkdir | Make a new directory | |
| more | Display a long file one screen at a time | |
| mount | Connect the file system partitions to the directory tree when the system starts | **-r** indicates that the mounted device is read-only.<br>**-t** specifies the type of file system. |
| mv | Move or rename files | |
| passwd | Change your UNIX password | |
| paste | Paste multiple files, column by column | |
| pr | Format a specified file before printing or viewing | **-a** displays output in columns across the page, one line per column.<br>**-d** double-spaces the output.<br>**-h** customizes the header line.<br>**-l***n* sets the number of lines per page. |
| printenv | Print a list of environment variables | |
| printf | Tell the Awk program what action to take | |
| pwd | Display your current path | |

**Table B-1**
(continued)

| Command | Purpose | Useful Options |
|---------|---------|----------------|
| **rm** | Remove a file | **-i** requests confirmation before deleting a file.<br>**-r** deletes a specified directory and its contents. |
| **rmdir** | Remove a directory | **-i** requests confirmation before deleting a file.<br>**-r** deletes a specified directory and its contents. |
| **sed** | Specify an editing command or a script file containing sed commands | **-a** \ appends text after a line.<br>**-d** deletes specified text.<br>**-e** specifies multiple commands on one line.<br>**-n** indicates line numbers.<br>**-p** displays lines.<br>**-s** substitutes specified text. |
| **set –o noclobber** | | Prevents files from being overwritten by the > operator |
| **sh** | Execute a shell script | **-n** reads commands without executing them. |
| **sort** | Sort and merge multiple files | **.+** designates the position that follows an offset (+) as a character position, not a field position.<br>**+n** sorts on the field specified by *n*.<br>**-b** ignores leading blank characters.<br>**-d** sorts in dictionary order.<br>**-f** indicates that a specified character separates the fields.<br>**-m** merges files before sorting.<br>**-n** sorts numbers arithmetically.<br>**-o** directs the sorted output to a specified file. |

**Table B-1**
(continued)

| Command | Purpose | Useful Options |
|---------|---------|----------------|
| **tail** | Display the last few lines of a file | **-n** *n* displays the last *n* lines of the specified file. |
| **test** | Compare values and validate file existence | **!** logical negation<br>**-a** logical AND<br>**-b** tests if a file exists and is a lock special file (which is a block-oriented device, such as a disk or tape drive).<br>**-c** tests if a file exists and is a character special file (that is, a character-oriented device, such as a terminal or printer).<br>**-d** true if a file exists and is a directory.<br>**-e** true if a file exists.<br>**-eq** equals to.<br>**-f** tests if a file exists and is a regular file.<br>**-ge** greater than or equal to<br>**-gt** greater than<br>**-le** less than or equal to<br>**-lt** less than<br>**-n** tests for a non-zero string length.<br>**-ne** not equal to<br>**-o** logical OR<br>**-r** true if a file exists and is readable.<br>**-s** true if a file exists and its size is greater than zero.<br>**string** tests for a non-zero string length.<br>**string1 = string2** tests two strings for equality.<br>**string1 != string2** tests two strings for inequality.<br>**-w** true if a file exists and is writeable<br>**-x** true if a file exists and is executable<br>**-z** tests for a zero-length string. |

**Table B-1**
(continued)

| Command | Purpose | Useful Options |
|---------|---------|----------------|
| **top** | Display a list of the most CPU-intensive tasks, such as the processor state, in real time | **-c** displays the command line that initiated each process. **-I** ignores any idle processes. **-q** displays output continually, with no delay between outputs. **-s** causes the top command to run in secure mode, disabling its interactive commands. **-S** runs top in cumulative mode, which displays the cumulative CPU time used by a process. |
| **touch** | Change a file's time and date stamp | **-a** updates access time only. **-c** prevents touch from creating a file that it does not exist. **-m** updates the modification time only. |
| **tput** | Format screen text | **clear** clears the screen. **cols** prints the number of columns on the current terminal. **cup** moves the screen cursor to a specified row and column. **rmso** disables boldface output. **smso** enables boldface output. |
| **tr** | Translate characters | **-d** deletes input characters found in *string1* from the output. **-s** checks for sequences of *string1* repeated consecutive times. |
| **trap** | Executes a command when a specified signal is received from the operating system | |
| **umount** | Disconnect the file system partitions from the directory tree | |
| **uniq** | Select unique lines or rows | **-d** outputs one copy of each line that has a duplicate. **-u** outputs only the lines of the source file that are not duplicated. |
| **wc** | Count the number of lines, bytes, or words in a file | **-c** counts the number of bytes or characters. |

**Table B-1**
(continued)

| Command | Purpose | Useful Options |
|---------|---------|----------------|
| | | -l counts the number of lines. |
| | | -w counts the number of words. |
| whatis | Display a brief description of a command | |
| who | See who is logged on to UNIX | -H displays column headings. |
| | | -i displays session idle times. |
| | | -q displays a quick list of users. |

**Table B-1:** Common UNIX commands

| Command | Purpose |
|---------|---------|
| **File Processing Utility** | |
| afio | Create an archive or restore files from archive |
| awk | Process files |
| cat | Display or join files |
| cmp | Compare two files |
| comm | Compare sorted files and show differences |
| cp | Copy files |
| cpio | Copy and back up files to an archive |
| cut | Select characters or fields from input lines |
| dd | Copy and convert input records |
| diff | Compare two text files and show differences |
| fdformat | Format a floppy disk at a low level |
| find | Find files within file tree |
| fmt | Format text very simply |
| grep | Match patterns in a file |
| groff | Process embedded text-formatting codes |
| gzip | Compress or decompress files |
| head | Display the first part of a file |
| ispell | Check one or more files for spelling errors |
| less | Display text files (pause when screen is full) |
| ln | Create a link to a file |
| lpr | Print file (hard copy) |

| Command | Purpose |
| --- | --- |
| ls | List file and directory names and attributes |
| man | Display documentation for commands |
| mkdir | Create a new directory |
| mkfs | Build a UNIX file system |
| mv | Rename and move files and directories |
| od | Dump formatted file |
| paste | Horizontally concatenate files |
| pr | Display and format files |
| rdev | Query or set the root image device |
| rm | Remove files |
| rmdir | Remove directory |
| sed | Edit streams (non-interactive) |
| sort | Sort or merge files |
| tail | Display the last lines of files |
| tar | Copy and back up files to a tape archive |
| touch | Change file modification dates |
| uniq | Display unique lines of sorted file |
| wc | Count lines, words, and bytes |
| **System Status Utility** | |
| chgrp | Change the group associated with a file |
| chmod | Change the access permissions of a file |
| chown | Change the owner of a file |
| date | Set and display date and time |
| df | Display the amount of free space remaining on disk |
| du | Summarize file space usage |
| file | Determine file type (e.g., shell script, executable, ASCII text, and others) |
| finger | Display detailed information about users who are logged on |

**Table B-2**
(continued)

| Command | Purpose |
|---------|---------|
| **free** | Display amount of free and used memory in the system |
| **kill** | Terminate a running process |
| **ps** | Display process status by process identification number and name |
| **sleep** | Suspend execution for a specified time |
| **top** | Dynamically display process status, like ps, but in real time |
| **w** | Display detailed information about users who are logged on |
| **who** | Display brief information about users who are logged on |
| **Network Utility** | |
| **ftp** | Transfer files over a network |
| **rcp** | Remotely copy a file from network computer |
| **rlogin** | Log on to a remote computer |
| **rsh** | Execute commands on a remote computer |
| **rwho** | Display the names of users attached to a network |
| **telnet** | Connect to remote computer on a network |
| **Communication Utility** | |
| **mail** | Send electronic mail messages |
| **mesg** | Deny (mesg n) or accept (mesg y) messages |
| **pine** | Send and receive electronic mail and news |
| **talk** | Let users simultaneously type messages to each other |
| **write** | Send a message to another user |
| **Programming Utility** | |
| **configure** | Automatically configure program source code |
| **gcc** | Compile C and C++ programs |
| **make** | Maintain program source code |

**Table B-2**
(continued)

| Command | Purpose |
| --- | --- |
| patch | Update source code |
| **Source Code Utility** | |
| ci | Create changes in Revision Control Systems (RCS) |
| co | Retrieve an unencoded revision of an RCS file |
| cvs | Manage concurrent access to files in a hierarchy |
| rcs | Create or change attributes of an RCS file |
| rlog | Print a summary of the history of an RCS file |
| **Miscellaneous Utility** | |
| at | Execute a shell script at a specified time |
| cal | Display a calendar for a month or year |
| crontab | Schedule a command to run at a preset time |
| expr | Evaluate expressions (used for arithmetic and string manipulations) |
| fsck | Check and fix problems on a file system (repairs damages) |
| tee | Clone output stream to one or more files |
| tr | Replace specified characters, like a translation filter |
| tty | Display terminal pathname, like the built-in command, pwd |
| xargs | Convert standard output of one command into arguments for another |

**Table B-2:** UNIX utilities by category

| Command | Purpose |
| --- | --- |
| ! | Leave vi temporarily |
| . (repeat) | Repeat your most recent change |
| / | Search forward for a pattern of characters |
| d$ or D | Delete from the cursor to the end of the line |
| d0 | Delete from the cursor to the start of the line |

| Command | Purpose |
|---------|---------|
| **dd** | Delete the current line |
| **dw** | Delete the word above the cursor. If the cursor is in the middle of the word, delete from the cursor to the end of the line. |
| **I** | Switch to insert mode |
| **P** | Paste text from the clipboard |
| **q** | Cancel an editing session |
| **r** | Read text from one file, and add it to another |
| **set** | Turn on line numbering |
| **U** | Undo your most recent change |
| **Vi** | Start the vi editor |
| **w** | Save a file and continue working |
| **wq** | Write changes to disk and exit vi |
| **x** | Save changes and exit vi |
| **x** | Delete the character above the cursor |
| **Y** | Copy (yank) text to the clipboard |
| **ZZ** | In command mode, save changes and exit vi |

**Table B-3:** Summary of vi commands

| Alt Commands | Purpose |
|--------------|---------|
| **Alt+<** | Move cursor to start of file |
| **Alt+>** | Move cursor to end of file |
| **Alt+B** | Move cursor back one word |
| **Alt+D** | Delete current word |
| **Alt+F** | Move cursor forward one character |
| **Alt+Q** | Reformat current paragraph using word wrap so that lines are full |
| **Alt+T** | Transpose word under the cursor with the following word |
| **Alt+U** | Capitalize all letters of the current word |
| **Alt+W** | Scroll up one screen |

| Alt Commands | Purpose |
|---|---|
| **Alt+X doctor** | Enter doctormode to play a game in which emacs responds to your statements with questions. Save your work first. Not all versions support this mode. |

### Ctrl Commands

| | |
|---|---|
| **Ctrl+@** | Put a mark at the cursor location. After moving the cursor, you can move or copy text to the mark. |
| **Ctrl+A** | Move cursor to start of line |
| **Ctrl+B** | Move cursor back one character |
| **Ctrl+D** | Delete the character under cursor |
| **Ctrl+E** | Move cursor to end of line |
| **Ctrl+F** | Move cursor forward one character |
| **Ctrl+G** | Cancel the current command |
| **Ctrl+H** | Use online help |
| **Ctrl+K** | Delete text to the end of the line |
| **Ctrl+N** | Move cursor to next line |
| **Ctrl+P** | Move cursor to preceding line |
| **Ctrl+T** | Transpose the character before the cursor with the one under the cursor |
| **Ctrl+V** | Scroll down one screen |
| **Ctrl+W** | Delete marked text. See Ctrl+@ (kept in buffer). Press Ctrl+Y to restore deleted text. |
| Ctrl+Y | Insert text from the buffer, and place it after the cursor |

### Ctrl Combinations

| | |
|---|---|
| **Ctrl+H+C** | Display the command that runs when you press a particular key |
| **Ctrl+H+T** | Run an emacs tutorial |
| **Ctrl+X, Ctrl+C** | Exit emacs |
| **Ctrl+X, Ctrl+S** | Save the file |
| **Ctrl+X, U** | Undo the last change |
| **Ctrl+Del** | Delete the character under the cursor |

**Table B-4:** Summary of emacs commands

# How to Install Red Hat Linux 6.0

This appendix guides you through a **workstation-class** installation of Red Hat Linux 6.0 onto a computer that is currently running Windows 95 or Windows 98. This is the simplest installation type and the best for first-time users. If you are replacing an operating system other than Windows 95 or Windows 98, or wish to perform a server-class installation, visit the following Red Hat Web sites:

www.redhat.com

www.redhat.com/corp/support/manuals

Successfully completing the steps in this appendix completely removes the existing Windows 95 or Windows 98 operating system from your computer and installs Red Hat Linux.

**Caution: This installation type erases *everything* on your hard drive. If you have data you wish to keep, perform a backup before starting the installation. You cannot recover data from the disk after you perform the installation!**

There are four major steps in this installation method:

- Gather information about your computer hardware and network
- Create a Red Hat Linux boot disk
- Prepare your hard disk by removing all existing partitions
- Install Red Hat Linux

You must follow the steps in the order they are listed.

## Gather Information About Your Computer Hardware and Network

The minimum hardware requirements for Red Hat Linux 6.0 are:

- An Intel x86 processor
- 16 MB of RAM
- 500 MB hard drive
- 3.5-inch floppy disk
- CD drive

Before you begin the Red Hat installation, you must gather information about your computer hardware, and the network it connects to, if any. Here are some specific things you will need to know:

- The type and size of your hard drive
- The amount of memory in your system
- The type of CD drive in your system (specifically if it has an IDE, SCSI, or other interface)
- The brand and model of your video card
- The amount of video memory on your video card
- The brand and model of your monitor, as well as the monitor's vertical and horizontal sync ranges (You can find this information in the monitor's manual)
- The type of mouse you are using (PS/2 or serial, two buttons or three)
- If your computer has a SCSI adapter, its brand and model
- The printer type you will use, if any. You also need to know how the printer connects to the computer. If you will print through a network, you need all the correct network connection information for the printer.

If your computer is on a network, you need to know:

- The type of network card your computer has. You also need to determine configuration information the card's driver may require.

■ Your computer's IP address configuration information. You need to determine if your computer has a static IP address or if it uses BOOTP or DHCP. You also need to know the IP address of your default gateway and primary name server. (If you have a secondary and tertiary name server, you need their IP addresses as well.) Your network administrator can provide all this information.

After you collect this information, you should compare it with Red Hat's hardware compatibility list. You can find the list on the Red Hat Web site at www.redhat.com/hardware. The hardware compatibility list shows all the devices that Red Hat Linux supports. If any piece of your hardware does not appear on the list, Red Hat Linux may not run on your system.

After you determine that Red Hat Linux supports your hardware, continue to the next installation phase.

## Preparing the Linux Boot Disk

The installation process starts from the Linux boot disk. You use a program named *rawrite.exe* on the Red Hat CD to make the boot disk.

To make the Red Hat Linux boot disk:

**1** Insert the Red Hat CD in the CD drive.

**2** Insert a blank floppy disk in drive A.

**3** Click the **Start** button, then point to **Programs**.

**4** Click **MS-DOS Prompt** on the Programs menu. An MS-DOS window appears.

**5** Change the default drive to the CD drive. If the CD drive is drive D, type **D:** and press **Enter**. (Likewise, if the CD drive is drive E, type **E:** and press **Enter**.)

**6** Type **cd \dosutils** and press **Enter**.

**7** Type **rawrite** and press **Enter**. You see the message:

Enter disk image source file name:

**8** Type **..\images\boot.img** and press **Enter**. You see the message:

Enter target diskette drive:

**9** Type **A:** and press **Enter**. You see the message:

Please insert a formatted diskette in drive A: and
press —ENTER— :

**10** Because the disk is already in the drive, press **Enter**.

**11** There will be a short delay while the program creates the boot disk. When the program ends, you see a DOS prompt. You now have a Red Hat boot disk.

**12** Type **exit** and press **Enter** to close the MS-DOS Prompt window.

## Preparing the Hard Disk

Before you can install Linux on your hard drive, you must make room for its partitions. This procedure deletes the existing partitions on your hard drive, so the Linux installation program can create its own partitions.

> Caution: As stated before, this type of installation erases *everything* on your hard drive. If you have data you wish to keep, perform a backup now. Removing your existing partitions permanently erases everything currently stored on your hard drive. You cannot recover data from the disk after you complete these steps!

For these steps you need a blank floppy disk. (Do not use the Red Hat boot disk you created earlier.) To remove your existing partitions:

**1**   Insert a blank floppy disk in drive A.

**2**   Click the **Start** button, then point to **Programs**.

**3**   Click **MS-DOS Prompt** on the Programs menu. An MS-DOS window appears.

**4**   After the **C:\Windows>** prompt, type **format a:/s** and press **Enter**. You are asked to insert a new disk for drive A and press Enter. Since the disk is already inserted, press **Enter**. Execution of this command takes several minutes. Once the disk is formatted, you are asked for a volume label. Press **Enter**. Next you are asked if you wish to format another disk. Press **n** and then press **Enter**.

**5**   When the format command finishes, type cd **command** and press **Enter**. Your prompt changes to C:\Windows\Command>.

**6**   After the prompt, type **copy fdisk.exe a:** and press **Enter**.

**7**   With the disk still in drive A:, restart your computer.

**8**   After the A:\> prompt, type **fdisk** and press **Enter**. If a message asks if you want to enable large disk support, type **N** for no and then press **Enter**. You see the DOS Fdisk menu.

**9**   Option 4 on the menu reads, "Display partition information." Type **4** and press **Enter** to select this option.

**10**   On the next screen you see a list of partitions. Under the "Type" column you see the type of each partition. You may see any of these types: primary-DOS, non-DOS, extended partitions, and logical drives. Under the "Volume Label" column you see the volume labels of each labeled partition. Note each type of partition listed and its volume label. You will need this information later.

**11**   Press **Esc** to return to the main Fdisk menu.

**12**   Option 3 on the menu reads "Delete partition or logical DOS drive." Type **3** and press **Enter** to select this option.

**13** You now see a menu of options to delete partitions. Each option lets you delete a different type of partition. Because you are installing Linux as the sole operating system, you delete all partitions you saw listed while completing Step 10. For example, to delete the primary DOS partition, you must select option 1 from the menu, so type **1** and press **Enter**. You see a screen that displays partition information and a message warning that you will lose data in the deleted primary DOS partition. You are asked, "What primary partition do you want to delete?" Type the partition number and press **Enter**. (The partition number is in the "Partition" column.) Next, you are asked to enter the partition's volume label. If the partition does not have a volume label, type it and press **Enter**. If the partition has a volume label, simply press **Enter**. Last, you see a message that asks, "Are you sure (Y/N)." Type **Y** and press **Enter**. This deletes the partition (along with data previously stored there), and you see the main Fdisk menu. You must repeat this step for each partition on the disk.

**14** Now you have removed all previously installed partitions and erased the the hard drive's contents. Press **Esc** to exit the Fdisk program. You are ready to begin the Red Hat installation described in the next section.

## Installing Red Hat Linux 6.0

The Red Hat installation program runs in "text mode" but displays screens that look like dialog boxes with buttons, scrolling lists, and other items common to graphical user interfaces. Although the program does not support a mouse, you can easily select items and activate buttons with keystrokes. Here is a summary of the keystrokes used during the installation process:

- Tab key: Highlights the next item on the screen
- Alt+Tab: Highlights the previous item on the screen
- Up-arrow and down-arrow: Scrolls through a list of selections, or move to the next item on the screen
- Spacebar: Selects the currently highlighted item, or deselects it if it is already selected
- Enter: Presses the highlighted button

You typically find these types of buttons on an installation screen:

- OK: Accepts the values entered on the screen and moves to the next screen
- Cancel: Cancels the current operation or the installation process
- Yes: Answers "yes" to the question that appears on the screen
- No: Answers "no" to the question that appears on the screen
- Back: Moves back to the previous screen

You are now ready for the final phase of the Red Hat Linux 6.0 installation:

**1** Remove the disk in drive A: and insert the Red Hat boot disk. Restart your system.

**2** When the system starts, you see a "Welcome to Red Hat Linux!" screen, which lists several installation options. The first option is, "To install or upgrade a system running Red Hat Linux 2.0 or later, press the <ENTER> key." Because you are installing Red Hat Linux, press **Enter** to select this option. The installation program takes several minutes to load. As it loads, various messages appear on the screen.

**3** When the installation program loads, another screen welcomes you to Red Hat Linux. Press **Enter** to continue.

**4** The next screen instructs you to choose a language. (The default selection is English.) The remainder of the installation process will use the language you choose. Use the up-arrow and down-arrow keys to scroll through the list of languages. When you find the language you want to use, press **Enter**.

**5** The next screen instructs you to choose a keyboard type. (The default selection is us, for United States.) The remainder of the installation process will use the keyboard type you choose. Linux will also use this keyboard type each time it boots. Use the up-arrow and down-arrow keys to scroll through the list of keyboard types. When you find the keyboard type you wish to use, press **Enter**.

**6** Next you must choose the installation method: LocalCDROM or Hard Drive. Use the up-arrow or down-arrow key to highlight LocalCDROM, and press **Enter**.

**7** The next screen prompts you to insert your Red Hat CD. Insert the Red Hat CD in the CD drive, and press **Enter**.

Note: If your system has a SCSI CD-ROM drive, a dialog box will open asking what type of CD-ROM you have. Once you make your selection, the program will determine the brand and model of CD-ROM you are using.

**8** After the CD is initialized, you see a screen that asks, "Would you like to install a new system or upgrade a system which already contains Red Hat Linux 2.0 or later?" Notice the two buttons labeled "Install" and "Upgrade." The Install button is highlighted, which means it is selected. Notice that when you press the Tab key, the next button is highlighted. You will use this method to choose screen elements in other sections of the installation. Make sure the **Install** button is highlighted, and press **Enter**.

**9** The next screen asks you to specify an installation class: Workstation, Server, or Custom. Use the up-arrow key to highlight **Workstation**, and press **Enter**.

**10** You now see a warning screen with the message, "All of the Linux partitions on your hard drive(s) will be erased." The Cancel button is selected by default. Press the **Tab** key to select the Ok button, and press **Enter**.

**11**  Again, you see a warning screen. The message, "Are you sure you want to do this?" appears. The No button is selected by default. Press the **Tab** key to select the **Yes** button, and press **Enter**.

**12**  For the next several minutes, various status screens appear while the installation program prepares your hard drive and installs the necessary software from the CD.

**13**  After the software is copied from the CD to your hard drive, the installation program probes your system for a mouse. If it finds a serial mouse, you see a screen with a message similar to, "Probing found some type of serial mouse on port ttys0." If it finds a bus mouse, you see a message similar to, "Probing found some type of PS/2 mouse on port psaux." If no mouse is connected to your system, skip to Step 15. Otherwise, note what type of mouse the installation program found (serial or PS/2), and press **Enter**.

**14**  If a mouse is connected to your system, the next screen lets you select the type of mouse you have. Use the up-arrow and down-arrow keys to scroll through the list of specific mice. If you see an entry for the precise type of mouse you have, highlight it and press **Enter**. If your mouse is not listed, select one of the Generic choices that best fits your mouse:

**Generic Mouse (serial)** for a two-button serial mouse
**Generic 3 Button Mouse (serial)** for a three-button serial mouse
**Generic Mouse (PS/2)** for a two-button PS/2 mouse
**Generic 3 Button Mouse (PS/2)** for a three-button PS/2 mouse

After you highlight the appropriate mouse type, press **Enter**.

**15**  The next screen asks, "Do you want to configure LAN (not dialup) networking for your installed system?" If you are connected to a local-area network and want to use your Linux system on the network, make sure the **Yes** button is selected and press **Enter**. Otherwise, skip to Step 21.

**16**  You are now asked to specify a driver for your network card. Use the up-arrow and down-arrow keys to scroll through the list of network cards. Highlight your card and press **Enter**. (If the installation program is able to automatically detect your network card, you will not need to specify the type of card. Simply press Enter and then proceed to Step 17.)

**17**  Depending on your network card, you may not see the screens described in this step. If not, proceed to Step 18. In many cases, your network driver requires its own configuration information in order to locate and communicate with the network card. For example, the driver may require that you specify the card's IRQ number and DMA address. The next screen tells you that your card driver may need this extra information, and lets you choose either Autoprobe or Specify Options. The Autoprobe option attempts to automatically configure the driver, and Specify Options lets you manually enter the values. If you know the values that your particular driver needs, select **Specify Options** and press **Enter**. You see a screen that asks for the values. (Exactly what this screen asks for depends on the network card you have.) If you do not know the values your driver needs, choose Autoprobe. If the system appears to lock up, you need to restart your computer and begin the installation process again. If this occurs, you must consult your network card's documentation to determine the configuration values it needs. When you return to this point in the installation, choose **Specify Options** and enter the values.

**18** After the network card is selected and configured, a screen asks for the Boot Protocol. You may choose from Static IP address, BOOTP, or DHCP. Use the up-arrow and down-arrow keys to highlight the correct option, and then press **Enter**. If you chose Static IP address, continue to the next step. Otherwise, go to Step 21.

**19** The next screen asks you to enter your computer's IP address, netmask, the default gateway's IP address, and the primary name server's IP address. Your network administrator can provide you with all this information. Enter the correct values, highlight the **Ok** button, and press **Enter**.

**20** The next screen asks for your network's domain name, your host name, and the IP addresses of your secondary and tertiary name servers. For domain name, enter the domain name assigned to your network. This is a name in the form of *campus.edu* or *course.com*. For host name, enter the host name you would like to assign to your machine. If you have a secondary or tertiary name server, enter their IP addresses in the last two fields. If you have no secondary or tertiary name server, leave these fields blank. Highlight the **Ok** button and press **Enter**.

**21** The next screen asks for your time zone. At the top of the screen is an option to set your hardware clock to GMT (Greenwich Mean Time). This option sets your computer's internal clock to GMT, which allows it to adjust the time for daylight savings. If you wish to choose this option, highlight it and press the space bar. An asterisk (*) appears next to it.

**22** Use the up-arrow and down-arrow keys to scroll through the list of time zones. Select your time zone, highlight the **Ok** button, and press **Enter**.

**23** The next screen asks if you want to configure a printer. If so, highlight the **Yes** button, press **Enter**, and continue to the next step. If you do not want to use a printer with your system, highlight the **No** button, press **Enter**, and skip to Step 33.

**24** You are now asked to select a printer connection. Your choices are Local, Remote lpd, SMB/Windows 95/NT, or Netware. Use the up-arrow and down-arrow keys to highlight the correct option, and press **Enter**.

**25** If you chose Local, continue to the next step. If you chose Remote lpd, skip to Step 27. If you chose SMB/Windows 95/NT, skip to Step 28. If you chose Netware, skip to Step 29. The next screen asks you to enter a name for the printer's queue and the name of the spool directory. The installation program provides default values. These are normally good values, so highlight the **Ok** button and press **Enter**.

**26** Perform this step if you are configuring a local printer. Next you are asked to identify the device your printer is attached to. A list of auto-detected ports is also shown. In the list of auto-detected ports, /dev/lp0 is the first printer port, /dev/lp1 is the second printer port, and /dev/lp2 is the third printer port. The installation program provides a default value for the port you wish to connect the printer to. If the value is correct, press the **space bar**, then press **Enter**. If it is not correct, enter the name of the correct port, press the **space bar**, and press **Enter**. Skip to Step 30.

**27** Perform this step if you are configuring a remote lpd printer connection. You see a screen that asks for the host name of the printer server and the name of the queue on the server in which print jobs will be placed. Enter the correct information, highlight the **Ok** button, and press **Enter**. Skip to Step 30.

**28** Perform this step if you are configuring an SMB/Windows 95/NT printer. You see a screen that asks for the following information: SMB server host, SMB server IP address, share name, your network user name and password, and workgroup name. Enter the correct values, highlight the **Ok** button, and press **Enter**. Skip to Step 30.

**29** Perform this step if you are configuring a Netware network printer. You see a screen that asks for the following information: printer server name, print queue name, your user name and password. Enter the correct values, highlight the **Ok** button, and press **Enter**. Continue to the next step.

**30** The next screen asks you to select the printer type you are using. Use the up-arrow and down-arrow keys to scroll through the list of printers. Highlight your printer (or one that is a close match), and press **Enter**.

**31** Next you see a screen that asks for paper size and screen resolution. Select the correct values for your printer. Another option reads, "Fix stair-stepping of text?" Stair-stepping is a common problem that occurs when DOS and Windows text files are printed on Linux machines. The printer performs a linefeed operation after each line is printed, but does not perform a carriage return. This causes the lines to appear in a stair-step fashion. Highlight this option and press the **spacebar** to select it. An asterisk appears next to the option. Highlight the **Ok** button and press **Enter**.

**32** The next screen shows all printer parameters you specified and asks you to verify your printer configuration. If everything appears correct, highlight the **Ok** button and press **Enter**. If you wish to change a parameter, highlight the **Back** button and press **Enter**. Continue to select the Back button on each screen until you reach the screen containing the information you want to change.

**33** The installation program now asks you to enter the root password. This will become the password for the superuser, or root account. As a security measure, the characters do not appear on the screen as you type them. You must type the password twice to confirm it. After you enter the password the second time, highlight the **Ok** button and press **Enter**. If the passwords you typed do not match, the program requires you to repeat this step.

**34** After setting the root password, you are asked if you want to create a boot disk. A boot disk can be used in emergencies, when the system will not boot from the hard drive for some reason. It is recommended that you create a boot disk, so highlight the **Yes** button and press **Enter**. (This is not the same boot disk you created at the beginning of the installation process. The boot disk you create now does not invoke the Red Hat installation, but simply boots the system and brings it to a login prompt.)

**35** The next screen instructs you to insert a blank floppy in the first drive. Remove the installation boot disk and insert a blank floppy in the drive. Press **Enter**. There will be a delay as the program creates the boot floppy. (If you see a "PCI Probe" screen, highlight Ok and press Enter.)

**36** The installation program now attempts to determine what type of video card you use. If it successfully detects your video card, you see the Monitor Setup screen described in Step 37. If it cannot automatically determine your system's card type, you see a screen that asks you to choose your video card. Use the up-arrow and down-arrow keys to scroll through the list of cards. When you find your video card, highlight it and press **Enter**. If your video card is not listed, you may choose Unlisted Card, which appears at the bottom of the list. You then see a screen that asks for specific technical information, such as the name of the card's chipset. You need your video card's documentation to complete this part of the setup.

**37** After you complete the video card configuration, you are asked to choose the monitor you are using. Use the up-arrow and down-arrow keys to scroll through the list of monitors. When you find your monitor, highlight it and press **Enter**. If your monitor is not listed, you may choose **Custom**. If you choose Custom, you will be asked to enter the monitor's horizontal and vertical sync ranges. You need your monitor's manual to determine these values.

Caution: Do not specify a sync range greater than that the monitor can perform. Doing so can damage the monitor!

**38** After you configure your monitor settings you must establish your screen configuration. You see a screen asking if you want the program to automatically establish the default screen resolution and color depth for your monitor. If you want the installation program to probe the system, highlight the **Yes** button and press **Enter** and then press **Enter** again. Probing the system can cause the computer to lock. If this happens, you must restart the system and begin the installation process again. (If this is the case, select **No** the next time.) If the probe succeeds, you see the screen described in Step 42. If you choose not to probe the system, or if the probe is unsuccessful and does not lock the system, you see the screen described in the next step.

**39** The next screen asks, "How much video memory do you have?" Highlight the correct amount and press **Enter**.

**40** Next, you are asked, "Which clockchip do you have?" **No clockchip setting** is the recommended choice, because Linux is usually able to determine this automatically. Highlight **No clockchip setting** and press **Enter**.

**41** If you see a screen entitled "Select Video Modes," highlight a video mode your card supports and press the **spacebar** to select it. Highlight the **Ok** button and press **Enter**. Depending on your system, you may not see the screen described in this step. If not, proceed to Step 42.

**42** The next screen lets you probe for a clock and contains two buttons: Probe and Skip. Highlight the **Probe** button and press **Enter**. If the system locks, you must restart the computer and begin the installation process again. (If this happens, select **Skip** the next time.)

**43** Next you see a screen indicating that X will start to test your configuration. X refers to the X Window system, a UNIX graphical user interface. Highlight **OK** and press **Enter**.

**44** At this point the display switches to graphics mode, and after a short delay you see a dialog box with the message, "Can you see this message?" Click the **OK** button if you see the screen. If you do not see the screen, the system eventually times out and takes you back through the video setup process.

**45** The next screen displays the message, "Xconfigurator can set up your computer to automatically start X upon booting. Would you like to start X when you reboot?" If you want your system to start the X Windows system automatically each time it boots, highlight **Yes** and press **Enter**. If not, highlight **No** and press **Enter**.

**46** The last screen indicates you are done. Remove the disk from the floppy drive and the CD from the CD drive. Press **Enter** to reboot the system.

**47** After the system restarts, you see a screen with a boot: prompt. Press the **Enter** key. Linux continues the boot process.

**48** When the boot process is complete, you can log in as root, using the password you set up during the installation process.

## Installing the Apache Web Server

To develop and test web pages with CGI scripts (as discussed in Chapter 9), you must install the Apache Web Server program. After successfully installing Red Hat Linux, follow these steps to install Apache.

To install the Apache Web Server:

**1** Make sure you are logged on as root.

**2** Insert the Red Hat Linux CD into the CD drive.

**3** Mount the CD drive by typing **mount /dev/cdrom** and pressing **Enter**.

**4** Type **cdmnt/cdrom/RedHat/RPMS** and press **Enter**.

**5** Type **ls apache\*.rpm** and press **Enter**. The output of the command should be the names of two files, in the form of apache-X.X.X-X.i386.rpm and apache-devel-X.X.X-X.i386.rpm (where the Xs represent numbers). The filenames will be similar to the following:

apache-1.3.6-7.i386.rpm   apache-devel-1.3.6-7.i386.rpm

Note that the actual numbers that are listed after apache- and apache-devel- on your computer may be different than those shown above.

**6** Type **rpm –i apache-X.X.X-X.i386.rpm** (where the Xs are the numbers you saw in the filename as a result of the command in Step 5) and press **Enter**. For example, if you saw apache-1.3.6-7.i386.rpm when you typed the command in Step 5, you will type **rpm –i apache-1.3.6-7.i386.rpm** and press **Enter**.

**7** When the installation is finished and you are returned to a command prompt, reboot the system by typing **shutdown –r now** and pressing **Enter**. When the system reboots, the Apache Web Server program will be running.

# Glossary

## Special Characters

**.bashrc file** A file in your home directory that you can use to customize your work environment and specify what occurs each time you **log on**. It contains a .bashrc program that executes each time you create a shell.

**/home partition** The home directory that provides storage space for all users' directories. A separate section of the hard disk, it protects and insulates users' personal files from the UNIX operating system software.

**/usr partition** A large section of the hard disk that stores all non-**kernel** operating system programs that make the computer useful: software development packages, networking, Internet access, graphical screen (including X-Windows), and a large number of UNIX **utilities**.

## A

**absolute path** A **pathname** that begins at the **root directory** and lists all **subdirectories** to the destination file.

**address** An exact location in a file or in memory.

**algorithm** A sequence of instruction or commands that produce a desirable result. You develop an algorithm by following the logic flow expressed in flowcharts and pseudocode.

**alias** A name that represents a command. Aliases are helpful in simplifying and automating frequently used commands.

**applet** A small software application, usually written in JAVA or some other programming language for the Web. The **GNOME** pager is an applet designed to run on the GNOME panel.

**argument** Provides UNIX and other operating systems with additional information for executing a command. On the **command line**, an argument name follows an **option** name, and a space separates the two. Examples of arguments are file and directory names.

**arithmetic operator** A character that represents a mathematical activity. Arithmetic operators include + (addition), - (subtraction), * (multiplication), / (division), > (greater than), < (less than), and a number of other characters.

**array** A variable that stores an ordered list of **scalar** values that are accessed with numeric subscripts, starting as zero.

**ASCII** An acronym for American Standard Code for Information Interchange, a standard set of bit patterns organized and interpreted as alphabetic characters, decimal numbers, punctuation marks, and special characters. The code is used to translate **binary numbers** into ordinary language and therefore makes information stored in files accessible.

**assembler**  Called by the **compiler** to convert the lines of code in a **source file** into **object code**.

**assembly language**  A low-level language that provides maximum access to all the computer's devices, both internal and external. Writing an assembly language program requires a great deal of coding and time. UNIX was originally written in assembly language.

**automatic variable**  A **variable** declared inside a function and local to the function in which it is declared.

**Awk**  A pattern-scanning and processing language that helps to produce professional-looking reports.

# B

**B**  A forerunner of **C**, this programming language was developed in 1970 for the first UNIX system to run on the DEC PDP-7 mini-computer. Its developer is Ken Thompson, a Bell Labs employee.

**backquote (') operator**  Encloses UNIX commands whose output becomes the contents of a variable. For example, TODAY='date' creates the variable TODAY, executes the date command, and stores the command's output in the TODAY variable.

**Bash shell**  LINUX's default command interpreter. Incorporating the best features of the **Bourne shell** and the **Korn shell**, its name is an acronym for "Bourne Again Shell."

**binaries**  The programs residing in the /bin directory that are needed to start the system and perform other essential tasks. Also called executables.

**binary digit**  A number composed of two numbers, 0 and 1. UNIX stores all data in the form of binary digits. Because the computer consists of electronic circuits in either an "on" or "off" state, binary digits are perfect for representing these states. Binary digits are also called bits.

**binary file**  A file containing non-ASCII characters (such as machine instructions).

**bit**  A short term for **binary digit**.

**bitmap**  Rows and columns of dots or bit patterns that graphics software transforms into an infinite variety of images. *See also* **GUI**.

**block special file**  A file related to devices, such as disks.

**body**  One of two parts of **HTML** code. (The other part is the **head**.) The body defines what appears within the browser window.

**bootstrap loader**  A utility residing in the /boot directory that starts the operating system.

**Bourne shell**  The first UNIX command interpreter, developed at AT&T Bell Laboratories by Steve Bourne.

**byte**  An acronym for binary term, a string of eight binary numbers. These numbers can be configured into patterns of **bits**, which in turn can be interpreted as alphabetic characters, decimal numbers, punctuation marks, and special characters. This is the basis for **ASCII** code.

# C

**C**  A programming language developed in part to overcome the disadvantages of **assembly language** programming, which requires a great deal of coding and time. The result is a high-level set of easy-to-understand instructions. UNIX was originally written in assembly language but further developed and refined in C, largely due to the efforts of Ritchie and Brian Kernighan of Bell Labs.

**C++** A programming language developed by Bjarne Stroustrup of AT&T Bell Labs, who added **object**-oriented capabilities and other features to the **C** language.

**C library** A collection of **functions** that perform file, screen, and keyboard operations, and many other tasks. To perform or include one of these functions in your program, you insert a **function call** at the appropriate location in your file.

**C shell** A UNIX command interpreter designed for C programmers.

**case logic** One of the four basic shell logic structures necessary for program development. Using case logic, a program can perform one of many actions, depending on the value of a variable and matching results to a test.

**case-sensitive** A property that distinguishes uppercase letters from lowercase letters (John differs from john). UNIX is case sensitive.

**CC** The **C compiler's name** in UNIX and Linux.

**CGI programming** An acronym for **Common Gateway Interface programming**.

**character special file** A file related to serial input/output devices, such as printers.

**child** A subdirectory created and stored within a **(parent) directory**.

**clients** Computers in a network running programs that depend on the network's **server** or host computer.

**code** A synonym for "binary term" or "**byte**," most often used in the context of **ASCII** codes.

**command** Text typed after the **command-line** prompt that requests that the computer take a specific action.

**command line** The on-screen location for typing commands.

**command mode** A feature of a modal editor that lets you enter commands to perform editing tasks, such as moving through the file and deleting text. The UNIX vi editor is a modal editor.

**Common Gateway Interface programming** A **protocol** or set of rules governing how browsers and servers communicate. Any script that sends information to or receives information from a server must follow these rules.

**compiler** A program that reads the lines of code in a **source file**, converts them to **machine-language** instructions or calls the assembler to convert them into **object code**, and creates a machine-language file.

**concatenate** To link. For example, by typing the cat command and then typing several filenames separated by single spaces, you can display the contents of all the files.

**configuration variable** A **variable** that stores information about the operating system and does not change value.

**console** The monitor connected directly to a computer.

**constant** A value in program code that does not change when the program runs.

**control string** Specifies how formatting should occur when using the screen output library function printf.

**core file** A type of **garbage file** created when an executing program attempts to do something illegal, such as accessing another user's memory.

# D

**decision logic** One of the four basic shell logic structures necessary for program development. Decision logic states that commands execute only if a certain condition exists. In this type of logic the if statement sets the condition(s) for execution.

**decrement operator (--)** A **C arithmetic operator** that decreases the value of a variable by a specified amount.

**default prompt** The prompt the system generated when the **system administrator** created a login account.

**dependent file** A **source code** file listed within **Makefile**.

**diamond operator (<>)** Accesses data from an open file. Each time the diamond operator is used, it returns the next line from the file.

**directory** A special type of **file** that can contain other files and directories. Directory files store the names of regular files and other directories, called **subdirectories**.

**domain name** A set of characters separated by periods and used to identify and access remote systems. An example is (Lunar.campus.edu).

**dot** A character that signifies the current **directory**. Two dot characters (with no space between them) signify the **root directory**. A dot used as the first character of the filename indicates the file is **hidden**.

# E

**editor** A program for creating and modifying computer documents, such as program and data files.

**electronic interfaces** The means for connecting **peripherals** to computers.

**environment variable** A **variable** that UNIX reads when you **log on**, which stores information about the characteristics of your work session. For example, the PS1 environment variable determines how your prompt appears. Other environment variables tell UNIX where to look for programs, which **shell** to use, and the path to your home directory. You can change the value of an environment variable as needed.

**equal sign (=) operator** Sets a value in a variable.

**executable file** A useable program, the result of the program development cycle.

**executable program file** A file containing pure binary or machine language that the computer can immediately use or execute.

**executables** The programs residing in the /bin directory needed to start the system and perform other essential tasks. Also called binaries.

# F

**false value** A value returned from a program function indicating that the function was not carried out successfully. A 0 represents a false value.

**file** The basic component for data storage.

**file decryption** An operation that restores a file to the state it was in before **file encryption**.

**file encryption** An operation that scrambles a file's contents into secret code and is a useful security measure.

**File Manager**  A graphical application for managing directories and files and for navigating the file system.

**file system**  A system's way of organizing

**files** on mass storage devices, such as hard and floppy disks. Its organization is hierarchical and resembles an inverted tree: in the branching structure, top-level files (or folders or directories) contain other files, which in turn contain other files.

**File Transfer Protocol (FTP)**  An Internet protocol for sending files.

**filehandle**  An input/output connection between a Perl program and the operating system. It can be used inside a program to open, read, write, and close the file.

**flat ASCII file**  A file that you can create, manipulate, and use to store data such as letters, product reports, or vendor records. Its organization as an unstructured sequence of bytes is typical of a **text file** and lends flexibility in data entry because it can store any kind of data in any order. Any operating system can read this file type. However, because you can retrieve data only in the order you entered it, this file type's usefulness is limited. Also called an **ordinary file** or **regular file**.

**flowchart**  A logic diagram that uses a set of standard symbols to explain a program's sequence and each action it takes.

**FORM tag**  In **HTML** specifies how you wish to receive information users entered as responses to your document. You can choose one of two methods: **GET** or **POST**.

**FTP**  An acronym for **File Transfer Protocol**.

**function**  A separate body of code designed to contribute to the execution of a single task. You can put together a number of functions to create a program. In some languages, functions are called subroutines or procedures.

**function call**  A feature that you insert in the appropriate location of a program file to specify and use one of the functions in the **C library**.

**function overloading**  A feature of the **C++** programming language that lets functions respond to more than one set of criteria and conditions.

# G

**g++**  The **C compiler's name** in UNIX and Linux.

**garbage file**  A temporary file, such as a **core file,** that loses its usefulness after several days.

**GET**  A method for receiving information users entered as responses to your **HTML** document. It transfers data within the URL itself.

**glob**  Similar to a **wildcard**, a glob character is used to find or match filenames. Glob characters are part of **glob patterns**.

**glob pattern**  A combination of **glob** characters used to find or match multiple filenames.

**GNOME**  An acronym for the **GNU Network Object Model Environment**.

**GNU Network Object Model Environment (GNOME)**  Produced by the **GNU project**, GNOME is a desktop environment that must be used with a Windows Manager.

**GNU project**  An organization created to develop a free, UNIX-like, operating system named GNU.

**Graphical User Interface**  Software that transforms **bitmaps** into an infinite variety of images.

**group id**  Gives a group of users equal access to files that they all share.

**GUI**  An acronym for Graphical User Interface.

# H

**hash**  A variable representing a set of key value pairs. A percent sign (%) precedes a hash variable.

**head**  One of two parts of **HTML** code. (The other part is **body**.) The head contains the title, which appears on the top bar of your browser window.

**header file**  A file containing the information the compiler needs to process standard input or output statements.

**hidden file**  A file that the operating system uses to keep configuration information and for other purposes. The name of a hidden file begins with a dot.

**high-level language**  A computer language that uses English-like expressions. COBOL, C, and C++ are high-level languages.

**host**  *See* **server**.

**HTML**  An acronym for **Hyper Text Markup Language**.

**Hyper Text Markup Language**  A format for creating documents and Web pages with embedded codes known as **tags**.

**hyperlink**  Text or an object in a Web document. When you click a hyperlink, another document loads and appears in the browser.

# I

**IDE**  Integrated drive electronics, the most popular electronic hard disk interface for **personal computers**.

**increment operator (++)**  A **C arithmetic operator** that increases the value of a variable by a specified amount.

**inline sort block**  A compact Perl notation that replaces an if-else statement and eliminates the need for a separate subroutine.

**input validation**  A process a program performs to ensure that the user has entered acceptable information.

**insert mode**  A feature of a modal editor that lets you enter text. The UNIX vi editor is a modal editor.

**Internet Protocol (IP) address**  A set of four numbers separated by periods (123.456.678.90) used to identify and access remote systems.

**interpreter**  A UNIX feature that reads statements in a program file, immediately translates them into executable instructions, and then runs the instructions. Unlike a **compiler**, an interpreter does not produce an executable file because it translates the instructions and runs them a single step.

**IP**  An acronym for **Internet Protocol**.

# K

**kernel**  The basic operating system, which interacts directly with the hardware and services user programs.

**kernel mode**  A means of accessing the **kernel**. Its use is limited to the **system administrator** to prevent unauthorized data from damaging the hardware that supports the entire UNIX structure.

**key words** Components of all programming languages, these words have special meaning and must not be used as variable or function names. *See* Table 10-1 for a list of C key words.

**Korn shell** A UNIX command interpreter that offers more features than the original **Bourne shell**. David Korn developed it at AT&T Bell Laboratories.

# L

**layering** A method of organizing software so that it surrounds the computer system's inner core, protecting its vital hardware and software and insulating the core and its users.

**line editor** An editor that lets you work with only one line or a group of lines at once. Although you cannot see the context of your file, you may find a line editor useful for tasks like searching, replacing, and copying blocks of text.

**line-oriented command** A command that can perform more than one action, such as searching and replacing, in more than one place in a file. When using a line-oriented command, you must specify the exact location where the action is to occur. These commands differ from screen-oriented commands, which execute relative to the location of the cursor.

**link** A means of joining multiple files that share a common field.

**linker** In program development, used after the **compiler** to link all object files that belong to the program and any library programs the program may use.

**localhost** A feature that helps you experiment with and test **HTML** documents, or Web pages, using a UNIX or Linux system. To use localhost, you need not be connected to the Internet. Located on your PC, localhost also assesses your PC's internal network configuration to ensure it's properly installed.

**log on** A process that protects privacy and safeguards a **multi-user system** by requiring each user to type a user name and password before using the system.

**log out** A process that tells a system that a user has finished using it. Commands for logging out vary from system to system; exit, CTRL+D, and logout are examples.

**logical structure** The organization of information in files, records, and fields, each of which represents a logical entity such as a payroll file, an employee's pay record, or an employee social security number.

**ooping logic** One of the four basic shell logic structures necessary for program development. In looping logic a control structure (or loop) repeats until some condition exists or some action occurs.

# M

**machine language** The exclusive use of 0s (which mean "off") and 1s (which mean "on") to communicate with the computer. Years ago, programmers had to write programs in machine language, a tedious and time-consuming process.

**macro** A set of commands that automates a complex task. A macro is sometimes called a super instruction.

**mainframe system** A large computer system with multiple processors that conducts input, output, processing, and storage operations for many users. Most widely used in large corporations and industrial computing.

**make utility** A UNIX utility that controls changes and additions to programs during program development. It tracks what needs to be recompiled using the time stamp file stored in all source files.

**Makefile**  A control file you create and the **make utility** uses. The file includes a list of all your source files and their relationship to each other, expressed as **targets** and **dependencies**.

**manipulation and transformation commands**  A group of commands that alter and format extracted information so that it's useful and appealing.

**methods**  Part of the new data class, objects, introduced in the **C++** programming language. Methods are a set of operations that manipulate data.

**modal editor**  An editor that lets you work in two modes: **insert mode** and **command mode**. The UNIX vi editor is a modal editor.

**mount**  To connect a file system to the directory tree structure, making it accessible.

**Multipurpose Internet Mail Extensions (MIME)**  A communications **utility** that supports sending and receiving **binary files** in mail messages.

**multitasking system**  A system that lets a user work with more than one program at a time. UNIX is a multitasking system.

**multi-user system**  A system in which many people can simultaneously access and share a **server** computer's resources. To protect privacy and safeguard the system, each user must type a user name and password in order to use, or **log on** to, the system. UNIX is a multi-user system.

# N

**network**  A group of computers wired together to let many users share computer resources and files. Combines the convenience and familiarity of the personal computer with the processing power of a mainframe.

**network operating system**  Controls the operations of a **server** or host computer, which accepts and responds to requests from user programs running on other computers on the network called **clients**.

**null character**  A single byte whose bits are all set to zero.

# O

**object code**  Binary instructions translated from program source code by a compiler.

**objects**  A new data class introduced in the **C++** programming language. Objects are a collection of data and a set of operations called **methods** that manipulate data.

**operand**  The variable name that appears to the left of an operator or the variable value that appears to the right of an operator. For example, in NAME=Becky, NAME is the variable name, = is the operator, and Becky is the variable value. Note that no spaces separate the operator and operands.

**option**  Directs UNIX and other operating systems to execute a command in a specific way. On the **command line**, an option name follows a command name, and a space separates the two. In UNIX option names begin with a hyphen and are **case sensitive**.

**ordinary files**  Files that you can create and manipulate. Includes **ASCII** files and **binary files**. Also called **regular files** or **flat ASCII files**.

**ordinary users**  All persons who use the system, except the **system administrator** or superuser.

# P

**parent** The **directory** in which a **subdirectory (child)** is created and stored.

**partition** A separate section of a disk, created so activity and problems occurring in other partitions do not affect it.

**PATH variable** Identifies a path and provides a list of directory locations where UNIX looks for executable programs.

**pathname** A means of specifying a file or directory that includes the names of **directories** and **subdirectories** on the branches of the tree-structure. A forward slash (/) separates each directory name. For example, the pathname of the file phones (the destination file) in the source directory of Jean's directory within the /home directory is /home/jean/source/phones.

**PC** An acronym for **personal computer**.

**peer-to-peer network** A networking configuration in which each computer system on the network is both a **client** and a **server**. Data and programs reside on individual systems, so users do not depend on a central server. The advantage of a peer-to-peer network is that if one computer fails, the others continue to operate.

**peripherals** Equipment connected to a computer via **electronic interfaces**. Examples include hard and floppy disk drives, printers, and keyboards.

**Perl** An acronym for Practical Extraction and Report Language, a UNIX programming language similar to C that uses features from the Awk and shell programs. Created by Larry Wall in 1986 as a simple report generator, Perl has evolved to become a powerful and popular tool for creating interactive Web pages.

**personal computer** A single, standalone machine, like a desktop or laptop computer, that performs all input, output, processing, and storage operations.

**portability** A characteristic of an operating system that allows the system to be used in a number of different environments. UNIX is a portable operating system.

**POST** A method for receiving information users entered as responses to your **HTML** document. It uses the body of the HTTP request to transfer data.

**preprocessor** Used after initial application development and before the compiler to make necessary modifications to the program and to include the contents of other files.

**preprocessor directive** A statement that you place in your program to instruct the **preprocessor** to modify your source code in some way. A preprocessor directive always begins with the # symbol. An example is #include, which tells the preprocessor to include another file in your program.

**process** To receive data from the standard input device (your keyboard) and then send output to the standard output device (your monitor).

**program development cycle** The process of developing a program, which includes (1) creating program specification, (2) the design process, (3) writing code, (4) testing, (5) debugging, and (6) correcting errors.

**protocol** A set of rules governing communication and the transfer of data between computers.

**prototype** A running model, which lets programmers review a program before committing to its design.

**pseudocode** Instructions similar to actual programming statements. Used to create a model that may later become the basis for an actual program.

# R

**record layout** The first task in the process of designing a new program, in which each field is named and identified by data type (for example, numeric or non-numeric).

**redirection symbol** The greater than sign (>). Typing > after a command that produces output creates a new file or overwrites an existing file and then sends output to a disk file, rather than the monitor.

**regular files** Files that you can create and manipulate. Includes **ASCII** files and **binary files**. Also called **ordinary files** or **flat ASCII files**.

**relational database** Contains files that UNIX treats as tables, records that UNIX treats as rows, and fields that UNIX treats as columns that can be joined to create new records. Using the join command, you can extract information from two files in a relational database that share a common field.

**relative path** A **pathname** that begins at the current working **directory** and lists all **subdirectories** to the destination file.

**RGB color code** A set of three numbers that specify a colors red, green, and blue components.

**root** The basis of the tree-like structure of the **file system** and the name of the file (root directory) located at this level. (The slash character (/) denotes this file.) Also, the **system administrator's** unique user name, a reference to the system adminis-trator's ownership of the root account and unlimited system privileges.

**root device** The hard disk partition that houses the UNIX root file system.

**root directory** The most basic file in the tree-like structure of the **file system**. (The slash character (/) denotes this file.)

# S

**scalar** A simple variable that holds a number or a string. Scalar variables' names begin with a dollar sign ($).

**scope** The part of the program where a **variable** is defined and accessible. The scope can be either inside or outside of a **function**.

**screen editor** An editor supplied by the operating system that displays text one screen at a time and lets you move around the screen to add and change text. UNIX has two screen editors: vi and Emacs.

**screen-oriented command** A command that executes relative to the position of the cursor. Screen-oriented commands are easy to type, and you can readily see their result on the screen. These commands differ from line-oriented commands, which execute independently of the location of the cursor.

**SCSI** Small computer system interfaces, pronounced *scuzzy*, a popular electronic hard disk interface commonly used on local-network **servers**.

**sed** A powerful UNIX editor used to make global changes to large files.

**sequential logic** One of four basic shell logic structures necessary for program development. Sequential logic states that commands execute in the order they appear in the program. An exception occurs when a branch instruction changes the flow of execution.

**server**   The computer that houses the **network operating system** and, as a result, can accept and respond to requests from user programs running on other computers in the **network** called **clients**. Also called the host.

**server-based network**   A centralized approach to networking, in which all **client** computers' data and programs reside on the **server**.

**shared library images**   Files residing in the /lib directory that programmers use to share code, rather than copying this code into their programs. Doing so makes their programs smaller and faster.

**shell**   A required interface between the user and the UNIX operating system. It interprets commands entered from the keyboard.

**shell function**   A group of commands stored in memory and assigned a name. Shell functions simplify the program code. For example, you can include a function's name within a shell script so the function's commands execute as part of the script. You can also use shell functions to store reusable code sections, so that you do not need to duplicate them.

**shell script file**   A file type based on the UNIX command-line history feature that recalls and reexecutes the commands you enter. The file contains command-line entries that you and others can repeatedly access and run sequentially as a set. Similar to an MS-DOS batch file.

**shell variable**   A variable you create at the command line or in a shell script. Valuable for use in **shell scripts** for storing information temporarily.

**source file**   A file containing source code, created with an editor like vi or Emacs and used for storing a program's high-level language statements. To execute, a source file must be converted to a low-level machine language file consisting of **object code**.

**spaceship operator** <=>   A special Perl operator for numeric sorts that reduces coding requirements.

**standard error**   A type of output that results when UNIX detects errors in processing system tasks and user programs and sends the error to the screen by default.

**standard error (stderr)**   A type of output that results when UNIX detects errors in processing systems tasks and user programs and sends the error to the screen by default.

**standard input**   Data received from the standard input device (the keyboard).

**standard output**   Data sent to the standard output device (the monitor).

**status line**   File status information that appears at the bottom of the screen. The vi editor's status line provides information on patterns you are searching for, line-oriented commands, and error messages.

**stderr**   An acronym for **standard error**.

**stdin**   An acronym for **standard input**.

**stdout**   An acronym for **standard output**.

**string**   A non-numeric field of information treated simply as a group of characters. Numbers in a string are considered characters rather than digits.

**subdirectory**   A **directory** created and stored within another directory. The subdirectory is considered the **child** of the **parent** directory.

**superuser**  *See* **system administrator**.

**swap partition**  A section of the hard disk, separated from other sections so that it functions as an extension of memory; that is, it supports **virtual memory**. A computer system can use the space in this partition to swap information between disk and RAM so the computer runs faster and more efficiently.

**symbolic link**  A name that points to and provides access to a file located in another directory. Many files in the /lib directory are symbolic links to files in system libraries. A 1 to the left of a file-name in a long directory listing identifies a symbolic link file.

**syntax**  A command's format, wording, options and arguments.

**syntax error**  A grammatical mistake in **machine-language** usage in a **source file**. Such mistakes prevent the compiler from converting the file into an executable file.

**system administrator**  The person who manages the system and is responsible for adding new users, granting privileges to **ordinary users**, deleting old accounts, and ensuring that the system performs efficiently. Having unlimited permission to alter the system, the system administrator is also called the superuser.

# T

**tags**  Code embedded in a document or Web page created with **Hyper Text Markup Language (HTML)**. When the document is viewed with a Web browser like Netscape Navigator or Internet Explorer, the tags give the document special properties like foreground and background colors, font size, and the placement of graphical elements. You can also use tags to place **hyperlinks** in a document.

**target file**  A file listed within **Makefile**. It depends on another file to determine if the **make utility** needs to take action to rebuild the target file.

**tcsh**  A free, shareware UNIX command interpreter based on the **C shell**.

**Telnet**  An Internet terminal emulation program.

**text editor**  A simplified word processor used to create and edit documents but has no formatting features for boldfacing and centering text, for example.

**text file**  Computer file composed entirely of ASCII characters.

**translate utility**  A utility that changes the **standard input** (characters you type on the keyboard) character by character.

**true value**  A value returned from a program function indicating that the function was carried out successfully. A 1 usually represents a true value, but sometimes any non-zero value represents a true value.

**user mode**  A means of accessing the areas of a system where all program software resides.

# U

**utility**  A program that performs useful operations like copying files, listing directories, and communicating with other users. Unlike other operating system programs, a utility is an "add-on" and not part of the UNIX shell, nor a component of the kernel.

# V

**variables** Symbolic names that represent values stored in memory.

**virtual file system** A system that occupies no disk space, such as the /proc directory. The system references and lets you obtain information about which programs and processes are running on a computer.

**virtual memory** An unlimited memory resource supported by the **swap partition,** where the system can swap information between disk and RAM, allowing the computer to run faster and more efficiently.

# W

**wallpaper** A graphic image you can choose to use as the background of your desktop area.

**wildcard** A special character used to represent any other character or, sometimes, a group of characters. Wildcards help you work with files whose names are similar or find a file whose exact name you cannot remember. Wildcard characters are also called **glob** characters.

**Windows Manager** The top layer of the X Window system and the user's interface to the system's components. It controls how windows appear and how users control them.

# X

**X Window system** A **graphical user interface** (GUI) that runs on Linux and many UNIX operating systems.

**X11** The eleventh version of the X Window system.

**Xfree86** A version of **X11** that was ported to the PC and on Linux.

**zsh** A free, shareware UNIX command interpreter based on the **Korn shell**.

# Index

## Special Characters

## A